Uncovering
Teacher Leadership

Uncovering Teacher Leadership

Essays and Voices From the Field

Richard H. Ackerman and Sarah V. Mackenzie, *Editors*

CORWIN PRESS
A SAGE Publications Company
Thousand Oaks, CA 91320

For information:

Corwin Press
A Sage Publications Company
2455 Teller Road
Thousand Oaks, California 91320
www.corwinpress.com

Sage Publications Ltd.
1 Oliver's Yard
55 City Road
London EC1Y 1SP
United Kingdom

Sage Publications India Pvt. Ltd.
B-42, Panchsheel Enclave
Post Box 4109
New Delhi 110 017 India

Printed in the United States of America.

Library of Congress Cataloging-in-Publication Data

Uncovering teacher leadership : essays and voices from the field / Richard H. Ackerman, Sarah V. Mackenzie, editors.
      p. cm.
Includes bibliographical references and index.
ISBN-13: 978-1-4129-3939-3 (cloth)
ISBN-13: 978-1-4129-3940-9 (pbk.)
      1. Teachers—Professional relationships. 2. Teacher participation in administration. 3. Educational leadership. I. Ackerman, Richard H., 1949- II. Mackenzie, Sarah III. Title.

LB1775.U436 2007
371.106—dc22

                                    2006026709

This book is printed on acid-free paper.

07 08 09 10 11 10 9 8 7 6 5 4 3 2 1

Acquisitions Editor:	Rachel Livsey
Editorial Assistant:	Phyllis Cappello
Production Editor:	Jenn Reese
Copy Editor:	Edward Meidenbauer
Typesetter:	C&M Digitals (P) Ltd.
Proofreader:	Caryne Brown
Indexer:	Ellen Slavitz
Cover Designer:	Scott Van Atta
Graphic Designer:	Lisa Miller

Contents

Preface

Uncovering Teacher Leadership: Essays and Voices From the Field

This collection of teacher leader voices brings together treasures from the past as well as contemporary gems. We bring to print these essays and stories as examples of the profound effect that teacher leadership can have on the quality of schools, not only as an influence on the schools themselves but also as a means of defining innovative leadership in the 21st century. Teacher leadership is not a separate entity, but part of a much larger continuum that gives it meaning. Collecting these voices mirrored many of the same challenges that schools face in marshaling the remarkable energies and talents of the teachers that work in them. It has been a humbling task because as far and wide as we have searched, we know there are remarkable stories yet to be told. The lessons in the stories of people in the field and in the essays by thinkers and writers on leadership are not the action-step or fix-it type. They surface the issues, expose some underlying ideas, provide different perspectives, and generate more questions about the inner work buried in this powerful phenomenon. The challenge for us is to honor the voices of teachers and give the term *teacher leader* real meaning today.

Teacher leadership itself continues to hold some ambivalence for teachers wondering about their role as leaders and shapers of responses to schoolwide pressures, all the while fully immersed in the demands of their individual classrooms. Teachers have untapped wisdom about the practice of teaching and deeply held beliefs about what is in the best interests of children and their learning. Outside influences, certainly, can build teachers' capacity—both in each individual and within a whole faculty—for leadership in governance, curriculum development, and reform. Principals, especially, are key to supporting teachers as they participate in leading colleagues. But teachers' inner resources and capabilities must be harnessed as well. They need to take risks, make mistakes, and reflect on their strengths and weaknesses both as teachers and as leaders. They must have courage, yet be vulnerable, fight the comfort of isolation and seek the critique of colleagues. For every leadership impetus outside the classroom there is equally strong inertia holding teachers there. Overwhelming responsibility for children's learning drains teachers mentally and emotionally; they may lack skill and confidence in dealing easily and effectively with other adults; power and authority issues, whether real or imagined, can undermine their sense of efficacy as leaders. Nevertheless, good teachers are increasingly aware of the need for their voices to be heard in many educational arenas. The challenges that teacher leaders confront are the same as those of all school leaders. They struggle for control over their work lives as they try to mobilize others on behalf of children and their learning. Although they may experience conflict with the school culture and within themselves, their goal is to catalyze others to work as hard as they do and care as deeply about what happens in classrooms and schools.

Teacher leadership still faces heavy odds today. It must compete not only with vested interests in traditional assumptions about leadership but also with schools that are still a bit uncomfortable with the idea of teacher leaders. It must endure school systems and bureaucracies that confuse certification with preparation and, sadly, the neglect of many school leaders themselves who think self-knowledge an expendable luxury. Fortunately, the domain of leadership and learning in schools is not restricted, and there are forms of enlightened action and leadership that lie ready and waiting within the lives of every teacher in a school. The practices of teaching and leadership demand no less.

Our understandings about teacher leadership come from years of working with teacher leaders as well as reading authors who have advanced the conversation through their published work. This volume draws on their stories, examples, evidence, insights, research, guidance, and wisdom. Organizing this collection has required creating a delicate interplay of voices along distinct but related pathways that honors the uniqueness of each and reveals more about the essential nature of teacher leadership. The goal is to offer teacher leaders insight into their situation by revealing some of the ways veteran writers have made sense of teacher leadership and leadership generally. The voices of teachers immersed in the experience of leadership echo their wisdom. In hearing the unique voices of teacher leaders, other educators—all teachers and leaders, too—may gain awareness of their own inner struggles as they strive to improve student learning.

The book is divided into five parts. We provide an introduction for each one to help the reader follow the "discussion." We have book-ended each part with "on-the-ground" leaders' voices. We see these beginning and ending pieces speaking to the theoretical and research-based articles by revealing practitioners' thoughts and feelings about their school leadership roles. At the end of each part, we include questions for reflection and conversation as well as protocols for helping people translate the ideas into meaningful action.

Part I, Looking at Teacher Leadership, reflects on what is meant by teacher leadership itself, revisiting and testing assumptions based on empirical studies as well as theoretical and interpretive work. Its six authors cast a wide net by looking at the way teacher leadership has been conceptualized through a steadily emerging knowledge base. Part II, Teacher Leaders Everywhere, explores the etiology of teacher leadership. The authors in this section provide distinctive and complementary rationales for the emergence, presence, and sustainability of teacher leadership.

Collected at the center of the book in Part III are stories of teachers who have allowed themselves to look into the heart of their leadership. These are snapshots of their sense-making. To gather these "raw" pieces we encouraged people we knew and contacted others through friends and acquaintances to cull through their diaries, blogs, and journals to bring to the surface once again the understandings they have of their own teacher leadership forged in the dailiness of their lives. The voices in Part III speak directly to teachers who are struggling with the tugs and pulls of leadership life. These slices of teacher leaders' inner lives tap into the teacher in all educational leaders who wrestle with the same thorny issues: What is my role? Who am I to take this on? What inner resources must I have to do this kind of work? Can I afford to be vulnerable when I step out of my comfort zone as leadership demands? These pieces expose the inner lives of teacher leaders. Throughout this section, Sarah facilitates the conversation by referring to other pieces in the book whose themes resonate with the teacher leader voice. Thematically, these stores are about growth, becoming, learning, and voicing a new identity as a teacher and a leader. They do not offer simple techniques for becoming leaders or recipes for quick successes. What they do is share, in the words of teachers, their inward and outward paths to cultivating their own voices in the service of responsible and responsive leadership at a time when our schools need it the most.

Part IV, Keeping the Teacher in the Leader, provides multiple perspectives on the organizational contexts of teacher leadership. The articles here, many written by teacher leaders-turned-researchers, explore the authors' most pressing questions and tensions about the experience of teacher leaders moving in and through leadership life. Part V, Nurturing Teacher Leaders, describes a number of integral ways organizations can support teachers and teacher leadership inside and outside of schools.

The book concludes with two pieces from Sarah and Richard. Sarah offers a new vision for teacher leadership, elaborating on the central idea many of the scholars and practitioners voiced: namely, all teachers can be leaders, and all leaders are teachers. Richard has the final word on teacher leadership.

Acknowledgments

This book has many authors. If there is a unifying message here, it is that there are teacher leaders everywhere. Thank you for allowing us to glimpse anew the extraordinary promise and possibility of leadership in teachers.

We want to offer special thanks . . .

To teacher leaders at the heart of this reader: Thank you for opening yourselves to us in your writing and continuing to rework and rewrite as we pushed you to articulate the stresses and strains of being a central leader in a classroom and part of a community of leaders in your schools. It is your perseverance that kept us going.

To our veteran authors: Thank you for the wisdom that inspired us to think more deeply about facets of teacher leadership and to set the stage for the kind of ongoing conversation we hope this collection of voices will generate.

To Roland Barth, friend, (especially) for inspiring this reader and for a remarkable career spent living the meaning of teacher leadership.

To our colleagues at the University of Maine College of Education and Human Development, Gordon Donaldson, Dianne Hoff, George Marnik: Thank you for being a steady source of support and inspiration for all our forays into teacher leadership and especially for the writing of this book.

The Corwin Press Team is a dream team.

Thank you Robb Clouse for your enduring faith in us and the idea of this book.

To Rachel Livsey, thank you for your thoughtful questions and gentle prodding.

To Edward Meidenbauer, thank you for your careful reading and constant communication throughout the editing process.

To Phyllis Cappello and Jennifer Reese, thank you for minding the details toward the final product.

From Richard:

To Sally, dear friend and editor extraordinaire, every word in this collection has been gifted with your stunning insight and graceful touch. Thank you for teaching me about teacher leadership and making this whole thing happen.

To my wife, Bobbi, and my daughter, Hannah Rose, the wisest and most beautiful teachers in my life.

From Sarah:

To Richard, thank you for suggesting the collaboration that led through myriad conversations and seemingly endless planning to this work. I enjoyed so much thinking with you about leadership, about writing, and about the vibrancy of our inner lives. You are a marvelous teacher and leader.

To my husband, Cal, thank you for your optimism and steadfast support. You kept me steadily moving toward the goal of getting this book to press.

To my daughter, Rebecca, whose foray into the publishing world showed me the kind of dedication I needed to proceed and to her husband, David, whose gentle questions about leadership helped me to think out loud about the human element of leadership, thank you.

To my family of teachers and learners, you provided the spirit I hope lives in this book. Thank you. You are all superb leaders. I have learned so much from you.

To teachers and principals at Freeport High School with whom I found roots and wings. Thank you for leading with me and nurturing my development as a teacher and leader.

The contributions of the following reviewers are gratefully acknowledged:

Tim Persall
Principal
Arden Road Elementary
Amarillo, TX

Michael Verdun
Principal
Lafayette High School
Red Lake Falls, MN

David Brom
Retired Principal
Champlin Park High School
Champlin, MN

Kari Dahlquist
Principal
Edina Public Schools
Edina, MN

Pru Cuper
Associate Professor
Keene State College
Keene, NH

Leonard Pellicer, Dean
College of Education and
    Organizational Leadership
University of La Verne
La Verne, CA

PART I

Looking at Teacher Leadership

"Each of us has a different conception of just what is meant by teacher leadership," Roland Barth observed in his groundbreaking and user-friendly monograph, included here, "The Teacher Leader." Each of us, it would seem, *still* does. The selections in Part I are not intended to offer the "one-best" definition of teacher leadership. However, in a distinctive but complementary way, each of these pieces provides a view of teacher leadership that represents some of the best thinking on the subject that has emerged over the past ten years.

To open this section, Elizabeth Wiley's "Surprising Outcomes or Why Do They Read *Macbeth?*" (from Donaldson and Marnik's *As Leaders Learn*) turns the question of what *is* teacher leadership into perhaps a better question all teacher leaders—past, present, and future—must ask: Can I make a difference?

Ann Lieberman and Lynne Miller's work represents the voices of teacher leadership advocacy. We have chosen to excerpt their chapter "What Research Says About Teacher Leadership" from their book, *Teacher Leadership*, because the chapter selectively reviews empirical studies as well as theoretical and interpretive work, which adds to the knowledge base and provides a "foundation for understanding the power, promise, and perplexities of teacher leadership" (p. 31).

"Teachers as Leaders: Emergence of a New Paradigm" is taken from a resourceful book by Frank Crowther, Stephen S. Kaagan, Margaret Fergurson, and Leonne Hann and presents an operational definition of teacher leadership that has stood up over time. The framework for teacher leadership they present derives from research in diverse school settings. As such, this selection provides, as the authors contend, compelling and thoughtful "confirmation of a capacity for professional leadership that has been obscured in the literature on educational leadership."

Marilyn Katzenmeyer and Gayle Moller's chapter, "Honoring the Uniqueness of Teacher Leaders," is excerpted from their prophetically titled book *Awakening the Sleeping Giant*. This chapter focuses less on what and how—technical and instrumental issues—of teacher leadership than squarely on the "who" question—the value of knowing "who I am" as a teacher leader. Finally, Laura Reasoner Jones ends Part I not with a "definition" of teacher leadership but perhaps more aptly, a mind-set for others to emulate. "I'm Not Like You" is an honest self-appraisal showing the humility of teacher leaders who recognize how much they still can and do learn from others.

1

Suprising Outcomes

Or Why Do They Read Macbeth?

Elizabeth Wiley

A high school teacher becomes the chair of her English Department and learns to balance ambition and colleagueship.

Four years ago, the English department was a fairly comfortable place. We knew all the rules—we were the good guys, our critics were the bad guys, the principal was a coward—and we spent our department meetings rephrasing those rules with the style, grace, and nuance (heavy on the nuance) that only English teachers can exercise in the late afternoon.

We had reason to feel besieged. People had often chosen to move to our community because the schools were good, and generally they'd been satisfied, or at least they'd been quiet about their dissatisfaction. In the past years, though, as our reputation climbed higher and higher (a phenomenon tied to the introduction of statewide testing), people seemed to

From Donaldson & Marnik, *As Leaders Learn: Personal Stories of Growth in School Leadership*, Chapter 2, pp. 12–18. © 1995, Corwin Press. Reprinted with permission.

feel duped. If we were the best in the state, why weren't their children learning more? Why couldn't they read and write better? And why, oh why, weren't their SAT scores higher? They called us lazy and inept. We called them overambitious and naive. Of course, because the two camps never talked to each other, all of this name-calling stayed sub rosa and we were able to be woodenly polite at soccer games and awards banquets.

Then we found a common enemy in our new principal. He was a good man with very good intentions—in fact, he was primarily responsible for most of the positive changes that happened, sometimes painfully, over the next few years—but he offended as many people as he pleased. It wasn't intentional; he simply lacked grace in dealing with people. His enthusiasm was seen as insensitivity; his candor, as arrogance. I've spent months wondering where his administration went wrong, and that's as close as I can get to the source of the trouble.

However complex the reasons, our initial reactions to the principal were based on simple things. We disliked him because he was in charge when the school board increased the English teacher load from four classes to five. Parents disliked him because he couldn't "schmooze." We assured each other that he was the trouble and did nothing more.

But then he moved into our territory. It's hard for me to stay mad at him here because he was rushing to my defense at the time, so I'll try to tell the story without embellishment. Historically, the chair of the English department has allotted course divisions after consulting with teachers. It's not very complicated; we all have our specialties and we usually teach pretty much the same load from year to year. The difficulty comes when a particularly large class moves through and adjustments must be made to the standard pattern.

It was June and the courses had been allotted. The switch from four to five classes was scheduled for the next year and the principal was making conciliatory visits to each of us before we disappeared for the summer. He told me that it was his hope that we could each keep the same number of students spread over five classes so that, although we'd have more preparations, we'd have no more papers to grade. I told him that my load was way up from 80 (our school board has really tried to limit our student load to 80, which is one of several reasons I like teaching here).

He checked the figures. It turned out that the chair of the English department was teaching three junior classes and two study skills courses for a total of 66 students. I had three senior classes and two freshman for a total of 110. I know that teachers too often get bogged down in comparing workloads, but I also know that teachers don't husband their energy, giving out less to each student when there are more of them in a class. We worry about each student, we plan lessons for individual interests, we call parents when we need information. We don't worry, plan, or call less when there are more students; we try to stretch our energies to cover them all. I was not looking forward to that much stretching.

Because I was on vacation and taking a course, what happened next is hazy to me. I've heard two versions, but because there are almost no points of agreement between the two I'll cut to the result. In September, I was teaching three senior classes, the chair had three junior classes, and we each had one freshman class and one study skills course. And she had resigned as chair of the department.

It was an awful year. First, we had no chair. Then the principal was going to chair our meetings. Then he asked us all to chair them jointly. Then our old chair was back, but our meetings were still devoted to licking our wounds. We didn't even do the ritualistic department bookkeeping (cleverly designed to keep us off awkward subjects like "What are we doing and why?"). By May, most of the department still wasn't speaking to the principal, and the chair had found a job in New Hampshire for the following year. You'd think that we would all be filing transfers to the math department, but when they asked for applications for the position as chair, three of the five of us applied.

CAN I MAKE A DIFFERENCE?

I don't know why I got the job, except that I was the only applicant who hadn't chaired a department before and they were relying on beginner's luck. I don't even know why I wanted it so badly. I love teaching, and I was learning more about it every day. Shifting my focus to being department chair might slow that down. But I was frustrated with going it alone and I thought I could help the department make a collective impact on kids. It seemed that I alone could do very little to affect my students' learning; they came to me from the void and disappeared into it again. Oh, I knew that they read *Romeo and Juliet* as freshmen and *Macbeth* as seniors, but I hadn't any idea what they were supposed to *know* when they came to me—or, for that matter, what they were supposed to know when they left. It was safer to teach them everything I could. Maybe, if I could use my role as chair to get us to talk, the other English teachers would drop some hints.

I had come into education in my mid-thirties, recruited into an experimental program to certify teachers who had had other careers. We, the other interns and I, had felt our way tentatively through our training and internships, learning the complicated ways of schools and making sense of them only through hours of discussion. Those discussions had supported, excited, and galvanized me through my first few years in the classroom. Maybe that's what I hoped to recapture in department meetings. I didn't hope for big changes quickly, though. My goal was to discuss the teaching of English by the following spring. We almost made it.

That first year I led by example. I was collegial, friendly, and collaborative with my fellow teachers. I gave them fliers for conferences and urged them to go. I passed out mailings from the Foxfire Network and the Coalition of Essential Schools and coaxed them into discussing them. I wrote up agendas that focused on authentic assessment and heterogeneous grouping. Upon reflection, I was arrogant, presumptuous, and rude.

These were all experienced teachers—much more experienced than I—and I presumed to tell them, through my not-so-subtle messages, that they needed to improve and that I knew exactly what form that improvement should take.

The summer after my first year as chair, several forces came together serendipitously to show me how wrong I had been: I read Stephen Covey's *Seven Habits of Highly Effective People* (1990), went to a summer institute, and spent nine days at a national conference on assessment run by some of the guiding lights of the reform movement. The last was particularly enlightening: They preached with a holier-than-thou tone that I found repulsive, yet familiar. Then I realized that that was what I must have sounded like to my colleagues in the English department.

I knew that I had been treating them badly, but treating them well couldn't mean going back to the status quo where we were all independent operators blaming any shortcomings on the kids or on the system. I still didn't know why my students read *Macbeth* or what I was expected to teach them; I couldn't even guarantee that they had really learned what I had taught. That's where the outcomes grant came in.

ONE SUCCESS CAN LEAD TO ANOTHER . . .

Recently we had been given a $25,000 grant through the Coalition of Essential Schools to write outcomes in every subject. The rest of the school had at least started on this task, but our department hadn't. I had reminded the members of the department regularly—probably in that same whining tone that makes me flinch now to remember—but they'd managed to shrug me off.

I had a long talk with myself—several, in fact—and because I walk when I talk, I was in great shape when fall rolled around. By then I had decided what mattered to me: that we have a good set of working outcomes by November, that we spend the rest of the year evaluating them, and that we begin working together as a team for the benefit of the students. So, in the best interests of everyone, I told a little lie.

Actually, it was more of a manipulation of the truth. I knew that the school board was interested in the progress of the outcomes and that the department would be more likely to work on them if they knew that the board was watching, so I called the superintendent and asked when she'd like the department to report to the board. She liked the idea so much that she put together a whole language arts presentation—K–12—and scheduled it for November.

At the end of August, I wrote to the members of the department telling them of the reporting deadline and informing them that we'd need to meet twice a month to get ready. I also told them that I knew that collectively we knew everything we needed to know to write outcomes that would work in the best interests of our students; we would be our own experts, our own consultants, because there weren't any better ones around. And I meant it.

They were wonderful—once they were convinced that I truly valued their expertise. We started with outcomes in writing research papers, partly because they were the least personal, partly because our wonderful librarian was eager to help. Most of us knew that we needed to teach our students how to write research papers, but none of us had ever developed the same careful lessons and units in this area that we had in reading, writing, and speech (the other outcome areas). In fact, with the exception of one teacher of American literature, most of us had hurried through research papers, remembering—and probably duplicating—our own unpleasant high school experiences.

We started with the Coalition injunction to plan backwards. What did we want seniors to be able to do in research by the time they left us? We envisioned self-motivated researchers, designing their own projects and presenting them to a panel of critics (why not dream big?). With some form of that as an end product, we worked backwards to the junior project, a lengthy paper that incorporated primary sources and was marked by a student-designed, original thesis. The sophomore paper would ask students to compare two systems—of belief, social order, mythology, whatever. The freshman research would be modeled on Ken McCrory's I-Search paper, a process that starts in a student's own expertise and pushes it into new territory.

When we were done, we not only had a design for challenging research outcomes and systems for helping students to meet those challenges, we had a model for working together that was both effective and pleasant. From there on, nothing could stop us. We sailed through those outcomes, arguing over sequence and wrestling with details, but working together. By November, we not only had a good working set of outcomes, we owned them.

EXPECT THE BEST, AND GET IT

Somewhere along the way, I had learned more about leadership than any workshop, any self-help book, or any lecture could ever teach. In describing others as whiny and self-centered, I'd only been describing myself. When I learned to honor my colleagues as professionals, they treated me professionally. It felt almost like magic, but it shouldn't have: We know that students reflect the expectations that adults have for them. And, as any teacher knows, most classroom lessons are metaphors for the rest of life.

Department meetings are still contentious, but now we're wrestling with bigger questions: How much can a department work together without inhibiting the creativity of individual members? Is teaching—as one colleague claims—an ephemeral art that can't be taught? If it is, how do we ever guarantee that students learn what they need to know? Where does community opinion come in? Should parents be consulted on major curriculum issues? Course assignments? And which parents?

I wanted to become chair because I wanted to provide leadership for the department; now I find myself looking for a higher vision of leadership—not from the principal or the superintendent; they've both been wonderful—but from the community, as interpreted by the school board. The greatest achievement of my tenure—the outcomes—came because we had a clear sense of what the community expected of us and what it wanted for its children. The most painful moments—arguments over standards, politics surrounding teaching assignments—came when the community was clearly ambivalent.

I'm not asking the board to take sides on all these issues but to continue to formulate a vision for the school that becomes paramount, that supersedes any squabbles, and that provides a touchstone for those of us who have to make the thousands of little decisions that cumulatively create a school. A good starting point would be for all of us to treat everyone involved in schools—staff, students, parents, community—with honor and dignity. It has worked for us in our department. I know it would work for our schools.

REFERENCE

Covey, S. (1990). *The seven habits of highly effective people: Restoring the character ethic.* New York: Simon & Schuster.

2

The Teacher Leader

Roland S. Barth

I'm just a teacher. If you want to talk with a leader, he's down the hall in the principal's office.[1]

I had come to visit this innovative middle school, especially interested in learning how decisions were made. After engaging a teacher in conversation for a while, I asked her: "Do you take on some leadership for this school?" Clearly the question struck a raw nerve within her. Her response abraded—and continues to abrade—a raw nerve within *me*. More important, this teacher's words identify and aggravate a very sore place within our profession. "I'm just a teacher." Indeed!

Robert Hampel spent four years studying ten schools within the Coalition of Essential Schools and found that different factions of teachers typically emerge within each school: the "cynics," the "sleepy people," the "yes-but" people—and the teacher leaders. Even within these reform-minded schools, he found that the teacher leaders never constituted more than 25% of a faculty.

---

1. All italicized quotations in this chapter are from teachers who attended a meeting in Providence, Rhode Island, on December 2, 1998, sponsored by the Rhode Island Foundation.

When we invited the 100 Rhode Island teachers at the Providence meeting to "stand up if you're a leader," perhaps two-thirds of them, with evident caution and hesitation, stood and identified themselves as leaders.

In our society, as in our schools, we are clearly uncomfortable claiming to be a leader. We are even more uncomfortable with those who claim to be leaders.

It is worth noting that those historical figures most widely celebrated as "teachers"—Moses, Socrates, Plato, Jesus, Gandhi, Martin Luther King—have also been indisputable leaders. In contemporary times, linking teachers with leadership, especially within the American schoolhouse, is neither so prevalent nor so acceptable.

A few years ago a doctoral student, after an exhaustive analysis of more than 250 major school reform studies, reported that the most prevalent recommendation for improving our nations' schools was that teachers should take on and share much more of the leadership of their schools. Then, and only then, it was argued, will schools be able to transform themselves.

But by and large, this is not happening. Although we might suppose that a teacher would jump at the chance to set up a computer lab for the school or to create a new block schedule, precious few opportunities for these kinds of schoolwide leadership are offered to teachers—and precious few accepted.

Something deep and powerful within school cultures seems to work against teacher leadership.

If schools would be better off with more teachers exerting more leadership, why has a culture developed in schools so unfriendly to even the idea of teacher leaders?

WHAT IS TEACHER LEADERSHIP?

Perhaps part of the caution, even reluctance, among teachers to stand as leaders in their schools is related to confusion about the meaning of "leadership" and "teacher leadership." What *is* the difference between being "just a teacher" and being a "teacher leader"?

A Carnegie Foundation study listed ten areas of decision making in which teacher involvement was essential to the health of a school:

- choosing textbooks and instructional materials
- shaping the curriculum
- setting standards for student behavior
- deciding whether students are tracked into special classes
- designing staff development and inservice programs
- setting promotion and retention policies
- deciding school budgets
- evaluating teacher performance
- selecting new teachers
- selecting new administrators

These are among the conditions of schooling that affect a teacher's ability to work with students, and they are the domains in which teacher leadership is most needed and least seen.

Each of us, I suspect, has a different conception of just what we mean by teacher leadership. I think of teacher leadership as the act of having a positive influence on the school as well as within the classroom. But I like the economy of the definition offered by one of the Rhode Island teachers: "initiatives by teachers which improve schools and learning" (Ruth Jernigan).

Speaking about a teacher's opportunities within the classroom, Haim Ginott (1972) once said:

> I've come to the frightening conclusion that I am the decisive ele-ment in the classroom. It's my personal approach that creates the climate. It's my daily mood that makes the weather. As a teacher, I possess a tremendous power to make a child's life miserable or joyous. I can be a tool of torture or an instrument of inspiration. I can humiliate or humor, hurt or heal. In all situations it is my response that decides whether a crisis will be escalated or de-escalated and a child humanized or dehumanized. (p. 15)

But can a teacher become an equally "decisive element" within the school? Does a teacher have comparable opportunity to influence, to humanize, or to dehumanize the collective whole? Many principals and teachers would say that teachers have such opportunities and exercise them regularly.

To be sure, some enjoy a corrosive influence by subverting. Some are "sleepy" and "yes-but" people. But all, I'm convinced, have the capacity to lead the enterprise down a more positive path, to bring their abundant experience and craft knowledge to the areas of schooling suggested by the Carnegie study. But I wonder how many principals and other administra-tors believe it. More important, do teachers believe it?

WHO BENEFITS?

Why do some teachers choose to have a positive influence upon their schools beyond the classroom? Why is the language of the burgeoning number of charter schools replete with phrases like "empowerment of teachers," "faculty participation in management," "authority of teachers," and "consensus management"? Something must be in it for somebody. As it turns out there's a great deal in teacher leadership for everybody.

The Principal

If there ever was a time when a principal could ride alone on a white horse, like John Wayne or Joan of Arc, and save a troubled school, those days are certainly over. The astonishing complexities and demands of the job are well known. I know of no administrator who doesn't need help in fulfilling this impossible job description. Parents, students, community members, universities, business partners, the central office—all have the potential to become wonderful resources for the principal. But the most reliable, useful, proximate, and professional help resides under the roof of the schoolhouse with the teaching staff itself.

When teachers pull an oar for the entire school—by setting up that computer lab, for instance—they offer valuable assistance to the overworked and overwhelmed principal and to the school itself. Ample evidence suggests that effective principals don't work harder than less effective principals: They work smarter. Principals who encourage and enlist teachers' leadership leverage their own.

The Students

If teachers begin to work together to learn new ways to teach and to learn, then the students will be the ones to benefit.

—Nancy Carnevale

The oft-stated, fundamental purpose of public education is "to equip our citizens to believe in and to participate fully in our democratic system." To accomplish this goal, we require students to take courses in civics, social studies, and citizenship. Given the often-cited statistics about low voter turnout, clearly not many students are graduating from our schools really believing in, let alone practicing democracy.

Few schools operate democratically. The governance is more akin to a dictatorship (albeit usually a benevolent one) than to a New England town meeting. I know. I used to be a benevolent dictator principal, and I used to be the faculty advisor to the student council. When student initiative went beyond keeping the school playground clean or installing larger lockers, on behalf of the faculty and administration, I ruled them out of order. Through such daily lessons, through what we teach in the "hidden curriculum," we succeed in conveying to students that democracy is a fraud.

If students do not experience their school environment as a democracy, neither do teachers. On the other hand, when teachers take on important schoolwide responsibilities, when they are encouraged and supported in such efforts, they take a huge step in transforming their school from dictatorship to democracy. This change in the leadership culture of the school is not lost on students. Ripple effects soon radiate throughout the building as teachers enlist student leadership to amplify their own. And the more the school comes to look, act, and feel like a democracy, the more students come to believe in and practice our democratic form of government. Students win in other ways.

The School

Schools develop cultures that promote and celebrate continuous learning for students only when teachers join the community of lifelong learners. To create communities of learners, teachers must model for students the most important enterprise of the schoolhouse—learning. A teacher who has stopped learning cannot create a classroom climate rich in learning for students. Yet, the dominant structure of a school—the repetition of classes, a reliance on textbooks and workbooks, "someone else" dictating what a teacher should do—is not one that can promote and sustain profound levels of adult learning. If their teacher is not a learner, students soon recognize that the message is "Do as we say, not as we do."

A powerful relationship exists between learning and leading. The most salient learning for most of us comes when we don't know how to do it, when we want to know how to do it, and when our responsibility for doing it will affect the lives of many others with whom we live and work. This is where teacher leadership intersects with professional development.

Teachers who assume responsibility for something they care desperately about—a new pupil evaluation system, revising the science curriculum, or setting up that computer lab—stand at the gate of profound learning.

Thus teacher leadership provides an inevitable and fecund occasion for teacher growth. The teacher who is always leading will be the teacher who is always learning. And the teacher who is always learning will generate students who are capable of both leading and learning.

When decision making is dispersed, when many minds are brought to bear on the knotty, recurring problems of the schoolhouse, better decisions get made about curriculum, professional development, faculty meetings, scheduling, and discipline. The better the quality of the decisions, the better the school.

Finally, the more educators feel a part of the decision making, the greater their morale, participation, and commitment in carrying out the goals of the school. Imagine a school where every teacher takes ownership for a portion of the entire organization! When many lead, the school wins.

The Teachers

I love to learn new things, and I'm an avid workshop participant. Most of the things I've learned . . . have found a way into my classroom and into the classrooms of many of the teachers and preservice teachers I work with. Spending time with other biology teachers and reading information from professional organizations and keeping in contact with other biology teachers on the listserv have helped me improve my own learning.

—Judy Hede McGowan

Most would agree that who the teacher is and what the teacher does within the classroom have a greater influence upon students' accomplishment than any other school factor. There is considerable evidence, also, that what the teacher does inside the classroom is directly related to what the teacher does outside the classroom.

We will learn in the pages that follow what benefits the Rhode Island teachers' experience as teacher leaders and how being a teacher leader enriches classroom work. Suffice it to say here that the lives of teachers who lead are enriched and ennobled in many significant ways.

Rather than remain passive recipients—even victims—of what their institutions deal to them, teachers who lead help to shape their own schools and, thereby, their own destinies as educators.

The teacher who leads gets to sit at the table with grownups as a first-class citizen in the schoolhouse rather than remain with the subordinates in a world full of superordinates.

The teacher who leads enjoys variety, even relief, from the relentless tedium of the classroom. An abundance of worthy, very different educational challenges await every teacher beyond the walls of the classroom.

The teacher who leads has an opportunity to work with and influence the lives of adults, as well as those of youngsters.

These are among the benefits for the teacher who teaches *and* leads. The teacher leader has much to give and much to gain. Empowerment, community service, recognition, parity, and stimulating variety are, indeed, benefits of consequence.

In sum, all teachers have leadership potential. And all teachers can benefit from exercising that potential. Schools badly need the leadership of teachers. Teachers become more active learners in an environment where they are leaders. When teachers lead, principals extend their own capacity; students live in a democratic, community of learners, and schools benefit from better decision making.

This is why the promise of widespread teacher leadership in our schools is so compelling for principals, students, teachers, and the success of schools themselves.

IMPEDIMENTS

The potential embedded in the concept of teacher leadership for enriching the lives of principals, students, teachers themselves, and their schools is evident. The idea is compelling. Why, then, do so few teachers contribute so little beyond their classrooms to the life of their schools? If it is such a good idea, why isn't everyone doing it?

There are reasons. Good ones. Many of them. They boiled to the surface with remarkable clarity, energy, and occasionally with anger, at the conversation in Providence. It is all very well to cite the virtues of teacher leadership, but the fact of the matter is, severe, crippling impediments stand in the way of realizing this dream. What teachers have to say about the barriers they experience to teacher leadership is important for our profession to hear.

Our Plate Is Full

Recently the only thing about our school that the majority of faculty members could come to consensus on was that our plate is full.

—Diane Kern

It's hard to care for a class of little bodies and still have time and energy to lead.

—Susan Naysnerski

Some of the conditions at work within the school culture that thwart teacher leadership come as no surprise. Responsibility upon responsibility has been added to each teacher's working day: responding to parents, overseeing afterschool activities, attending professional development activities, and of course maintaining standards. The list is staggering. As one teacher told me, "When was the last time someone said to me, 'Sandra, you are *no longer* responsible for . . . '? It's always an add-on."

In this context, the "opportunity" for chairing a schoolsite council, setting up a computer lab, or taking charge of a staff development day does encounter a full plate. The fact of the matter is most teachers are overwhelmed with existing duties. School leadership is an add-on, a desirable add-on perhaps, but an add-on nonetheless. When choices must be made, many teachers understandably choose to teach, not lead.

Time

There seems to be a preponderance of non teaching duties that today's teachers are asked to handle. Teachers are fed up with the school's red tape. They feel they are being pulled in many different directions without the time to accomplish meaningful work.

—Michael Neubauer

An obstacle I face is that there never seems to be enough time to get together in my building to talk and share ideas.

—Wendy Lombardi

For systemic change to occur, colleagues need time, quality time to work together.

—Sharon Webster

It *is* all about time. Time is *why* the plate is full. Time in schools is in finite supply and in infinite demand. For most, time is a question of living within the allotted 24 hours in a day. How many teachers have been heard to say: "I would love to chair the committee, but I don't have time"? For most it is the truth. There simply is not enough time to do it all, let alone do it all well.

Others feel they have or could make time, but they expect to be paid for it: "They are reluctant to try it if it requires more time without compensation" (Sharon Webster).

Some unions don't look kindly at teachers who take on additional leadership functions without pay. They set and enforce limits on teachers' allocation of uncompensated time and draw attention to those who breach the limits. Many find they can exert more power by saying "no" than "yes." And why not? Such an "add-on" mentality eventually leads to the schoolhouse equivalent of a sweatshop. Because teachers have so little to say in what they do, it is not surprising that their union would step in to protect them.

> (Our) union uses restraints of the contract to convince teachers to follow time limits in their work in schools. Doing "extra" jobs (jobs that are unpaid or not in the contract) that are often the very work that can improve student learning is discouraged. (Ruth Jernigan)

Teachers also lead demanding lives outside of school. Three-quarters of teachers nationwide are women, many of whom bear major responsibility for their children. Others are fathers, spouses, or caretakers of elderly parents. Still others hold outside jobs to make ends meet.

The plate *is* full. The clock *is* depleted. Most of the work of the teacher leader is uncompensated. Thus, it is not difficult to understand why a majority of teachers confine themselves to their classrooms.

All of this leaves unexplained the puzzling paradox that those teachers who seem to have the least time and most on their plates are the very ones who always seem ready and able to take on the additional work of school-wide leadership. Like most principals, I soon discovered that if something had to get done, I needed to find a "busy person" to do it.

The Tests

> *Administrators, school committee members, teachers, and indeed, the entire "system" itself—we are all being held hostage by the test scores.*
>
> —Vin Doyle

The current wave of "accountability" and "standards" has been widely translated into standardization, tests, and scores. Increasingly, the feeling in the schools is that everything must be sacrificed upon the altar of the standardized test. Accountability is ratcheted up and up by constant, comparative scrutiny of the scores by teacher, by grade level, by school, by district, by state, and by nation. The public, it seems, will have its pound of flesh, and it will come in the form of improved performance by students on standardized tests.

Standardized tests are having a chilling effect upon both the teaching profession and the inclination and ability of teachers to assume broad leadership within their schools. Every moment of every teacher's day is being analyzed by others to discover what change might raise a student's scores.

It is virtually impossible, of course, to link a teacher's leadership of a professional development day with salutary effects on the achievement level of that teacher's students. "What's my responsibility for such a day got to do with raising my students' scores to the 85th percentile?" has become a common, debilitating question.

In the short run, demonstrably, very little. So the teacher, mindful of what the system values and rewards, chooses to forgo responsibility for shaping the professional development day. The tyranny of the tests rules the day, every part of the day, and its tentacles work themselves into aspects of schooling that go far beyond class content. It is possible that the test scores will rise, but at costs, unfortunately, that will not be factored into the equation. The discussion has gone so far off track that the unquestionably valuable concept of standards has been divorced from all that goes into building the kind of school culture that leads naturally to the attainment of those standards.

Colleagues

The Rhode Island teacher leaders were resolute in their belief, ground out over years in the crucible of the schoolhouse, that full plates, time crunches, and standardized tests are not the only, or even the most severe, barriers they face when sailing into the uncharted and dangerous shoals of school leadership. Their greatest concern was reserved for far more critical and influential elements within their schools: those with whom they work. If they can get by the Sirens of time, tests, and tight budgets, their reward is the Scylla and Charybdis of fellow teachers and administrators who, together, wield an immense power to extinguish a teacher's involvement in school leadership.

It is sad, but sometimes we are our own worst enemies. (Judy Hede McGowan)

The reports of the Rhode Island teachers, similar to what I hear from teachers elsewhere, suggest various school climates surrounding teacher leadership, which range from supportive to indifferent to inhospitable to toxic. Unfortunately, the balance is skewed toward the latter.

There are many reasons that the teacher who would lead encounters resistance from other teachers. Opposition often comes in bizarre, enervating, and discouraging forms. Some are passive—inertia, caution, insecurity, primitive personal and interpersonal skills—whereas others are active.

Inertia

Newton's first law seems to apply to people as well as to inanimate objects. "A body at rest will remain at rest unless acted upon by an outside force." Inertia is endemic in most academic institutions.

> It seems that when the status quo is threatened by anything new, an immediate systemic defense mechanism comes to life. Even when people appear willing to try something new, they eventually revert to the status quo. (Vin Doyle)

> The biggest challenge is trying to get to teachers in my building who are set in their ways. There are some teachers who are not willing to listen to new ideas or strategies. The few have made it hard for the rest of us to try new things. (Wendy Lombardi)

Caution

Coupled with institutional inertia is another quality familiar to many school cultures: aversion to risk. It can be as unsafe to lead as it can be unsafe to follow the lead of another, especially when neither is an officially "designated" leader. In the world of teacher leadership, danger abounds.

A few schools see the connection among risk-taking, leading, and learning, and working to build "a community of risk takers." Posted prominently on the wall of the hallway of one school is a big sign: "Anything worth doing is worth doing badly... at first." In another school, I found these words emblazoned on the wall of the faculty room: "Throughout history the most common, debilitating human condition has been cold feet." And one courageous district circulated hundreds of cards to administrators, teachers, students, and parents on which was boldly printed:

> I BLEW IT. I tried something new and innovative, and it didn't work as well as I wanted. This COUPON entitles me to be free of criticism for my efforts. I'll continue to pursue ways to help our district be successful.

These good examples notwithstanding, I'm afraid caution is much more common. A Rhode Island teacher reported that he had given up pursuing his project because it had been dependent on his teaching a certain class, which got scheduled to someone else at the last minute. The more he thought about it, however, the more he found himself asking hard questions about himself:

> Why didn't I go to the superintendent and explain what the schedule change was doing to my work? Why didn't I go to the teacher who got assigned to that class to see whether we might pursue the work together? Why didn't I ask the students if they had any ideas about how we could salvage the project? Instead, I threw up my hands, railing against the "system" when I should have been helping make the "system" work for me and for my students.

Each of these responses carried risk. From the teacher's startling admission, it was clear that, in retrospect, he wished he had taken those risks.

Ours is a very cautious profession top to bottom. Lack of risk-taking among the role models in an environment intended to promote the ultimate risk-taking—learning—constitutes yet another strand of the hidden curriculum.

Insecurity

Coupled with inertia and caution is insecurity. The Rhode Island teachers were outspoken about the prevailing insecurity they experienced among many teachers in their schools.

As one teacher said:

> When a teacher is truly passionate about her work, others are threatened because they don't feel it, or can't impart it to their students. Sometimes I feel impeded in my work by teachers and administrators who are threatened by my enthusiasm.

A kind of taboo among teachers in many schools makes it difficult for one person to step out from the others. Many teachers don't possess the courage or self-confidence that allows them to violate this taboo.

Personal and Interpersonal Skills

> *I really think teachers need to rely on each other for knowledge and an exchange of ideas. Teachers need to build a network of support. We need to be able to communicate.*
>
> —Wendy Lombardi

A final source of passive resistance to the teacher leader, found in many schools, is the primitive quality of the relationships among teachers. Few teachers would characterize themselves as collegial. Many seem to lack the personal, interpersonal, and group skills essential to the successful exercise of leadership. The following story suggests the extent of the deficiency:

> Recently, I sat with a group of educators from several different school districts to talk about student reading responses and to share our craft knowledge about what we believe is exemplary student work at the grade level that we teach. I thought that all teachers would love to talk about student work and about classroom practice, so I envisioned a worthwhile conversation with colleagues that I could use. I was completely taken aback at how miserably the morning went.
>
> Two teachers sat red-faced and unable to contribute comfortably for at least an hour. One teacher was combative and only wanted to share if the sharing was on her terms. One teacher interrupted others more than once. The majority of the group felt the need to defend why their students did not do as well on this test as they would have liked.
>
> I began to share my thoughts on the task, hoping to encourage the group towards open communication about the student work, but realized through reading body language and listening carefully to the contributions of individuals that the group was not going to be comfortable sharing. This task was too risky for a majority of members. (Diane Kern)

Active Resistance to Teacher Leadership

> *In every school community there are veteran teachers who have "been there, done that." Some are well practiced at sitting back and waiting for new ideas to die; others act to make sure the ideas die. Whatever the discussion, the first group dismisses most, if not everything, that is suggested. The second group actively sets up roadblocks. Want to reorganize the day?* Can't. *The contract doesn't allow it. Want to form interdisciplinary teams?* Can't.
>
> —Sharon Webster

Inertia, risk aversion, lack of confidence, primitive adult relationships all thwart teacher initiatives toward school leadership. Collectively, they provide a kind of backdrop on which more active forms of resistance from teachers play out.

> Colleagues who do not want to be involved in a change idea will sometimes sabotage the efforts of a teacher who is actively pursuing that change. (Ruth Jernigan)

> I asked several teachers to get together once a month after school to share ideas, lessons, etc. Everyone thought it was a good idea

until we tried to set a date. No one could agree on a day because some people had other jobs, children at home, afterschool clubs, etc. It was very difficult.

When we finally agreed on a date and got together, it turned into a gripe session. Some complained about the discipline, others about administration. Although these were legitimate concerns, it wasn't what this meeting was intended for. I became very frustrated. The once-a-month meeting soon stopped. (Wendy Lombardi)

Sometimes even the strong support of the principal is insufficient to cushion the teacher leader against the formidable opposition of other teachers. One teacher told the following story:

Our building administrator, as usual, was supportive and encouraged us to take the lead in discussing this topic. We did some research, attended a conference, and spoke with a couple of schools already involved in looping, and finally brought the topic to a faculty meeting for discussion. We made a presentation to the faculty following this research.

The reaction of other teachers, who had been informed and updated about the upcoming discussion, was disappointing and disheartening. Most were silent. Those who did speak were unsupportive. There was an unwillingness to even engage in a discussion on a topic. Which we thought should be, at the very least, of interest to educators.

I was disappointed. I was even more disappointed (although not surprised) to learn that there had been a great deal of discussion about the topic in the teachers' room, but the discussion had not been with those of us who were initiating the discussion.

The persistent, insistent array of means teachers can employ to wet-blanket the best intentions of others is daunting and discouraging. Many are left perplexed by the unfriendliness of their school's culture to teacher leadership. They have experience, as one teacher put it, that "leadership can turn to ostracism." (Patrick Kelly)

Passive and active resistance by other teachers, when played out on the stage of full plates, insufficient time, lack of compensation, and standardized tests, all but brings the curtain down on teacher leadership. Many become content with trying to become a distinguished leader in their tangible classrooms, where they can lead young people in relative safety and with considerably more control and satisfaction. They opt out of being leaders in their schools or within their profession.

OPPORTUNITIES

Happily, fellow teachers also hold the power to unlock teachers' leadership potential and to foster its growth. That power is linked to the basic disposition of a school toward the value of teacher leadership. Far more than workload, time, or tests, it is the nature of a school's culture—"the way we do things here"—that ultimately determines whether and by what means teachers will participate in the school community as leaders beyond their classrooms.

One definition of leadership I like very much is "Making happen what you believe in." Teachers believe strongly in many things. If a teacher believes in strengthening parent involvement in the school, say, and wants to make that happen, there are several choices. As these Rhode Island teachers, undaunted by the impediments, clearly document, there are many ways to lead. These educators reveal a repertoire of hopeful means by which they are having a positive and significant influence on their schools as teacher leaders.

LEAD BY FOLLOWING

Many teachers choose to follow, even though they have the ability to lead.

—Diane Kern

Perhaps the least risky, demanding, complicated, and therefore the most common way to influence the life of one's school beyond the classroom is to follow the lead of others. By selectively enlisting behind the efforts of fellow teachers, one teacher can help others to move mountains and occasionally even more massive geological formations such as schools.

In our American culture, however, it's as difficult to identify oneself as a "follower" as a "leader." Indeed, most of us were raised in households where being a follower was always cast in a negative light. Of course, it's the way one follows and the leader one chooses to follow, rather than following itself, that determines whether one's decision to follow is strong and principled or weak and pedestrian.

Following may seem like a modest contribution on the part of the teacher leader, but it often constitutes a significant, affirmative, even courageous form of leadership. For anything of consequence to get done in schools, many are needed to contribute in a hundred subtle, periodic, and reliable ways to "stand up and be counted." This can mean showing up and speaking out at an important public meeting, signing petitions, writing letters, and participating in the cheering section. The success of those at the front of the line depends upon the support of others behind them. "Followership" is an art form yet to be discovered by many educators. More schools will improve when more teachers turn their considerable energies to judiciously following others.

JOIN THE TEAM

Referring to his colleagues who gathered for our meeting in Providence, one educator noted:

> These teachers are team players. They have an ability to bring those around them into the process. Thus begins the process of change. By providing the same support and enthusiasm they bring to the classroom, they build the next step in the process: teams of teachers and students working toward common goals. (Vin Doyle)

Another teacher put it this way: "If schools are going to be run by a committee, then I want to make damn sure I'm ON the committee."

So they join a collective effort, not as followers, but by sharing leadership with others. Teams offer some safety in numbers for the cautious, companionship for the gregarious, challenge for those attempting to influence others, and greater hope of making a significant difference through combined strength. They also often lead to better decisions because more perspectives are considered.

> Colleagues who work in teams or feel a community in the school will often spend more time trying to understand ideas that lead to change. (Ruth Jernigan)

When a teacher shares common ground with the purpose of the team and with other members of the team, frustration with long meetings and disagreements can be tolerated, and it may be possible, as a team member, to "make happen what you believe in." We have all experienced the astonishing influence of a single member of a team. And we have all seen examples of the extraordinary influence a team can have upon a school. This is why many find greater satisfaction from being a part of a high-performing team than from solitary accomplishment.

LEAD ALONE

> *I plan to continue to do my work in my own quiet way and try to influence as many people as I can by my example.*
>
> —Nancy Carnevale

Because they may be dissatisfied with following the lead of others, and because they experience impatience and frustration trying to work with colleagues as team members, and perhaps having been thwarted or ignored by administrators, many teachers set out to influence their schools, more or less alone. They hope others will follow their example. Often they take this course of necessity, only after pursuing, unsuccessfully, "the correct route."

One of the Rhode Island teachers described it this way:

> In the past, I have taken the *correct route* to try to get things done. I go to the principal and get told no. Then I write a letter to the school committee and the superintendent and get ignored. Then I just go and do it myself. I have decided to just get it myself. Maybe it's not right, but it gets the job done.

Many teachers conceal their attempts to improve their schools, such as applying for a grant to get the school wired into the Internet. They become covert, guerrilla warriors. For them it is safer, simpler, and faster, and perhaps more exciting to go underground, only to disclose what they have done when success is certain. This way, their efforts do not depend upon enlisting the support of others, and they risk no public failure should their project prove unsuccessful. If the effort succeeds, however, the impact of the guerrilla leader is often blunted, or at least compromised, by the clandestine nature of their work. There is no one to share in the celebration, as there was no one to share in the project.

Despite the many impediments faced by the teacher who sets out to lead alone, a great many find success.

LEAD BY EXAMPLE

> *If we do not lose our enthusiasm for what we do, and continue to push on, more people will join the team.*
>
> —Denise Zavota

Different from their guerrilla cousins, teacher leaders who stay out of the open are more likely to have a positive influence upon the larger school community when they take the risk of providing a constant, visible model of persistence, hope, and enthusiasm, and by the way they pursue worthwhile goals. By their example, they influence others.

> The best teachers I have known have shown leadership by holding out their excitement for teaching like a beacon and by keeping it focused on student welfare. Their model inspires other teachers. It also brings other teachers along with them in their zeal. (Helen Johnson)

Leading by example is perhaps the purest form of leadership and the one over which each of us has the most control. The bumper sticker tells us that "You can't lead where you won't go." The flip side, known so well to these teachers, is that "You can lead only where you will go."

WHAT IT TAKES

The Rhode Island teachers suggest that their success as teacher leaders is related to three factors.

Have a Goal

Teachers who can identify and clearly delimit a goal, who care passionately about and can convincingly articulate what change they want to see in the school are likely to experience some success, especially if they recognize how others might find benefit from that change. For example:

> I had a goal to try to get a scanner purchased for my school. I decided to create a school Web page so my principal could see the benefit of it. She loved it and has agreed to make the purchase for the scanner, a color printer, and a digital camera. I will be running a faculty workshop on how to use this new equipment. (Lisa Zavota)

Persist

> *Tenacity, persistence, and handling rejection well are admirable qualities of a teacher leader.*
>
> —Michael Neubauer

Teachers who succeed in influencing the school are tireless, incessant, and undeterred by the obstacles that seem to leap from behind every bush. Commitment to their cause is stronger than the hurdles they encounter.

> I have learned that persistence generally pays off. Obstacles should never be seen as insurmountable. Defeat can only happen with capitulation. I suppose that Don Quixote may be an imperfect role model, but he has his qualities. (Ron Porier)

Learn to Enjoy Half a Loaf

Tilting at windmills can be a dangerous activity, especially if one gets so tangled in the dream that satisfaction can come only with total fulfillment. The real world of school seldom allows total fulfillment of anyone's dreams. The teacher leaders who succeed, in addition to being purposeful and persistent, seem to be able to settle for, and to even celebrate, small, partial success.

> When we built our first weather station, many teachers came to me and said it wouldn't last and that kids would trash it. It hurt, but I was stubborn and felt it was worth a shot. It took quite a while to train my students in the proper way to take measurements, much longer than I had anticipated. Then it was time to start transmitting data.
>
> Unfortunately, the teachers who thought it would never work were right: the station was trashed. We picked up the pieces and rebuilt the station again only to have it trashed over the summer. The following fall we rebuilt it for the third time only to find that our phone line was pulled because the school was installing a 56K line in the building. While I was trying to decide if I could handle transmitting the data from home, the station was destroyed for the final time. It was hard listening to the *I told you so's*, but it was still worth the effort.
>
> The GLOBE computer is constantly in use in my classroom, and the activities I learned have found a place in my curriculum even if my students and I could not participate in the project the way I wanted to. I've even shared some of the activities at workshops so the whole experience was not a total loss.
>
> It was not my most successful project, but I learned that it was OK to try new things. I don't like to fail, but I did learn from the failure. (Judy Hede McGowan)

Teachers who define success as an increment of change in the desirable direction, rather than as accomplishing everything they set out to, experience success, feel "it was still worth the effort," and are likely to engage in subsequent initiatives.

When it comes to changing a school, these then are among the options and the strategies available to every teacher: lead by following, join the team, lead alone, lead by example, or don't lead at all. Some teachers may see these as deliberate, intentional choices; others select by default. And some may go with one choice this time, another the next. Each offers different advantages and disadvantages to the teacher and the school.

THE PRINCIPAL

A teacher may sometimes choose to exercise leadership independently, but few initiatives can be undertaken without the school principal. Administrators have a disproportionate influence upon teacher leadership— for better or for worse.

The Rhode Island teachers are unambiguous about the importance of the school principal, not only in leading a school, but in creating an environment that encourages—or discourages—others to lead as well. The leader of the school clearly has the capacity to enable or to curtail teacher leaders.

Barriers

It is disheartening that many teachers experience their school administrator, and especially their principals, as severe obstacles to their leadership aspirations. They see principals holding tightly and jealously to power, control, and the center stage.

> Leadership from any other sphere often causes a negative reaction unless, of course, the idea comes from the administration and the leadership is appointed by the administrator. (Ruth Jernigan)

There are understandable reasons why principals guard with authority. Principals have worked long and hard to get where they are. First as classroom teachers, then through countless nights and weekends and summers in expensive administrative preparation programs, then through an arduous job search. Now that they have secured their position as leader of the school, they protect it tenaciously as their special province.

And, just as it is risky for a teacher to assume leadership, it is risky for a principal to share leadership with teachers. Because principals will be held accountable for what others do, it is natural that they want evidence in advance that those empowered can get the job done well. Principals also are mindful of how much care, feeding, and hand-holding must go into helping the teacher leader. Why set up and tend a new committee to hire that new teacher? Given their own time crunch, many principals find it more efficient to make the decision by themselves.

For all of those reasons, many principals control carefully whether and on whom they bestow responsibility for important decisions. They offer leadership opportunities to teachers who are most likely to support the principal's agenda and who will not divert attention or energy by pursuing their own. As one teacher said, "The administrators' task is to influence a *chosen few* and have them advocate their position on issues indirectly."

But a pattern of repeatedly anointing the "chosen few" overloads the few while squelching the leadership potential of the unchosen many. The principal's tendency to control also gives rise to the guerrilla teacher leader, who, because she will never be invited by the principal to lead, *must* work surreptitiously. Although they may not be aware of it, many principals transmit forbidding, unwelcoming messages about teacher leadership.

Part of me feels that administrators do not want to hear the voice of the teacher. (Susan Naysnerski)

A principal's disposition toward sharing leadership with teachers (or others) is probably related to personal security. One California study concluded that the weaker the principal, personally, the less the principal is likely to share leadership. Stronger, more secure principals are more likely to share leadership. It makes sense.

Culture Builders

Other principals who preside over precisely the same kind of schools and who work under an identical job description find ways not only of encouraging but of inspiring a culture of teacher leadership within their schools. Happily, the stories of the Rhode Island teachers are full to the brim with examples of these visionary principals.

The school administration has been most supportive when I have initiated any type of leadership within the school.

This support has been of various types: Time has been provided to meet with others, to attend conferences, and to otherwise investigate issues; money has been provided when needed. Most important, administrators have encouraged and supported the type of risk-taking which is involved in teacher leadership. (Denise Frederick)

Both my principal and superintendent have encouraged and mentored my growth as a teacher leader. (Sharon Webster)

My current principal has been very supportive of new teaching methods and ideas as well as the use of technology in the classrooms. She seems honestly committed to change. (Judy Hede McGowan)

His style inspires you, makes you reflect about your teaching, supports you, and brings out your best. And he has only one goal, that which is best for the students and staff. (Helen Johnson)

Some administrators embrace the energy of staff members to join in leadership roles and provide much support for people who want to take the lead. They show support for grant writing or support for organizing a group to work on an idea. The positive power of administrators and teachers working together to improve schools is awesome. (Ruth Jernigan)

Indeed! Far more than either one going it alone. If teacher leadership is crucial to the health and performance for a school, principals are crucial to the health and the performance of teacher leaders.

Just what do principals do that has such a powerful influence on the development of teacher leaders? They "support." But what, exactly does support mean?

Expectation

Principals who support teacher leadership really believe in it and articulate this as a goal of the school. The participation of teachers as leaders is more likely to occur if their principal openly and frequently articulates this vision at meetings, in conversations, in newsletters, in memos to the faculty, and at community meetings. "Teacher leadership is not only welcome here, it is *expected.*"

Debbie Meier, the principal at the Mission Hill pilot school in Boston, says that a school is a community. By virtue of the fact that its teachers are citizens of that community, they take responsibility in some way for the well-being of the school. That's what members of a community do.

High expectations have been associated with academic achievement of youngsters. We are beginning to believe that "all children can learn." Similarly, when principals expect teachers to become committed and responsible school leaders, they instill the equally lofty message that "all teachers can lead." And all teachers do lead.

Relinquish

Principals have in their bottom drawer a few marbles of authority that came with the job and a few more that they have earned over the years. Some principals play these marbles alone. Others don't play them at all, making few decisions and allowing others to make fewer. The principals who support teacher leadership make sure that all the marbles are played by as many players as possible. Principals have learned that when they relinquish some of the marbles to teachers, they unlock and enlist the latent, creative powers of the faculty in the service of the school.

Entrust

Teachers will not become leaders within the school community if when the going gets rough and an angry parent makes a phone call, the principal violates the trust, disempowers the teacher and reasserts his or her authority. It takes only a single incident of having the rug pulled from beneath a teacher leader before the teacher—and the entire faculty—secedes from the community of leaders.

Empowerment

It is common for a principal, when confronted with a sudden problem—for example, a reprimand from the fire chief and superintendent after a plodding school evacuation drill—to set up a new procedure and then recruit a trusted teacher to monitor and maintain it. Yet the fun, the learning, and the commitment around leadership come from brainstorming and devising one's own solutions and then trying to implement them. Principals elicit more leaders and more leadership if they invite teachers to address the problem before, not after, the principal has determined a solution.

Inclusion

To address a nagging school issue, the principal often selects a trusted teacher who has handled similar problems successfully. But by relying on a tried and proven teacher, the principal rewards competence with even more work. In a short time, the overburdened teacher concludes, "My plate is full," and retreats to the classroom.

Principals who build a school culture in which teacher leadership can flourish are more likely to take on an important school issue with a teacher who feels passionately about that issue. One teacher's passion may be fire safety; another's the supply closet. Still another's might be serving as the conduit with the local press, as an able facilitator for discussions among parents, or as the sleuth with a knack for finding new professional development opportunities for colleagues. One person's junk is another's treasure. Nobody knows what everyone knows.

Too often, the criterion for bestowing leadership on an individual is evidence that the person knows how to handle the problem. Yet innovative solutions also come from teachers who don't know how to do something but want to learn. This is where leadership and professional development become one. It is also the same principle of good learning that we try to impart to our students. It's called experiential learning. If the teacher is committed to learning, the principal and other faculty members have both an opportunity and responsibility to help that teacher develop new leadership skills.

When a principal accords opportunities for leadership to untried (and perhaps untrusted) teachers who express passionate interest or concern about an issue, everyone can win. The oft-chosen teacher is overburdened no longer. The teacher who feels strongly about an issue and is now entrusted with resolving it comes alive as an adult learner and leader. Rather than being excluded or becoming a guerrilla, the teacher joins the community of leaders. And the principal's efforts this year to help induct new teacher leaders will be rewarded next year by less drain on the principal's time and energies because the principal shared the work of leadership with others who welcome it. These efforts will also be rewarded with the recognition that comes to teacher and principal alike for an improving school.

Protection

As we have seen, teachers who reveal themselves as leaders, and thereby distinguish themselves from others, violate a taboo and place themselves "at risk." Principals must find ways to run interference and protect them from the assaults of their fellows. A teacher calls a meeting; the principal attends to support and shows the flag. A teacher wants to share at a faculty meeting her craft knowledge about creating a multicultural curriculum, the principal "asks" that teacher to address the faculty. When it's clear to the school community that leadership is being shared and that the principal values others taking leadership, everyone is safer.

Responsibility for Failure

If, as inevitably happens, a teacher stumbles in a schoolwide effort, the principal has several options. One is to blame the teacher and remove the responsibility. This may help the principal in the short run, but in the long run few teachers will choose to stick their necks out again. Alternatively, the principal can assume the lonely and self-punitive position of captain of the ship: "The ship has gone aground; I'm responsible."

But teacher and principal can share responsibility for failure as well as for success. Usually a school community deals more kindly with mistakes made jointly by teacher and principal than by either alone. The important question is not "Whose fault is it?" but rather, "What happened and what can we learn from it so we can do better next time?"

When principal and teacher share a foxhole, the outcomes are often collegiality, staff development, safety, trust, and higher morale. Much can be gained from stumbling . . . together.

Success to the Teacher

It is important that the principal share with teacher leaders responsibility for success as for failure. Principals have plenty of opportunity each day to be on center stage, visible to the school community. Teachers have few and need more. The principal who hogs the limelight and deprives the teacher of deserved recognition thwarts the development of teacher leaders. Let the teacher bask in the glory of a new, distinguished fire evacuation system or take the credit for helping open a door to a summer fellowship for a colleague! Good principals are more often hero-makers than heroes.

Conversations among the Rhode Island teachers suggest a rich repertoire of ideas and practices available to principals who want to demonstrate that schools can be democracies as well as teach about them. This is what teachers mean when they say, "Support from my principal has been a huge factor in my becoming a teacher leader."

Teachers and Principals

The concept of shared leadership in schools goes to the heart of the principal-teacher relationship. So what shall it be? Superordinate to subordinate? Adversarial? Supportive? Collegial? Cooperative? Clearly there is nothing inherent in the role of principal that causes either curtailment or support of teacher leadership: It is how the principal chooses to perform the job. By their day-to-day actions, principals build the culture of their schools. That pattern of behavior can embed teacher leadership in the school's culture, cast a wet blanket on it—or have no influence at all.

Leaders influence through *positional* authority, which comes with the job description. And they influence through *personal* authority, which they earn by who they are and how they conduct themselves. One way many teachers become leaders in their schools is by leaving the classroom and assuming positions as assistant principals and principals. They acquire positional authority.

But I wonder if principals are aware of how often they present to teachers an image of school leadership as something undesirable, if not reprehensible. By their example, many principals discourage teachers who would be principals or teacher leaders. Several Rhode Island teachers expressed a disturbingly negative perception of the role of the school principal.

> I think many talented individuals remain in the shadows because they hear colleagues talk about administration in a negative way. (Lisa Zavota)

> Unfortunately the job of a school administrator has become one that seems to have less and less to do with educational issues and more and more to do with managerial issues. I have no interest in being involved in this aspect of education. (Denise Frederick)

> I will never be a principal because I would be losing the one thing that makes everyday of my life a pleasure: going to my class. (Nancy Carnevale)

Rightly or wrongly, teachers seem to extend their judgment of the principalship to leadership in general. The logic seems to be: "To be a leader is to be like an administrator. I don't like the plight of administrators. I want none of it for myself. Therefore, I will stay away from teacher leadership."

A healthy, productive learning community should not have so many of its most valuable citizens recoiling at the thought of assuming the top leadership role in that community. Teachers might not feel "up" to the position of principal, but feel they should see it as something they respect and admire and something that symbolizes the best profession the school has to offer. Principals who would elicit leadership from teachers in their schools would do well to consider what image of leader—and of leadership—they project to others, and to try to come to terms with their own leadership.

It is not surprising then that many teachers who want to offer leadership in their schools do not want to become a principal or to even *like* a principal. So how might more teachers reconcile their crucial schoolwide responsibilities? And how might more teachers be sustained rather than discouraged in their final efforts to lead?

To capture the potential of these teachers, the profession needs to invent, expand, and honor other opportunities so there will be more choices than "either" principal or teacher. If greater teacher leadership is to be attained in our schools, educators will also have to explore multiple conceptions of the role of the teacher: team leader, lead teacher, teacher researcher, master teacher. There is no more important form of "school restructuring."

And our profession needs to reinvent the principal or, perhaps, return the position to something akin to its original state as "principal teacher" or "head master," and thereby further blur the distinction between teacher and leader. In some schools, there are no restrictions about administrators teaching; almost everyone, even the head of school, remains in the classroom as well as in an administrative post. Just as all teachers can lead, all principals can teach!

The potential residing in teacher leadership for the benefit of the schools and of the teachers themselves will be realized only when many means exist to acknowledge and value personal authority as well as positional authority within the schoolhouse.

RECOGNITION

I personally think teachers are crying for respect. They want to feel they are valued and productive members of the school community.

—Michael Neubauer

Teachers will not for long go through the heroic efforts of leading schools in addition to teaching classes if the consequence of their work goes unnoticed, unrecognized, or unvalued by others.

I find it disheartening that so many outside of schools believe schools are incapable of renewing themselves, when these same skeptics extinguish the candles of the very educators most capable of reforming the schools. Teacher leadership has the unique capacity to strengthen teachers, the teaching profession, and the schools themselves all at the same time.

Yet a profound ambivalence about teachers pervades our profession. On the one hand, teachers are viewed—and treaded on—by many policymakers, board members, and administrators as semiskilled workers who need to be more technically trained and retrained, more closely monitored, more regulated, and more often evaluated against ever more prescriptive requirements and standards.

On the other hand, teachers are coming to be viewed by other reformers, administrators, and colleagues as professionals, deserving greater opportunity for more leadership, more participation in important decisions, and greater self-governance. They are being invited to "sit at the table with the grownups."

The former limited, mechanistic, conception of teacher as assembly line worker depletes the number and quality of those who choose to enter the profession and the spirit of those already there. And it begets a corps of teachers who find they must keep "two sets of books." One set shows compliance with those things that help them retain their jobs; the others record what they genuinely believe is best for youngsters. The constant dissonance between the two and the attendant deception combine to mute the voices of teachers in the important debates swirling around American education. In the scrutiny and reform of no other profession is the thinking of its members so absent. Is it any wonder teachers hesitate when asked to "stand up if you are a leader"?

Positive recognition comes in many forms: a title like "Master Teacher"; additional compensation; reduced teaching load; responsibility for a budget; allocation of prime space; an appreciative note from a parent; acknowledgment by the principal in the school newsletter; writing for publication about the work of teacher leadership or about taking some responsibility for the profession beyond one's school.

It's ironic that teachers, principals, and parents see clearly the value of *student recognition* and have assembled an array of ways to offer recognition to students, from gold stars to scholarships, while developing no comparable offerings for the outstanding work of teachers. Recognition of teachers' efforts, including their efforts as leaders, is in precious short supply in the culture of most schools. Recognition costs little, sometimes nothing in dollars, but when the alarm rings at 6:00 A.M., it is among the reasons a teacher keeps bounding out of bed with alacrity.

The consequence of expecting teacher leadership without recognizing and rewarding it is obvious. Teachers are telling us pure and simple: "I will commit and sustain the investment of time, energy, risk-taking, tedious meetings, inconvenience, intrusion on my classroom and into my personal life. I will pull my oar as a school leader if what I do is acknowledged and valued by those around me."

A DIFFERENT FUTURE

In the near future, many new teachers will be needed to staff America's schools because much of the entire teaching profession will retire. Thus, the coming decade brings with it a profound opportunity to *re-create* the teaching profession. How would we like it to become?

Most would agree with Ruth Jernigan, a Rhode Island teacher who said, "The talents and skills of students, staff, and parents in schools are underutilized." Schools are, indeed, full of an overabundance of underutilized talent. When teachers lock their cars in the lot each morning, too many of them also lock up astonishing skills, interests, abilities, and potential. Then they go inside and teach five classes of beginning algebra and monitor the lunchroom.

Teaching algebra is critical to the school itself, and so is the fulfillment of supervisory duties. Yet an opportunity resides with each of those 2.2 million new teachers, and with the veterans as well, to become far more for their schools, and for themselves, than "just a teacher," with the leaders residing down the hall in the principal's office. Each of these teachers can become—and must become—a school-based leader and reformer. For only when we transform and re-create the teaching profession in this way will we be able to transform and re-create the nation's schools.

Teachers face a choice about whether, in addition to classroom teaching, they will attempt to influence the entire school. A subtle yet definitive calculus determines the outcomes of the decision.

Teachers who choose to confine their work to the classroom *win.* They have more time and energy to devote to their teaching, to each of their students, and to their responsibilities at home. They are immune from the interpersonal conflicts with other teachers and with the principal. They enjoy a measure of safety in the relatively risk-free sanctuary of the classroom, where they may be accountable for pupil achievement but not for their own achievement as a leader. And they may enjoy a measure of sanity each day in the often turbulent and chaotic world of the schoolhouse. This is the path followed by the majority of teachers.

Other teachers—a smaller number, to be sure—take a different path. They choose to supplement their work as classroom teachers by assuming responsibility, some of the time, for some of the issues that are integral to the health and character of the entire school. By participating in the larger arena, these teachers *lose* what the larger group wins: time, energy, freedom from interpersonal hassle, and immunity from public criticism for efforts that might not succeed. And they probably lose, as well, a measure of sanity in their days at school and at home.

But the teachers who choose this path also *win.* They experience a reduction in isolation, which comes from frequent companionship and collegiality among other adults; the personal and professional satisfaction that comes from improving their schools; a sense of instrumentality, investment, and membership in the school community; a new learning about schools, the process of change, and themselves, which accompanies being a leader; and professional invigoration and replenishment, which spill over into their classroom teaching. These teachers become owners and investors in the school, rather than mere tenants.

These are two very different paths, taken for very different reasons, and with very different implications for the teacher, the school, and the profession.

Even with new job descriptions, titles, and generous recognition, even by expecting all teachers to lead, it is difficult to transform teachers who are used to seeing their domain as the classroom and the leader's domain as being "down the hall in the principal's office."

With those 2.2 million new teachers coming into view on the horizon, schools and school systems can post any job description for "teacher" they choose. They can expect of the new arrivals any kind of professional work that offers hope of transforming schools into communities of learners. These prospective teachers have not yet been inoculated by the prevailing school culture against leaders or against leading. We can expect, if we choose, that all teachers will lead. Subject for negotiation need be only the manner in which each will take on some important responsibility for the betterment of the entire school community.

With our nation's schools under relentless scrutiny, with all of the probing and prodding, with all the well-placed concern, a remarkable gap exists for teachers to fill. Most concerned people know what they don't want in schools; a smaller number know where the reforming of schools ought to lead us, and very few know how to get there. There are many right answers, and we are most likely to find them when we ask teachers to step into various kinds of leadership roles and to articulate for the public and for the profession just what school and teaching might become.

As one Rhode Island teacher put it so well:

Education needs leaders who feel it in their souls, not just those who get up there and talk. (Nancy Carnevale)

The bottom line remains: All teachers can lead! Many teachers want to lead. Schools badly need their ideas, invention, energy, and leadership.

REFERENCE

Ginott, H. (1972). *Teacher and child: A book for teachers and parents.* New York: Macmillan.

3

What Research Says About Teacher Leadership

Ann Lieberman and Lynne Miller

Teacher leadership has been the subject of a good deal of attention and scrutiny in the past two decades. In this selective review of the research, we focus on empirical studies as well as more theoretical and interpretive work that we believe adds to the knowledge base. To that end, we have found it useful to divide the literature into three broad categories or themes:

- *Individual teacher leader roles* and *organizational realities:* empirical studies of the roles individual teacher leaders play, what skills the roles require, how these roles bump up against the structures and norms of the bureaucratic school organization, and how teacher leaders earn legitimacy within the school organization.
- *Learning in practice:* descriptions of how teachers learn on the job and in specific contexts to become leaders, interpretive accounts of the

From Lieberman & Miller, *Teacher Leadership*, 2004, Jossey-Bass. Reprinted with permission of John Wiley & Sons, Inc.

nature of professional learning, and descriptions of how learning in practice is enacted in new teacher leadership roles.

- *Teacher leadership and reshaping school culture:* descriptions of broadened conceptions of teacher leadership, which place it at the center of efforts to renew the culture in schools and build professional communities.

INDIVIDUAL TEACHER LEADER ROLES AND ORGANIZATIONAL REALITIES

Most of the early research on teacher leadership focused on individual teachers and the nature of the leadership they assumed, making only passing mention of the organizational context or wider school reform issues. In fact, Smylie (1995) reported that of over two thousand published articles on teacher leadership, most were descriptions of teacher roles and the organizational constraints that teachers faced in those roles.

Individual Teacher Leader Roles

In the 1980s, Miles, Saxl, and Lieberman (1988) studied teacher leaders in order to identify the skills and capabilities of faculty who had taken on change agent roles in three different reform efforts in a large city. The teacher leaders in the study had a broad range of abilities and experience before they assumed leadership roles, and they came equipped with a repertoire of effective interpersonal skills and an impressive array of academic credentials. They were knowledgeable about curriculum, because most had gained some experience in administrative and organizational pursuits. However, they quickly discovered that building collegial relationships was a complicated process; they had to acquire a new cluster of skills to help them gain acceptance from teachers and principals and to forge communications across role groups. The new skills included building trust and rapport, making an organizational diagnosis, using resources, managing the work, and building skill and confidence in others. The teacher leaders also came face-to-face with the social realities of teaching in most school organizations and came to see, with new insight, how isolated teachers were and what this isolation did to them.

Wasley (1991) performed an in-depth study of three teacher leaders, each with a different focus, geographical location, and role. Her study revealed that these leaders, despite their disparities, shared common problems: difficulty in working within bureaucratic systems, lack of incentives for teachers to assume new roles, and teachers' resistance to becoming involved in reform efforts. Wasley concluded that in order for teacher leadership to become a reality, teachers must be given real support for their work. Further, she suggested that school culture be altered to accommodate these new roles. Whereas the Miles, Saxl, and Lieberman study pinpointed the skills and abilities that teachers developed, Wasley's research got at the dynamics of leadership as it was practiced over time. She offered an inside look at teacher leadership that demonstrated both the obstacles and the potential for teachers who reached out beyond their classrooms.

Teacher Leadership and Organizational Constraints

Descriptions of new roles for individual teacher leaders and how they negotiated school organizations were helpful to a point. But questions remained. What caused conflict? Ambiguity? Discomfort? Burnout? Or even success? Wasley raised some of these very issues, and a new group of researchers explored them further. Their research started with the recognition that teachers performed their leadership in the context of their schools, and it looked to the organization as the stage upon which the work was accomplished. The research found that the bureaucratic, hierarchical nature of schools often conflicted with the collegial nature of the reforms that teacher leadership was designed to bring about. The researchers concluded that structures endemic to schools made it difficult for teachers to become authentic leaders.

Focusing on organizational elements, Smylie and Denny (1990) documented the certainties and uncertainties associated with the roles of thirteen teacher leaders in a district. They described how these leaders adjusted to the tensions and ambiguities in their roles as well as to the organizational factors that supported or constrained their new work. They found that although teachers were supported by the district and were knowledgeable about classroom practice, they were uncertain about their role within the organization—whether other teachers knew or understood their work as teacher leaders or whether the expectations of the principal regarding their role matched their own. Smylie and Denny uncovered tensions about the proportion of time to be spent on classroom responsibilities versus leadership responsibilities and how the role of teacher leader related to the principal's role. Smylie and Denny concluded that organizational factors, such as the lack of time to adequately address their leadership functions, made it difficult for teachers to perform the new tasks assigned to them.

This organizational perspective helped explain why some teacher leaders suffered role conflict and ambiguity and found it difficult to do their jobs: Not only were they trying to support change and build collaborative relationships, but they were also taking on the traditional bureaucratic and institutional norms of the school. There were powerful organizational forces at work that either supported or thwarted teacher leadership.

The Quest for Legitimacy

Little (1995) explored the question of organizational legitimacy for teacher leaders when she documented the evolution of leadership in two secondary schools in the process of restructuring. She identified two key issues: "contested ground" and leadership legitimacy. She also found that teacher leaders were caught between strategies of commitment and strategies of control. According to Little, when teachers advance a restructuring agenda, they must work toward collaboration, experimentation, and flexible use of time and space within an environment that also supports the bureaucratic controls of evaluation and curriculum alignment. This becomes the "contested ground," the ground between the two opposing forces that operate in the school and on the teachers. Teachers who lead must somehow learn to negotiate between these two forces and move their school forward despite the strong pulls to maintain the status quo. In secondary schools, Little reports, it is subject-matter expertise that gives teachers their legitimacy to lead.

Bartlett's study of teacher leaders in two schools further explored the concept of "contested ground" that Little had uncovered (Bartlett, 2001). She examined two reforming schools, both of which supported teacher leadership. One school, although it allowed powerful teacher roles, lost much of its leadership because teachers found that they could not teach and lead at the same time. The demands of the two roles took too great a toll on their personal and professional lives. The will and the support for teacher leadership were there, but the structures, time, and distribution of work were not. In the other school, there were better provisions for teacher leadership, but ancillary tensions intruded on the lives of teacher leaders. Bartlett's study graphically illustrated how the absence of appropriate structures and culture makes it difficult for teacher leaders to negotiate reasonable personal and professional lives.

Little and Bartlett (2002) referred to this dilemma as "the Huberman Paradox," an acknowledgment of the work of Michael Huberman, an international scholar who looked at teacher careers over time and across continents. Huberman (1993) found substantial differences between the lives of teachers who ended their careers with a sense of serenity and satisfaction and those who exited with feelings of disenchantment and bitterness. The teachers who were most content spent their years in teaching tinkering at the classroom level. Those who were most bitter spent their time engaging issues at the school and district levels. The paradox is this: on one hand, teachers were stimulated by their involvement in reform work and leadership in their school; on the other hand, that very work led to burnout, disaffection, professional conflict, and disappointment (Bartlett, 2001).

Spillane, Hallett, and Diamond (2003) also studied how teachers assumed leadership roles and gained legitimacy within the school organization. Using observations of eighty-four teachers in Chicago's elementary schools, they found that teachers constructed others as leaders based on the interactions they had with them. As a rule, teachers valued subject-matter expertise in other teachers and were most comfortable assigning leadership roles to peers who demonstrated a certain level of expertise. Unlike principals who came by their leadership through formal organizational positions, teachers who were subject-matter experts became leaders because they had accrued the cultural, social, and human capital necessary to lead within the school. The work of Spillane and his colleagues articulated a clear path to teacher leadership within the organizational confines of a school.

Miller and O'Shea (1991) documented other paths toward teacher leadership. In their study of four teacher leaders in one elementary school, they uncovered four diverse warrants for leadership: (1) *leadership through experience:* a veteran teacher is acknowledged as a leader by virtue of her time in the system and her reputation as a classroom teacher; (2) *leadership through knowledge:* a relative newcomer is granted authority by "dint of her intelligence, her driving curiosity, her search for new knowledge, and her power as a classroom teacher" (p. 202) to transform theory into practice; (3) *leadership through vision:* a midcareer teacher is valued for his ability to imagine new ways of assessing, displaying, and communicating student progress and his willingness to involve others in making his vision a reality; (4) *leadership through respect for children:* a librarian invents a role for herself and is awarded credibility as an advocate for tying student self-knowledge to academic learning through her visible and direct work with children and through presenting demonstration lessons in classrooms. Like Spillane, Hallett, and Diamond, Miller and O'Shea concluded that teachers come to leadership informally through the construction of peer interactions. They also found that "each teacher followed a unique trajectory, . . . each led from a particular strength, . . . each was rooted in classroom practice . . ." (1991, p. 209). Legitimacy was earned, not granted.

LEARNING IN PRACTICE

A second body of scholarship focuses on how teachers learn their new roles and how to enact them. Researchers from fields outside of education were the pioneers in studying professional learning and how it occurs. They began with the observation that professionals learn by actually doing the work and reflecting on it. Gawande's description of how surgeons learn their craft stands as an apt description of such a process. Reflecting on one of his first surgeries, in which he couldn't get it right, he reported, "In surgery, as in anything else, skill and confidence are learned through experience—haltingly and humiliatingly. Like the tennis player and the oboist and the guy who fixes hard drives, we need practice to get good at what we do. . . . We want perfection without practice. . . . Learning is hidden, behind drapes and anesthesia and the elisions of language" (2002, pp. 18, 24).

Gawande's account resonates with the ways that teachers learn to become leaders: on the job, through experience and practice, by trial and error, seldom visible and often hidden. Although they are taught theories and skills in preparation for their work, teacher leaders learn most of what they need to know in the process of performing the work. The concept of learning in practice is now viewed as foundational to teacher leadership; it rests on the idea that learning is more social, collaborative, and context-dependent than was previously thought. In the next two sections, we explore the roots of this concept and its implications for understanding how teachers learn to become leaders.

Theories of Reflective Practice and Situated Learning

Schön (1983) laid the foundation for understanding learning-in-practice when he coined the term *reflective practice*, which is now commonplace in the literature, as a starting point for developing a theory of learning in the professions. For Schön, learning took place on the job, where people developed "theories in use" that were derived from their own experience in practicing their craft. He argued that professionals did not apply knowledge; they created it. Often spontaneous and sometimes chaotic, the process of reflective practice allowed people to uncover what they already understood and knew how to do—what Polanyi (1967) had called "tacit knowledge"—and to build on that knowledge by making it more explicit so that it could expand learning and deepen practice. Learning, in this view, was not the transmission of knowledge from an expert to a novice; rather, learning was discovery. It made the private public and the implicit explicit (Schön, 1991, p. 5).

By situating learning within specific professional settings, Schön opened the door for educational researchers to examine the development of teachers' learning as it occurred under different conditions and to explore the connections between learning and context. By focusing on what teacher leaders actually did in different settings, researchers were able to develop understandings about why teacher leaders encountered difficulty within bureaucratic organizations and assumed leadership roles with more ease in smaller learning communities. In the first instance, leadership responsibilities were considered an add-on to an already heavy teacher workload. In the second instance, teacher leadership was supported by the provision of adequate time, space, and resources and by the establishment of responsibilities that fell within a reasonable set of expectations. In the learning-community settings, teachers assumed leadership as part of their work, not in addition to it.

Professional Learning Within Communities of Practice

Lave and Wenger (1991) added to the idea of learning in context. Their social theory of learning rests on three processes—learning, meaning, and identity—that occur side by side in communities of practice in which social practices are espoused and enacted. "Learning is both social and collective, rather than individual and social" (Lave, 1996, p. 149) and comes about by social participation. It cannot be designed; it happens through experience and practice. In plain terms, people learn from and with others in particular ways. They learn through practice (learning as doing), through meaning (learning as intentional); through community (learning as participating and being with others); and through identity (learning as changing who we are).

Borrowing from Schön, Wenger (1998) views practice as both explicit and tacit, including both what people say and observe and what is left unsaid and begs for explanation. It includes "subtle cues, . . . untold rules of thumb, . . . sensitivities, embodied understandings . . . and shared world views" (p. 47), as well as a community willing to share the work publicly. Central to learning in communities of practice is "the construction of identities" (p. 280) within a community of practice where newcomers can absorb "how masters of their trade talk, walk, work and generally conduct their lives; how people who are not part of the community of practice interact with it; what other newcomers are doing; what newcomers need to learn to become full practitioners; increasing understanding of how, when, and about what old-timers collaborate, collude, and collide and what they enjoy, dislike, respect, and admire" (Lave and Wenger, 1991, p. 98). Professional learning so constructed is rooted in the human need to feel a sense of belonging and of making a contribution to a community where experience and knowledge function as a part of community property. "Such participation shapes not only what we do, but also who we are and how we interpret what we do" (Wenger, 1998, p. 4).

Hargreaves (2003) deepens our understanding of communities of practice when he compares them to what he calls "performance sects," approaches that he characterizes as valuing results over process and viewing learning as transfer rather than as the making of meaning and identity. In their efforts to train teachers to master standardized scripts and externally imposed rules, performance sects deny them the authority that comes from the joint construction of knowledge that occurs in a community of practice.

Learning new roles within such a community requires what Lave and Wenger term *legitimate peripheral participation* (Wenger, 1998). *Legitimate* refers to the rightful place that is accorded the newcomer by the full-fledged members of the community. *Peripheral participation* refers to the stance that the newcomer assumes. Neither a full participant nor an uninvolved observer, the newcomer has the advantage of rehearsing new roles and taking risks in a community of support and assistance. Thinking of professional learning as a legitimate and peripheral form of participation for newcomers is a significant shift.

Rogoff (1994) commented that such a perspective offers an alternative to both the teacher-centered and student-centered approaches that have dominated the discourse about learning. In this new iteration, neither the teacher nor the student has the strong authority position; instead the community is responsible for the learning of its participants. This helps to explain why learning to lead is eased for teachers who are part of professional communities and why it is more difficult for teachers who function individually within their school organization. Moore (2004) states, "It turns out that organizations, in and of themselves, may be poor settings for learning. . . . The very glue that organizes a group of people—roles, responsibilities, norms, and procedures—limits the feedback and errors that lead to learning. To learn, the practitioner must have a place 'in the balcony' from which to watch the action, critique the performance, and reflect on what needs to be done next. That is why collegial relationships and networks of practice are invaluable to the ongoing development of the school leader" (pp. 87–88).

TEACHER LEADERSHIP AND RESHAPING SCHOOL CULTURE

The third body of literature that we will consider explores broadened conceptions of teacher leadership and views teacher leaders as engaged in the work of reshaping the culture of schools. It focuses on teacher leadership roles that involve the reconstruction of relationships and meaning, the transformation of conditions for teaching and learning, and the development of an ambitious new view of the profession.

Teacher Leadership and Reculturing Schools

In 1995, Fullan wrote about the necessity of extending the notion of teacher leadership. He advocated moving away from a narrow view of a single individual trying to make a dent in a bureaucratic system toward a more complex perspective that involves multiple levels of leadership, all engaged in reshaping the culture of the school. Working together as a cohort rather than as individuals, teacher leaders can build a new collaborative culture. Such a culture would have the capacity to support the diverse leadership approaches and configurations necessary to "reculture" a school (Fullan, 1995).

Fullan mapped the professional work of teacher leaders by identifying six domains of teacher leadership work: knowledge of teaching and learning, knowledge of collegiality, knowledge of educational context, opportunities for continual learning, management of the change process, and a sense of moral purpose (Fullan, 1994, p. 246). It was clear that no one person could assume all that leadership required. In order to be enacted, teacher leadership had to be shared. Fullan's expanded notion of teacher leadership not only lifted the burden from individuals but also provided the criteria for distributing the professional work of leadership throughout the teaching force in a school.

Lambert (2003) also wrote persuasively about broadening the concept of teacher leadership. She offered a view of "constructivist leadership," which is grounded in "relationships, community, learning and purpose" (p. 14).

She saw the concept of leadership as being in transition, in line with Fullan's notion of "reculturing." In Lambert's articulation of leadership, it is not a role but rather "performing actions . . . that enable participants in a community to evoke potential in a trusting environment; to inquire into practice; to focus on constructing meaning; or to frame actions based on new behaviors and purposeful intention" (p. 13). Under this definition, many people in an organization or school could perform acts of leadership. Leadership, understood broadly, could build an environment for the continual learning and participation of the adults as well as their students.

Both Fullan and Lambert pointed to a new direction in understanding and supporting teacher leadership. They replaced the limited vision of teacher leadership as an individual enterprise trapped in existing school organizations with a broader conception of teacher leadership as groups of teachers intentionally working together to transform the very cultures in which they work and lead.

Teacher Leadership as Building Community

A view of teacher leadership that is closely related to reculturing schools encompasses building a professional community. McLaughlin and Talbert (1993) first used the term *professional community* when they reported on a five-year study of secondary schools in California. They found high school departments where such communities existed, in which groups of teachers talked openly about their students and the problems they were having, discussed curricular and pedagogical approaches to making changes together, taught one another different strategies and practices, and committed themselves to collective discussion and action with their peers as colleagues. These high school departments were in sharp contrast to the norm of loose collections of teachers who each worked alone.

Westheimer (1998, p. 12) further defined community as involving interaction and participation, interdependence, shared interests and beliefs, concern for minority views, and meaningful relationships. In his now-classic study of two middle schools, Westheimer further refined his concept of community. Both schools had strong professional communities but were unlike in kind and culture. The forms of participation and interaction differed in each school, as did the ways that members expressed shared interests and handled conflict and minority opinion. The first school, "Brandeis," was a community that was tied together by respect for individual rights and differences. The other school, "Mills," was " . . . driven by a strong collective mission and collective values" (Westheimer, 1998, p. 120). Brandeis teachers looked within their own community of teachers and sought support from one another; Mills teachers extended themselves externally and gained support from the larger community. Professional community for Brandeis was procedural and conforming. For Mills, it was characterized by joint work, broad leadership responsibilities, and strong identification with the larger community.

Westheimer drew several lessons from his study. First, beliefs matter. The Mills teachers believed in a communal ideal; the Brandeis teachers believed in individual rights and innate abilities. The differences in beliefs permeated the culture of the school. Second, structures matter. The Mills teachers developed structures that encouraged innovation. Their structures tended to support a culture of participation. For Brandeis, there were fewer structures for both participation and conflict; Brandeis teachers developed forms for participation, which Hargreaves (1994, p. 195) calls "contrived collegiality," that were imposed, required, and ordered rather than developmental, integrated, and part of the life of teachers. Westheimer's study uncovered how professional communities can differ in their cultural commitment to participation, shared visions, and ways of working together.

Little (1990) analyzed the conditions under which teachers acted as colleagues within a community and described how they move from independence to interdependence. She developed a continuum that began with storytelling and scanning (the occasional opportunistic contacts that teachers have), moved to aid and assistance (giving help and advice) and then on to sharing (exchanging materials, strategies, and ideas) and finally to joint work (collective action based on shared responsibility such as an interdisciplinary team). Her analysis demonstrated that an authentic professional community in schools tended to develop over time with increasing levels and complexity of teacher engagement and was powerful in changing the norms of privacy.

Grossman, Wineburg, and Woolworth (2001) conducted a three-year study of a large secondary school that illustrates the pangs of developing a professional community. The research focused on what happened when twenty-two teachers from the English and social studies departments participated in a book group that was created specifically for the purpose of building community and studying it at the same time. Community was defined as providing for the learning of students and the learning of adults. As the teachers worked through the "inevitable conflicts of social relationships, and formed structures to sustain relationships over time" (p. 3), they confronted the cultural and vocational impediments that were involved in building a community across traditional boundaries. The study documented the dynamics of the growth of a community from its inception and identified a number of fault lines of conflict among the teachers. Conflicts arose over differences in disciplines, gender and racial differences, and difficulties in learning to work and learn together. The researchers also uncovered a lack of capacity to do what they termed the "social work" of building a community and the necessary social norms of genuine civil discourse. This study presented a powerful narrative of how a professional community is formed. It described the dynamics of beginnings and the evolution from subgroups and factionalism to a mature community through the exposure and working through of differences. It highlights what it takes for teachers to persist and learn to take responsibility for their own growth and that of others.

Promising New Teacher Leadership Roles

The shifting conceptions of teacher leadership is represented in research that documents three promising new roles: teacher as researcher, teacher as scholar, and teacher as mentor. Teacher as researcher derives from a genre of research that creates new knowledge from direct teacher practice and reflection rather than from more removed methods of observation and interpretation. As a form of leadership, teacher research attends to both process and results and leads to improvement in classrooms that can extend to the whole school. The seminal work of Cochran-Smith and Lytle (1993, 2001) describes how teacher research and inquiry not only leads to an articulation and improvement of individual work but also influences the school culture. Because it generates knowledge that is local, contextual, and immediate, it resonates with the dilemmas of practice that other teachers experience. Teacher research is a form of reflective practice. It not only creates new knowledge, allowing teachers to see their practice in a new light and improve on it, but it also makes inquiry a critical component in teacher learning and school redesign.

Teacher as scholar builds on the idea of teacher as researcher and expands it (Shulman, 2000). The Carnegie Foundation for the Advancement of Teaching, in a program known as the Carnegie Academy for the Scholarship of Teaching and Learning (CASTL), expands the idea of teacher research to include scholarship as a central tenet of the work of teaching. Scholarship is characterized by the necessity of making one's work public in some form, being amenable to having it critiqued, and passing it on to others so that they can build on it. CASTL researchers found that when teachers studied their own practice and made it publicly available to others, they felt far more efficacious about their teaching and they approached their peers in substantially different ways.

When leadership has scholarship at its foundation, it is more about expertise, credibility, and influence than it is about power, authority, and control. Teacher scholars influence others by collaboratively studying practice, reading other researchers' work, and making their own work available as a source of discussion and action by their colleagues. They promote learning-in-practice for others as they enact it for themselves (Hatch, Eiler, & Faigenbaum, 2003).

Teacher as mentor or coach is another leadership role that allows teachers to make their work public and assist in the reconstruction of the profession. It is important to note that the terms *mentor* and *coach* have been appropriated by some of the "performance sects" that Hargreaves (2003) describes. In those instances, mentors and coaches work from predetermined scripts to transmit the one right way or the "best practices" that authorities, who are far removed from the context of particular classrooms, have established and sanctioned. Strong and St. John (in press) report on a project in which mentors assume a more complex and ambitious role as guides for new teachers and as agents for reculturing schools.

The Santa Cruz new Teacher Program, which developed under a statewide initiative, releases veteran teachers from classroom responsibilities to serve as full-time advisers to groups of fourteen beginning teachers. The program has been very successful in easing the entry of new teachers into the profession and in keeping them: 94 percent of the 1992–93 and 1997–98 cohorts of newcomers were still in education after six years—89 percent in teaching and 5 percent in other roles (Strong & St. John, in press). Just as important, however, is the program's emphasis on creating systemwide norms and practices that promote career-long learning and inquiry into practice. To that end, the program engages advisers in their own induction program. Here they learn and practice the skills as coaches, classroom observers, and group facilitators that they need to be effective with their advisees. With strong links to administrators and to the participating sites, the program for mentors doesn't leave them to fend for themselves; it ensures that they learn their new roles as members of communities of practice, and it also prepares them to confront organizational realities that affect new teachers in particular and their own teaching and the teaching profession in general.

Originally conceived as a form of teacher empowerment, teacher leadership has earned its place in the professional literature. It has grown in sophistication and complexity over time. The studies reviewed in this chapter demonstrate an unfolding of descriptions, interpretations, and theories that began with stories of individual leaders striving to "make a dent" in the school organization, moved on to analyses of how new organizational roles were learned and enacted, and culminated in new conceptions of the role and its responsibilities. When taken together, the research provides a foundation for understanding the power, promise, and perplexities of teacher leadership.

REFERENCES

Bartlett, L. (2001). *A question of fit: Conceptions of teacher role and conditions of teacher commitment.* Unpublished doctoral dissertation, University of California, Berkeley.

Cochran-Smith, M., & Lytle, S. (1993). Teacher research: A way of knowing. In M. Cochran-Smith & S. Lytle (Eds.), *Inside/outside: Teacher research and knowledge* (pp. 41–62). New York: Teachers College Press.

Cochran-Smith, M., & Lytle, S. (2001). Beyond certainty: Taking an inquiry stance on practice. In A. Lieberman & L. Miller (Eds.), *Teachers caught in the action: Professional development that matters* (pp. 45–56). New York: Teachers College Press.

Fullan, M. (1994). Teacher leadership: A failure to conceptualize. In D. R. Walling (Ed.), *Teachers as leaders: Perspectives on the professional development of teachers* (pp. 241–253). Bloomington, IN: Phi Delta Kappa Educational Foundation.

Fullan, M. (1995, November). *Broadening the concept of teacher leadership.* Paper presented at the National Staff Development Council, New Directions Conference, Chicago, IL.

Gawande, A. (2002). *Complications: A surgeon's notes on an imperfect science.* New York: Henry Holt.

Grossman, P., Wineburg, S., & Woolworth, S. (2001, December). Toward a theory of teacher community. *Teachers College Record, 103,* 942–1012.

Hargreaves, A. (1994). *Changing teachers, changing times: Teachers' work and culture in the postmodern age.* New York: Teachers College Press.

Hargreaves, A. (2003). *Teaching in the knowledge society: Education in the age of insecurity.* New York: Teachers College Press.

Hatch, T., Eiler, M., & Faigenbaum, D. (2003). *Expertise, credibility, and influence: How teachers change the system.* Unpublished paper, Carnegie Foundation for the Advancement of Teaching, Stanford, CA.

Huberman, M. (1993). *The lives of teachers.* New York: Teachers College Press.

Lambert, L. (2003). Shifting conceptions of leadership: Towards a redefinition of leadership for the twenty-first century. In B. Davies & J. West-Burnham (Eds.), *Handbook of educational leadership and management* (pp. 5–15). London: Pearson Education.

Lave, J. (1996). Teaching, as learning, in practice. *Mind, Culture and Activity 3*(3), 149–164.

Lave, J., & Wenger, E. (1991). *Situated learning: Legitimate peripheral participation.* Cambridge, UK: Cambridge University Press.

Little, J. W. (1990). Teachers as colleagues. In A. Lieberman, (Ed.), *Schools as collaborative cultures* (pp. 165–193). New York: Falmer Press.

Little, J. W. (1995). Contested ground: The basis of teacher leadership in two restructuring high schools. *Elementary School Journal, 96*(1), 47–63.

Little, J. W., & Bartlett, L. (1995). Contested ground: The basis of teacher leadership in two restructuring high schools. *Elementary School Journal, 96*(1), 47–63.

Little, J. W., & Bartlett, L. (2002). Career and commitment in the context of comprehensive school reform. *Theory and Practice, 8*(3), 345–354.

McLaughlin, M. W., & Talbert, J. (1993). *Contexts that matter for teaching and learning.* Stanford, CA: Context Center for Teaching and Learning in Secondary Schools.

Miles, M., Saxl, E., & Lieberman, A. (1988). What skills do educational "change agents" need? An empirical view. *Curriculum Inquiry, 18*(2), 157–193.

Miller, L., & O'Shea, C. (1991). Learning to lead. In A. Lieberman (Ed.), *The changing contents of teaching* (pp. 197–211.). Chicago: University of Chicago Press.

Moore, M. (2004). *The role of legitimate peripheral participation in school leader preparation* (working title). Unpublished doctoral dissertation, University of Maine, Orono.

Polanyi, M. (1967). *The tacit dimension.* London: Routledge.

Rogoff, B. (1994, Fall). Developing understanding of the idea of communities of learners. *Mind, Culture and Activity, 1*(4), 209–229.

Schön, D. (1983). *The reflective practitioner: How professionals think in action.* New York: Basic Books.

Schön, D. (1991). *The reflective turn: Case studies in and on educational practice.* New York: Basic Books.

Shulman, L. (2000). From Minsk to Pinsk: Why a scholarship of teaching and learning? *Journal of Scholarship and Teaching, 1*(1), 48–52.

Smylie, M. A. (1995). New perspectives on teacher leadership. *Elementary School Journal, 96*(1), 3–63.

Smylie, M. A., & Denny, J. W. (1990, August). Teacher leadership: Tensions and ambiguities in organizational perspective. *Educational Administration Quarterly, 26*(3), 235–259.

Spillane, J. P., Hallett, T., & Diamond, J. B. (2003). Forms of capital and the construction of leadership: Leadership in urban elementary schools. *Sociology of Education, 76*(1).

Strong, M., & St. John, L. (in press). *Research working paper no. 3.* Santa Cruz, CA: Santa Cruz New Teacher Program.

Wasley, P. (1991). *Teachers who lead: The rhetoric of reform and the realities of practice.* New York: Teachers College Press.

Wenger, E. (1998). *Communities of practice: Learning, meaning, and identity.* Cambridge, U.K.: Cambridge University Press.

Westheimer, J. (1998). *Among schoolteachers: Community, autonomy, and ideology in teachers' work.* New York: Teachers College Press.

4

Teachers as Leaders

Emergence of a New Paradigm

Frank Crowther, Stephen S. Kaagan, Margaret Ferguson, and Leonne Hann

Within every school there is a sleeping giant of teacher leadership, which can be a strong catalyst for making change. By using the energy of teacher leaders as agents of school change, the reform of public education will stand a better chance of building momentum.

— Marilyn Katzenmeyer and Gayle Moller (1996, p. 2)

NEEDED: A NEW PARADIGM OF THE TEACHING PROFESSION

Even a cursory reading of the educational literature leads to the conclusion that the way the teaching profession is currently viewed is ill founded and out-of-date—in a word, wrong. Although the challenges confronting schools worldwide are greater than ever before, and many teachers

From Crowther, Kaagan, Ferguson, and Hann, *Developing Teacher Leaders: How Teacher Leadership Enhances School Success,* Chapter 1, pp. 3–16. (2002) Corwin Press. Reprinted with permission.

possess capabilities, talents, and formal credentials more sophisticated than ever before, the responsibility and authority accorded teachers have not grown or changed significantly in decades.

Thus a new paradigm of the teaching profession is needed, one that recognizes both the capacity of the profession to provide desperately needed school revitalization and the striking potential of teachers to provide new forms of leadership in schools and communities. The Teachers as Leaders Framework (Table 4.1) that represents the core of this chapter—and, indeed, of this book—substantiates the assertion that teacher leadership is an idea whose time has come. This assertion was advanced by Katzenmeyer and Moller (1996) in the first edition of their landmark publication, *Awakening the Sleeping Giant: Leadership Development for Teachers.* They claimed that the teachers have the potential to exercise new and dynamic leadership in schools, thereby enhancing the possibility of social reform. They introduced the metaphor of a sleeping giant to illustrate not just the current dormant status of teacher leadership but also the power it might exert if aroused.

In the 5 years since publication of *Awakening the Sleeping Giant,* teacher leadership has drawn considerable attention worldwide and has acquired a degree of legitimacy in the educational literature if not in educational practice. But what does *teacher leadership* mean? Sherrill (1999) has pointed to the ambiguity surrounding the term in the literature, asserting that "teacher leaders are referred to as clinical faculty, clinical educators, teachers-in-residence, master teachers, lead teachers, and clinical supervisors" (p. 57). In our view, teachers' proficiency in areas of specialized competence, such as those identified by Sherrill, may point to the growing maturity of the profession, but it does not directly provide direction for teachers aspiring to lead school reform. New, dynamic, defensible conceptions of teacher leadership are required as a matter of immense professional urgency. The search for this new paradigm informs this chapter.

This chapter is an optimistic and confident assessment of the teaching profession. It is grounded in highly successful, real-life school practices. It presents a view of educational leadership that is idealistic, realistic, and suited to the complex needs of school communities in a rapidly changing world.

TWO SNAPSHOTS

To begin, we profile two schools where teacher leaders have exercised distinctive forms of leadership to shape meaning for their students and communities.

Snapshot One: Greenhills State High School

Greenhills has 500 students and is situated in a small, economically depressed rural town. Because it is attractive in many ways, the casual visitor to Greenhills could be forgiven for not discerning that the

Table 4.1   The Teachers as Leaders Framework

Teacher Leaders

Convey convictions about a better world by

- articulating a positive future for students
- showing a genuine interest in students' lives
- contributing to an image of teachers as professionals who make a difference
- gaining respect and trust in the broader community
- demonstrating tolerance and reasonableness in difficult situations

Strive for authenticity in their teaching, learning, and assessment practices by

- creating learning experiences related to students' needs
- connecting teaching, learning, and assessment to students' futures
- seeking deep understanding of tacit teaching and learning processes
- valuing teaching as a key profession in shaping meaning systems

Facilitate communities of learning through organizationwide processes by

- encouraging a shared, schoolwide approach to pedagogy (teaching, learning, and assessment)
- approaching professional learning as consciousness raising about complex issues
- facilitating understanding across diverse groups while also respecting individual differences
- synthesizing new ideas out of colleagues' dialogues and activities

Confront barriers in the school's culture and structures by

- testing the boundaries rather than accepting the status quo
- engaging administrators as potential sources of assistance and advocacy
- accessing political processes in and out of the school
- standing up for children, especially marginalized or disadvantaged individuals or groups

Translate ideas into sustainable systems of action by

- organizing complex tasks effectively
- maintaining focus on issues of importance
- nurturing networks of support
- managing issues of time and pressure through priority setting

Nurture a culture of success by

- acting on opportunities for others to gain success and recognition
- adopting a no-blame attitude when things go wrong
- creating a sense of community identity and pride

surrounding community has endured a long-term slump in its primary industrial base, that it has one of the highest levels of economic disadvantage in the nation, and that as many as three generations of some families have experienced persistent unemployment.

According to a veteran teacher at the school, students used to "come to school with their shoulders drooped." It was in this context of limited opportunity and low levels of motivation that teacher leaders undertook to provide the material out of which success stories are made.

Where it all began is still not entirely clear. Perhaps it was the Student Aspirations Program, through which a small group of teachers built a system for student mentoring and peer support. This involved identifying students' interests or talents as a starting point for building self-esteem and proficiency and, ultimately, for broadening their horizons for future endeavors. Over the years, the Student Aspirations Program became part of the fabric of the school, changing regularly as new teachers, with new interests and capacities, joined the community. Conceivably, it was only when the school motto—*success breeds success*—began to infiltrate the thinking of the whole school community that students' expectations and self-belief started to change.

A second possibility is that credit for initiating the turnaround should be assigned to the current principal. Among his considerable talents is his ability to convince students that personal demeanor—dress, speech, manners—is very important to their achieving enhanced levels of academic and post-school success. He also insisted that every achievement, no matter how small, or in what field, was worthy of celebration. Thus he had no difficulty convincing Nancy and Lisa, two young teachers, of the impact of their public-speaking initiatives and organized-sports competitions on student motivation, self-expectation, and school pride. Nor did he have difficulty accommodating the school resources committee's recommendation that finances be made available to facilitate access to on-line career information for students and the community to improve career opportunities for all.

The positive effects of synergistic leadership at Greenhills State High are numerous. First, the school has achieved marked recognition for its academic, cultural, and sporting successes, having been honored in a statewide showcasing competition. Second, it has undertaken significant educational innovations in which teachers have challenged themselves to improve their teaching practices. Third, community surveys indicated that it has become regarded as the center of local community life to an extent seldom achieved by a high school.

The teacher leaders we observed at Greenhills were able to articulate clearly their goals and strategies. They spoke convincingly of the "we can do anything" mind-set of the student body, the inseparability of school and community, the sense of reward that goes with overcoming immense odds, and the teamwork of the teachers, matched by the facilitative support of the principal. They regarded their school as unique, and they treasured that uniqueness, despite, or maybe because of, the human disadvantage, and even despair, out of which it had emerged.

The question we asked ourselves as we left Greenhills was, "Could this dynamic leadership come from elsewhere in the community, or does it point to something distinctive about the teaching profession?" Certainly, our analysis of the leadership processes in place at Greenhills, supported by the views of teachers and school administrators, is that the magic of Greenhills resides substantially in the power of teachers—through their pedagogical and community-building practices—to transform their schools and enrich their communities.

Snapshot Two: Sunbeach Elementary and Middle School

Sunbeach has 300 students and is located in a small town that nestles in tropical bushland. The questions asked and answered there were, "Can a classroom teacher single-handedly inspire and coordinate a literacy program that enhances student achievement across an entire school? If so, what sort of leadership does it take?" The lessons learned from this remarkable story say a great deal about teacher leadership and its potential to contribute to the revitalization of schools:

> Loretta returned from the professional development day buoyed by new ideas and possibilities. What she had observed was an integrated approach to literacy that built on basic skills and seemed ideally suited to the needs of students in her remote rural school, with its large number of transient students. As a learning support teacher, however, she had no formal authority on which to build and sustain a schoolwide innovation. But Loretta's boundless enthusiasm for literacy innovation was matched by her determination. She had energy, passion, and optimism. And she was a thoughtful educator, well respected by her colleagues. She immediately shared her ideas and enthusiasm with the principal, Paul, who encouraged her to test them out with the school staff. The school's curriculum team was more questioning, drawing attention to likely incompatibilities with teaching styles, the extreme difficulty of creating a schoolwide approach to literacy, limited resources, the absence of a training program, and the largely untried nature of the innovation itself.
>
> A colleague, Claire, told Loretta about an advertised funding opportunity and coordinated, under difficult circumstances, the preparation of a successful grant application on her behalf. In a matter of weeks, Loretta had an implementation plan drafted, a training strategy designed, a community communications process in operation, and a school management team in place.

The communications process was particularly innovative, enabling parents to gain access on-line to weekly reports on their children's progress and to reciprocate with information they regarded as relevant. For many parents, particularly those of non-English-speaking students, this aspect of the program provided practical interaction with the school that was unprecedented. Six months later, authoritative testing, conducted with the assistance of a nearby university, provided clear evidence that students' literacy levels had improved. The teachers and principal decided to expand the initiative.

The exceptional success of the Sunbeach literacy program, sustained over time and across grade levels, can be linked to a number of factors. Among them were Loretta's indisputable personal dynamism and drive to address a glaring student need in the school; a professional learning experience that made its mark; the political advocacy of her colleague Claire; the strong facilitative support of the principal, Paul; a school staff open to suggestions; the availability of funds; external advice and encouragement at critical junctures from a neighboring university; a high degree of task orientation and organizational capacity on the part of a teacher leader and her colleagues; and a district director noted for his entrepreneurial stance.

The pervasive view of the school staff was that, without Loretta's inspiration, conviction, and organizational skill—and without Claire's support in confronting barriers—they would not have achieved anything significant. Indeed, other schools in the district, where the innovation was tried, reported no change in student achievement after a similar period of implementation. Our conclusion? There are surely teachers like Loretta and Claire in many schools, but distressingly few bring about the notable successes that these two achieved. When the extraordinary nature of their achievements is better understood, when such achievement is named as true leadership and accorded the recognition it deserves, we believe that it will become a contagious force.

PROBING THE WORK OF TEACHER LEADERS: AN EXHILARATING ENDEAVOR

The material in the two snapshots is both extraordinary and commonplace. Probing the work of teacher leaders is exhilarating in that it reveals aspects of the teaching profession that are largely obscured in the educational literature and in current practice. Several long-held assumptions are challenged in the process. The principals and staff at Greenhills and Sunbeach articulate and model a conviction that public education can provide the best possible opportunities for students, and that factors like isolation and economic disadvantage are no excuse for mediocrity.

The snapshots focus on ways that classroom teachers have brought about significant educational and social change in their schools and communities. The featured teachers involved both their professional and civic communities in the construction of new knowledge that inspired confidence and laid the foundations for heightened aspirations and enhanced levels of student achievement. In effect, the sketches offer a glimpse of the futuristic social transformation advocated by reformists like Drucker (1994) in the United States, Hargreaves (1994) in Canada, and Beare (2001) in Australia. Transformation of this order can occur relatively painlessly when teachers assume the mantle of leadership, and it can be very powerful.

The two snapshots present the work of a small cadre of teachers in a manner that defies the traditional mind-set that teachers do not have the capacity, inclination, or opportunity to do leaders' work. The featured teachers displayed conviction, courage, reasonableness, professional knowledge, and a wide range of persuasive and interactive skills. The "I'm just a teacher" syndrome that has come to characterize self-concept in the teaching profession worldwide is far removed from these descriptions.

At the same time, the material in these two snapshots is relatively commonplace. Our research has established that teacher leadership exists in its own right. Katzenmeyer and Moller (1996) provide a powerful picture when they compare teacher leadership to a sleeping giant and assert that where teacher leadership is alive and well, schools flourish. We agree and can see clear signs that the giant is rousing. Will it be a friendly giant? What should we now be doing to prepare for its arrival and ensure its productive impact in our schools and communities?

Here we are clear that the sleeping giant of teacher leadership is indeed rousing, its image discernible, its movement palpable. These developments we regard with enthusiasm but also with a degree of trepidation, because they could dramatically reshape the school workplace, the status of the teaching profession, and the place of schools within communities.

TEACHERS AS LEADERS FRAMEWORK

Our definition of teacher leadership:

> Teacher leadership facilitates principled action to achieve whole-school success. It applies the distinctive power of teaching to shape meaning for children, youth, and adults. And it contributes to long-term, enhanced quality of community life.

The Teachers as Leaders Framework presented in Table 4.1 emphasizes two aspects of this definition: (a) the values of teachers who enhance student outcomes and elevate the quality of life in their schools and communities, and (b) the power of teaching to create new meaning for people in schools and communities.

The framework presents an idealized image of how teacher leaders exercise influence in their school communities. It reflects the essence of the work of teachers designated as leaders in their schools, their communities, and their profession. In a sense, the framework is a hypothetical portrait, because no one teacher leader whom we observed fulfills all six elements. Yet all the teacher leaders whom we studied exhibited aspects of the six elements in some way, at some time in their work. The framework can thus be regarded as both idealized image and pragmatic guide to action.

Many teachers, perhaps most, do not meet the formidable requirements of the definition and the framework in its entirety. In particular, we recognize that consciousness of the power of teaching to shape meaning systems is not well developed in many schools or, indeed, throughout the teaching profession. Some would argue, legitimately in our view, that many educational innovations cause teachers' professional skills to atrophy (Apple, 1992) rather than to enrich their understanding of their marked capabilities.

There are good reasons that some teachers may not seek to link their work to the dynamics of communities in the way our definition prescribes. For example, teachers may choose to pursue subject-matter specialization, research, administration, or a range of other challenging occupational avenues that do not necessarily lead to teacher leadership as defined here. Moreover, some teachers who exert leadership at a certain juncture in their careers, or in a particular educational context, may not choose to do so at another time or in another context.

Furthermore, the capabilities required to exercise influence on professional processes of learning and on community agencies are complex. One cannot assume that all teachers have the energy, confidence, or experience to engage influentially at all times. Finally, our research suggests that teacher leadership occurs most readily in supportive organizational environments. But environments that support and nurture teacher leadership are not endemic to many schools.

Despite these drawbacks, there are far more classroom teachers who do meet the demanding requirements of this definition than one might assume. (See Table 4.1 for a portrait of the teacher as leader.) These individuals and collegial groups have, for the most part, been overlooked in the development of leadership theory in recent decades, and have been largely bypassed in the development of policy governing schools. These oversights have cost us all dearly. They have inhibited educational reform and helped to marginalize the teaching profession.

THE FRAMEWORK IN ACTION

The teacher leaders whom we studied, and whose work is captured in the Teachers as Leaders Framework, regarded themselves as ordinary citizens, bound by the usual limitations and imperfections. Yet they were doing what appeared to their colleagues, principals, and communities to be extraordinary things. This combination of the ordinary and the extraordinary is reflected in the connections between the material in the snapshots and the elements of the framework. Teacher leaders have certain characteristics in common—which we will now discuss.

Teacher Leaders Convey Conviction About a Better World

At Greenhills, preparing students for a better future provided the motivation for the teacher leaders. They understood the generally severe disadvantage of students' backgrounds and felt responsible for preparing students for the world of work. Lisa explained it this way: "As teachers, we can help these kids realize that they can do anything that kids in advantaged high schools can do. Getting the confidence is the key step for students in making the break."

At Sunbeach, Claire told us, "My motivation in supporting the literacy program came about because I am committed to getting a better deal for public schools."

Some colleagues saw Claire's stance as provocative, but she did not shy away from asserting it publicly. The principal, Paul, reinforced her in subtle ways, emphasizing the complexity of teachers' work: "I personally couldn't do what these teachers do. It is incredible how they take these kids and teach them such extraordinarily complex processes."

Explicit in both of these teaching-and-learning settings is the capacity to create new meaning and new forms of socially useful knowledge. The ability to meet what is, perhaps, the most challenging and, for some, frightening requirement of a knowledge-based society is, therefore, apparent. Teachers are the professionals into whose laps the responsibility most directly falls for helping children realize their talents and opportunities. But that responsibility implies the introduction of new values, new understandings, and new capabilities—a daunting challenge.

Evident at both Greenhills and Sunbeach is leadership that drew on distinctive personal attributes of teachers, leadership grounded in a vision of a positive and optimistic future for disadvantaged students. But it was not personal attributes or vision alone that constituted leadership in these two situations. Rather, leadership, as we observed it, was also exercised through interactive processes that were centered on serious professional and communal dialogue and trust.

Teacher Leaders Strive for Authenticity

At Greenhills, the Student Aspirations Program was, in some respects, an integrating force in the school, linked to all subjects and to extracurricular activities, such as debating, work experience, sports, personal development, and personal mentoring. It was based on educational principles and on teachers' perceptions of students' needs to take responsibility for their own learning, to study relevant content, and constantly to expand their view of the world. What emerged was distinctive to the school: As one teacher noted, "Once you become a part of Aspirations, you are a changed person as well as a changed teacher. The way you interact and engage is different from what it would be anywhere else."

At Sunbeach, Loretta recognized that to be effective, the literacy program had to be a schoolwide initiative. She emphasized the integration of the program into regular classroom literacy activities and coordinated it with parent literacy initiatives. The question "Will it work for *all* of our kids?" was a focus of staff dialogue during this trial period. Ultimately, Loretta's insight and conviction influenced other teachers' approach to literacy.

Authenticity in teaching, learning, and assessment practices took on a number of meanings in our snapshot studies: shared understanding of learning goals across the school; learning goals grounded in students' needs and evident in teachers' practice; an integration of teaching, learning, and assessment; and actions justified by authoritative educational theory. This is an imposing set of criteria, in part because it extends the boundaries of classroom instruction in a number of directions—engaging the broader community in shared learning, the creation of new forms of pedagogy, and the extension of academic ideas into community action.

Teacher Leaders Facilitate Communities of Learning

At Greenhills, community apathy toward the school turned into expansive support once successes became evident. The teacher leaders themselves derived strength and confidence from one another. In fact, the informal alliance of teachers and administrators working as equal partners proved to be the root of the school's success. From this highly visible and successful alliance, community agencies were easily linked into Aspirations and other school programs.

At Sunbeach, too, an informal professional group (a teacher, a learning-support teacher, and the principal) initiated a highly successful innovation. Elementary teachers were the first formal group to be integrated into this collegial network. It was further expanded in response to the expressed interest of individual teachers, following staff discussions on the merits of the program. This program was also extended to include a cluster of nearby schools.

Rosabeth Kanter (1994) wrote that "like romances, the formation of alliances rests largely on hopes and dreams—what might be possible if certain opportunities are pursued" (p. 95). The teacher leaders we observed demonstrated practical capacity to build alliances and networks in many forms, thereby engendering the creation of new ideas, dreams, and opportunities that would not otherwise have existed.

Teacher Leaders Confront Barriers

When Lisa approached the Greenhills principal to ask for one more chance for a highly disruptive student who was threatened with exclusion, she epitomized the social-justice orientation of Greenhills teacher leaders and their preparedness to extend ideals into social action. This orientation included a wide range of activities, including provision of basic food and laundry services for needy students. The principal summed up the advocacy role of teacher leaders as follows: "I regard the teachers here as the guardians of the culture. They take personal responsibility for managing projects that fit the school's vision."

At Sunbeach, Claire located two significant funding sources to support the innovative literacy program, and coordinated the grant application process. Her colleague Loretta, who had conceived the literacy project, generated an extensive training program for the staff and organized the planning that led to a smoothly running operation. Loretta's capacity for social action was apparent in her statement that even without the facilitative support of the principal, "I would do it in some form myself."

These examples capture the essence of teaching against the grain that some theorists have articulated in projecting images of teacher leadership. They manifest conviction, courage, and strategic skill that might not be expected of most teachers and, thus, might be generally discouraged. They are, however, essential to teacher leadership and to the pursuit of enhanced schooling and quality of life in our communities.

Teacher Leaders Translate Ideas Into Action

At both Greenhills and Sunbeach, the teacher leaders whom we observed articulated deep concerns regarding the sustainability of the innovations with which they were associated. In both instances, they translated their concern into direct actions that contributed to the ongoing implementation of their innovations. Thus at Sunbeach, Loretta mobilized staff development processes, with the support of a deputy principal, and also engineered a range of highly successful community awareness programs. At Greenhills, teachers managed all aspects of the Aspirations program, including curriculum, community service, publicity, and budget. In creating and sustaining productive relationships with school administrators and with external constituencies, and in using the Aspirations program to enrich the self-perceptions of a severely disadvantaged community, these teachers could be said to have entered the arena of metastrategy that we draw on elsewhere and that Limerick, Cunnington, and Crowther (1998) regard as fundamental to leadership in postindustrial organizations.

Teacher Leaders Nurture a Culture of Success

At Greenhills, the teacher leaders collectively emphasized a "we can do anything" attitude. This had a demonstrable impact on students' self-esteem and achievement. Even seemingly insignificant achievements were held up as evidence that all students can achieve beyond normal expectations when they are encouraged and recognized. The Greenhills principal provided us bemusedly with this example: "Even a student taking a cow to the Blackbutt Fair can provide a basis for building confidence. These shows bore me silly except for what I can do for the school just by being there."

Successes of past students in the outside world were also offered regularly as evidence that success breeds success and that small achievements can turn into bigger ones, once a start is made.

At Sunbeach, Loretta's infectious optimism energized others. The school's successes in the national Innovation and Best Practice Project (IBPP) were presented as proof that it is quite realistic to articulate and pursue lofty expectations. When Loretta and Claire prematurely terminated an IBPP research contract, they did so in the confident spirit of Sunbeach: "People are not to blame for failing to achieve high expectations. It is more likely the processes *we* [emphasis added] have in place that are flawed." Amid the disillusionment and anxiety that creep into our lives, success may be hard to recognize and equally hard for many of us to acknowledge. But leaders routinely recognize and acknowledge success. Teacher leaders do so to enhance confidence, induce high expectations, and extend horizons for their students. In the process, the uncertainty of the emerging knowledge-based society becomes not a threat but a promise for a better future.

CONCLUSIONS

In this chapter, we have presented a definition of teacher leadership and a related framework that derives from extensive research in diverse school settings. We regard this definition and framework as confirmation of a capacity for professional leadership that has been obscured in the literature on educational leadership and in most professional development programs for practicing and aspiring educational leaders.

In the eyes of their colleagues, principals, and communities, the teacher leaders whom we studied have a remarkable impact on their schools and communities. The Teachers as Leaders Framework captures these ordinary people doing extraordinary things. Their leadership is well suited to a postindustrial world where hierarchy in organizational relationships will decrease in importance, and the capacity to help communities enhance their quality of life through the creation of knowledge will increase.

REFERENCES

Apple, M. W. (1992). *Teachers and texts: A political economy of class and gender relations in education.* New York: Routledge.

Beare, H. (2001). *Creating the future school: Student outcomes and the reform of education.* London: Routledge/Falmer.

Drucker, P. (1994). The age of social transformation. *Atlantic Monthly, 274*(5), 53–80.

Hargreaves, A. (1994). Changing work cultures of teaching. In F. Crowther & B. Caldwell (Eds.), *The workplace in education: Australian perspectives.* Australian Council Educational Administration Yearbook. Sydney: Edward Arnold.

Kanter, R. (1994, July/August). Collaborative advantage: The art of alliances. *Harvard Business Review, 72*(4), 96–108.

Katzenmeyer, M., & Moller, G. (1996). *Awakening the sleeping giant: Leadership development for teachers.* Thousand Oaks, CA: Corwin Press.

Limerick, D., Cunnington, B., & Crowther, F. (1998). *Managing the new organization: Collaboration and sustainability in the post-corporate world.* Warriewood, Australia: Business & Professional Publishing.

Sherrill, J. (1999). Preparing teachers for leadership roles in the 21st century. *Theory Into Practice, 38*(1), 56–61.

5

Honoring the Uniqueness of Teacher Leaders

Marilyn Katzenmeyer and Gayle Moller

Becoming a leader is synonymous with becoming yourself. It's precisely that simple, and it's also that difficult.

—Bennis (1989, p. 9)

An underpinning assumption in this book is that an invitation to teacher leadership should be extended to all teachers. The reality of the nature of adult life is that teacher leadership may not be for every teacher at all points in a career. Acknowledging the transitions in the personal lives of teachers recognizes that there are times at which a teacher may be eager to participate, and there may be other times when the teacher must retreat from these responsibilities. One young teacher we know admitted that she had to be selective in her participation in some events and not in others. As a mother of young children, she knew she needed

From Katzenmeyer & Moller, *Awakening the Sleeping Giant: Helping Teachers Develop as Leaders,* Chapter 4, pp. 57–72. (2001) Corwin Press. Reprinted with permission.

to do this to maintain balance in her life, yet she also felt that teachers' opting out of leadership roles left a smaller group of people to take on the workload. This group was often made up of the same people over and over again.

As a teacher walks through the front door of a school, a whole person enters the community of teachers, administrators, students, and other staff members. Teachers used to be encouraged to compartmentalize their personal and professional lives, but this is no longer recommended. We now understand that the "work self" exists in concert with other facets of a teacher's life, and attempts to isolate them are absurd. Hargreaves and Fullan (1996) say that "teaching is bound up in [teachers'] lives, biographies, with the kinds of people they have become" (p. 25). This uniqueness affects how they will approach their work and carry out leadership roles. Because of the importance of personal assessment for success in leadership roles, a major component in the development of teacher leaders is asking "Who am I?" (Figure 5.1). To thrive as teacher leaders, teachers must recognize the factors that influence how they and their colleagues work,

Figure 5.1   Personal Assessment

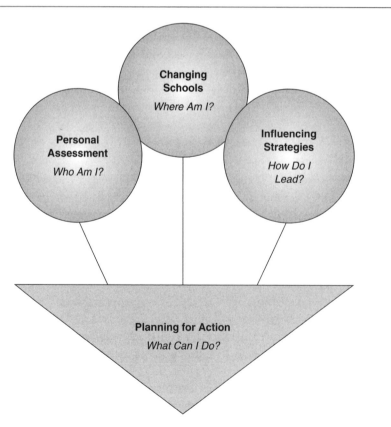

learn, and change in the workplace. Although the external context in which they function influences teachers, the reactions to the context and consequent decisions to make behavioral changes happen internally. A teacher confided, "Self-assessment made a difference in my life." Teacher leaders who learn to use this information find that it is helpful professionally and personally.

Educational change occurs not only school by school, but also, and more important, person by person. A faculty consists of people with differences in teaching skills, philosophies on how students learn, career needs, work perspectives, willingness to interact with others, adult development levels, and personal lives (see Figure 5.2). Teachers cannot presume to lead others before they understand themselves. When they spend time in self-assessment activities, teachers soon recognize that their colleagues may have different sets of values, beliefs, concerns, philosophies, and behaviors or may be at different stages of development. This insight led one teacher leader to share about a troublesome relationship with a fellow team member:

> I don't feel threatened by my peers and I give it my best shot. I feel much more confident and skillful in working successfully with a teacher on my team. She and I are working better together, and I am able to listen and see her point of view. More important, I am able to help her in being part of our team.

Figure 5.2   Factors Contributing to the Uniqueness of Teacher Leaders

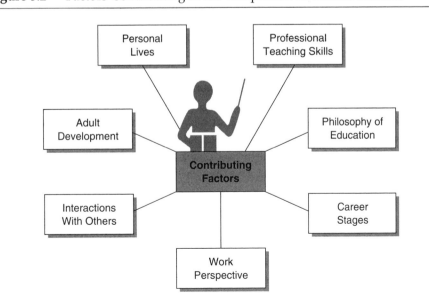

PROFESSIONAL TEACHING SKILLS

Before other teachers will accept a teacher's leadership, that teacher must be successful with his or her students. Excellent teaching skills are necessary to lead effectively with students in the classroom and to establish credibility with peers and administrators. Competent teachers diagnose situations within the classrooms, then select instructional strategies to match student needs (Wasley, 1999). The strategies will not be found in the lesson plans, but the teacher's ability to effectively adjust the instruction reflects a high level of skill development. If a teacher is not proficient in teaching skills, then the focus in the classroom is on daily survival. This teacher will need to develop classroom expertise before leading beyond the classroom.

Teachers confident in their own abilities want to collaborate with colleagues. They are willing to explore new strategies and to expose their own insecurities about their teaching practice. Teachers who can be honest about their struggles in teaching are usually the ones who win the respect of their colleagues. Many teachers feel that they should know the answers—after all, they are teachers. Teaching, however, is an uncertain craft (Rosenholtz, 1989), and when a respected teacher reveals uneasiness, it makes others feel they are not alone in feeling frustration.

One teacher described a teacher leader: "She has always been successful first with students. She always seems to know what she is doing and how to approach things in a quiet and supportive, dependable, enthusiastic way." As teachers become secure in their professional teaching skills, they are ready to reach out beyond the classroom to share with others. As one principal commented, "To me the highest accolade teachers can have is when their peers ask for help from them."

PERSONAL PHILOSOPHY OF EDUCATION

School reform challenges teachers to confront what they believe about education. Because our philosophies guide our actions, this is an important step in teachers' development. Earlier in this book, we shared our assumptions about teacher leadership; similarly, teachers bring a set of assumptions to their teaching. Rarely are teachers given opportunities to examine their own assumptions and then to compare them with their actual practice. For example, teachers' views of education may be based on their experiences as young students. Teachers may remember success in their own schooling. It is difficult for them to think differently about schools when traditional education served them so well. School reform efforts at times call into question teachers' assumptions about these past positive experiences. If they excelled as individuals competing for academic grades, then it may be distressing to embrace cooperative learning.

These assumptions will influence the decisions teachers make and how they will lead others.

Little (1993) recommends that teacher leaders examine the underlying assumptions of school reform and compare the congruence of these underlying assumptions with their own existing beliefs, values, and practices. Inviting teachers to compare what they say they believe with their actions can also test their assumptions. For example, experienced teachers who say "beginning teachers should be supported" may find that their actions are incongruent with this belief. They may be reluctant to confront the practice of placing novice teachers with the most difficult classes in their school. We all experience discomfort when we realize that, although we say we believe one thing, our assumptions drive our practices in the opposite direction.

Teacher leaders may think that all teachers share their beliefs about discipline, homework, or other areas of concern. It is eye opening for teacher leaders to see how their assumptions may be unlike the views of their colleagues. Teachers are even more disturbed when they discover they do not share the predominant values of their schools. The focus of the school may be proclaimed through a lofty mission statement, but the actual practice in the school may violate the expressed values. Until this dissonance is resolved, teacher leaders may not be comfortable working toward common goals for the school. Some teachers leave schools to find another position in a different school that has values congruent with what they believe.

A strategy we use to help teachers examine their belief systems about teaching and learning is the *Philosophy of Education Inventory* (Zinn, 1996). At first, the title of the instrument brings back memories of teacher education programs, and teachers believe that they will be discussing "ivory tower" theory. After completing the instrument, the teachers compare scores with colleagues and discuss how they may prefer different teaching methods or hold different beliefs about their roles with students. Then teacher leaders begin to see the practical use of examining these underlying beliefs. They recognize differing philosophies of colleagues and see that the differences can cause conflict in the school decisions about curriculum, instructional practices, and assessment.

STAGES OF CAREER DEVELOPMENT

As teachers move through their careers, they have different needs. Teachers may enter the profession at a traditional age or later in life, when they decide to move from another career into teaching. With the current emphasis on teacher recruitment, school districts are attracting people from other professions to enter teaching. A teacher's career stage can influence his or her willingness to take on leadership roles. Super, Thompson, Lindeman, Myers, and Jordaan (1988) describe four stages of career development and the concerns related to each stage. The stages are not always sequential. Some teachers skip stages, and others repeat them at particular points in their careers. A teacher who moves to a new position to teach a different type of student, learns new instructional content, or makes a lateral move from another profession may change stages.

Exploration Stage

Teachers entering our profession have different concerns than someone who has taught for 20 years. The individual recently graduated from the university will watch other teachers to decide the best way to survive in a school. It takes time to learn the social protocol for working with both students and other teachers. If the preservice program at the university emphasizes a teacher's responsibility toward school improvement, beginning teachers may take on limited leadership roles at the start of their careers. We work with teachers with fewer than three years of experience who are actively involved as members of school improvement teams. This early interest in teacher leadership should be encouraged as a means of helping to retain outstanding teachers. Many beginning teachers with previous work experience bring the expectation of being involved in leadership roles.

Establishment Stage

As teachers become comfortable with organizing and delivering instruction, they may decide to move their interest outside the classroom to work with other colleagues. These relationships can be positive influences on the improvement of instruction or may remain as informal social interactions not related to teaching and learning. A teacher leader may elect to work with a teacher on the same grade level, serve as a department chairperson, or join the school's governance structure.

Maintenance Stage

The "graying" of the teaching force (Sikes, 1992) implies that there are many teachers who are at this career stage. These experienced teachers face three options. First, they can remain unchanged and teach as they have taught for years. Second, they can update their knowledge and skills to improve their performance in the classroom to meet today's challenges. Finally, these teachers may decide to move beyond maintenance to improve their professional skills and influence school change on a broader scale. We have observed examples of teachers with more than 25 years of experience who become renewed through learning a new approach to teaching that is successful with their students.

Disengagement Stage

Toward the end of a teacher's career, the concerns may change depending on involvement in leadership roles. Teachers may take on more responsibility at this stage or may begin to plan for their retirement and to reduce their leadership contributions. Teachers who maintain a level of commitment to improvement in the school can be outstanding resources. If they have the respect of other teachers in the school, these teachers can influence those with less experience or those with fewer skills. Some teachers at this stage recognize the need to prepare others to fill the leadership roles they will vacate at retirement.

Withdrawal

At any time a teacher may withdraw from involvement. If interventions are to be successful with teachers who withdraw, they should occur early (Steffy, 1989). Unfortunately, the symptoms are hard to detect, because teachers who begin to withdraw become quiet and blend in with a compatible group of peers. Inviting teachers at this stage to accept even limited teacher leadership roles may be enough of an incentive to prevent them from moving into deeper levels of withdrawal.

Teacher leaders benefit by understanding their own movement through career development stages. This helps them clarify the concerns they may be feeling at various times in their careers. As leaders, teachers have an obligation to support their colleagues. Knowledge of career stages also helps teacher leaders select appropriate strategies to use when helping others.

Many teachers we work with are at the stage of exploration regarding their roles as teacher leaders. They are rethinking their careers and trying to decide how they will pursue their desire to increase their sphere of influence. The traditional option has been the route to administration, but now many teachers choose to make lateral moves by providing leadership as teachers.

WORK PERSPECTIVES

Teachers are influenced by their perspective on work as well as by career stages. Staw's (1986) longitudinal study found that a person's disposition as a teenager can predict an attitude toward work in middle and late adulthood. Perhaps people are not as malleable as one would like to think they are. To change an attitude toward work requires strong interventions. It often takes a critical incident to change a person's perspective. For example, a teacher's own child may experience difficulties in a traditional school environment, stimulating that teacher to suddenly see the benefit of increased commitment to change in education.

Teachers may have begun their careers with an idealistic view, but after years of disappointment in trendy innovations they may protect themselves by refusing to accept change. Why should they become involved again? These are the teachers who become the cynics, yet they can be valuable resources during decision making about a new change effort. These teachers, if encouraged, can ask the difficult questions that may prevent a school from moving from one educational fad to another.

Teachers' work perspective affects how they balance work and other parts of their lives. For instance, some teachers may view their responsibility to teaching as secondary to other life obligations. In contrast, other teachers may believe teaching is a mission and devote extra time and effort. Different perspectives on work can influence the leadership responsibilities these two groups of teachers may choose to accept. The first type of teacher may want to provide leadership within the classroom and, perhaps, help a few colleagues. The other group of teachers may take on the leadership roles in groups within the school, which frequently require additional time beyond the regular workday. Those teachers who make large commitments toward school improvement may be impatient with teachers who do not. Teacher leaders must understand that not all teachers have the same level of interest in their work or are at a stage in their lives that permits them to make the commitment.

INTERACTIONS WITH OTHERS

Teacher leadership demands frequent interactions with other adults. This may be uncomfortable for some teachers. One teacher leader told us, "During faculty discussions, I didn't hesitate to share. I was surprised that I took a risk—just the willingness to share and being open was a change for me." Interactions beyond the everyday conversations with others who work nearby force teacher leaders to deal with diverse ideas and speak out about their own beliefs.

Teachers working in collegial work environments are more effective (Bodone & Addie, 1999), but working alone should not be construed as an unhealthy way to work. Hargreaves (1993) questions the negative connotation given to teachers working alone. Teachers may prefer working by themselves for many reasons. Like the general population, some teachers are energized by contact with others and some are not. Teachers sometimes choose to work alone to conserve their most valuable resource, time.

On the other hand, there are teachers who would like to work together, yet the structure of the work environment does not encourage collaboration. These teachers want to be "in the know" about the happenings within the school. Sometimes these teachers want knowledge to lead positive change, but other teachers may use this as an excuse to seek control that leads to negative consequences. One experienced teacher leader we know wants to be deeply involved in all aspects of the schools; she is impatient with teachers who choose not to be part of the decision making but then complain about the decisions being made. She believes that teacher leaders need to be a part of the solution, not part of the problem.

Selecting the best match between the desire to interact with others and a specific leadership role contributes to the success of that teacher. Those who prefer to work alone may be interested in roles such as developing grant proposals or writing curriculum materials. In contrast, the teacher who wants to interact with others may be more interested in facilitating teams, speaking at community group meetings, or becoming a trainer. As teachers examine their own needs, they will become clearer about the kinds of leadership activities that suit their individual styles.

ADULT DEVELOPMENT

Each day, adults have opportunities to reflect and grow. Individuals can choose to develop, or they can continue to view the world from an existing perspective. More than 40 years of research from developmental psychology reveals that just as children have developmental needs, so do adults. Teachers' developmental stages influence their interactions with students, parents, and other staff members, as well as their ability to lead others.

Leithwood (1990) structured a summary of the work of three developmental psychologists, resulting in a stage model that briefly describes adult growth. Table 5.1 provides descriptions adapted from his work.

Table 5.1   Adult Development Concerns

Stage 1: Self-Protective	Stage 2: Conformist
• Must obey rules, but tries to get own gain • Most questions have one answer • Fear of being caught • Blames others	• Needs approval in order to meet expectations of others • Feels guilty breaking rules • Tends to go along with the group and not accept individual differences
Stage 3: Conscientious	**Stage 4: Autonomous**
• Understands multiple possibilities • Recognizes there are exceptions to rules • Future-oriented	• Fully independent • Understands the interdependence of relationships • Accepts others as they are

SOURCE: Adapted from Leithwood (1990).

The stages of development appear to be tidy categories, but adults are unpredictable and cannot be pigeonholed. Each of us is unique and exhibits behavior represented in different stages. Though other models exist, Leithwood's (1990) synthesis offers insight to teachers' stages of development. Teacher leaders who are at the self-protective stage may find open and honest communication to be more uncomfortable than their colleagues find it. Teachers at the conformist stage tend to honor the status quo, finding it difficult to embrace change unless other teachers with whom they identify want the change. Group decision making is a chore for these teachers, because they find different perspectives on issues annoying. In contrast, the teacher at the conscientious stage values consensus and would be effective as a facilitator or group member. At the autonomous stage, teachers not only see value in others' viewpoints, but draw strength from them. They may seek schoolwide leadership responsibilities. As teachers move into higher levels of adult development, we find that they are less dependent on experts for solutions to problems. Instead, these teachers solve their own problems, often in collaboration with other colleagues. The more mature teacher will seek out experts only to fill in the gaps in his or her problem-solving strategy.

Adult development is complex. Teachers find the right time to examine what is happening in their lives, both personally and professionally, and then choose to change or maintain their current perspective. A principal described a teacher leader in his school: "I see a big difference in the last two years. She has a calm way of dealing with the team. She smoothes over hurt feelings, and the little problems are resolved." This teacher leader chose to learn, and those around her benefit from her development.

PERSONAL LIVES

Teacher leaders involved with governance and decision making put in long hours doing excellent work with their students and providing schoolwide leadership. Just as do other adults, teachers have struggles with life issues. Children, elderly parents, marital difficulties, second jobs, community involvement, and other personal worries occupy the minds of teachers as they shoulder leadership obligations. Often, concerns are expressed about students who live in difficult family situations, but teachers may experience similar types of problems. Teachers' reluctance to take on leadership roles may stem not from a lack of interest, but from a desire to protect the time they need to balance work and personal responsibilities. Teachers welcome options in their level of involvement in leadership responsibilities.

Zinn (1997, p. 45) studied supports and barriers to teacher leadership. One area in which she found impeding factors was personal consideration and commitments. The factors in this area included:

1. Family or other responsibilities that compete with leadership roles (i.e., crises, child-rearing, single parenthood, aging or infirm parents, illness of one or more family members)

2. Personal health issues or concerns

3. Lack of family support for leadership efforts

4. Cultural or religious values that discourage leadership

The reality of teacher leaders' lives may compel them to move in and out of leadership roles. Dependence on a few teacher leaders in a school puts the school's reform efforts at risk because of these possible circumstances. Care must be taken to build the leadership capacity of all teachers in the school so that when a teacher leader must attend to personal issues, there are other teachers to assume the lead.

ACKNOWLEDGING DIVERSITY

Being able to successfully influence colleagues will require teacher leaders to understand how to work with others who are different from them. Departments and organizational and academic divisions of schools are highly segmented within schools. It may be difficult for teachers to engage with other teachers across these structures (Cambone, Weiss, & Wyeth, 1992). There are schools in which teachers seldom work with other teachers or may not even know the names of teachers in the same building. Certainly the increasing ethnic diversity within our schools and communities also suggests that these skills are of primary importance to teacher leaders.

We encourage teacher leaders to learn skills that will make them sensitive to seeing others' points of view. A first step could be providing experiences that focus teachers' attention on the diversity of educational philosophies at a specific school. Teacher leaders become alert to the various sets of beliefs and values that their colleagues, administrators, and parents bring to school. In our work of developing teacher leaders, we have found that the instrument *Philosophy of Education Inventory* (Zinn, 1996) helps teachers to measure their personal educational philosophy. Learning about the philosophies of others leads teachers to a deeper understanding of the different perspectives they encounter in making change happen at their schools. Practice with influencing those who have different beliefs and experiences with education invites the teachers to learn to effectively work with other people in their schools and in their communities.

Teachers work with a broader group of stakeholders, including parents, students, and business and community representatives—all of whom bring their own perspectives to the school setting. In addition, teacher leaders work with others who come from diverse cultural and socioeconomic backgrounds. The neighborhood school in which everyone basically looked and thought the same no longer exists in most communities. Ovando (1996) observes that relationships for teacher leaders are affected by many factors, including the context, beliefs, and culture of the school.

Learning skills to approach others who are different can enhance teacher leaders' abilities to work collaboratively with others. We suggest that teacher leaders learn to articulate and acknowledge the differences that exist, rather than ignoring them. For example, the English department and the social studies department may think differently about grading. Or the businessperson on the school improvement team may not share the views of a teacher in the group. Once the differences are articulated, teacher leaders must learn to reveal their values and views by being open and honest with others. For example, the physically handicapped teacher might share with colleagues the beliefs she holds about ways to work with differently abled children. The teacher who holds a humanistic philosophy of education may articulate his views on the new state testing program. Finally, teacher leaders should seek to understand all viewpoints. Valuing individuals for the diversity they bring to the situation can be essential to the success of teacher leaders. We came up with an acronym, ADS (Figure 5.3), to aid teacher leaders in using skillful communication in situations where differences exist.

We find that teachers recall the value of understanding differences as a highlight of their leadership development experience. A teacher in one of our leadership sessions shared the following poem to describe his or her feelings:

The beauties of nature come in all colors.
The strengths of mankind come in many forms.
Every human being is wonderfully unique.
All of us contribute in different ways.
When we learn to honor the differences and appreciate the mix,
We find harmony.

—Anonymous, 1994

Figure 5.3   Acknowledging Diversity

Acknowledge differences.

Disclose values and views.

Seek to understand and include others.

In our experience, teachers find it beneficial to enhance their abilities to listen, to empathize, and to examine issues from the perspective of others. Given the diverse environments in which teachers are trying to make change, these skills become valuable tools for teacher leaders to learn.

VALUE OF KNOWING "WHO I AM"

Experience with thousands of teacher leaders has taught us that personal assessment does not stop with understanding about oneself, important as those insights may be. The meaningful learning for these teachers has been in how they view their colleagues and their relationships with these colleagues. They recognize and acknowledge the differences that exist among their colleagues, and they learn that diversity is to be valued. We not only emphasize the importance of acknowledging these differences, but also invite teacher leaders to reveal their own assumptions to encourage a deeper understanding of others.

Teacher leaders can look at their own assessments and predict how others may be the same or different; they can then use this information to be more effective with others. The insights help teacher leaders to know themselves better. Often they conclude that leadership involves changing one's own behavior to be productive with diverse individuals or groups. By acknowledging others' perspectives, teacher leaders honor the uniqueness among their colleagues.

CONCLUSION

The uniqueness of the individual must be honored as each teacher considers moving into a leadership role. Many factors surface as teachers assess where they are in their professional and personal lives. Not all teachers are willing to accept teacher leadership responsibilities, and this may be due to circumstances unknown to others in the school. Teachers are unique and bring their personal history to the workplace, which affects their interest in assuming new leadership roles. Many teachers seek out leadership roles. Principals must recognize and respect the differences and then identify leadership roles that could match the reluctant teacher's level of interest.

In our experience, the development of teacher leaders begins with personal knowledge. Teachers need an opportunity to assess their teaching skills; philosophy of education; work perspectives, career, and adult development stages; and the challenges in their personal lives. With knowledge about themselves, teachers can see that other faculty members are not just being difficult but truly come from diverse perspectives. Important insights about self and colleagues result in teacher leaders' beginning to value the differences. Teacher leaders use listening and communication skills to increase their proficiency in working with these alternative perspectives.

Attention to the organizational environment in which these teachers work is also necessary. If the school workplace does not reflect a rich learning climate for both students and staff, teacher leadership will not flourish. Teachers seek positions in schools that have environments to support the individual differences discussed in this chapter. If the goal is to improve all schools, then all schools need to provide healthy environments for adult growth and development.

APPLICATION CHALLENGES

For Teachers

1. If you are exploring the notion of being a teacher leader yourself, keep a journal about the skills, knowledge, and experiences you have. Decide where you are in terms of professional skills and career stages. Where do you see a role for yourself in providing leadership at your school site? What might be an opportunity for you to contribute your time and energy?

2. Identify a couple of reluctant teacher leaders at your school. Consider what aspects of their personal lives might influence their readiness or willingness to be involved. Consider family obligations, health, outside interests, and their stages of adult development.

3. Create a graph of your faculty members and analyze the numbers of teachers at each of the four stages of career development. Use this information to guide the strategies you select as a teacher leader. How would you relate differently to beginning teachers than to teachers near the end of their careers?

For Principals

1. Matching the needs of the individual with the needs of the organization is a complex undertaking. Think about those teachers on your staff who may not be fulfilling their potential to be leaders. How could you match their skills and talents with real needs at your school? Meet with existing teacher leaders for a discussion about their roles. Encourage them to talk through their feelings as you support them.

2. Establish an informal mentoring program for new or transferring teachers to help them adjust to the school culture. Encourage teacher leaders to act as mentors to individuals who wish to be helped.

3. Conflicts will naturally arise within a faculty facing substantive changes in the school. Treat these situations as opportunities for all to learn. Do not back away from conflict. Differences can be as important as consensus in unpredictable change situations. Use your knowledge of differences to help your faculty understand what might be going on. Look for individual and group learning that can result from working through a conflict together.

For Superintendents and District-Level Administrators

1. Teachers who are prominent, active, and visible in your schools and communities are less likely to suffer from teacher stress and cynicism in the middle to late career stages. Determine actions you can take that support this level of involvement and to ameliorate forces that are obstacles.

2. Teacher leadership is less likely to be sustained without rewards and incentives. Examine your district's practices about these issues. Try to be creative in identifying what rewards and incentives would be motivating for your district's teacher leaders. Seek their input.

3. Work more closely with the colleges and universities that train teachers for your schools. Form partnerships and work collaboratively to produce teachers who see themselves as agents of educational change.

4. Invite your teacher union leaders to discuss ways you can work together to provide leadership development opportunities for teachers.

For College and University Professors

1. Develop strategies in your courses to include personal assessment of communication styles and leadership approaches for teachers. Teachers who know themselves are more likely to understand and work well with their colleagues and students. Encourage your students to maintain a portfolio of assessment information about themselves.

2. Case-study research on teachers at different levels of adult development or career stages would be instructive to both university faculty members and students. Think about how this research could be accomplished by faculty or graduate students.

REFERENCES

Bodone, F. M., & Addie, K. L. (1999, April). *Teaching in a standards-based system: Teachers' voices can influence policy, preparation, and professional development.* Paper presented at the annual meeting of the American Educational Research Association, Montreal, Quebec, Canada.

Cambone, J., Weiss, C. H., & Wyeth, A. (1992). *We're not programmed for this: An exploration of the variance between the ways teachers think and the concept of shared decision making in high schools* (Occasional Paper No. 17). Cambridge, MA: Harvard Graduate School of Education.

Hargreaves, A. (1993). Individualism and individuality: Reinterpreting the teacher culture. In J. Warren & M. W. McLaughlin (Eds.), *Teachers' work: Individuals, colleagues and contexts* (pp. 51–76). New York: Teachers College Press.

Hargreaves, A., & Fullan, M. G. (1996). *What's worth fighting for in your school?* New York: Teachers College Press.

Leithwood, K. A. (1990). The principal's role in teacher development. In B. R. Joyce (Ed.), *Changing school culture through staff development* (pp. 71–90). Alexandria, VA: Association for Supervision and Curriculum Development.

Little, J. W. (1993). Teachers' professional development in a climate of educational reform. *Education and Policy Analysis, 15,* 129–151.

Ovando, M. N. (1996). Teacher leadership: Opportunities and challenges. *Planning and Changing, 27*(1/2), 30–44.

Rosenholtz, S. J. (1989). *Teachers' workplace: The social organization of schools.* New York: Longman.

Sikes, P. J. (1992). Imposed change and the experienced teacher. In M. Fullan & A. Hargreaves (Eds.), *Teacher development and educational change* (pp. 36–55). Bristol, PA: Falmer.

Staw, B. M. (1986). Organizational psychology and the pursuit of the happy/productive worker. *California Management Review, 20*(3), 63–74.

Steffy, B. (1989). *Career stages of classroom teachers.* Lancaster, PA: Technomic.

Super, D. E., Thompson, A. S., Lindeman, R. H., Myers, R. A., & Jordaan, J. P. (1988). *Adult career concerns inventory.* Palo Alto, CA: Consulting Psychologists Press.

Wasley, P. (1999). Teaching worth celebrating. *Educational Leadership, 56*(8), 8–13.

Zinn, L. F. (1997, March). *Support and barriers to teacher leadership: Reports of teacher leaders.* Paper presented at the annual meeting of the American Educational Research Association, Chicago, IL.

Zinn, L. M. (1996). *Philosophy of education inventory.* Boulder, CO: Lifelong Learning Options.

6

I'm Not Like You

Laura Reasoner Jones

When I was a little girl, my family spent every summer at my grand-mother's cottage at Bass Lake in northern Indiana. When school let out the Friday of the Memorial Day weekend, my four brothers and sisters and I would all be taken to the doctor's office to get our polio vaccine updates. We would then come home, pack our books and old clothes, and go to sleep in our new summer pajamas, eager for the next day. Our parents would come into our rooms early in the morning, lift each of us into the old station wagon while we slept, and start the long drive north while it was still cool. I would wake up in the back seat of the car, not exactly sure where I was, but knowing I was on my way.

My journey toward becoming a teacher leader started without my knowledge also. It too was a trip with a silent beginning. I don't think I rec-ognized that I was moving in that direction until I was well over halfway there, and I had to stop and think about it before I went forward again.

Prior to moving into the Technology Specialist position I currently hold, I worked for 17 years as a preschool special education teacher for a large suburban school system, the twelfth largest school system in the country. As the years progressed and I improved in my job, I volunteered for many roles outside of my normal teaching duties. I coordinated the Pediatric Resident Visitation Program, chaired the Local Screening Committee, started the neighborhood outreach program in my local com-munity, evaluated the pre-intervention program to see if we were effec-tively serving families, and mentored both new teachers and new mentors. After school hours, I started and ran an afterschool girls math/science club for my daughter's elementary school, developing a teacher research project and a Web site around it. But all of that didn't seem to be enough.

In the spring of 1999, the National Board for Professional Teaching Standards offered a pilot program to validate the upcoming certificate in Exceptional Needs. My out-loud excuse for doing this was the $150 they were paying for participation, which I promptly spent on toys for my preschool students. But as I look back, I realize that no other special education teacher I knew was willing to do this—money is clearly not the motivator people think it is. I think I really did it out of curiosity and a need to challenge myself.

So, when the Exceptional Needs certificate was validated and opened up the next year, I was primed and ready to be one of the first candidates in the country to earn this certification. And when I achieved it, and published my diary of the experience in the *Washington Post Sunday Magazine,* a whole new world opened up to me.

I applied for and was chosen to be the Teacher in Residence at the National Board to run its American Telephone and Telegraph Foundation grant-funded program with Apple Computer, Inc., creating the Digital Edge Learning Interchange video library of National Board Certified Teachers, integrating technology into their accomplished teaching. This was a huge leap for me. I had never even opened up a laptop. I left my comfortable job in preschool to commute on the subway, learn digital video editing, manage 35 teachers who lived all over the country, and wear dresses every day. I was way out of my comfort zone, and I was scared to death. In fact, I remember telling myself that I had to do this to set an example for my 17-year-old daughter, who was getting ready to apply to college. If I couldn't take a risk and change my life, how could I expect her to leave home and go away to college?

After a few weeks in the new job, I met one of my preschool teaching colleagues for coffee before she went to see her students. She asked me how it was going, and I remember saying, "You know, you are one of the best teachers we have. You really need to go for your National Board Certification." And she looked me right in the eye and said, "Oh, no, I couldn't. I'm not like you."

I thought about that comment over and over during the next two years as I traveled all over the United States learning about digital video, presenting for Apple and the National Board at national conferences, and writing exhibit content. I could feel myself changing every month, becoming more confident and feeling more capable. I began to feel that I could hold my own in a room full of nonteachers and that I had something to offer. But I kept thinking, "What did she really mean, 'I'm not like you'?"

She and many other people I worked with in preschool special education were people I respected for their teaching expertise. I went to them for advice, for answers to tricky problems. They were my experts. So what was she saying?

As I thought about the comment and saw the changes in myself, I began to see one difference between us. For my own personal happiness and professional satisfaction, I needed to work beyond the classroom. I needed to be doing something that had a measurable effect on more people than my students—on their families, on their communities, or on teachers in general. This didn't mean that she or any of the other teachers that I respected were better or worse than I was; it just meant that we really were different. They were very happy to work very well with their own assigned students; I preferred to work with both my own students and the community at large, either the people in my small town or the larger professional community. It wasn't enough to do my job well as she and many of my teaching colleagues did. No, I needed to do more for more people. And thus I recognized my role of leadership as a teacher.

I found that my ease at being a teacher leader and working for more than the students I was assigned had become smoother and more rewarding as the pressures at both work and home eased. My daughters grew up and started to drive. Day care and carpooling were things of the past, giving me lots of time on my hands. At the same time, I found that my day-to-day job responsibilities had become so effortless that I could spend more of my time at work taking on extra tasks to benefit the students in general or managing programs for all the staff.

When I left the preschool program to be on "loan" to the National Board, my colleagues and I realized exactly how much extra work I had been doing. It took five different people to take over the extra jobs and tasks I had been doing—local screening, teacher research, resident visitation program. . . . and I had been doing all of that for no extra pay and no additional benefits like space or time. What was I thinking?

When I came back after two years, I had the opportunity to reinvent myself, to choose the extra jobs I wanted to do. And I also had the opportunity to choose to do nothing extra, to just do the job as assigned, as many of the 33 teachers I worked with did.

Here was the crucial moment of decision—what did I really believe in? Did I feel that teachers did too much without compensation? Did I think that silently supporting this work ethic was really the way to run a school system? Or did I still believe that it was my responsibility to contribute as much as I could to the greater good of the program?

After much thought, I decided that I was fully awake now and well on a journey to a destination that I liked. I could look around and see where I was both professionally and personally and make an active choice about how I wanted to spend my time and my talents. So I chose extra jobs that used my newfound technology skills—building a Blackboard site, creating digital portfolios of my preschoolers, running a teacher research group, among other things. These jobs fulfilled me and met my need to contribute to the community and the program.

As I remember my friend's comment, I know now that I am "not like her," even though she is an exceptionally good teacher that all of us should try to emulate. But to be true to myself, to be "like me," I need to work outside of the teaching role and contribute as much of myself as I can.

Questions for Reflection and Conversation

- Are you a leader in your school? In answering this question for yourself, how are you "constructing" a definition of teacher leadership?
- How would you assess your own developmental readiness to take on the challenges of teacher leadership?

We have found protocols—simply put, a plan for proceeding, but lately used as a synonym for structured conversation—to be very useful in our educational leadership classes and in leadership coaching. The point, of course, is to have a rich conversation, but protocols can also serve to prompt individual reflection. The National School Reform Faculty (http://www.nsrfharmony.org/) provides a wealth of protocols that we have used and adapted.

We have modified "The Qualities of Educational Leadership Exercise" of the ATLAS Principal Institute (available from the NSRF Web site) for our use with teacher leaders.

1. Take a few minutes to think about the most rewarding experiences you have had as a teacher leader. What are the qualities of leadership that made these experiences so memorable? What are the critical characteristics of the leadership experiences for you as a teacher, learner, or leader? Write down 3–5 one-word descriptors of the qualities that are most important to you as a leader, a teacher, and a learner.

2. Gather in groups of 2–3 and share one of your most rewarding experiences. After you have each told your stories, reflect together on what role respect, trust, and relationship had in shaping the experiences.

3. Take a few minutes to think about a leadership issue that you are struggling with right now. How might you use the elements of respect, trust, and relationship to influence how you will respond to your current dilemma? Make a note of one thing you will do with regard to this situation based on a new insight.

4. Share your new insights with your partner(s).

PART II

Teacher Leaders Everywhere

There is the children's fable of the old man who searched far and wide for a treasure only to learn in the end it was buried in his home. Like him, we know there are teacher leaders everywhere. Finding them requires looking carefully and compassionately at teachers and the work of teaching within schools. The contributions that occupy Part II offer different ways of seeing teacher leaders everywhere.

Nancy Flanagan's "Teacher Professionalism: Diamonds on the Souls of our Shoes" sets the tone for this section by making the case that the challenge of teachers seeing themselves as teacher leaders rests more with a world that hasn't fully conceptualized what teachers do in the classroom as a professional occupation. "Teaching is soul work, work that opens windows on eternity," Flanagan says in a passionate argument for a more enlightened conception of what it means to be a professional teacher. Michael Fullan builds on this theme more broadly in his chapter, "Leadership to the Fore," from *Leadership & Sustainability,* arguing "If you think context, you can change context." Michael Fullan's chapter enlarges the world of leadership by describing how every person in a system, including and especially teachers, can become "system thinkers in action" and thus bring more sustainable leadership to schools and school systems.

A constructivist perspective on leadership is offered by Linda Lambert and coauthors in "Teaching as Leading," from *Who Will Save Our Schools?* This chapter echoes a theme that resonates throughout this collection; namely, that teaching itself "is an act of leadership" and that "how we choose to practice leadership must relate directly to how we teach" (p. 121).

Our colleague Gordon Donaldson wrote "What Teachers Bring to Leadership: The Distinctive Assets of Teachers Who Lead." He carefully explores and analyzes the unique gifts that teachers bring to school leadership, arguing well that teachers *are* leaders and have always exerted strong leadership in our school. Finally, Barbara White's "Leading From the Parking Lot" makes the case for seeing teacher leaders everywhere (*especially* in the parking lot)!

7

Teacher Professionalism

Diamonds on the Souls of Her Shoes

Nancy Flanagan

Several years ago, after giving a speech on leadership to an audience of award-winning teachers, I was approached by a woman in a business suit and heels. After saying how much she enjoyed my remarks, she suggested I rethink my "teacher" terminology in future talks, saying emphatically, "I'm not a teacher—I'm a professional educator." We exchanged further pleasantries, but what I really wanted to say in reply was something my preadolescent students frequently exclaim: *As if.*

When it comes to teacher professionalism, wishing (and hoping, or even labeling) doesn't make it so. We can call ourselves education professionals, but the words themselves carry no more weight than "hair care professionals." Those of us who see ourselves as teacher leaders, who understand the intellectual complexity and social importance of the work of teaching, feel that we are true professionals. It is the rest of the world that has a problem conceptualizing what we do in the classroom as a professional occupation. If we want to make that transition, however, recreating our beloved vocation into a nationally accepted profession, with all the respect and benefits accorded to professions in America, we must do it ourselves. Certainly, no one will do it for us.

My teaching colleagues are fond of pointing out the poor working conditions in our very average school. We are isolated from other adults and have—at best—limited access to tools other workers take for granted: a telephone, adequate technology (and, more important, on-site technological training and support), privacy, and reasonable bathroom and lunch breaks. We sit on the floor with 5-year-olds and eat our USDA-surplus cafeteria lunches in the allotted 23 minutes over brown paper towels. It's not a glamorous job by any means, but these rudimentary, even shabby, circumstances and lack of amenities don't in any way classify our actual work. After all, if a doctor is practicing in a third world country under primitive conditions, her work is still considered highly professional.

Professionalism is not defined by trappings—we cannot dress or speak ourselves into being professional; hanging our diplomas on the wall and ordering business cards are not enough. A telephone in every classroom will not make us professionals—in fact, neither would an executive secretary and reserved parking slot for every teacher. We need to stop dreaming about the glitzy accoutrements of professions, attractive as they are, and turn our eyes to the real prize in teaching professionalism: control over our own work.

I've been thinking about some hallmarks of what it means to be professional:

- shared control over who enters the field and established, acknowledged standards of professional practice;
- communal belief in ongoing professional learning, actually using research to make decisions, and a personal obligation to share new information and techniques (as opposed to keeping the cool ideas to yourself, in hopes of making your evaluation just a little brighter than your colleagues' this year);
- lively conversation and healthy debate over critical issues in the field (rather than desultory chat about bus duty and the PTO meeting);
- the opportunity to influence policy decisions where the rubber meets the road, in the classroom rather than central office or the state capitol;
- discretion over use of limited time and resources;
- a voluntary work ethic—independently managing our own work; having access to our work space on weekends, because our work life is determined by doing the job right, not by the dismissal bell or an antiquated building security system.

None of these are part of typical teaching practice in my school. The very essence of what I do every day—choosing curriculum, assessing student performance, delivering instruction—is increasingly determined by someone who has not even met the unique students I serve. It is no surprise that many teachers resist professional development—often, it's just one more thing that someone else has decided is important.

If we want to re-create the dynamics of teaching into something that looks and feels like a profession, I don't believe we can wait for political leaders, newspaper columnists, or the superintendent to suddenly notice our vital importance to the national well-being and invite us into the conversation. We must do what other professions did to establish their legitimacy: roll up our sleeves and start telling powerful stories of how teaching has changed, how complex it has become, and what fabulous teaching looks like. Remember that doctors were not always regarded as highly trained specialists using a body of precise technical knowledge—they were once considered little more than barbers with an extra blade or two. Their transformation into a respected profession came through their own insistence on publicly defining excellent medical practice and more than a touch of public relations magic. We can also—individually and collectively—become true professionals.

The first step for me was reading, and then believing, the National Board for Professional Teaching Standards cornerstone document, "What Teachers Should Know and Be Able to Do," a foundational statement supporting teacher professionalism through accomplished practice. Becoming a National Board Certified Teacher was *my* personal transformational journey, but all of us must endorse standards of professional practice before we can hope to call ourselves professional teachers. We need to acknowledge that there are levels of accomplished practice and openly declare that some teachers are more skillful and effective than others. Opening the doors of our classrooms with a willingness to measure our own practice against high standards is frightening—it takes courage to expose what's been hidden. When I looked critically at my practice through the lens of professional teaching standards, I was shocked to see gaps and significant areas of weakness. As I struggled to fix the flaws the process had revealed, I also wondered what would happen if every teacher had to justify habits and decisions by holding them up to high and rigorous standards. Setting the bar high would radically change the system.

Maybe we need to begin at the gate, limiting entrance into teaching, through more stringent screening and training. I have had the excruciatingly uncomfortable experience of failing a student teacher—a nice young woman, completely unsuited to teaching. As teacher leaders, we can no longer turn a blind eye to substandard, ineffective teaching. If we want to become professionals, we must accept responsibility for protecting and uplifting *teaching*, rather than teachers.

Behaving professionally has sometimes led me out of the classroom and out of my comfort zone. Professionals create their own challenges, starting networks of vigorous, informed dialogue about current issues and forming active partnerships to leverage change. The holy grail of professional teaching, however, is a genuine voice in policymaking at all levels. If I define teacher leadership only as work done in the school and classroom to improve instruction and learning, I am missing a critical piece of what it means to be a professional: autonomy, the power to make decisions based on the research I trust most—my own experience and expertise.

Why is this conception of professionalism worth pursuing? Not just for our own satisfaction, although many teachers would relish the opportunity to manage their own work and professional growth. The reason is clear: The teacher is the critical factor in student learning. Teacher quality trumps all other variables, including class size, socioeconomic factors, and per-pupil allotment. There is no better investment in our children and our future than improving teaching. Professionalizing teaching would pay dividends far beyond a contented teacher workforce; valuing teacher expertise will release new creativity and energy to build and fine-tune better conceptions of teaching and learning.

Parents have long understood the essential value of great teaching, the blend of deep content and deep caring. When exemplary practitioners speak, parents (who have firsthand knowledge of their skill and power) listen. This cornerstone of mutual respect can help us elevate the profession. Parents are the group most personally invested in a demonstrably qualified teacher for every child and may serve as our allies in the quest to achieve professionalism. They can also provide those powerful stories and images of transformation in the lives of children—and a story can be worth a thousand test scores.

The most important reason to pursue this professional vision of teaching? Although it is sometimes humble—and humbling—labor, my teaching is soul work, work that opens windows on eternity. When we walk as professionals, we set our own course, and so gladly accept the weight and privilege of that influence. We find value and beauty in our work of excavating minds, looking for diamonds, when we have defined that work ourselves. Why would we settle for anything less?

8

Leadership to the Fore

Michael Fullan

As society places higher and higher expectations on the performance of public and private agencies, leadership is bound to come to the fore. The question is, what kind of leadership is needed for sustainability? In a nutshell, we need a critical mass of leaders at all levels of the system who are explicitly cognizant of and committed to pursuing in practice the implementation of the elements of sustainability. Systems change on an ongoing basis only if you have enough leaders who are system thinkers. This is what is meant by "thinking outside the box." If you think context, you change context. Let's be very careful here: You can't think precisely enough about context unless you are also *acting* in this enlarged arena. When great thinking and action go hand in hand, the concepts get larger and they also get more meaningful because they are grounded in concrete strategies and actions.

Almost 20 years ago, Peter Block (1987) argued that "cultures get changed in a thousand small ways, not by dramatic announcements emanating from the boardroom" (p. 98). Not fully true. It requires the thousand small ways *and* boardroom policies. Sustainability is a team sport, and the team is large.

From Fullan, *Leadership and Sustainability: System Thinkers in Action*, Chapter 3. (2005) Corwin Press. Reprinted with permission.

In this chapter, I take up where we are now and set the stage for what individuals can do and what systems can do to bring the right kind of leadership to the fore.

WHERE WE ARE

Almost everyone agrees that leadership is the key to reform. And then they make mistakes. The most egregious error is the search for the super leader. The title of Khurana's (2002) study of 850 CEOs captures the problem: *Searching for a Corporate Savior: The Irrational Quest for Charismatic CEOs*. As he puts it:

> Perhaps the most fundamental—and fundamentally irrational—attitude underlying the closed CEO market is the belief in charismatic authority itself. The attraction of charismatic leaders is that they promise a solution to all of our problems if only we follow the leaders with unwavering certitude....
>
> For all its manifest defects, charismatic authority has always been alluring for the single reason that it avoids accountability and responsibility for outcomes. (pp. 207–208)

Ironically, the poorer the performance of the company (or school district), the more likely boards will make the fundamental mistake of hiring high-profile CEOs, virtually guaranteeing that continuous improvement over time will not happen:

> When a company performs badly, institutional investors [the public, school board] are likely to demand that the CEO resign and be replaced by someone who is from outside the firm. The external CEO search process that ensues is characterized by unusual secrecy; anxious attention to the expectations of outsiders . . . ; a focus on an extremely small number of candidates, people who are already high-profile leaders; and an emphasis on the elusive, culturally based qualities of "leadership" and "charisma" at the expense of concrete knowledge of a firm and its problems. (Khurana, 2002, p. xii)

Similarly, Collins (2001) found that charismatic leaders are negatively associated with sustainability. He distinguishes between Level 5 leaders "who build enduring greatness" and Level 4 leaders who "catalyze commitment to a vision and to standards" (p. 20). As Collins laments,

> One of the most damaging trends in recent history is the tendency (especially by boards of directors) to select dazzling, celebrity

leaders and to de-select potential Level 5 leaders [who appear less flashy]. (p. 39)

We don't have comparable in-depth studies of superintendents and principals, but the carousel of superintendent turnover certainly reflects the ad hoc search for the leader who will finally right the ship (see Andy Hargreaves, 2004). David Hargreaves (2003), taking up Collins's (2001) findings, makes a similar point:

> When English headteachers are being appointed, they are expected by the governing body to articulate a clear vision for the school, which they promise they will implement if appointed.
>
> Significantly, very few Level 5 leaders were appointed from within the company, whereas among school headteachers, it is more common to appoint from outside than inside. We may have it wrong in education in assuming that "fresh blood at the top" is a lever of school improvement. While this may apply to schools that are (close to) failing, it may need an insider to take a good school to greatness because it builds on what they inherit rather than striving towards a different vision against the inclinations and preferences of the staff. An insider may have a better grasp of the school's weaknesses and is thus able to face the facts brutally and so do something about them. (p. 42)

Sustainability is very much linked to continuity of deepening direction over time. We can describe Collins's Level 5 leaders in these terms: The main mark of an effective principal is not just his or her impact on the bottom line of student achievement, but also on *how many leaders he or she leaves behind who can go even further.* These are not mutually exclusive. Level 5 leaders have a dual focus on performance and development of leadership in others.

There are, however, very few Level 5 leaders (in any sector), which means that there are too few leaders available who are working on developing leaders beyond themselves. In cases of high turnover, such as in education, this is a disastrous situation. Stated differently, it is not turnover per se that is the problem, but rather *discontinuity of direction.*

We can also consider the issue of sustainability from a different angle and ask about "succession." Studies of succession in the principalship are rare, with Andy Hargreaves, Moore, Fink, Brayman, and White's (2003) recent study being an exception. In a review of literature, and in case studies of succession in six high schools, Hargreaves et al. (Hargreaves & Fink, in press) drew disturbing conclusions:

> Four sets of findings emerged from the study. First, succession can bring about *planned continuity* in a school's development where it is doing well, *planned discontinuity* where a school has been

underperforming or resting on its laurels, and *unplanned continuity* or *discontinuity* where little thought has gone into the succession process at all. *Planned continuity* was a rare phenomenon and mainly occurred when successful schools groomed insiders to continue the work of the existing principal. *Planned discontinuity* temporarily turned underachieving schools around, but principals were rotated out of their schools too soon, before their work was done, and the schools quickly regressed. In these and other cases, many cases of succession were ones of *unplanned discontinuity* with the prior principal's achievements, and *unplanned continuity* with the mediocrity that preceded them. (Hargreaves et al., 2003, Executive Summary, pp. 1–2; emphasis in original)

In short, there is not much planned continuity going on at all, and when there is, it is short term or weak. There is nothing to inspire us that many Level 4, let alone Level 5, leaders will be spawned. As Andy Hargreaves et al. (2003) conclude,

Sustainable leadership maintains improvement from one leader to the next and spreads across many leaders and schools in a district, not just one or two. What our evidence suggests instead is that principal succession today is not an episodic crisis but a chronic process. Its suddenness and frequency short-circuit most improvement efforts, and its predictable regularity creates longer-term staff cynicism about any and all attempts at change. (p. 80)

The consequences of the failure to focus on succession are amplified under circumstances of high turnover. In every jurisdiction, the current decade represents a massive exodus from the principalship. Williams (2001) found that more than 80% of current elementary and secondary principals in Ontario, Canada, will retire by 2009 (two thirds by 2006). In the United States, it is estimated that 40% of current principals will retire in the next 6 years (Wallace Foundation, 2003). In England, 45% of head-teachers and deputies are over 50 years of age, which means there will be a large exodus over the next 10 years (Hartle & Thomas, 2003). In New South Wales, Australia, the mean age of current school principals is just over 50 (Scott, 2003). And so it goes.

It is not so much that there is a shortage of certified principals to fill the vacancies, but rather a shortage of principals with the qualities to help develop the sustainability transformation we are talking about in this book. In the United States, Roza (2003) found that there is not a dearth of certified candidates for the principalship, but rather, two other fundamental issues. First, was a problem of distribution:

Some districts and schools are avoided by prospective principals. Districts and schools with the fewest applicants are typically those with the most challenging working conditions, higher concentrations of poor and minority students, and lower salaries for principals. (p. 7)

A second and equally troubling problem concerns the leadership qualities (as distinct from technical eligibility) of prospective principals:

A serious gap exists between what superintendents say they want in new principals and the experiences human resource departments rely on to screen candidates. . . .
    Superintendents are more interested in the leadership experience and talent of prospective principals than in candidates' administrative or management skill. (Roza, 2003, p. 9)

Regardless of who does the hiring, are there enough candidates with the *leadership* qualities that will be required to take us into new levels? The answer, given the analysis in the previous pages, has to be "no."

Given the dearth of Level 5 leaders, there are two basic problems. First, there are scores of teachers who are working under difficulty; that is, since high-quality leaders help make working conditions energizing and make school improvement exciting, principals who do not possess these qualities do not improve the working lives of teachers.

Second, we can't gain on the problem, because it takes Level 5 leaders to produce more Level 5 leaders. We need to cultivate leaders who can combine Level 4 leadership (catalyzes commitment to visions and standards) and Level 5 leadership (builds enduring greatness). Amalgams of Level 4 and 5 leadership can lead, mentor, and reproduce a critical mass of new leaders who can turn the tide toward powerful new forces for sustainable reform.

Reports from the Office for Standards in Education (OFSTED, 2003a, 2003b) in England found that leadership at the school level had improved over the past 7 years but that there were still many schools where work was not managed effectively. Of course, we are talking about even greater expectations—not management, but leadership that promotes the conditions of sustainability.

Finally, if we ask the question, aren't we demanding too much of the principalship by expecting sustainable leadership? The answer is "yes" *under the current system*. This does not have to remain the case in the future. I reckon it takes about 10 years of cumulative development to become a highly effective school leader. If such development occurs, the job becomes more doable and more exciting because of what can be accomplished. We know, for example, that experts expend less energy in dealing with complex matters because they more easily and subconsciously recognize patterns and intuit effective responses (Ackerman, Pipek, & Wulf, 2003). They become more efficient and more effective because of their (reflective, developmental) experiences. If we then can multiply the opportunities for would-be and practicing principals to obtain new learning experiences—through, for example, strategies described in this book—we enable more and more leaders to develop accordingly. And the more that leaders develop in this direction, the more similar leaders they, in turn, produce. Once these developments reach a critical mass, *the context changes.* As this happens, less energy will be required to yield positive results, with self-generating or sustainable reform becoming possible.

To recap:

1. Leadership is to this decade what standards-based reform was to the 1990s.

2. The main mark of an effective leader at the end of his or her tenure is not so much the impact on the bottom line (of profits or student achievement), but rather how many good leaders he or she leaves behind who can go even further.

3. It is not turnover of leaders, per se, that is the problem, but rather discontinuity of direction.

4. While almost everyone agrees that leadership is key to success, there is insufficient clarity about what the role should be and to what short- and long-term ends.

5. The current "system" is random at best and dysfunctional at worst; put harshly, the current system is guaranteed to produce disruptive leadership rather than to generate cumulative continuity necessary for going deeper over time, which is essential for sustainability.

WHAT INDIVIDUALS CAN DO

Individual sustainability concerns the ability to keep on going without burning out. The key to doing this is not an all-out marathon, but rather cyclical energizing. To do this, leaders need to seek sources and situations that push the limits of their energy and engagement, coupled with rituals or periodic breaks that are energy recovering.

Loehr and Schwartz (2003) argue for *The Power of Full Engagement.* Leaders have a double reason to address cyclical energizing, because not only does this affect them, but it also has far-reaching consequences for those with whom they work:

> Leaders are the stewards of organizational energy. . . . They inspire or demoralize others first by how effectively they manage their own energy and next by how well they mobilize, focus, invest and renew the collective energy of those they lead. (p. 5)

Loehr and Schwartz (2003) make the point that we need to seek and harness four sources of energy—the physical, emotional, mental, and spiritual. But instead of urging leaders to maximize energy, they call for cycles of high performance and recovery:

> We grow at all levels by expending energy beyond our ordinary limits and then recovering. Expose a muscle to ordinary demand and it won't grow. With age it will actually lose strength. The limiting factor in building any "muscle" is that many of us back off at the slightest hint of discomfort. To meet increased demand in our lives, we must learn to systematically build and strengthen muscles wherever our capacity is insufficient. Any form of stress that prompts discomfort has the potential to expand our capacity—physically, mentally, emotionally or spiritually—so long as it is followed by adequate recovery. (p. 13)

On "the use it or lose it" dimension, we do need to revisit and stretch our moral purpose: Why did I become a leader in the first place? What do I do to develop and support leaders? How can I share outside my school in order to help other schools develop? In short, fuel and be fueled by our emotional and spiritual sources of energy.

With respect to mental or cognitive energy, work with others to tackle the adaptive challenges. Accessing ideas and mobilizing collective energy to address a complex problem can be exciting and satisfying as you grapple with an important matter that has yet to be solved. Work on your emotional intelligence: Emotionally intelligent leaders live longer and more effectively in complex times.

The cluster of energy sources just discussed is very close to one of the eight guidelines in my *Change Forces With a Vengeance* (Fullan, 2003): "Mobilize the social attractors—moral purpose, quality of relationships and quality knowledge" (p. 24). In short, there are a small number of powerful, positive sources of energy that we can seek out and immerse ourselves in.

There are things you should not do. If you are in a toxic or distrustful culture, you can get ahead by outwitting others, looking after number one, or hoping others will fail. As Peter Block (1987) said, "Why get better at a bad game?" (p. 9). It is not just morally wrong. Let's consider energy. There is actually no shortage of energy in a negative culture. When people are out to get each other, they don't complain about lack of time. Negative actions are amazingly energizing (think *rage*): Aside from their short-term damage, negative actions deenergize us over time. Indeed, negative energy can lead to illness and early death. It is positive energy fully exploited that is related to longevity and hence greater sustainability.

A second recipe for burnout in yourself and those with whom you work is what Goleman, Boyatzis, and McKee (2002) call the "pace-setting" leader. Pacesetters are leaders who expect excellence and exemplify it, who push people to the limit, and who are constantly searching for new ideas. Not bad for short-term performance, but fatal for sustainability:

Our data show that . . . pacesetting poisons the climate—particularly because of the emotional costs when a leader relies on it too much. Essentially, the pacesetter's dilemma is this: The more pressure put on people for results, the more anxiety it provokes. Although moderate pressure can energize people—the challenge of meeting a deadline, for instance—continuous pressure can be debilitating. . . . Although pacesetters may get compliance—and therefore a short-term, upward blip in results—they don't get true performance that people will sustain. (p. 73)

The argument, then, is that the skillful and balanced management of energy is the key to sustainability. Overuse is burnout; underuse is atrophy. Tim Brighouse, the former Director of the Birmingham Education Authority, in England, and now the "czar" of transforming the London education system, divides the world into energy creators, energy neutrals, and energy consumers (Brighouse & Woods, 1999). He summarizes their characteristics:

Energy creators

- Are enthusiastic and always positive
- Use critical thinking, creativity, and imagination
- Stimulate and spark others
- Practice leadership at all levels
- Are able and willing to scrutinize their practice and willing to make their practice accessible to others
- Wish to improve on their previous best

Energy neutrals are

- Competent, sound practitioners
- Willing to [address] the task
- Good at "maintenance"
- Sometimes uncomfortable accepting examination of their practice by others
- Capable of improving on their previous best

Energy consumers . . . tend to

- Have a negative view of the world
- Resent change and practice blocking strategies
- Use other people's time excessively
- Not feel good about themselves
- Be unable and unwilling to critically examine their teaching practice
- Appear not to want to improve on their personal best. (p. 84)

The goal of would-be individual leaders, of course, is to become more and more like "energy creators" and especially to be aware of how they can cultivate energy creation in other leaders they are in a position to mentor. We know the sources of energy creation: moral purpose, emotional intelligence, quality relationships, quality knowledge, physical well-being—all mobilized to engage the mind and heart in attempting to solve complex adaptive challenges.

There is less acknowledgment in the change literature of *energy recovery*. Virtually all the positive press on leadership is about developing and energizing people, and little on strategies of recovery. Because of this neglect, even the most motivated leaders will not last and will not leave lasting legacies.

I provide here some initial ideas about energy recovery, but the broader call is that the massive attention currently being paid to leadership needs to include a conceptual and strategic focus on cycles of energy renewal.

It seems to me that there are two types of energy-recovery strategies: One is built into daily or weekly routines, which we could call "rituals" (after Loehr & Schwartz, 2003); the other is more cyclical, which I will refer to as "periodic."

Loehr and Schwartz (2003) refer to "positive energy rituals," which are highly specific routines for managing energy:

> The sustaining power of rituals comes from the fact that they conserve energy. . . . In contrast to will and discipline, which imply pushing ourselves to action, a well-defined ritual pulls us. We feel somehow worse if we don't do it. Think about brushing your teeth or taking a shower or kissing your spouse goodbye in the morning. . . . If we want to build into our lives new behaviors that last, we can't spend much energy to sustain them. (p. 169)

And:

> The power of rituals is that they insure that we use as little conscious energy as possible where it is not absolutely necessary, leaving us free to strategically focus the energy available to us in creative, enriching ways.
>
>   Look at any part of your life in which you are consistently effective and you will find that certain habits make that possible. If you eat in a healthy way, it is probably because you have built routines around the food you buy and what you are willing to order at restaurants. . . . If you are successful in a sales job, you probably have a ritual of mental preparation for calls and ways that you talk to yourself to stay positive in the face of rejection. . . . If you sustain high energy despite an extremely

demanding job, you almost certainly have predictable ways of insuring that you get intermittent recovery. Creating positive rituals is the most powerful means we have found to effectively manage energy in the service of full engagement. (pp. 14–15)

Eating habits, physical fitness, meditation, reflective journal writing, and taking short time-outs all qualify as positive rituals. Leaders who are to be effective over the long haul will need to establish their own combinations of rituals.

Periodic recovery consists of cycles of activity that take place over longer periods of time. Since all effective leaders are immersed in daily relationships, getting away from the group now and then can be a great source of personal renewal. The psychologist Anthony Storr (1988) shows how solitude can be a source of personal meaning and creativity:

The capacity to be alone is a valuable resource when changes of mental attitude are required. . . . In a culture in which interpersonal relationships are generally considered to provide the answer to every form of distress, it is sometimes difficult to persuade well-meaning helpers that solitude can be as therapeutic as emotional support. (p. 29)

Solitude, says Storr (1988), facilitates "learning, thinking, innovation, and maintaining contact with one's own inner world" (p. 29).

As we contemplate promoting and balancing full engagement with renewal, we come to the intersection of the individual and the system. If the system is relentlessly demanding, or for that matter, if it is casually permissive, it is not possible to become or stay productively engaged. In one study, Flintham (2003) talks about "when reservoirs run dry" in referring to why principals leave the headship. These school leaders "had key messages regarding the value of . . . professional development reinforced by strategic reflection opportunities and an infrastructure of peer support to reinforce this" (p. 3).

We are about to turn to the system side of the equation, but the message for the individual leader is to push the system by "getting better at a good game." Look for ways to cultivate other leaders as you focus on performance; participate in networks and other knowledge-sharing opportunities as these involve. I won't go so far as to say that if enough individuals get good at this new game that sustainability will replace survival in leadership, but we won't get any breakthroughs in the absence of individuals doing their part.

In addition to individual effort, we need, as I have argued, a more direct and explicit focus on changing *systems*.

WHAT SYSTEMS CAN DO

Systems consist of individuals, so what does it mean to say that systems must change, and, furthermore, that they must change toward sustainability? My answer is that you do this through leaders at the system level and all other levels, becoming *explicitly conscious* that they are engaged in widening people's experiences and identification beyond their normal bailiwicks. The proposition is that the key to changing systems is to produce greater numbers of "system thinkers." If more and more leaders become system thinkers, they will gravitate toward strategies that alter people's system-related experiences; that is, they will alter people's mental awareness of the system as a whole, thereby contributing to altering the system itself.

I do not think we have made any progress at all in actually promoting systems thinking since Peter Senge (1990) first raised the matter. Let's consider Senge's first description:

> Human endeavors are also systems. They . . . are bound by invisible fabrics of interrelated actions, which often take years to fully play out their effects on each other. Since we are part of the lacework ourselves, it is doubly hard to see the whole pattern of change. Instead, we tend to focus on snapshots of isolated parts of the system, and wonder why our deepest problems never seem to get solved. Systems thinking is a conceptual framework, a body of knowledge and tools that has been developed over the past fifty years, to make the full patterns clearer, and *to help us see how to change them effectively.* (p. 7; my emphasis)

We will come back to the italics later, but most of us will recall that systems thinking is the fifth discipline, which integrates the other four disciplines: personal mastery, mental models, building shared vision, and team learning.

Philosophically, Senge (1990) is on the right track, but it doesn't seem to be very helpful in practice:

> [Systems thinking] is the discipline that integrates the disciplines, fusing them into a coherent body of theory and practice. It keeps them from being separate gimmicks or the latest organization fads. Without a systemic orientation, there is no motivation to look at how the disciplines interrelate. . . .
>
> At the heart of a learning organization is a shift of mind—from seeing ourselves as separate from the world to connected to the world, from seeing problems as caused by someone or something "out there" to seeing how our own actions create the problems

we experience. A learning organization is a place where people are continually discovering how they create their reality *and how they can change it.* (pp. 12, 13; my emphasis)

With at least a decade of work, I don't think we have made any significant gains on defining the problem, let alone doing anything about it. The fifth discipline "fieldbook" takes up the issue of application (Senge et al., 2000). We see once again that "the discipline of systems thinking provides a different way of looking at problems and goals—not as isolated events but as components of larger structures" (p. 78). There is then a discussion of how the term *systems thinking* has been used in a confusing manner, with the new suggestion that there is actually a continuum of seven approaches: "systemwide thinking," "open systems thinking," "human systems thinking," "process systems thinking," "living systems thinking," and "feedback-simulation" (Senge et al., 2000, p. 79).

This doesn't seem to be a "continuum," and more important from the perspective of the new theoretician seeking system impact, there is nothing practical to go on. If anything, the situation seems more confusing.

In the fifth discipline fieldbook, systems thinking is applied to staff development:

All too often there is little communication across grade levels and across content areas. A child gets an experience in one year that might not relate to the next year's experience. This situation makes the school particularly vulnerable to tests, because each year's instructor feels that he or she alone must prepare the kids for assessment. But aligning curriculum across levels requires using the skills and technologies of systems thinking and mental models; you have to get agreement among all the teachers about where the starting level for students exists and how fast to carry them along the development path. . . .

If you're a systems thinker in school planning, then you focus not on particular practices but on building collaborative relationships and structures for change. You need mechanisms and a process that allow people to talk, across grade levels, departments, and schools within a system. (Senge et al., 2000, p. 394)

It is not so much a criticism of Senge's (1990) work as it is a commentary on the field of system thinking to note that we are not making any progress at fostering it in practice. Here is my take:

1. Yes, we know that current systems are working in isolation with terrible results, but we have known that for years.

2. Yes, collaboration is key, and "you have to get agreement among all the teachers," but how do you do that, not to mention agreement among districts, governments, and the public?

3. Systems thinking is not just a cognitive endeavor in order to discover the whole picture and long-term trends. As my italics from Senge's quote emphasize, the goal is to understand the system and change it for the better.

4. Systems thinking means not only that given individuals or organizations can appreciate and take into account the larger system but also that individuals and organizations can be engaged with others outside themselves in order to change the very system that surrounds them.

5. For systems thinking to have its intended effect, it can't be for a small group of specialists; it must be made practically accessible to the large group of new and emerging leaders.

Earlier, I said we need powerful concepts of change but that the power will be realized only if the concepts can be rendered understandable by typical intelligent leaders, not by a subgroup specializing in the topic. I said that for every abstract concept, we need to be able to point to a corresponding concrete policy or strategy that is intended to advance the concept in practice.

Thus, one core goal is to identify ideas and strategies that will promote systems thinking. Systems thinking in practice, in turn, is the key to sustainability. On the practice side, I maintain that it is possible and necessary to give leaders experiences that increase their ability to take the larger picture into account. When leaders get such experience, they obtain an increment in systems thinking, and when the latter happens, they are more inclined to share and to identify with others in pursuit of larger, more meaningful system goals. When this happens, systems themselves change for the better.

We need to be clear. I am not talking about producing armchair system thinkers. It will be "system thinkers in action" who count. They may not have the best elaborate theories of how systems evolve over the long run, but they will be in the midst of action with a system perspective. And they will interact with others to promote system awareness through their actions and conversations.

As we focus on system sustainability, one critical aspect to address is what cyclical energizing means at the organization and system levels. Just as individuals have to enter cycles of push and recovery, so do systems. What this means has not been addressed in the literature. It will include not aggravating the overload problem by piling policies upon policies, working on alignment so that the deenergizing effects of fragmentation do not take their toll, taking time out to review and consolidate gains, celebrating accomplishments, investing more resources as success accrues, and, of course, fostering the development of leadership at all levels of the organization and system.

More generally, I have suggested eight correlated strategies for sustainability. Elements of these strategies are already in place in some jurisdictions. Networks and collaboratives, for example, can increase leaders' capacities to see wider and farther, provided that they also contribute to leaders' clarity and coherence of system purpose and dynamics. Leaders at the system level need to engage other levels so that policies and strategies are shaped and reshaped, and the emerging bigger picture is constantly communicated and critiqued. They need to give other leaders within the system many experiences to widen their interaction and knowledge base and to question central direction. Local leaders for their part must push outward to lead lateral capacity building and vertical exchanges with higher levels of the system as a whole.

In short, in a would-be sustainable world, "leadership to the fore" means the proliferation of systems thinkers in action.

REFERENCES

Ackerman, M., Pipek, V., & Wulf, V. (Eds.). (2003). *Sharing expertise: Beyond knowledge management.* Cambridge: MIT Press.

Block, P. (1987). *The empowered manager.* San Francisco: Jossey-Bass.

Brighouse, T., & Woods, D. (1999). *How to improve your school.* London: Routledge.

Collins, J. (2001). *Good to great.* New York: HarperCollins.

Flintham, A. (2003). *When reservoirs run dry.* Nottingham, UK: National College for School Leaders.

Fullan, M. (2003). *Change forces with a vengeance.* London: Routledge/Falmer.

Goleman, D., Boyatzis, R., & McKee, A. (2002). *Primal leadership.* Boston: Harvard Business School Press.

Hargreaves, A. (2004). *The carousel of leadership succession.* Manuscript submitted for publication.

Hargreaves, A., & Fink, D. (in press). *Sustainable leadership.* San Francisco: Jossey-Bass.

Hargreaves, A., Moore, S., Fink, D., Brayman, C., & White, R. (2003). *Succeeding leaders.* Toronto, Canada: Ontario Principals Council.

Hargreaves, D. (2003). *Education epidemic.* London: Demos.

Hartle, F., & Thomas, K. (2003). *Growing school leaders: The challenge.* Nottingham, UK: National College of School Leaders.

Khurana, R. (2002). *Searching for a corporate savior: The irrational quest for charismatic CEOs.* Princeton, NJ: Princeton University Press.

Loehr, J., & Schwartz, T. (2003). *The power of full engagement.* New York: Free Press.

Office for Standards in Education (OFSTED). (2003a). *Leadership and management: Managing the school workforce.* London: Author.

Office for Standards in Education (OFSTED). (2003b). *Leadership and management: What inspection tells us.* London: Author.

Roza, M. (2003). *A matter of definition: Is there really a shortage of school principals?* New York: Wallace Foundation.

Scott, G. (2003). *Learning principals.* Sydney, Australia: University of Technology.

Senge, P. (1990). *The fifth discipline.* New York: Doubleday.

Senge, P., Cambron-McCabe, N., Lucas, T., Smith, B., Dutton, J., & Kleiner, A. (2000). *Schools that learn.* New York: Doubleday.

Storr, A. (1988). *Solitude.* London: Flamingo Press.

Wallace Foundation. (2003). *Beyond the pipeline.* New York: Author.

Williams, T. (2001). *Unrecognized exodus.* Toronto, Canada: Ontario Principal's Council.

9

Teaching as Leading

Linda Lambert, Michelle Collay, Mary E. Dietz,
Karen Kent, and Anna Ershler Richert

In many parts of the United States, the teacher's voice is beginning to be heard in conversations about re-structuring schools. Although teachers, because they work directly with children, may have the greatest effect on the success of the school, they are seldom called on to lead the process of school reform. Therefore, many teachers do not see themselves as leaders of adults or of the profession. Furthermore, the more visible teacher leaders are continually encouraged to leave the classroom and work directly with adult colleagues.

Our assumptions about the need for formal leadership and authority in schools are implicit in current educational practice: Teachers work with children, and designated leaders work with adults; teachers are isolated, have little time set aside to prepare their lessons and complete administrative tasks, and have virtually no time designated for adult interaction. A newly certified teacher is expected to shoulder the same responsibilities as a 30-year veteran, revealing our tacit belief that experienced teachers do nothing differently than newcomers. Teachers who survive this enculturation and still surface as able adults are seen as "true leaders" and urged to become administrators. This tradition of school leadership predates this century with little change in recent years.

From Lambert et al., *Who Will Save Our Schools?: Teachers as Constructivist Leaders,* Chapter 7. (1996) Corwin Press. Reprinted with permission.

The lack of professional status for those who remain in teaching is reflected in current tensions that face teachers who choose to stay in classrooms. Can they really provide leadership from the teacher's role? Or does the gendered nature of teaching or the child-centered focus of the work limit potential to lead? Our conversation about the constructivist leader opens doors to new possibilities for career teachers to be school leaders and for formal leaders to remain engaged in the activities of teaching and learning that initially drew them to the profession. We believe that good teaching is itself constructivist leadership and that teachers are key participants in facilitating the construction of knowledge in schools. This chapter focuses on the teacher's leadership role as meaning maker with children and as meaning maker in school-level leadership. This foundation must be firmly anchored before teachers will open their doors to their roles as reformers.

Earlier we identified the dominance of the female gender in teaching as a major context issue. To further make sense of the emergent roles of teacher leaders, we must understand the journey teachers have taken to become professionals. The role of teacher is closely linked with children, and the nurturance of children has not often been framed as leadership. Historically, leadership theories and beliefs have been steeped in the metaphors of the "great men" role models studied in social studies textbooks, in graduate education in leadership and organizational theory, and in contemporary business "how-to" books. As women have taken more formal roles in leadership, they have been influenced by these traditions of leadership. Until recently, women in formal leadership have accepted the same Western, Newtonian approaches to leadership as men. In the late 20th century, however, theories of leadership have begun to evolve as a growing understanding of, and respect for, more holistic and integrated leadership approaches have emerged. Teachers, traditionally perceived as followers, are contributing to a more organic model of organizational reform and change.

Because schools have been female dominant and male led, women and men teachers have accepted roles as followers of primarily male principals. This condition may contribute heavily to the failure to place responsibility for school reform in the hands of teachers. Whereas some regions report a growing number of women in formal leadership roles, the national picture shows only modest changes (Bell & Chase, 1993; Schmuck & Shubert, 1995). The gendered difference between leader (male) and follower (female) widens the chasm of power and authority and replicates industrial divisions between management and staff. Although many teachers now seek advanced degrees while remaining in the classroom, thereby bringing a greater foundation of knowledge and expertise to the role of teacher, mainstream cultural beliefs about appropriate roles of women and men continue to limit understanding of teaching as a profession. These limitations hinge partly on beliefs about whether women can even be professionals (Preston, 1991). Despite these deeply ingrained practices, change in educational roles is occurring.

Evidence of change in both assumptions about the role of teacher and organizational practices in schools can be seen in the number of experienced teachers who attain advanced degrees and remain in the classroom. Since the early 1960s, the percentage of teachers holding a master's degree or six-year diploma has more than doubled (Darling-Hammond, 1990). The knowledge base attained in graduate study can move a teacher from one who is subjected to orders to one who is a decision maker, from factory hand to one who is responsible for a greater societal good. Title and role, such as principal and teacher, still separate management from staff; but in recent years, teachers have sought opportunities to extend their capacity in the classroom and are usually as knowledgeable as their principals, if not more so. This professional transition has provided more opportunities for teachers to be seen as leaders. More important, diverging roles encourage teachers to see themselves as leaders.

A second important change is the slow but steady efforts of teachers to establish collegial relationships within their schools. The nature of the industrial model school limits collegial interaction between adults. Teachers who value opportunities to enhance their professional status struggle to overcome the organizational structures that limit this development. Experienced teachers are dependent on strong collegial relationships for their continued development (Kent, 1985, as cited in Little, 1990).

A third important change that supports the contributions of teachers to new images of leadership is the epistemological movement toward constructivist teaching and learning in schools. As teachers gain courage to collaborate in the construction of new learning with their students, they can envision collaborating with colleagues in the same way. As we have noted, collegial interaction is possible only in a culture of mutual respect and care for the other. It is not feasible in authoritarian or hierarchical structures. As we re-imagine learning in constructivist ways, we know more about how to construct knowledge with children than with adults. Although one experience doesn't necessarily precede the other, the sheer number of hours teachers spend with children provides many more opportunities for learning about constructing learning with children than with adults.

These changes give us faith that teachers, in the current context of educational reform, are uniquely poised to effect real change in schools. Although they have always been so poised, the changes in our thinking about systems and reform described in this book are creating real opportunities and support for teachers to see themselves as change agents. Teachers have called the question and are seeking answers. It must be teachers themselves, however, who begin to present their work with children as leadership. One hundred years of tradition will not slip quietly away,

Are teaching and leading the same? We know that in effective classrooms, adults and children construct knowledge together, develop shared meanings, and are participants in creating a learning community. Adults provide these opportunities for construction of new knowledge because they are leading children along a pathway to knowledge. Adults who lead other adults hope for the same capacity building and growth in knowledge for the members of their organizations. There are lessons from teaching that can inform our understanding of learning and leadership.

HOW ARE TEACHERS CURRENTLY LEADING?

Teachers talk about children. They talk about individual children, about how different children learn, and about what strategies might lead those individual children into new understandings of their world. Teachers talk about their roles as facilitators of the learning of others, as stewards of communities of learners. They seldom discuss budgets, policies, or turf—topics that are more common at administrative meetings. If we look beyond the client and the context, however, we may see some interesting parallels in the construction of knowledge, or meaning making, by teachers and administrators. The beliefs they share may be the keys that unlock successful school restructuring.

We believe that good teachers are constructivist leaders. In her discussion about the role of teachers in school restructuring, Rallis (1989) describes the leader as a "catalyst, guide, interpreter, and facilitator for a process" (p. 201). Many teachers, especially those who work with younger students, embrace those terms. The practicing teacher is herself a constructivist leader in the school, modeling learning for students and sharing learning with other adults in the school community. A parallel practice may emerge between leadership with adults and leadership with children as the role of teacher-leader, one who creates an environment in which participants are encouraged to make their own meaning from their own experiences. Many teachers cite the importance of building of relationships with children, "in order to reach them." This time-worn adage holds much truth, because new learning does not occur in a linear, decontextualized setting. Learning is reciprocal, as both "teacher" and " learner" become teacher and learner (Freire, 1970).

The research that informs this conversation comes from two sources: a study of first-year teachers describing how they are learning to teach and a study of experienced teachers who have recently completed a Master of Arts in Education and have chosen to stay in the classroom. These first excerpts of teacher talk are taken from interview transcripts in a yearlong ethnographic study of new teachers. New teachers talked about their roles within teaching as counselor, empowerer, and learner. We see the early stages of "catalyst and guide" in the words of teachers articulating beliefs and making meaning of their role as teacher. These young teachers are engaging with individual students to construct learning opportunities. Their reflections about the children's learning and their own learning are completely intertwined.

TEACHERS DESCRIBE THEIR ROLE

The teachers in this first section were participants in a study of five new teachers who were enrolled in a resident-year master's degree program. They had already obtained a license, were completely responsible for a classroom, and looked much like any other first-year teacher. They met on a weekly basis for seminar and with their supervisor each week in their classroom. The text that follows came from individual interviews conducted throughout their first year of teaching. Susan, Thad, Marilyn, and Terry taught in small, rural districts, whereas Barbara was in a suburban, blue-collar area. The geographic setting was the northwestern United States.

Susan taught English 7 and 8 and home economics in a tiny rural high school of about 200 students grades 7 through 12. She described the dilemma of a senior named Annie, who had recently chosen to walk with a different friend in the graduation ceremony and had alienated her peers:

> So Annie's hurting from that. She says the whole class hates her. Annie's feeling victimized right now. And I'm hearing from other people that she brought it on herself, and so I want to say, "It's going to be OK." I try to get in my counselor mode.

Susan paid close attention to the emotional state of this young woman, and her focus in this remark was to nurture and support this student through a difficult time. She saw her role as counselor and named it as such.

Another new teacher, Marilyn, reflects on a 7-year-old in her charge:

> I think I've brought Hanna out of her very quiet shell. You know what I've been doing, I've been giving her lots of hugs.

Again, the focus is on the role of teacher as counselor, one who nurtures and supports children in their quests to become themselves. The focus for these teachers is the child's environment, an awareness that a high level of anxiety will diminish opportunity for learning. An important role for the teacher is creating a trusting environment for learning.

In this next conversation, Barbara discusses a young man in her fifth-grade class. She had previously expressed her intent to teach her students to become responsible for themselves:

> If I could get him in a situation where I could push him over that little hump, have him finish something and feel good about it, maybe he would take that initiative on, become more self-motivated. I think students have to learn to resolve problems

themselves, but when I see that they're struggling with that, and they're not getting anywhere, sometimes I will give them tools to resolve their problems.

In these descriptions, new teachers are quite aware of their role as guide or catalyst. The act of teaching begins with identification of these students' emotional needs, as these three teachers articulate in their analyses. After giving a description and an interpretation of the child's behaviors, these teachers made choices about which values to encourage. Those values came from teachers' individual beliefs, from the culture of the school, and from the expectations of the greater society. The literature on constructivist education suggests a need for the development of shared values and beliefs. Within the learning community of the classroom, these teachers begin with individual needs, make choices and decisions that reflect their own values, then lead the students toward a collaboratively constructed, rather than a predetermined outcome. Qualities desired in a leader, such as vision and management skills, are required to create such a constructive environment. Yet the teacher is engaging the other participants, who are children, in the act of constructing knowledge. And because they construct the learning together, the traditionally distinct roles of leader and follower are not useful. Understanding that all individuals are capable of leading and participating provides a more helpful interpretation for constructivist teaching and leading.

Another quality of a teacher who is a constructivist leader is the capacity to share power. Again, metaphors from corporate, masculine cultures are not sufficient for the classroom. A woman caring for children is seen as "providing for." A thoughtful leader values expanded capacity in the other members of the community, especially if they are youngsters. In this next example, Susan demonstrates a strong commitment to empowering the learner. Her classroom activities were structured to create an environment in which young adolescents would become more individual in their thinking:

My seventh graders are so self-confident right now that they don't feel like they always have to group together and always believe the same way to be liked by each other.

In this excerpt, Susan assumes she has framed actions that will embody new behaviors, in her and in her students. Her students are able to build community with each other in a more healthy, interdependent way.

Any teacher or parent of adolescents has bemoaned the "peer problem" as their children become teenagers and look to each other, rather than to adults, for guidance. Each of us has struggled with the right form of leadership for this age group, a form that is recognized both by the young people and by the adult community as appropriate for a time of transition.

The qualities of a "guide" are especially useful, because adult role modeling can be the most powerful balance for students.

For Thad, with a fifth-sixth split class of young adolescents, the notion of "guide" proved elusive. In one conversation, he described appropriate classroom atmosphere as "definitely no spitwads, no throwing things ... if an assignment comes up, the kids will greet it with, if not with enthusiasm, at least with acceptance." A positive ambience would be "just a feeling of peace, that the kids are working it out, or just playing a game, or just talking between them, really getting along." In response to a question about his role in creating such an atmosphere, he replied, "I have a major role. Because, I don't see the kids creating it for themselves." Whereas his classroom teaching proved a fairly negative and unsuccessful experience, he described having greater success as a scout leader "taking kids into the wilderness, where they have to listen up the first time. I say something and that's it." Exerting authority felt comfortable to Thad in the outdoor setting where the cues about what the children needed were evident to him. Thad described a hike he took with the fifth graders at the end of a very tough year:

> So I bought treats—chips, juice, and apples—and we went hiking up the creek a ways. And I said, "OK, what have we learned from times we have gone out in the woods before? Keep in a line, keep together, have a person at the head of the line and the tail, and just be really organized."

Inside the classroom, Thad was insecure about his role as "authority," whereas outside, traditional leadership seemed a comfortable fit. In this case, "guide" was not collaborative but authoritative.

In the next excerpt, we are reminded that younger children need a leader who values them and believes in their ability to accomplish tasks. Marilyn and Barbara had a similar empowerment agenda for their students. Marilyn reflected at the end of her first year:

> If I teach second grade again, I'd let them do more of the actual teaching, have them do more of the investigating and the reporting, even from the beginning ... just let them take more responsibility.

This teacher faced a personal dilemma of returning the responsibility of constructing new knowledge to the children. She was a teacher who initially tried to package every piece of learning in small, bite-sized pieces, and only through trial and error did she begin to relinquish that grip.

This shift could also be portrayed as a "break set" behavior on Marilyn's part. New teachers carry the image of "teacher up front" from their years as students and are therefore socialized to provide answers to questions. Her choice to give "more responsibility" is a choice to share the construction of new knowledge, not to hand it over prepackaged. This is also a choice to be a different kind of teacher, or leader. The confidence to make this shift in per-spective comes from different sources, we believe. Daily life in the classroom is itself a disrupter of the stereotype of teacher, as experienced teachers see results from collaborative instruction that they will not see from direct instruction. Alert teachers soon realize that instruction delivered from the front doesn't take. The repertoire of teaching strategies expands as new teachers become more willing and able to change the ways they structure learning. Confidence in one's emerging role as a collaborator is also essen-tial, as children and adolescents respond positively to invitations to share the creation of the environment for learning.

Finally, acceptance by senior colleagues is critical for new teachers. Until they feel some sense of membership in the association of teachers, they may not be willing to try out new behaviors. Even so, a teacher who builds capacity in others rather than behaving in the more traditional role of teacher as teller is often criticized by colleagues who retain a different view of the role of teacher and may find himself or herself "teaching against the grain" (Cochran-Smith, 1991). If teachers feel criticism while "teaching like leaders," what implications are there for those who see themselves as leaders teachers? Barbara summed up her beliefs this way:

> I like to find more seeds to plant and find ways of pulling out that kind of learning rather than just give them a book and have them read questions and write answers.

Barbara is not only a guide but a facilitator of the learning of others. For the learner to construct knowledge, each must be nurtured by other learners in a safe environment. Barbara concluded:

> The more responsibility that I can get students to take on, the better I feel, because I feel they're more prepared to deal with the outside world.

A key to constructivist leadership by teachers is the belief that they must facilitate the conditions for learning, not do the work of learning for their students. In a culture in which teaching is telling, teachers are sometimes con-sidered lacking the ability to discipline if they are found supporting active learners. A colleague may wonder aloud from the doorway, "Who's in charge here?" As any teacher leader can tell us, facilitating the learning of others is much harder than telling. Facilitation is also much more effective and satis-fying if the goal of the teacher and leader is to build strength in others. In a community of learners, adults must be trusted to support the learning of children without threat of criticism by colleagues and administrators. The presence of a true community of learners is necessary for this trust building.

Constructing knowledge is a multifaceted process for the classroom teacher, and the context of the learning of others frames individual teacher development as well. As we have discussed in our chapter on learning communities, one must acknowledge one's own growth as a learner and the effects of others on our learning. This understanding requires reflection on one's own learning and behaviors as a leader or collaborator with others, as well as reflection on the learning of others. Some may assume that only experienced teachers have the maturity to reflect on their own learning, yet these beginners reflected copiously while still on the earliest leg of their professional journeys. Statements of self-examination and reflection were found throughout interviews with these new teachers. In this interview, Terry wondered how she could possibly get through the third-grade curriculum before the end of the year:

> And I thought, "All right, I gotta do this. I gotta do this, I gotta do this, I can't do it all in one day, I can't do it all in one year!" Yeah. I've lightened up! I decided, "What are my priorities?"And I decided my priorities are that they learn how to read, and learn how to write, and actually write with some sort of idea of being able to proof and see what their writing's about.

These first attempts at self-dialogue reflect early efforts to reconstruct old assumptions in a school culture not given to breaking set with myths. In Terry's case, her traditional school staff sent clear messages for appropriate teacher behavior, such as the janitor who forbade her to have a braid rug in her room. The same clear messages were sent to students, for example, by the principal, who flashed cafeteria lights off to modify the lunchtime behavior. Through reflection on her beliefs about learning, she was able to challenge her own assumptions and make decisions about which norms to challenge and which to work in more subtle ways. Only with some experience was she able to judge her work with a sense of ownership and responsibility.

Terry recalled more self-talk after the school year ended, valuing contact with each student:

> It felt like I was achieving what I needed to do. It felt much better looking at the kids as individuals, and with only 10 kids, I kept telling myself, "If I couldn't connect with each kid every day, I was nuts, what was wrong with me?"

Terry was well aware that her rural school class size was tiny, and that once in suburban school, she would be challenged to relate to 30 children. Again, the importance of making meaning of these first, tentative steps in a remote, rural setting with few children was evident to this new teacher, who would be required to transfer these understandings to a new school the following year.

HOW DO WE BEGIN TO SEE OURSELVES AS LEADERS?

Studies of professional induction teach us much about how newcomers find their way in a complex profession like teaching (Bullough, Knowles, & Crow, 1991; Ryan, 1986; Zeichner & Gore, 1989). We also learn about how we begin to see ourselves as leaders. If teaching is leading, perhaps new teachers can instruct us about the importance of personal development and self-knowledge for leaders. Many of the reflections by new teachers were about making sense of their novice status. Marilyn shared her thoughts:

> And here I am and I have to teach these kids, even though it's a small group, yet I felt, "I'm going to teach these kids, and I'm not ready!"

Marilyn definitely had the skills required to impart knowledge using traditional methods, but she had much less confidence about whether children would actually learn. Susan mused over her emerging relationships with young people from 13 to 18 years old:

> I was trying to find the continuum [of authority] of where I could be with them [high school seniors] and with my junior highers. I didn't feel like I could "come down on them" because I didn't feel like I was the expert in the class. . . there were so many factors.

Early in her first year, Susan recognized that, at 24, she was only a few years older than her students. What were the implications for her making sense of her role as teacher? Her mythic teacher model was described in a portrayal of a favorite teacher who was an older, male minister. For her, the choice to construct meaning together was a nonchoice. She couldn't be that older, wise man; she was almost a peer with her high school students. In Susan's case, her age and the social context of a high school classroom forced her to reconstruct her old myths about teaching.

All teachers, young and experienced alike, struggle to know enough to be "leading" learners. Outside the classroom, teachers find that people within and outside the profession seem to have expectations of them beyond what they might have for other professions. Within school, teachers' aides, nonteaching staff, and parents play a critical role in shaping teachers' beliefs about their abilities. Outside of school, community members, friends, and the media play an additional, if more abstract, role in reflecting back beliefs about the role of teacher. Barbara talked about her experiences in social settings:

> I'll be around people that aren't teachers, and they'll ask me a question about, "What's the highest mountain in a certain area?" and I can't tell them. They look at me like, "Well, you're a teacher."And I think, "Golly, what am I doing teaching? I should know these things."

The public nature of schooling allows anyone the freedom to judge teachers and leaves teachers vulnerable to anyone with an opinion about schools. Because the classic stereotype of teachers and leaders is that they should know all, they are not often invited to express ignorance or to engage in a type of learning that requires the public vulnerability that can accompany constructivism. If teachers allow themselves to feel victimized when others frame their roles, it will be hard to move toward more interactive ways of making meaning.

New teachers understand quickly that there is much to learn about who one is, how one teaches, and how much "content" each has yet to learn. How they choose to respond to their own learning becomes central to how they construct the learning environment for their students. For instance, if a new teacher has confidence that he and his students can participate together in new learning, new topics of study are within reach. If teachers are fearful about areas of little expertise, they may not seek more knowledge, with or without the students. A glimpse of this phenomenon can be seen in teachers' perceptions of literacy in language and mathematics. Most elementary teachers are confident about language and will experiment with creative constructions of meaning making, whereas in mathematics, a discipline described by many adults as a weak area, teachers tend to stay close to the text. The acceptance of constructivist methods of learning can create a culture in which professionals can say, "We can learn together!"

One place where teachers learn about not having "correct" answers is in their role as meaning makers. Meaning is made in relationship with others, and building such authentic relationships is central to success in constructivist leadership. In their descriptions of this role, there are clues about effective leadership in schools. Many of the new teachers' descriptions of their work are really descriptions of their relationships with their students. They are not describing management; they are describing "caring for" (Grumet, 1980; Noddings, 1984). They discuss their interactions with children as humanistic rather than bureaucratic or regulatory. The literature on teacher satisfaction cites positive relationships with students as a key element. According to Lieberman and Miller (1990), "The greatest satisfaction for a teacher is the feeling of being rewarded by one's students. In fact, most of the time the students are the only source of rewards for most teachers" (p. 154). Although these authors speculate that professional isolation or the need to be liked are reasons that teachers turn to students for feedback, perhaps the opportunity to construct learning together within a trusting relationship is a more positive spin on this professional dependence on students.

Susan described a boy whom she had confronted for some misdeed:

I know this child was never disciplined in the traditional ways of being spanked or being told no. . . . He's a charmer, and I like him, but he doesn't see that because I make him do things he doesn't want to do. He sees me as someone real tough, mean. And at the same time, we have good eye contact: I know he likes me.

Susan's goal in this case was to provide guidance and set expectations, much as a parent would. She owns her responsibility to do so yet remarks on how the boy is relating to her.

Barbara revealed her thinking about the emotional development of a girl in her fifth-grade class:

> There are some kids in here, for instance Jessica, who is an individual thinker, but her individual thinking doesn't hurt other people in the classroom. She's not disrespectful of other people, so I admire her.

Barbara saw Jessica as an individual and as a member of a community of learners.

Marilyn talked about Hanna, a little girl who required special attention on an hourly basis:

> Well, she came to me in tears, "They didn't let me do anything. My brother never lets me do anything." Yeah, she never gets to do anything. She has older brothers. I said, "So did you tell them how you felt?" She said, "No." This child needs a hug and compassion, not lots of instructions.

Marilyn begins with the most basic needs of the child. These characteristics of "caring for" are important to relationship building, rather than problematic.

Much of the research on teacher development in relation to the client, or student, focuses primarily on the new teacher's ability to "manage" the classroom. This industrial image, one of patriarchal leadership, assumes a stance that teachers are middle management and students are workers on an assembly line. Indeed, one can peer into some classrooms, with their straight rows and dittoed worksheets, and choose the term *manage* without fear of misunderstanding. In these excerpts, however, new teachers were peering into mirrors of their own souls as they looked into the eyes of their students. In each student's journey, these teachers found a piece of their own story, and they drew on their own life histories to parent, guide, and counsel the children (Collay, 1988). In so doing, they found themselves healed from wounds that had occurred in their own lives as learners. Teaching and learning, especially in the constructivist philosophy, require dialogue (Freire, 1970) and social interaction, requiring the whole person to enter the process. Only teaching that is telling allows the presenter the freedom of remaining distant.

Vygotsky (1962) and others have debated the nature of learning in schools, attempting to separate independent or innate learning from learning that occurs because of interactions with other children and adults. We believe that learning is interactive and that adults and children make meaning and construct knowledge as members in a community. The excerpts above demonstrate "teacher talk," or how young teachers made meaning of their interactions with children. Few people would call the act of empathizing with a 7-year-old leadership. Yet, if we recall the words of Rallis (1989) about the role of teachers as "catalyst, guide, interpreter, and facilitator for a process" (p. 201), there is certainly a purposeful dimension to the guidance of others. Teaching and learning with others is the setting in which young teachers make sense of who they are becoming as adults. They and the other members of their learning communities construct a time, a place, and a feeling about each other and about their sense of place.

Mature teachers not only demonstrate leading children by maintaining their focus on humanity, but they also move more boldly into the roles Rallis describes: catalyst, guide, interpreter, and facilitator. With maturity and sophistication, however, they interact with and influence the community of adult learners as well as the children in their classrooms. The second study that informs this chapter is a series of interviews with midcareer teachers who have completed a Master of Arts in Education. The geographic setting is the upper Midwest, with teachers representing districts that are urban, suburban, and rural. The average age of the participants is 40, and the group reflects the average American elementary schoolteacher: primarily white, female, and Christian. Their age is more telling than their years in service, because most are mothers who stayed home to raise children at some point in their careers. This degree does not lead to the principalship, so it tends to attract teachers who explicitly state that they have no desire to become principals. Yet their stories demonstrate tremendous acts of leadership in their schools—from the catalyst, guide, interpreter, and facilitator roles mentioned earlier to radical acts of disruption.

EXPERIENCED TEACHERS AND LEADERSHIP

The new teachers in the previous study focused their learning primarily on students as individuals. Experienced teachers who choose more visible roles of leadership, however, speak more about interactions with colleagues, reciprocal activities, and seeking shared meaning or common purpose. The first experienced teacher presented here is Fran, an English as a Second Language (ESL) teacher in an urban school. Fran worked with non-English-speaking Southeast Asian kindergarten students. She became aware of her students' potential involvement with gang activity because her husband was on the police force, and she was very knowledgeable about the juvenile system. Fran researched her topic for two years, becoming an expert within her graduate cohort and her urban district. After she completed her thesis and the program, I asked her if she had presented her recommendations to her staff. She replied, "Not terribly much. I've done a fair amount with my own students here. Oddly enough, never to staff, never as a staff inservice presenter. I've done staff inservices with other buildings." When I asked her if she anticipated making more formal presentations of her work, she said,

> I've gone to see other staff. I gave a presentation at the TESOL [Teachers of English to Speakers of Other Languages] conference. I'm a member, and that one was kind of interesting because there was feedback that certainly our district should use new forms of teaching. I presented at the Hmong parents' meeting. But of course there's no money involved.

Fran's thesis was original, theoretically sound, and was the quality of a doctoral dissertation. Within her own building, however, she was not seen as an expert, at least not one that might conceivably be paid for her services. More important, she did not see herself as a leader. There are a few interpretations we can make here. One might be that Fran still sees herself as "just a kindergarten teacher" after many years in the same building. Teachers who teach the youngest children or those with disabilities— limited English proficiency is often categorized with other disabilities if one examines policy closely—have the lowest status in a school, and Fran may have internalized those beliefs.

Midlife female teachers who seek advanced degrees and remain in the classroom are seldom acknowledged for new expertise the way a teacher turned principal is. There are few visible turning points for midcareer professionals who remain in the classroom. District administrators, who spend great sums of money on outside experts, may not have the information about internal experts, and site-level leaders may not be socialized to advocate for teachers who may be more knowledgeable than they are themselves. Teachers who do serve in leadership roles without formal appointments (e.g., teachers on special assignment) do so at their regular salary, reinforcing the standard that only principals with licenses and formal appointments can be leaders.

Fran may have chosen not to make public her changing perception of herself from a teacher without remarkable special expertise to one who brings expertise to her school community. Experienced teachers develop areas of expertise, but the nature of the profession does not encourage formal dissemination of teacher knowledge. Teachers like to talk about new ideas with colleagues, but not at the risk of stepping away from the others by cloaking themselves in the mantle of expert. Teachers who are identified by principals as leaders or experts risk loss of association with peers and may find that the risk is not worth the acknowledgment. We believe that the pervasive "egalitarian ethic" (Lieberman, Saxl, & Miles, 1988) held by teachers and the culture of schools must be acknowledged and addressed in movements of educational reform. Fortunately, leadership as we have conceived it does not require expertise as much as it does mutual respect, listening, posing questions, and making sense of teaching together.

In addition to the school culture that rewards fitting in, school administrators have historically played a role in problematizing teacher leadership. For instance, in urban districts in Minnesota (and in many other districts throughout the United States), a role called Instructional Assistant has emerged in recent years. Teachers take on administrative tasks while retaining a regular teacher's salary. This is a place where teachers' unions might take a position on teacher leadership. The dilemma posed by this practice is that teachers need and deserve opportunities to practice roles of formal leadership, yet bureaucratic procedures cannot allow them the extra pay made available for administrators. This practice confuses our efforts to create opportunities for all members of the community to lead and to participate.

Another veteran teacher, Nancy, described her current role as a teacher of sixth graders in a suburban school. She had recently completed her thesis on gender equity in schools and remarked about that experience:

> The master's program reawakened my interest, it rejuvenated my confidence, it allowed me to not just sit back and accept what people say and accept directives without really thinking about it. I'm interested in making some changes and raising awareness in other people, whether it be through workshop situations or through conversation, as well as in my own teaching.

Nancy's commitment to engage colleagues in a common purpose is evident in the following story. She and her colleague had designed a gender equity workshop for their colleagues, submitted a grant proposal to their district, and were asked to present their materials in workshops. In addition to making formal presentations, her informal behaviors had also changed: "I have aligned myself professionally with other people who are in the process of doing graduate work or who have just completed their graduate work." Her colleagues were people who were also active learners, rather than those who accepted things the way they had always been.

These veteran teachers have become expert in an area, owned knowledge of the broader profession, and still have not found the means by which to make a formal contribution in their own schools. The expectations they have of themselves, as well as the expectations of others in the organization, have limited their opportunities to contribute. It is important to many teachers to find entry points to participation through their expert knowledge. In the cases of both Fran and Nancy, experienced teachers with newly won knowledge have taken the first step in gaining expertise. Being knowledgeable, though, is not enough. Each must enter the next stage of development and reconstruct his or her professional image. Ways in which teachers can lead through their expert knowledge might include writing articles for local publications; teaming with a colleague to offer a workshop; working as alumni presenters in their graduate programs, where they offer credible role models to those who follow them; or developing courses and offering them in institutes or continuing studies courses. Thus, individual learning becomes individual acts of owning one's expertise through interactions with children and adults in settings such as these. Leadership processes can and should be shared and equitable, yet the skills of leaders include offering one's own knowledge to others. We believe that these intermediate steps may yet be necessary as teachers make the transition from "independent contractor" to member of a learning community. Formal knowledge acquired through graduate study was a key in their success at taking first, critical steps in efforts to become recognized as formal leaders.

Graduate education offers the safety of a learning community that may be less politicized and problematic than some school cultures. In addition to formal course work conducted seminar-style, which offers a culture of dialogue and shared colleagueship, students are asked and encouraged to present their new findings in formal settings within and beyond the academy. Publications of their work in newsletters and short articles for other members of the graduate program are supported. Thesis committees include an advocate or formal leader from the school site, so that each teacher has a link to the next stage of implementation. The importance of advocacy or mentorship for midcareer teachers cannot be overstated.

The experienced teacher must work within a learning community in the professional setting of the school or district. Having acquired experience and knowledge, the community of the school is the place where new ways of practicing "colleagueship"occur. Teachers construct new knowledge with their peers, retaining what is good about their work and having the courage to introduce new ideas to old colleagues. This critical step doesn't happen easily. The constructivist approach to learning and teaching provides a more culturally acceptable way for teachers to lead. The learning community is the setting in which teachers and students are supported in their efforts to construct their own knowledge.

In this last example of teachers leading, a veteran teacher who chose to stay in the classroom has made the transition from informal to more visible leadership. Nina is a 24-year veteran who was on the design team that built her school in the late 1970s. Nina has welcomed and bid good-bye to several principals in that time and had been asked by her current principal to design staff development activities for her colleagues. This invitation followed several years of detachment from school activities as she completed her master's degree and during which school administrators had been perceived as ineffective. Nina's case represents the elements of constructivist leading. She first outlined "the reciprocal processes that enable ... " then created a series of conversations in which "participants in an educational community constructed meanings . . . " and finally "led toward a common purpose of schooling."

Nina had invited Michelle Collay, the Director of Graduate Education at Hamline University, to work with her on a specific inservice activity for a staff just emerging from a period of frustration and disengagement caused by several changes in administration. This conversation took place one year after the inservice day that represented the beginning of a more active role as leader in her school. When Michelle asked Nina why the principal had engaged her to work with the staff, Nina described a principal who had "met with quite a bit of resistance initially. She's had negative feedback, defensiveness from staff members." Apparently the principal's efforts to provide leadership had met with little success. Nina felt that teachers naturally resist change efforts from the top: "Plus, coming from the principal, it's different than coming from colleagues."

The inservice session she planned was an outgrowth of her thesis, planning a school structured around student happiness and a re-visioning of the school's mission. Teachers had become disillusioned with their status as a "reassignment school"—that is, a school into which students from across the district who weren't placed at magnet schools get placed. Michelle asked Nina to recall steps she had taken to prepare herself and Michelle for the professional development session to re-vision the school:

> I think I talked with people on an informal basis, passing in the hall-way or whatever, finding out what issues were important to them. I think I even surveyed the staff, just a little piece to find out where people wanted to go, looking at some redirection. I think we even had some discussions at staff meetings and in other places. Prior to your coming, we did some preplanning to get a sense of what to do. And then Anne [the principal] had certain specific things in terms of our strategic school plan that we needed to incorporate.

We see in her language the tentative "I think." This represents an early stage of owning one's leadership, of choosing language carefully to retain her status as "one of the teachers," rather than a teacher who is becoming an authority, or a teacher who is aligning herself with ineffective administration. Although she was not as direct about owning the steps she took, she did express confidence about her ability to find out what her colleagues valued.

Nina and Michelle had talked about the importance of incorporating the school elders in the planning so that she would not be isolated as a teacher leader and so that other senior teachers would be honored for their historical contributions. Her next statements reflect her careful efforts to create a map of the school history with her colleagues to elicit their support and demonstrate her respect:

I did some background research on the school; I pulled all those folders to get a sense of where we had been. One senior teacher and I talked about memories of the annex, the farm school. I talked to Linda, who I taught with when we first started. It was a country-type school; we ate lunch together in the office. When I started talking about this inservice with other senior teachers, they said, "Oh yeah, those were the best years of our teaching!" I think that really did help. I don't think they felt intimidated by their involvement with the session.

Applying her fine teacher skills, Nina perceived her role with colleagues as a catalyst or facilitator of their staff development activities. She did not "carry the agenda" but rather solicited the hopes of others in her community. Nina also talked about the collegial atmosphere among the teachers, who could work well together and share ownership. At the inservice, she and Michelle modeled that approach as they co-led the first session:

In the morning, we [Michelle and Nina] worked as a team, so there wasn't just one of us hanging out there. In the afternoon, it was the same thing with Kathy and myself. It didn't feel like there was just one person saying this is the way it's going to be. I think that's a lot of it.

Nina felt that she couldn't "stand up in front" and instruct or give answers to colleagues. She stated a value for a style of leadership described by Robertson (1992) in her work on the role of gender in leadership styles: "Women's leadership styles are expressed through communication patterns which are more typical of collegial than autocratic endeavors. Women's language patterns appear to create a consensual and participative atmosphere for decision-making" (p. 52). As a teacher and colleague, Nina was successful with this approach to leadership.

This next reflection contains some of the reasons why Nina has the ability to "evoke potential in a trusting environment." Whereas the recent history of the school had been disrupted by mistrust, the senior teacher group was credible and trustworthy. When Michelle and Nina talked more about trust building and how she had earned her status as senior teacher, Nina said,

Longevity is part of it! One person said, "Go talk to Nina, because she doesn't just talk about changing something, she does something!" I think of the way I try to interrelate to the people in the building. I tell the truth, I'm respectful, I don't act like I know everything. And I've been here a long time. I came with the building! And professionally I think I'm a good teacher. And I think other people recognize that.

As Nina reflected on the traumas of her teaching day with second graders, she added ruefully, "Maybe not every day!" We talked more about teachers who have longevity and experience but do not garner the respect Nina was describing:

> There are people who have been in the building for a long time. They just kind of sit back and let other people do the work; they won't take a position on anything. They're not risk takers; they're not going to put their head on a chopping block or speak up at a staff meeting. They stick with the same old things; they won't try some new things. I think those people look at teaching as a job, rather than as a vocation or a blissful experience or what your journey in life is. And there is a difference!

In these remarks, we see evidence of the importance of vision for anyone in a leadership role. Experience, longevity, and just knowing the history don't seem to be enough. Having the courage to speak her truth and to move toward a goal were central to Nina's perception of herself as a leader. Michelle had talked with Nina about the context of their interview being "constructivist leadership" and her belief that teachers undertake approaches with children similar to those that good leaders take with adults. When she asked Nina, "If you were to put language on what you do with adult colleagues, what language would you use?" Nina answered,

> I'm real active in committees that make a difference in the building, committees that can get change going. I'm not afraid to say something in the staff room. I'm not afraid to take a stance, even though I have been in the past. I'm not afraid to shoot my hand up and say, "Hey, wait a minute. Maybe there's another possibility."

Michelle was curious about whether this more proactive stance Nina described was a recent thing. Nina said,

> It's been since I got into graduate school. Since I got into the master's program and began getting into all the information in education, and talking to people in other schools, it gives you a base of current knowledge. You ground yourself better, you come across as if you know something, and you question more.

Again, the role of graduate education for Nina cannot be underestimated. In a community of learners motivated by the same thirst for knowledge, Nina, along with Fran and Nancy, gained a level of confidence that translated into inquiry and action. We closed the session with a comparison of teacher leadership for children and for adults, something Michelle had asked Nina to think about at an earlier meeting:

What do I do with the staff in terms of leadership? I do about the same thing I do in the classroom! That's what I do. You structure things for success, you interrelate to people in certain ways, you're positive, you try to facilitate them through where they need to go, you allow them leadership, you give them choices and options. If you really sat down and listed all the things you do with children in classrooms, if you're effective with kids, a lot of it is all there. It's just a different level.

There are two important and parallel strands to Nina's perception of her role as a "teacher who leads." The first strand is the importance of the credibility earned by her long-term membership in the school community. In the first part of her reflection, she revisits the history of the school, and her longevity is named as an important factor in her ability to lead. Other factors that are important include "I'm truthful, I'm respectful, I don't act like I know everything." Her stance allows reciprocal behavior to remain central to interactions and, therefore, offers potential for interdependence. These values that Nina states give her recognition and respect by others. She is a team player in how she hears what others have to say and includes them as equals. These characteristics are evident in classrooms designed for constructed knowledge and are central to the success of all members of the community. A teacher who values student confidence and success over merely completing basic assignments offers such a learning community to students. This learning community is holistic and open, not linear and closed.

Second, Nina states the importance of "voice." She is not afraid to "take a stance." This ability to risk criticism by others does not come early in practice, at least it did not for this teacher. Nina cites her graduate education as if key to her confidence as a professional: "You ground yourself better, you come across as if you know something, and you question more." Each of us must feel confident that our voice carries weight, that we speak from a place of knowing, and that we can back our claims with real information.

With the strength of credibility among peers, confidence in hard-won knowledge about the profession, and a sense of voice, what else is necessary for constructivist teacher leaders to succeed?

CONCLUSION

Teaching is an act of leadership, requiring an understanding of one's role, a commitment to empowering all learners, the skills of facilitation, and the willingness to inquire about and reflect on one's own learning. Teaching and learning are highly relational, interactive, and grounded in the lives of the participants. Constructivist leaders are teachers. Those who teach will recognize the following social interactions necessary for learning described by Wells and Wells (1992):

> Like the culture itself, the individual's knowledge, and the repertoire of actions and operations by means of which he or she carries out the activities that fulfill his or her perceived needs, are both constructed in the course of solving the problems that arise in goal-directed social activity and learned through interpersonal interaction. Human development and learning are thus intrinsically social and interactive. (p. 29)

A constructivist leader recognizes and values this framework for learning. From first-year teachers who are capable of leading children through their learning and of constructing self-knowledge about that leadership role, to experienced teachers who are skilled in their colleagueship with other adults, we have seen exemplary approaches to leadership—if we choose to name what they do as such. As teachers make meaning with their students, they are participants in the collaborative construction of knowledge. It is ironic that, even though teachers' leadership is often dismissed as child care, we can look to classroom teaching as a source for metaphors of the roles of leaders. If we accept teachers as leaders, what can we learn from teaching practice about leadership?

New metaphors for leadership are necessary. The term constructivist leader offers many possibilities beyond those we have inherited from the patriarchy. Rallis (1989) believes that metaphors of leading, which include "steward, captain, visionary, evangelist, manager, or instructional leader are inadequate because they suggest leadership is confined to a role or described by a set of skills or tasks to be accomplished" (p. 203). Teachers, as constructivist leaders of children's and adults' learning, can lend different metaphors for leadership. Their contributions, however, will not be embraced within old paradigms of school organization. "The espoused theory of teacher leadership would be undermined if theories in action stress teacher compliance as opposed to creative risk-taking" (Cliff, Johnson, Holland, & Veal, 1992, p. 906). Only when the school community is itself a learning community as a result of constructed knowing and shared meaning will the contribution of teachers be considered leadership.

Is it possible to imagine school communities where all adults teach all other participants in learning? Sacken (1994) calls our attention to the importance for school leaders to stay closer to children—and, therefore, to retain opportunities to construct meaning with all members of the school community: "People who want to contribute to the well-being and future of children simply must work with them. At the least, they should not be paid more not to work with them" (p. 669). The historic paradigm of stratified leadership is with us still. And the creation of new or different metaphors for leadership remains the challenge before us.

How we choose to practice leadership must relate directly to how we teach. Different models of leadership can be derived from teaching, and the role of leader will allow for many kinds of participants. In a collaborative process with colleagues studying the characteristics of constructivist leaders, we hoped to draw together the common traits between teaching and leading. We must look to our classrooms as the beginning point rather than as the end point:

> Our position is that for substantive and widespread change to occur, we must start with a vision of what we want to occur in classrooms and schools, and then begin to question which existing structures support or facilitate that image and which must be altered. (Cohn & Kottkamp, 1993, p. 260)

Teachers have much to contribute to our thinking about leadership and leading. The traditions of constructivist education offer a powerful catalyst for our thinking about the work of teachers and their roles as leaders. This conversation has always attracted people of many philosophies, but the voices of teachers are being heard above the din.

REFERENCES

Bell, C., & Chase, S. (1993). The under-representation of women in school leadership. In C. Marshall & P. Zodhiates (Eds.), *The new politics of race and gender: The 1992 yearbook of the politics of education association* (pp. 141–154). Washington, DC: Falmer.

Bullough, R., Knowles, G., & Crow, N. (1991). *Emerging as a teacher.* London: Routledge.

Cliff, R., Johnson, M., Holland, P., & Veal, M. (1992). Developing the potential for collaborative school leadership. *American Educational Research Journal, 29*(4), 877–908.

Cochran-Smith, M. (1991). Learning to teach against the grain. *Harvard Educational Review, 61*(3), 279–310.

Cohn, M., & Kottkamp, R. (1993). *Teachers: The missing voice in education.* Albany: SUNY Press.

Collay, M. (1988). *Dialogue as a language of learning: An ethnographic study of teacher socialization.* Unpublished doctoral dissertation, University of Oregon, Eugene.

Darling-Hammond, L. (1990). Teachers and teaching: Signs of a changing profession. In W. R. Houston (Ed.), *The handbook of research on teacher education* (pp. 267–290). New York: Macmillian.

Freire, P. (1970). *Pedagogy of the oppressed.* New York: Continuum.

Grumet, M. (1980). *Bittermilk.* Amherst: University of Massachusetts Press.

Lieberman, A., & Miller, L. (1990). The social realities of teaching. In A. Lieberman (Ed.), *Schools as collaborative cultures: Creating the future now* (pp. 153–163). London: Falmer.

Lieberman, A., Saxl, E., & Miles, M. B. (1988). Teacher leadership: Ideology and practice. In A. Lieberman (Ed.), *Building a professional culture in schools.* New York: Teachers College Press.

Little, J. W. (1990). Teachers as colleagues. In A. Lieberman (Ed.), *Schools as collaborative cultures: Creating the future now* (pp. 165–193). London: Falmer.

Noddings, N. (1984). *Caring: A feminine approach to ethics and moral education.* Berkeley: University of California Press.

Peston, J. (1991). *Gender and the formation of a women's profession: The case of public school-teaching.* Working Paper Series, Wellesley College Center for Research on Women.

Rallis, S. (1989). Professional teachers and restructured schools: Leadership challenges. In B. Mitchell & L. Cunningham (Eds.), *Educational leadership and changing contexts of families, communities, and schools: Eighty-ninth yearbook of the National Society for the Study of Education* (pp. 184–209). Chicago: University of Chicago Press.

Robertson, H. J. (1992). Teacher development and gender equity. In A. Hargreaves & M. Fullan (Eds.), *Understanding teacher development* (pp. 43–61). New York: Teachers College Press.

Ryan, K. (1986). *The induction of new teachers.* Bloomington, IN: Phi Delta Kappa Educational Foundation.

Sacken, D. (1994). No more principals! *Phi Delta Kappan, 75*(9), 664–670.

Schmuck, P., & Shubert, J. (1995). Women principals' view on sex equity: Exploring issues of integration and information. In D. Dunlap & P. A. Schmuck (Eds.), *Women leading in education* (pp. 274–287). Albany: State University of New York Press.

Vygotsky, L. (1962). *Thought and language.* Boston: MIT Press.

Wells, G., & Wells, G. (1992). *Constructing knowledge together: Classrooms as centers of inquiry and literacy.* Portsmouth, NH: Heinemann.

Zeichner, K., & Gore, J. (1989). *Teacher socialization.* East Lansing, MI: National Center for Research on Teacher Education.

10

What Teachers Bring to Leadership

The Distinctive Assets of Teachers Who Lead

Gordon A. Donaldson, Jr.

M any teachers are understandably leery of choosing to lead. Here's
the way Martha, a midcareer teacher, put it:

> I see [principals] being pulled in a lot of different directions, and
> I see the job becoming much more managerial than being that
> professional leader, the educational leader . . . If I could be a
> principal . . . an educational leader to teachers, an educational sup-
> port where I still got into the classroom, where I helped . . . give
> that peer evaluator, peer assistance, peer coaching kind of stuff, I'd
> be really interested in something like that. I still would have that
> connection.

Martha feels pulled by a desire to help make her colleagues stronger
teachers, a desire reinforced by colleagues encouraging her to think about
becoming a principal. But she's pulled back from such a career move by a
very big "If": She wonders if she could really work as the kind of leader
she defines as "an educational leader to teachers."

As teachers ponder the possibilities for having wider influence on learning than they can have within their own classrooms, they often encounter this duality. On one hand, leadership is conventionally understood to be what principals do; if you ask who the leader of a school is, most folks will point to the principal. On the other hand, if you invite teachers to reflect on how leadership works for them and who their leaders are, they will conjure up other images beyond administrative ones.

In the following pages, I explore the assets that teachers, perhaps uniquely, bring to school leadership. In my view, teachers have always exerted strong leadership in our most successful schools. It has been our loss that we haven't recognized either the power or the richness of this "other kind" of leadership. Now, when we are so clearly feeling the limits of administrative leadership, it is imperative that we understand and practice more consciously what Martha calls "educational leadership for teachers."

THE LIMITS OF ADMINISTRATIVE LEADERSHIP

The school principalship has taken a fast and bumpy ride in its short history in U.S. schools. Invented in the 1920s for the larger city schools then being built, the principal's role was largely viewed as a managerial one, focusing on assuring uniformity of practice, a secure environment, and a measure of quality control. The many small schools in the U.S. had no principals—or full-time principals, at least. Changes in the 1960s prompted a growing expectation that principals had curricular leadership roles and, with the Effective Schools movement in the late 1970s, "strong leadership" from the principal came to be seen as an essential quality of a good school (Sergiovanni, 1996).

A great many hopes rode on principals in the '80s and '90s. They were to do it all: be the first and last word in the behavior system; handle the budget; manage buildings, equipment, and co-curricular programs; facilitate community relations; evaluate teachers and staff; and ensure that the instructional program was effective. The word *leadership* began appearing in school administration writing during the '80s, capping a transformation in the hopes of many that schools could be led by principals to serve every child, and to high standards.

It is common knowledge now that this aspiration for principals was unrealistic. No single person, particularly in larger schools with more heterogeneous populations, could succeed at all these expectations. So we now face a "leadership crisis," insufficient numbers of qualified applicants for principals' positions; many of the best teachers in our schools, like Martha, viewing administrative positions as no place for real leadership. As reforms keep coming and government and community expectations that every child achieve to standard grow less flexible, the need for Martha's type of leadership "for teachers" grows.

Listening to teachers explore their own capacity as leaders has made clear to me that administration does not offer many of them opportunities to lead that promise to sustain and fulfill them. It is also clear that many teachers are willing to think outside the box about how leadership can function in schools. My analysis of data from a study of 60 midcareer Maine teachers (Mackenzie, Cook, & Morrell, 2004) reveals some important themes in their assessments of the principal role:

- It's a position in which you have to "put up with" a lot, where you're often "complained to," and where "you get all the negatives."
- It's a position in which the number and variety of responsibilities are "mind-boggling" and, frankly, impossible for one person to accomplish.
- It's a position in which the daily activities are very different from those that motivated teachers to get into teaching in the first place: "going to meetings," dealing with bureaucracy, and doing "everything I dislike about teaching: budgets, answering to school board members who are ignorant of the ways kids learn, dealing with behavior."
- It's a position in which you have to inspire and supervise adults; as one teacher put it, "I don't like being responsible for other people when they are adults who should be responsible for themselves."
- It's a position from which you can have considerable influence, shaping priorities for staff, students, and community and "advocating for kids."
- For some, it's a position that does provide opportunities for coaching and nurturing colleagues and improving student learning.
- But for many, the principalship is not personally sustainable: It would "drive me crazy"; "I wouldn't enjoy it much"; and "I'd miss the kids too much."

It is time we paid attention to these sentiments from teachers. After all, when we think about leadership in schools, it's primarily *teachers* who are being led! So, who do teachers regard as leaders? What is it that these leaders do? How does this "leadership for teachers" function so that teachers feel inspired to improve and supported in their improvement? And how can it be practiced so it is sustainable for our very best educators— so that leading and teaching are not an either-or choice?

THE ASSETS TEACHERS BRING TO LEADERSHIP

Many of the Maine teachers referenced above, when asked about moving toward a principalship, echoed the following remarks: "I love what I'm doing in the classroom," "I'm not ready to leave the kids," and "I'm a good bridge between teachers and administration in my school." Teachers' sense of reward and fulfillment stems fundamentally from seeing their students succeed and from colleagueship with other educators in this important work (Darling-Hammond, 1997; Johnson, 1990). So, teacher leadership, to be sustainable for the leader, needs to stay close to students, teaching, and learning.

This vibrant connection to the classroom and its work, of course, is the single greatest asset that teachers bring to school leadership. I see three sets of opportunities for teacher leaders to shape the environment of the school and the practices for learning and teaching that are vital to success for every child. These are unique leadership opportunities for teachers; principals, except in rare instances, cannot seize them as fully. They are relationship-building, protecting the learning mission, and stimulating invention in the classroom. These themes are described and referenced more fully in Donaldson (2006) and supported by the seminal work of Katzenmeyer and Moller (2001).

Relationship Building

Leadership, particularly in schools, is first and foremost a relationship. If teachers and others are to share a commitment to acting together to improve learning for all children, their working relationships must be strong enough to sustain that action (Bryk & Schneider, 2002). Of all the adults in the school, teachers have the best opportunities to cultivate open, respectful relationships with one another. Administrators are saddled with supervisory responsibilities and expectations to exercise authority and power. Their relationships are constrained by past administrators' example, by policy, and by labor-management history. Teachers, plain and simple, have the best opportunity to be leaders with one another.

How? By taking advantage of the following opportunities. First, teachers' relationships begin with an expectation of equality, affirmation, and collaboration. Teacher leaders cultivate these relationships so that they sustain frontline educators, both as people and as teachers. Schools are like any workplace. They are a mini-society made up of clusters of staff shaped by interests, friendships, and work patterns. Often, these group affiliations shape teaching philosophies and practices; personal and professional differences can cripple a faculty's ability to grow. Or widely respected teachers who move freely among the faculty can use their relational trust and influence to cultivate relationships that sustain a common focus on kids, learning, and a positive culture.

These are powerful teacher leaders. By dint of their naturally earned influence, they project and model healthy relational and professional norms in their approach to their colleagues. They can see staff divisions as opportunities for creating alternative approaches to improving practice as well as for bringing to the surface the challenges they all face building a thoughtful—and diverse—community of practice. A teacher's leadership begins with establishing authentic respect for other teachers and inviting reciprocal respect in return. Our most influential teacher leaders do this naturally; many others can do it by being more planful about relationships with and among their colleagues.

Second, teachers work elbow-to-elbow with one another. They teach next door, they are on a grade-level team or department, they share committee assignments, and they participate together in the teachers' association. Their relational world is a web of face-to-face contacts around personal and professional issues that matter to them. Teacher leaders seize these daily opportunities to listen, to share, to enlist colleagues' thinking and assistance in the persisting tasks of reaching all children. Their work happens in small, daily ways made possible because the relationships they have with fellow teachers keep them connected. Sharing work and sharing kids gives teachers the potential to influence one another's practice through these daily, small connections. This influence—often reciprocal—is the essence of relational leadership.

Protecting the Learning Mission

Leadership isn't just about strong working relationships. Working together in common commitment to children and learning turns relationships to the pursuit of professional goals. Teacher leaders have unique opportunities to keep the focus of their collective work on kids, on learning, and on the effectiveness of that work.

First, they demonstrate their own vision and their own commitment to it by sharing with colleagues the challenges they face with the children they teach. They bring to discussions, faculty meetings, and casual conversations what concerns them most about how they are doing with their kids or how their teaching team is doing with their cohort of children. They talk about their challenges and seek assistance from others. And when meeting agendas are diverted to noninstructional topics, as they often are, teacher leaders speak up to return them to kids and learning. Teacher leaders, sometimes stridently, insist that time together be devoted to working on ways to make all teachers more successful with children.

Second, teacher leaders find creative ways to gain time and resources so the groups they work with can address the teaching challenges they face and celebrate their successes. That is, they advocate with principals, support staff, central office, and even the community for conditions that will permit their colleagues to do their jobs better. They are voices for children and for learning in the schoolhouse, the district, and the community. They are skilled at extracting resources to support professional development, team-planning time, assistance to release teachers from clerical or supervisory duties—all in the service of the school's achievement of the learning mission.

Stimulating Invention in the Classroom

In addition to relationship building and protecting the learning mission, teacher leadership can uniquely shape the real work that goes on in classrooms. Teacher leaders working in small groups and in daily ways that maintain the focus on learning and kids meet with many opportunities to mobilize their colleagues to invent new ways to work with their students and their curricula. Teacher leaders are working beside their colleagues, not above them. They are close to the action and not saddled, as principals often are, with having to change the whole school or with imposing top-down solutions on other teachers.

Opportunities to stimulate invention abound for the teacher leader who shares open working relationships with colleagues that focus on kids, teaching, and learning. They encourage colleagues to bring their persisting teaching challenges to team meetings, to professional development experiences, and to fellow teachers who can help. This problem-solving mindset includes making meetings safe places for teachers to share their frustrations and vulnerabilities about kids they cannot reach or parents who are not cooperating. Most important, teacher leaders bring *their own* persisting classroom challenges to their colleagues, seeking assistance and support from colleagues in the same way that they make themselves available to help their colleagues.

Teacher leaders are essential to a culture of continuous improvement. As we have learned about schools that use assessment data, schedules that allow for problem solving and planning, and team structures for instruction (DuFour, Eaker, & DuFour, 2005; Garmston & Wellman, 1999), we are seeing how teachers function as leaders, often without any formal or structural designation that they *are* leaders. Again, the colleague whose expertise as a teacher and whose skills as a collaborator and coach draw teachers to her or him for professional assistance and support has achieved an enviable and very influential role in shaping the success of the school.

Each of the opportunities to lead I have described is more easily seized by a teacher than by an administrator. Together, they blend into a package of relational, purposive, and practical activities that, I believe, form the heart of teacher leadership. When teachers pursue respectful working relationships with all their colleagues, when they champion learning and teaching, and when they engage directly in the search for answers and solutions to classroom challenges they and their colleagues face, the result must be that their colleagues feel encouraged, supported, challenged, and helped to be better teachers in very concrete ways. In a word, that is, they feel led.

BEYOND ROLE: THE SPIRIT OF LEADERSHIP

I have written about three types of school leader role: administrative leadership, formal teacher leadership, and informal teacher leadership. Principals fill *administrative leadership* roles; they report directly to other administrators and are legally responsible for the performance of school staff. *Formal teacher leaders* fill quasi-administrative roles such as department chair, team leader, or standing committee chair; these roles have job descriptions and are paid positions obligating these leaders to school administrators for the delivery of services. They are primarily teachers who have subcontracted for some management responsibilities. Finally, *informal teacher leaders* have no formal titles or job expectations other than those attributed to them by other teachers, administrators, and parents. Their influence stems from how others view them, not from any ascribed authority or power that comes with the position.

Teacher leaders, whether formal or informal, bring to their work the assets that I describe in the previous section. But the institutional expectations for formal teacher leaders position them differently than informal leaders. The kind of leadership they can provide benefits in some ways from their quasi-administrative status: they can access budgets and the principal's authority to get things done; they can require colleagues to participate in desirable activities; they sometimes have release time to devote to team or departmental work that teachers would otherwise have to do. But they are also hampered by their institutional obligations. They are neither fish nor fowl; they don't have administrative authority, yet have administrative duties; colleagues can be resentful of them, their pay, and their reduced teaching loads (Wasley, 1991).

Each type of leadership, however, brings with it both assets and liabilities. I have summarized these in Table 10.1. Educators who aspire to lead might be best advised to approach their work knowing that each of them, alone, doesn't have the whole package. He or she cannot have the whole package. Instead, what schools need if they are to transform themselves is leadership from all three roles. And what they need most are leaders of all three types who understand how important they *all* are to the success of their school—how, that is, they must work in a *complementary leadership relationship*.

Whereas we know a lot about the assets and liabilities of administrative leaders and have learned of late about those of formal teacher leaders, informal teacher leaders remain a precious yet unrecognized leadership resource in most schools. The special value informal teacher leaders bring to this mix stems from the spirit they evoke. They make individual competence a collective responsibility. No teacher's work is understood to be her or his work alone because it really does take a whole school to educate every child well. These teacher leaders exude a "can-do" spirit about their own learning and their own invention of better practice. They invite

Table 10.1   Assets and Liabilities of Teacher and Principal Leaders

	Informal or Natural Teacher Leaders	Formal or Designated Teacher Leaders	Administrators or Principal Leaders
Building Relationships	+ happen naturally; strong "voluntary & permissive" − occurs in pockets; may undercut schoolwide collaboration	+ small teams; collaboration grows from common work − staff feel forced to collaborate; uncertain authority	+ sanction connections among people; officially value relationships − power interferes; staff is too large to build trusting, open relationships
Growing Commitment to Purpose	+ groups form around natural "community of interest" − interest may not reinforce school-wide purposes	+ shapes mission of work team; keeps team members focused − can develop "cross-purposes" to other teams/school-wide purposes	+ has everyone's attention; can keep grand purposes in the forefront − get compliance, not commitment; group too large to "test" purpose and reaffirm commitments
Nurturing Action-in-Common	+ natural sharing/support lead to innovation/growth; spontaneous action − haphazard; doesn't include everyone; may not reinforce student improvement	+ working teams innovate together; access to resources − can develop new practices that conflict with other teams; can resist formal priorities/ leaders	+ promote and coordinate school-wide learning & innovation; commit resources to support them − compliance, not learning; get coercion, not authentic innovation

NOTE: + = asset; − = liability; Summarized from Chapters 5, 6, & 7 of *Cultivating Leadership in Schools* (Donaldson, 2006)

colleagues into their own classrooms, consult with colleagues about their own struggles, and celebrate with colleagues their own breakthroughs. They cultivate a community of practice by behaving as committed professionals (Barth, 2003; Meier, 2002).

They don't wait for a uniform plan to improve curriculum, instruction, and assessment to be drawn up (and left to gather dust). For many informal teacher leaders, the formal world of the school is too cumbersome, too slow and irrelevant to the on-the-ground changes they and their colleagues can make. So they rally those around them through conversations at lunch or in the hall and willingly put to use any ideas, materials, and suggestions offered. Their commitment to their own improvement is palpable in their daily search for a better way—both in their own classrooms and in the classrooms of those around them.

This is what gives colleagues the notion that these teachers *are* leaders. They are respectful of collegial relationships, but that does not mean that they hold back from voicing their commitment to high learning ideals. It means that they, courageously in some schools, make their commitments public and that they bring the educational challenges they face and the school faces into discussions and spaces shared with colleagues. And they are not self-conscious about their own search for better teaching techniques, new ideas for assessment, unusual ways to present material and engage children in mastering skills. These are teachers about whom others can say, "She helps me be a better teacher. She helps us all do the best we can do by kids."

REFERENCES

Barth, R. (2003). *Lessons learned: Shaping relationships and the culture of the workplace.* Thousand Oaks, CA: Corwin Press.

Bryk, A., & Schneider, B. (2002). *Trust in schools: A core resource for improvement.* New York: Russell Sage Foundation.

Darling-Hammond, L. (1997). *The right to learn: A blueprint for creating schools that work.* San Francisco: Jossey-Bass.

Donaldson, G. (2006). *Cultivating leadership in schools: Connecting people, purpose, and programs* (2nd ed.). New York: Teachers College Press.

DuFour, R., Eaker, R., & DuFour, R. (Eds.). (2005) *On common ground: The power of professional learning communities.* Bloomington IN: National Educational Service.

Garmston, R., & Wellman, B. (1999). *The adaptive school: A sourcebook for developing collaborative groups.* Norwood, MA: Christopher-Gordon.

Johnson, S. M. (1990). *Teachers at work: Achieving success in our schools.* New York: Basic Books.

Katzenmeyer, M., & Moller, G. (2001). *Awakening the sleeping giant* (2nd ed.). Thousand Oaks, CA: Corwin Press.

Mackenzie, S. V., Cook, S., & Morrell, B. (2004). *A view from the inside: Continuing the conversation about teaching in Maine schools.* Augusta, ME: Maine Educational Leadership Consortium.

Meier, D. (2002) *In schools we trust: Creating communities of learning in an era of testing and standardization.* Boston: Beacon.

Sergiovanni, T. (1996). *Leadership for the schoolhouse.* San Francisco: Jossey-Bass.

Wasley, P. (1991). *Teachers who lead: The rhetoric of reform and the realities of practice.* New York: Teachers College Press.

11

Leading From the Parking Lot

Barbara H. White

I was getting tired of teacher leadership, at least the way it was evolving in my school. Being a teacher leader placed me in a position where challenges and personal learning were almost continuous. That was the beneficial part of the experience because the opportunities for personal and professional growth were so numerous, frequent, and rewarding. However, the position also put me in a situation where I often seemed to have to face conflict and overt confrontation. I realized that I had to find other ways to be a full-time teacher and a full-time teacher leader that would allow me to nurture the relationships I valued with my colleagues and still forge ahead with changes I believed necessary in our school and defined in the school reform grant I had coauthored. Our grant allowed for and encouraged feedback from the faculty to help define the outcomes and goals. We had carefully constructed the grant expectations so systematic changes could occur but also so that the specific details and plans would be determined by the faculty, not by a small group. Sometimes understanding when to take the lead and when to stand back is one of the biggest challenges. Moments when one must make that choice provide some of the most valuable opportunities for personal growth.

A critical incident that illustrates both the need for effective communication and my increased ability to detach involves a seemingly innocuous survey. I put out a brief survey to find out which of the various methods of communicating with the teachers were most favored or helpful to them. Because effective communication was one of the areas our leadership team realized was a weakness in our school, we wanted specific feedback to help us address and improve the problem. The members of our leadership team had been hearing the scuttlebutt that we were not communicating frequently or efficiently enough with the faculty. In completing the survey, most of the faculty simply responded briefly, and a few added helpful comments that specifically stated how we could communicate with them better. However, one teacher took the opportunity to tell us all that she was thinking. She filled the half page survey and continued her comments, in bold red ink, for an additional full page. She had consistently been one of our "naysayers." It did not seem that the goals of our grant and school reform initiatives meshed with her vision of what we should do for our students. Yet, she is a dedicated teacher with the students' best interests in mind. My first reaction to her response was frustration that she didn't recognize our attempts to improve communication and that she had taken the opportunity to be hypercritical on what was a focused and specific survey. As I read her red inked comments, I initially felt it was my personal failure that I hadn't been able to more successfully "bring her onboard" concerning the systemic goals and vision some of us saw for the school. However, after rereading her note several times, I began to see it in a different light. I realized that if she was feeling that high level of frustration, I had a responsibility to acknowledge her concerns and to consider her perspective. I also realized that I might learn more from her honest, if sarcastic, response than many of the others' perfunctory responses.

Michael Fullan (2005) sums up the lesson I learned. Leaders "don't mind when naysayers rock the boat"; "doubters sometimes have important points." Good communication goes two ways. Sometimes the naysayer is the person whom we can learn the most from in both professional and personal ways. I believe in this concept, but living it isn't necessarily easy for the leader. When I could detach myself from the personal aspects of this situation, I gained valuable insight. I had to consciously step back from thinking about all the positive things I thought the leadership team and school reform team were doing and try to consider her message objectively. I realized that her message was more about the situation than about me or the leadership team. Some of the issues were beyond my control and that of the leadership team, but some directly related to us. In fact, my insight was confirmed when she stopped me in the hall and we talked about her survey responses. Some very valuable, honest communication took place in that hall. The other teacher even offered to rewrite her response to eliminate the sarcasm before I shared the results with the faculty. This conversation reminded me of Roland Barth's observation that some of the more meaningful meetings take place after the official faculty meeting—in the parking lot—or in this case in the hallway of the school (Barth, personal communication, October 14, 2004).

A couple of notable incidents of others getting involved to varying degrees support the small successes I felt in mobilizing others and in helping me step back when possible. The first event was a result of that hallway talk with the "naysayer." She suggested that the faculty needed time to get some issues out into the open. From our hallway conversation, we designed a faculty forum that I facilitated. I set up fairly rigid guidelines concerning our purpose, which was to brainstorm in order to identify issues that were of concern to the faculty. I was afraid people would feel "gagged" if I did not open it up for full discussion and problem solving. That strategy was based on our belief that several of the recently implemented initiatives were simply too new to begin talking about their specific strengths and weaknesses. However, the climate of this meeting was positive, even when negative observations surfaced, and the meeting was productive. The feedback from the faculty was informative and honest. The leadership team received helpful information that aided us in assessing where we were as a school and where we wanted or needed to go to accomplish our stated goals. I had opened the meeting by saying one of our colleagues had suggested the forum, but I did not identify her because I didn't know if she would be comfortable with that. However, at the conclusion of the meeting, she openly took credit for the suggestion. I was pleased that she, our naysayer, voluntarily did that and publicly took ownership of her part in planning a productive, positive meeting about school reform even if she had mixed feelings about specific initiatives.

Another example of others becoming more active and allowing me to step back is when two colleagues volunteered to help plan and facilitate a faculty "Taking Stock" session in April. The purpose of this session was to evaluate the successes and identify the continuing challenges involved with our newly implemented changes. These two colleagues are knowledgeable and skillful but have been reluctant to take a leadership role in the school change initiatives. Their willingness to facilitate part of this meeting was a real bonus because the faculty did not seem to view them as closely related to the initiatives and seemed to believe they could be more objective. We met several times to carefully plan the meeting so we would get feedback that would be helpful and not just end up in complaints or perennially unsolvable problems. The meeting was a good example of when facilitation can best be executed by someone who is not viewed as having too much ownership of the issues. I was able to take a backseat and still gather the information we needed in a positive, productive way. My colleagues successfully conducted a meeting that had the potential of being counterproductive if not facilitated carefully and purposefully.

The challenges of being a teacher leader are innumerable. However, when I focus on the two that were most significant to me lately, I realize I have to think about when to lead and when to stand back. Being able to encourage others to step forward and take the lead when they have the expertise, knowledge, and comfort level to do so is a rewarding and challenging part of leadership. Learning to lead from behind and, when out in front, looking back to see who is following are two of my most important realizations as a teacher leader in a challenging role and school.

REFERENCE

Fullan, M. (2005). *Leadership and sustainability: System thinkers in action.* Thousand Oaks, CA: Corwin Press.

Questions for Reflection and Conversation

- What are the assets and liabilities you bring to "informal" teacher leadership in your school?
- What might you do to foster a culture of greater shared leadership in your school?
- Having read these pieces, consider using a protocol to focus on and create a plan for your leadership development. You can certainly work through these questions on your own, but exploring them with others who are interested in their own leadership growth promises a deeper experience. Answer these questions to create a learning plan for your leadership development.

  1. To make a difference in my school:
     - What do I believe is critical to improve learning for students?
     - What do I want to commit to?

  2. Where and how can I exert influence in the school?
     - What opportunities do I have to shape an impact?
     - What is my role?

  3. What are some strategies I could pursue?

  4. In implementing these strategies, what challenges might I face?

  5. Given these challenges what do I need to learn?
     - What knowledge do I need to acquire?
     - What skill do I need to improve or develop?
     - What understanding of myself or clarity about my beliefs do I need?

  6. What steps will I take to learn, develop skill, and deepen my understanding?

  7. How will I get feedback on how well I am progressing?

PART III

The Heart of Teacher Leadership

I n the following short pieces you will read interior monologues of teacher leaders. These stories reveal the many voices of teacher leaders as they grow in their leadership with colleagues and administrators. The essence of teacher leadership can be expressed in the African phrase *Ubuntu* (loosely, I am you and you are me). Teacher leaders live and work with other people, and their connection with others is where their leadership lies. Colleagueship, the role of the individual in and of the collective, concerns them most. They are not white knights who stride in and save the day. In fact, they shy away from representations of the teacher as hero or martyr. They are the ones who chip away at tasks and problems with their colleagues. They want more than anything to share in the success of and responsibility for the learning of all students in a school. It is through their own learning that they do that. They long to be in a situation reflective of democratic empowerment and work hard to move their schools in that direction, in tandem or, sometimes, in tension, with their principals and colleagues.

Teacher leaders derive satisfaction and enjoyment from exploring new curriculum and assessment ideas as well as ways of improving practice with their colleagues. This is not to say that teacher leaders herd like sheep. They are capable of stepping out from the pack if necessary or using their individual voices to raise the consciousness of peers and administrators. But they know their strength derives from their classroom teaching. From that perspective, they can speak knowingly and effectively to fellow teachers about what they all value.

We highlight here the intrapersonal challenges teacher leaders face, but of course these challenges have much to do with interpersonal issues.

Conflict of some kind is often the center of their struggle and their learning. Teacher leaders swirl in ever-changing relationships with colleagues and supervisors. They want control over their work lives and what is near and dear to them—improving teaching and learning. They may be in conflict with the culture or the structure of the school, with others or within themselves. A large concern is how best to catalyze others to work as hard as they and care as deeply about what happens in classrooms and schools. The tensions derived from their relationships allow teacher leaders to grow and learn from their experiences, yet sap their time and energy and, sometimes, cause pain and undermine their patiently optimistic view of colleagues (York-Barr & Duke, 2004).

Because teacher leadership has come of age, we no longer see teacher leaders as principal interns or middle managers who direct the work of their teaching neighbors or department members. The third wave of teacher leadership (Silva, Gimbert, & Nolan, 2000) does not mean a change in one's role; it means a change in perspective, a confidence coupled with humility in one's practice, and a commitment to improved learning for one's students and all students in the school. Teacher leaders have faith in their colleagues that they can and want both to learn and to lead. Their modus operandi is linked to those fundamental beliefs.

Some teacher leaders can be seen as Pollyannas, but there is, below the surface even in the Pollys, a steely realism that helps them understand where others are on the leadership continuum even as they continually push and prompt their fellows to keep on learning—about students, themselves, best practices, and schools as organizations. We see, as they do, the challenges for teacher leaders are the same as those for all leaders.

REFERENCES

Silva, D. Y., Gimbert, B., & Nolan, J. (2000). Sliding the doors: Locking and unlocking possibilities for teacher leadership. *Teachers College Record, 102*(4), 779–804.

York-Barr, J., & Duke, K. (2004, Fall). What do we know about teacher leadership? Findings from two decades of scholarship. *Review of Educational Leadership, 74*(3), 255–316.

Introduction to
"The Courage to Lead"

*T*odd West's simple, honest storytelling reveals his vulnerability. The frankness of the piece is startling, perhaps, except to other teacher leaders who know the feelings well. As so much of the literature about teacher leadership shows, teachers who step out of the acceptable pattern of quiet acquiescence with the status quo—among both administrators and peers—take big risks. They feel stung or deeply hurt, as Todd does, when their advocacy on behalf of students is seen as rudeness or disloyalty. Todd discovers the courage of teacher leadership that Parker Palmer advocates.

> One of the major challenges in educational reform is for teachers—who see themselves as working in service to the young—to see themselves also as leaders in service to our schools and society. By embracing a larger leadership role, teachers would not dilute but deepen their commitment to children and youth. If more and more educational leaders were to rise from the ranks of teachers—transforming both our schools and the way our society supports them—the ultimate beneficiaries would be our young people, the most precious asset any society has.
>
> —*Parker Palmer*
> *Foreword,* Stories of the Courage to Teach:
> Honoring the Teacher's Heart
>
> —*SVM*

12

The Courage to Lead

Todd West

This may seem a bit odd, referring to a book that I haven't read when trying to explain some of my most significant leadership development, but I am going to anyway. The book I am referring to is *The Courage to Teach* by Parker Palmer. I have never read this book; all I know is the title. The concept "courage to teach" resonated with me, but the title planted in my mind became "the courage to lead" as I learned more about Palmer and his book by experiencing a Clearness Committee. I am not writing about that experience, however. I am going to do my best to explain a new understanding of my leadership that has only recently dawned on me and that I am still trying to clearly articulate to myself.

I will admit that at first the idea of "courage" in teaching—and in teacher leadership—seemed a bit weak. I mean, come on, when the going gets tough you get going, and you just get it done. While courage is admirable, it is something that firefighters and orphans need, not leaders in schools. But in the last school year, courage has become a recurring theme when I think about how I am a leader.

This need for courage was imperceptible at first, nothing more than just a few bad encounters with a few people that left a kind of sting afterwards. One instance involved an attempt to get a bank of computers into my classroom. Another one occurred about the same time. I advocated for myself and some other teachers that we needed more time to get our grades done before the school mailed home progress reports. Both cases involved our dean of students, who was in charge of technology and also printing and mailing report cards. In each instance, I had to challenge the decisions that this administrator made. I told her that I thought her decision was wrong and that I was not going to take no for an answer. I kept pushing because I honestly believed that in both situations I had the best interests of students as my priority.

After a few days, the administrator asked to speak to me privately. She told me that "several teachers" had come up to her and asked why I was being so rude to her this year. I was totally taken aback. Had I confused assertiveness with rudeness? Had I lost sight of polite society in my attempts to better my students' situation? I quickly spoke with other teachers and administrators, asking them to give me feedback on my recent behavior. I was especially interested in what my principal thought, since he had witnessed several of my interactions with this administrator. Everyone agreed that I had been professional and assertive, yet respectful.

It became clear to me that this administrator's way of "putting me in my place" was to call upon unknown, unnamed teachers who had witnessed my being rude to her, but that is beside the point of this story. What was most confusing to me was that I had been personally attacked, in a purely negative manner, by a supervisor because I had failed to see things her way and kept pushing the issue. I had often heard people talk of the "politics of the school," and I had always been "in the loop," so to speak. But I had never before been the victim of such politics, especially on an emotional level. It is one thing to have your ideas or methods questioned, but to be labeled as rude by a supervisor for disagreeing has the power to make one stop and think, "Do I really want to keep going down this path?"

This year was also a contract year for us, and money was tighter than usual. Negotiations were a little more tense than usual. One point of contention involved the policy and procedure for Reduction in Force (RIF). It seemed that our RIF policy was linked to our evaluation system. Teachers got "half credit" for straight seniority and "half credit" for the quality of their evaluations. In that way, a low-performing veteran teacher could be replaced by a high-performing rookie. The school board wanted to keep the RIF policy the way it was; the veteran teachers who ruled the roost in the teacher's association wanted a straight seniority system.

I was quite outspoken at association meetings that I thought that the RIF policy should remain linked to our evaluations and be based, at least in part, on merit. I was the only member of the association to voice such an opinion, although later several teachers told me that they had supported me "in spirit." Well, that didn't help much because I was quickly labeled a heretic at the association meetings. One colleague stood up and screamed at me, "You are anti-educator. Everything you say is on their side." He then picked up the contract, hurled it to the floor, and yelled, "You must not care about anything in that, and you obviously don't appreciate what it has gotten you." Again, I was completely blindsided. I felt that I was advocating what was best for the school, not just teachers. But by not toeing the party line, I was soon seen as out of line.

I began to realize, however, that all of the "bad encounters" had something in common: They all involved a situation in which I was trying to take a leadership role in the broader school community, outside the social studies learning area. In retrospect, I think I was "overstepping my bounds" by asking people who were "outside my sphere of influence" to address certain issues. In many ways, our school has a broad, decentralized structure for leadership. However, like most organizations, people become territorial: People who try to lead across the school without being in the position of a "whole school leader" (principal, assistant principal, dean of curriculum) are looked at as overambitious "players" trying to "climb the ladder."

The result has been a deep-down hurt that makes me question whether I want to put myself in the same position again. At times, after certain interactions with certain people, I leave the room feeling, "Well, if that is what they think, screw them. I won't be a leader on this project. I will just keep doing what I am doing, and retreat within the walls of my learning area or classroom. If they want me, they can come find me." I have never had those feelings before. I had always seen myself as someone who kept plugging along, perhaps even playing the political game that goes on in schools, but never being *hurt* by the political game. Why were people attacking me for trying to take a broader leadership role in the school? I thought that it would be seen as a good thing that I was trying to address problems and issues that were outside my "domain." The literature and research I read pointed out the importance of leadership coming from within the faculty and not just the administration. That was what I was providing, so why was it being met with resistance?

Although many people talk about "leading from behind," I guess I am beginning to feel that such an approach to leadership is not always possible. At times, a leader needs to be out front, either to be visible or to blaze a trail. Being out in front of the group, by definition, means being alone. And being alone means being vulnerable.

I am at a point, however, at which I question how vulnerable I want to make myself. I have a colleague who is doing great things for the school and taking a variety of leadership roles. She seems to get burned at every turn, though. I can see that it hurts her. I wonder how many more times she can stand being burned before she just gives up. How many times can I get burned before I give up?

In hindsight, I guess I have decided that I can get burned at least one more time, because I am taking on even more leadership opportunities that would be classified as "whole school leadership." A lot of this has to do with a change in administration (new principal) that is creating many subtle leadership opportunities for those who are so inclined.

As with most everything, I think there is a direct correlation between confidence and courage. As I feel more confident with my abilities and my role, that confidence, in turn, gives me more courage to expand my leadership role. But the courage is a wary courage; I am always concerned that the next action I take may stir the embers and get me burned again. When I speak my mind at faculty meetings or in the lunchroom, I always do a quick cost-benefit analysis to see if it is worth making myself vulnerable on an issue. Should I choose this battle or save my comments for another time?

And that is where the courage comes in. Leaders are willing to get burned. Leaders are willing to make themselves vulnerable, and do it again and again and again. There may be no safe haven for leaders because often the act of leading means leaving the safe havens behind. You must have courage to keep stepping out in front of the pack, knowing that you may indeed be left out there all alone in the cold. It is similar to the courage that a prizefighter must have, constantly having to pull yourself up off the canvas even though you know full well the other guy has another right hook with your name on it. But, if you stay on the canvas, you don't have any chance of getting the prize either, so you have to find the courage to keep getting up.

Introduction to
"On the Balcony"

*A*s Ron Heifitz (Leadership Without Easy Answers, *Belknap, 1994) has pointed out, when the going gets tough, leaders cannot withdraw. They have to be able both to stay in the action and be above the action. From the balcony they are more able to consider alternatives and make effective decisions that will move the group forward rather than mire it further or send it hurtling backwards. Lieberman and Miller (Part I) cite Moore* (The Role of Legitimate Peripheral Participation in School Leader Preparation, *unpublished doctoral dissertation, 2004) who describes how difficult it is to learn in an organization because what holds people together often interferes with honest communication.*

Kathy Stockford describes her first "out of body" experience, in which she learned, "If I can keep my head and concentrate on the people in my group and focus on their needs rather than my own, I can stop and think long enough to ask the right questions and to receive the right answers." She found the right words and tone to nurture her colleagues' further growth as a team and showed her ability to see the big picture, which involved maintaining good working relationships in order to advance the goals of the organization and this work group within it.

—SVM

13

On the Balcony

Kathy Stockford

W e were sitting together in our last department meeting of the year. We had many loose ends to tie up, things like summer maintenance requests, final summer order revisions, and schedules for the following year. The meeting took place during the last week of probably the toughest year in any of our careers thus far. Our department had been developing, reviewing, and revising (*endlessly* revising!) assessments to be included in our district's local assessment system in order to satisfy a statewide mandate of a standards-based education system.

When I had become department chair four years before, the nine English teachers at the high school were not considered a cohesive group of colleagues. We might even have been called a fragmented or difficult group by teachers outside of our department. We had never really been required to engage in meaningful collegial work. However, I had made it my personal priority to create a climate in which we teachers could work together, learn, grow, and share critical insights about our work. English teachers in general are creative, informed, opinionated, unique individuals. They value diversity, and I knew that bringing us together would be a tall order, to say the least. Nevertheless, I received many compliments from colleagues and administrators concerning our development as a department, especially during the fourth year of my position as chair.

At our high school, departments are required to design Adequate Yearly Progress Goals. The writing is left up to the department chairs, as is the end-of-year report on the goal. During the previous end-of-school year meeting,

I had proposed that we create a bank of reading strategy lessons. Each of us would submit four lessons for each of the courses we teach. We could measure the effectiveness of the lessons through grade 11 state assessment scores and grade 9 CTBS (Comprehensive Test of Basic Skills) scores. I typed up the goal, submitted it to department members at our first meeting of the school year, received their feedback, revised it, and finally received their approval. I made sure that all the teachers received a copy of the goal and sent a copy to my principal and superintendent.

Although the ninth-grade teachers worked very collaboratively and completed their lessons early, I could tell by November that not everyone was participating. I sent out a reminder and brought it up at the November department meeting. The general response was something like, "No, there's no problem. I am doing strategy lessons; I just don't have them written down for the bank yet."

I was afraid to push too hard because I knew they were also working diligently on grade-level common assessments. I also knew that both endeavors were important, and none of these teachers had let me down before. I wanted to demonstrate my trust by giving them time to compile the lessons.

I continued to receive lessons from department members and kept them in a file in my desk, but I have to admit that teaching, taking courses, being involved with district-level committee work, and developing the English department's assessments diverted my attention from our department goal. In March, I reviewed the bank of reading strategy lessons and realized that four of the nine teachers had still submitted nothing. I sent these four teachers a polite reminder to submit their lessons prior to spring break. At least two of these teachers spoke to me face-to-face and said their work would be completed.

However, as the break came and went, I forgot about the deadline, and apparently so had the four others. Nothing was turned in, and I had not noticed it.

The year careened out of control. The district assessment system committee was meeting once or twice per week during May and early June, and each meeting brought requests for more work, more revisions, and more time. I completely lost my focus on the Adequate Yearly Progress Goals in trying to meet these other state- and district-imposed deadlines.

Back to the last department meeting of the year . . .

I had sent a notice once again to the four teachers who had yet to complete their lessons and bring them to the meeting. I obsessed the day and night before about how to approach the subject if they just downright refused to do it. How could they? They had given input on the goal in September! I had heard their concerns and rewritten the goal! I had asked if they needed help! I had sent reminders! What was the problem?

I considered moving my top priority to the end of the agenda. When the teachers came in, however, with long faces, looking as if they had been dreading this as much as I was, I decided to tackle the toughest issue first—the failed goal.

After we ate our snacks and shared informal debriefings about the day's events, I took out my file and listed who had and who had not met the goal, and I asked what we, as a department, could or should do about it now. One teacher said that he was just too overworked and stressed to meet "the stupid goal" and that he did not care if I used that exact quote in our report. Another teacher, near tears, was clearly angry that I had made her level of nonparticipation public. She said that she had just forgotten and that I had not reminded her enough times. Another teacher said that he was unsure about the goal and that I had not made it clear to him. The fourth teacher remained silent with glaring eyes and arms folded across her chest. The other teachers, those who had completed their goals, were also silent but upset. What was going to happen to the slackers who had clearly not done their portions of the group goal?

As I sat there in this circle of teachers, I could almost feel myself pushing away, pushing back, pushing out of this circle. I looked from face to face and became aware of how alone I was. Three teachers blamed me for their inattention to a department goal; one burned holes through my self-worth with her hateful stare; and the rest did not come to my rescue. And why should they? They were the members and teachers of the department; I was the leader. It was my job to fix the problem and fix the department.

Here I was, in the most frightening place on earth for me—sitting in the hot seat with eight of the most important people in my school life expressing varying degrees of frustration with me. They stared at me waiting for a response. I think if I had found myself in this position prior to my department chair years, I might have burst into tears, fled the building, and found a quieter, more peaceful job repotting plants at the Agway down the street from my home. This time, however, I was aware of a force separating my head from my heart, separating the old, emotional me from the thinking, problem-solving me. I felt as if I was involved in this situation while I watched myself in this role from afar.

When I watched from outside, I realized that I was clearly not the only one feeling stress. As the formal leader of this group of people who had learned to work together and, by trusting each other, had grown to be a highly respected department in our high school known for its collaborative efforts and products, I needed to focus on their needs and not my own. I had to make a choice, and I had to make it quickly. I also needed to make the right choice because I sensed that this was a pivotal point in our group development.

I unfolded my arms, allowing the blood to return to my fingers and wrists, and faked a smile, which eventually became genuine. I said, "Clearly, if we did not meet our goal, and I am the leader of this department, then at least a portion of this is my responsibility and my failure. Can you please give me some ideas as to how we could all avoid this very uncomfortable place next June? Can we think about how I could facilitate or ensure the success of our goal next year?"

English teachers in a group setting are rarely quiet for long, but for the second time in this one meeting, they were silent. Stunned might be a better choice of words judged by their open mouths and big eyes. Then their arm and neck muscles relaxed. They stretched out their legs and munched on their snacks. They had clearly expected an emotional response or counterattack.

Instead, I had solicited from them their suggestions concerning my personal improvement in the area of leading a group to successfully complete a task and meet deadlines. I had at first been afraid that the ninth grade teachers would lose faith in me, but all three of them were clearly pleased. No one wanted an all-out war, although everybody had been expecting one. Their relief was palpable. This meeting that was headed for a train wreck transformed into a problem-solving, team building session.

Introduction to "Teacher Leadership: Noble Aspiration or Myth?"

*S*o often we read of the frustration of teacher leaders who poke their heads out of their classrooms and encounter realities they do not want to face: colleagues who are not as dedicated or as effective as they; fellow teachers who view their efforts as suspect; principals who are unwilling to give up authority for decisions that relate to teachers and the learning of their students. Teacher leaders have to make peace with these realities in order to forge ahead; when they do so, they often proceed with renewed vigor because they have discovered the courage of their convictions. Occasionally teacher leaders throw in the towel, though, and close their doors because they feel burned or beaten in the process of speaking out or up.

Hank Ogilby, on the other hand, wishes he could close his door because he feels he should—if he is to do a good job as a teacher. It is a version of the Huberman paradox, recounted by Lieberman and Miller in their review of research on teacher leadership (Part I). Contentment with teaching as a career comes from remaining in the classroom, not involvement in reform or school leadership initiatives. Hank argues for a separation of the roles of teaching and leading—at least in the cost-effective way teacher leadership has been practiced so far—in order to do justice to the primary job of teachers, promoting learning.

—SVM

14

Teacher Leadership

Noble Aspiration or Myth?

Hank Ogilby

I think that if you asked the folks I work with, or parents in my community, or even acquaintances in the world of educators, they'd all say, "Oh sure, Hank is the quintessential teacher leader." Perception is funny that way. I could be the biggest phony of all time in the classroom, the most ineffective teacher on the planet, but because I've presented a certain persona, I have become—even in my own eyes—the prototypical teacher leader. It sounds great. "I teach. I touch the kids every day. Yet miraculously, I lead as well. I shape the larger school beyond my classroom!" Wow, I must be quite a swell guy. But how effective am I at either of these roles? How realistic is it to expect teachers to be real educational leaders within their schools? I accept the mantle of teacher leader and recognize the power of my skills and talents in both capacities, but I wonder, I really wonder if the concept of the teacher leader isn't more of a myth or a fiscal necessity than it is good educational practice.

As I get older, and lean more into my profession, one of my favorite mantras has become "Teaching is a full-time job." And I believe this in my core of cores. There is the perception, sadly, that teaching is a part-time job, thus that teachers can take on a variety of extra responsibilities, like coaching, or advising, or leadership. Now this perception would hold a great deal of truth if all these tasks took place between late June and Labor Day, but they don't. During the other parts of the year, teachers are teaching. And this is what they should be doing. That is what parents expect us to be doing, what taxpayers pay us for, and what sincere educators *want* to be doing. Teaching is a full-time job.

The conundrum is that the longer that I've been in the profession, the more adept I've become at juggling my teaching with a variety of other roles. I'm a pro! I'm a veteran! I'm a master teacher! I'm a teacher leader! Wow. But am I a better teacher? Always? With all classes? All kids? Nope. I know I'm not. I know that I often have to make decisions between something new in the classroom and nonclassroom-related tasks. Yeah, yeah, I can hear the voices and rationalizations now: "But you're helping the whole school"; "You're spreading your expertise throughout the building and to other classes." Maybe so, maybe in some small way, but that does not necessarily negate or counterbalance the reality that I'm not doing all that I can for my classroom. As I have become more and more of a teacher leader, I am less able to do more and more for students in my classroom. It's a simple physics problem, but often it manifests itself as more of a rationalization, a moral struggle that we usually give in to because "No one else is going to accept this role," or because "If I don't do it, who will?"

We suffer from reformers who proclaim that schools need to structure themselves on the business model. If schools were more product-oriented, they would be much more efficient. Our results would be more reliable and certifiable. But think about the business model. It is the classic pyramid. A board of directors, a CEO, a few presidents and executives, about one hundred vice-presidents, a plethora of project managers, a battalion of worker bees, and then, finally, the product. Now think about the educational model. We are missing the entire middle section of the pyramid! Most schools have a board of directors (school board), a CEO (superintendent), a president (principal), a vice-president (assistant principal), and then we go right to the worker bees (teachers) and the product (students). No executive structure! No cadre of vice-presidents. No band of super-efficient project managers. We feebly attempt to insert deans as assistants to the executives, teacher leaders as vice-presidents, and department heads as project managers. We may give folks a bit of a title for this, and maybe a stipend, but rarely any extra time (especially teacher leaders). Thus, the concept of teacher leadership seriously challenges my notion that teaching is a full-time job. The business model requires a dramatic increase in school budgets. In my very small school of 40 teachers and two administrators, to make the pyramid proportional, I think 10 to 15 midlevel managers are in order, at salaries between the top executives and the worker bees, thus at about $60,000 each. We're on our way to a million-dollar add-on to next year's budget! But . . . wait . . . ooooooh, look . . . Whooosh! I just heard the ax fall! That 600 or 900 thousand just got lopped off! Too bad. But, it's okay, say the business efficiency experts: "Teachers are only part-time workers! They get the summers off! They can do all the extra work! They can become 'teacher leaders'!"

Am I cynical? Maybe so. But I really think that I've got the answer to all that ails American education—probably because I'm a teacher leader, because I've been enrolled in leadership programs and held leadership positions *while* maintaining my primary responsibility as a classroom teacher. The answer is actually simple! Smaller class sizes and student-teacher ratios, a larger professional management structure, and increased pay. That's it! Let teachers teach. Make the job very competitive, with professional pay, and give teachers a reasonable workload. And when teachers want leadership roles, say NO! No, no, no! Tell them that their job is much too important. They need to focus every molecule of energy on their students, every molecule! Tell them that students and their learning are just too important! Then tell this body of professionals (maybe some former teachers, products of universities or leadership programs) to do everything they can to create a structure and environment that best support the teachers and student learning. These folks should be the cutting-edge leaders: exploring new models, visiting schools, and working as a comprehensive decision-making body to ensure that the worker bees and the "products" achieve the best "outcome" possible. And these folks should get some serious money. These folks are the vice-presidents. They really know the business; they've been in classrooms as both teachers and learners for most of their professional lives. They are the best of the best. They are real "teacher leaders," but they need to be relieved of one *very* serious duty and obligation (teaching) to fully pursue another very serious responsibility (leadership). We should not, as a society, be so cheap and penny-wise as to blur the two responsibilities. The work is just too important. There is just too much at stake.

So is the notion of teacher leadership a myth? Counterproductive to good educational practice? Certainly not in every way. But as a structural norm? As a best-practice method of running a school? Yes. The heart of all schools is teaching and learning, which must be preserved, protected, honored, glorified, and rewarded. As demands within schoolhouses become greater (learning results, outcomes, IEPs, 504s, No Child Left Behind, Highly Qualified teachers), so have the "opportunities for leadership" (one of my principal's favorite euphemisms). We teachers have many more "opportunities for leadership," maybe more than ever in the history of education. But if we seize these opportunities, will we benefit kids? Are all these opportunities noble aspirations that will enhance teaching and learning within our schools? Or is it a myth to think that we can ask the same number of employees to do more and more and still somehow produce the same or better quality education in the classroom? Of course it is a myth. In general we live in a society that doesn't really support education, I mean fully support it.

So what are we "teacher leaders" to do? For me, right now, it's the teacher thing. Inspiring kids to be learners. That is the greatest leadership that I can offer my students, my community, and maybe even my colleagues. I hold on to my mantra that teaching is a full-time job. And a hard one. I can always be better, more creative, more inspirational if I can commit all my time to it. And I'll try, knowing full well that I'll be pulled away by a variety of "leadership opportunities," opportunities that indeed may diminish the quality of teaching and learning in my classroom. Maybe someday, some tectonic shift will invite a new structure into our worlds, and there'll be all these midlevel leadership positions waiting for all of us teacher leaders. I'll teach maybe one class a day, and then mentor a few young teachers, and be on the curriculum and instruction committees, and meet with school leadership council weekly, and serve on the accreditation committee, and maybe participate as a curriculum department member. And of course I'll get a new, bigger paycheck. That'll be great! But . . . oh wait . . . I do all of this now!?! Except for teaching only one class, and that paycheck thing. Ooops, then I guess, at least by definition, teacher leadership is no myth at all.

Introduction to
"The Golden Rule of Leadership"

*C*an leaders be collaborative or promote collaborative leadership if they themselves have not experienced it? We know how difficult the concept of collaboration is to grasp and how much definitions vary. Collaboration is more talked about than practiced, so, like many things, it becomes the goal rather than the tool for reaching goals. Sam Moring's story about developing his understanding of collaboration parallels how often congeniality is mistaken for collegiality in schools. Crowther, Kaagan, Ferguson, and Hann (Part I) say that facilitating a community of learning means teacher leaders must confront barriers. Sam had to surmount an internal obstacle to being truly collaborative. He emphasizes how much of a paradigm shift it is for teachers to be authentically involved in decision making and how much leaders have to develop not only their own but others' capacity for effective participation in collaborative processes.

—SVM

15

The Golden Rule of Leadership

Samuel Moring

Collaboration and I go way back. I have been collaborative for a long time, or so I thought. Then I began working on my master's degree in 2001, and my eyes opened. Over the past 4 years I learned that what I thought was collaboration was not. In the process I found a whole new purpose and direction for my school leadership.

As a new teacher, a student teacher, or even an employee in other fields, I have always felt comfortable going to others for help. My definition of collaboration involved simply asking someone for help or getting reassurance on an issue. Colleagues viewed my willingness to seek out help from others as a major interpersonal strength. People thought of me as a good listener, as open-minded, and as a team player just because I would show up on their doorstep and ask them for help. However, the appearance was not reality. Inside I did not value the input I was getting from others. There was no true, active listening on my part and certainly no group decision making. It was all me taking the easy way out and seeking out others for superficial reasons. Several times I sought advice from veteran staff members about problem students. Even though I sat and listened to their words, I had already decided what I was going to do; I just wanted to hear their views before I enacted my plan. I do not think I was disingenuous; I think I did not understand that collaboration is a two-way street.

As a group member, I sought out others due to my lack of experience. If I was unsure of the right move, I might seek out help from a colleague, but again, that process was not motivated by mutual growth, but by personal gain. The help I sought was more for affirmation of myself than for gaining the new perspectives and group ownership that come with real collaboration. All too often in leading groups, I engaged people in some sort of brainstorming so that we appeared collaborative. But all along I would be biding my time and waiting to push the group in a direction I had already predetermined. While working on curriculum evaluation in small groups, I had already seen the data our groups had collected and made my determinations about what the data told us. No matter what activities I designed to be "collaborative," I was funneling my agenda though the group.

Collaboration became a crutch for me. I could rely on others to back me up and support my ideas because they continually validated the process. This strategy built my professional confidence. However, it undermined my learning because I had a false understanding of what collaboration was all about. Rather than valuing the input of the group, I valued the image that came from appearing to collaborate. I did not see any value in the process time that is necessary for true collaborative work. I valued products only. I sought out the goal of a task and got there as quickly and efficiently as possible. I cared little for the human element of the process, focusing only on the work. I did not understand that there needs to be a diversity of learning styles, leadership styles, and opinions for collaboration to be effective. People around me were not being trained in collaborative group work, so they bought in to my routine and enjoyed it. It was different at least from the principal's reading them the riot act at a staff meeting. Whether they really had more to say in the course of action or not, my style gave them the feeling of having a say in their work.

For a few years, I served as my school's assistant to the principal. My first year in that role was my third year of teaching, so I was not really a fountain overflowing with collaborative experience. From time to time I was called upon to hold staff meetings or stand in for the principal at meetings, and, as usual, I was entirely task-oriented. My priority in running a staff meeting was to get through the items *I* had on *my* agenda. I did not consider the group's needs, only what I had to get done. I believed I was being collaborative, but my understanding was incomplete.

With experience came more and more opportunities to run groups and to practice collaborative skills. A major shift in learning about collaboration came when I was asked to form a task group to evaluate a district program. For the first month or so of that project, meetings adhered strictly to the written agenda (which I had planned). If I planned for us to discuss survey results and question bias, that is exactly what we did. My peers were either too nice to speak up or too lulled to sleep by the habits we had all fallen into.

Because I was involved in a graduate program in educational leadership, I learned plenty about my own leadership. As my experience and knowledge base grew, my work with the program-evaluation group improved. By the end of the evaluation our process had become the focus of our work, and my partners had taken control of the direction of the group. Their ideas became as important as mine, and their goals came to the forefront. The focus of the work became how we worked together in addition to the task itself. Rather than working on what I needed to get done, *our* needs outweighed *my* needs. I could see the resources that other members brought to the group. I was impressed by their ideas and realized how much stronger our work was when their ideas directed us.

What changed? I think a few things factored into my shift in perspective regarding collaboration. One of the biggest was an increased opportunity to run groups and practice the skills of collaboration. It takes repeated effort to run a meeting with no prescribed goal in mind or to run a meeting with the goal of accomplishing something by including everyone's ideas. It takes even more effort to realize that the goal you had for the group may not be the best goal at all. It is gut-check time when one of your group members comes up with a new idea that is a total opposite of yours and you have to take it and run with it.

For a person like me, who chews on his pen, bites his lip, and jiggles his knee, I realized that I needed to come up with some ways to keep from moving meetings along too fast. I needed to let others have their processing time and allow them to contribute to the group at their own pace. My job in the collaborative process became more facilitative, pushing others to vocalize their ideas and pushing my plans to the back burner. I learned that by facilitating and getting others used to the process, I was being more, not less, collaborative. Had I tried to push the group *my* way, to suit my needs, the group might have been task efficient, but all of my coworkers would likely have been frustrated by their lack of input. They would only be working toward my goals and I, in theory, could always do that on my own.

In addition, I had to delve into my core beliefs about collaboration. I have had a wide range of teaching and administrative experiences over the past few years. While I have always believed in the idea that teachers are essential to decision making in schools, I never really got the idea that decisions should center on collaboration. It seemed like common sense to me that teachers, being the people who have the most student contact time in schools, should have the greatest say in decisions about the school. However, tried and true school practice runs opposite to that line of thinking. We learn through experience in schools that administration makes the decisions and if you come up with a plan that strays from the status quo, you had better run it past the principal first. We have also learned from experience that teachers' ideas are not highly valued—they are somehow second rate. Collaborative leadership requires a total restructuring of this style of thinking, but it takes time for collaboration and shared approaches to decision making to become part of the culture.

So after several years of practicing collaboration and learning from people with whom I collaborate, I have become a believer. Collaboration is a working environment that embraces shared decision making, teacher empowerment, and equality in power roles. Collaborative school leaders believe, "None of us is as smart as all of us." We all bring a wealth of knowledge to school in a diverse range of specialties. Think about the opportunity that is available each and every day to school leaders in harnessing all of those different ideas and perspectives.

Collaboration has become an integral part of my leadership philosophy. In the old days I was frustrated as people endlessly looped through the same discussions over and over. I jittered my knee, chewed my pen, and paced around the room in frustration. Now I encourage that discussion so that everyone in the school is on the same page and has the same understanding of the task at hand. If people are not ready to make a decision, I am comfortable with postponing until we can discuss it further. That is a big step for someone as task-oriented as I.

Though productivity is still important to me, I understand that our school will grow and improve more through collaboration. We work together to change the school for the better, and it becomes *our* school. The students are *our* kids. We take ownership and are empowered to succeed and make our school better for every person in it. I had to understand and then enact my beliefs to realize what they meant and truly believe them.

As a school leader, my behavior has changed. Other teachers needed to see me using the skills I was advocating in order to trust that they were effective so they could feel at ease. Teachers need to feel comfortable in order to try something new. Taking the time and effort to be collaborative and building a supportive climate shows your colleagues how much you care about their input and value them as professionals. Care and compassion are reciprocal. The more you show you value others and their ideas, the more they will value yours. It is sort of a Golden Rule of leadership.

Introduction to
"A Year in the Life of
a Teacher Leader:
Enacting Core Beliefs"

*T*eacher leaders find it relatively easy to articulate and then examine their core beliefs about teaching and learning. They have grist for their explorations in reflecting on their classroom practice. Codifying their platform of leadership practice, however, often gives them pause. They do not feel they are in a position to shape the structure and culture of a school enough to be able to test their beliefs about how schools should be led. When teacher leaders come to grips with their role in the leadership of the school, they can articulate their theories in action about school leadership that are closely connected to what they believe about teaching and learning.

As Terry Young describes in this piece, his being able to reflect on and speak articulately about his classroom experience helped other adults understand and then act more effectively in the larger school context. Terry's journal weaves many of the themes found in articles in other sections of this book, but it echoes most fully Joanne Dowd's article about the "netherland" of teacher leadership (Part IV). Teacher leaders are confident in their beliefs about teaching and learning: nurture relationships, have courage, take risks. Yet the sense of being in a netherland—always below others and subject to their authority—plagues teacher leaders and speaks to the need, as Nancy Flanagan points out (Part II), for a new vision of teacher professionalism.

—SVM

16

A Year in the Life of a Teacher Leader

Enacting Core Beliefs

Terry Young

These are entries from the journal I kept during the year I moved to a middle school from an elementary school in the same system. I had been a recognized leader in my previous school and was happy when the superintendent asked me to cofacilitate a districtwide committee looking at revamping the supervision and evaluation process.

September 23, Frustration as a "Cofacilitator"

Today I met with the districtwide committee to look at the teacher evaluation system. I am in a very interesting position because I have the title of cofacilitator. Unfortunately, I share this title with an administrator in the district. I am a facilitator in name only. I have no real power. I had no input around who would be on the committee or the agendas of the meetings.

My assigned job was to lead the group in a discussion around effective teaching and list criteria for what an effective teacher looks like in hopes of moving the group toward a philosophy statement. The problem was that by the time it was my turn the direction had moved so fast that the committee was already discussing what system to adopt. The sense was, "Why reinvent the wheel?" My reaction—So people will own what they create!!!—fell on deaf ears.

I was blown away that there were five administrators present; they met in one group while the other two groups were comprised of teachers, and all seemed to think that this worked well. The strength of the personalities in the room ran over me like a wave. I still feel bruised.

October 17, Becoming a Facilitator

It is all about causing ripples in the water—not large splashes. I don't teach so that my students have mastery of content at the end of the year. I teach to create lifelong learners. The same can be said for me as a leader. I want my perspectives as a leader to promote the learning of teachers and, in turn, student learning.

I tend to shut down during meetings. I am energized by people who agree with me but left stagnant by people who disagree with me. I think it is a defense mechanism because I am fearful that some will consider me too passionate. I get lost in all the jabber. I have trouble when people are more assertive than I am. I need to continue to be involved in the conversation without zoning out during discussions I view as useless.

I approached the planning of the next meeting believing that I needed to take a risk and be honest. We had spent the previous meeting going through the motions of setting up our districtwide system. When I met with the cofacilitator today, I was brutally honest. I told him that I was concerned because I felt that the last meeting did not go well. I was disconcerted that administrators sat together and teachers sat together. I told him that if we were going to set up the system as we did at the last meeting, we didn't need a committee. He and I could have sat down over a beer and cranked it out.

I was shocked that the administrator agreed! He agreed that how it went down the wrong path, and he didn't know what to do. He couldn't turn it around. I emphasized that I understood and felt helpless as well. Nevertheless, we developed a plan together.

October 21, Compromising

But when it came to planning the upcoming meeting, I realized how hard it is to really collaborate. The principal wanted to have a discussion around targets and one about whether to use standards or a continuum in teacher self-assessment. I told him that I didn't think I could lead the discussion around a standards-continuum debate because I didn't believe that was the next step. I decided to present the target portion instead. Part of me felt like quitting, but I realized it had to be a joint effort, and I was getting some of what I wanted.

October 25, Taking Stock

Reflection on the whole process left me with mixed emotions:

The other cofacilitator was correct in that we didn't need to identify the tension within the group. It was enough to mix the groups up. I was right when I asserted that evaluation can't be an "I Gotcha" and still promote teacher learning. I made the right decision not quitting the committee—If I'm not there, nobody will say the things that should be said.

For the next meeting: I think I need to focus with the same intensity as this past meeting because it truly helped me prepare and crystallize my thinking. However, I need to work on not letting myself get upset to the point of feeling sick.

November 23, The Reign of the Status Quo

I have a few observations about why change is so slow in public schools or in any organization for that matter. The reason change doesn't happen is it is easier not to change. There are little ripples, and then you hit a wall and feel like giving up. It feels as if we are pushing against a brick wall. I don't feel like accepting the common adage "Change takes time" when it puts children at risk.

I don't know how to balance how I really feel with the need to build positive working relationships with the people I work with. I know that I need positive relationships or nobody will listen to me, but I run out of patience. An example: Team leaders had to list all "at-risk" students. One teacher described an eighth-grade student as "clueless" when she was asked to describe a student's learning style. I am starting to believe that we teachers are our own worst enemies.

December 1, The Glass Ceiling

I have started compiling ideas for a book called *Underground School Reform: Visions From Below the Glass Ceiling*. We had a staff development day to promote a culture of trust. Neither of my administrators or the secretaries participated in these trust-building activities. The irony was they were the people nobody trusted. They watched while the rest of us, the teachers, participated.

I can remember too many staff development training sessions when an administrator introduced the facilitator or speaker and then left the room. Afterwards, the "leader" would then ask select staff members how it went. When you start to analyze the message this sends, you can go on forever seeing the damage this behavior can have on a school culture. Breaking the glass ceiling for one teacher is not enough. It needs to be broken for all teachers and administrators so that they can both cross over from leader to learner freely. Teachers need to be able to cross over into the role of a title-less leader; likewise, leaders need to be able to cross over into the world of learners. The two complement each other to promote a community of learners.

February 3, Struggling With Core Beliefs

I feel strongly about my beliefs around teaching and learning, and as long as they stay in my head, they are safe and free of judgment. I wonder if it is another form of my fear around risk-taking. Although I know that questioning will make beliefs stronger, it is still risky to share.

One of my beliefs is that learning needs to be free of rewards that supposedly motivate learning. I believe that when students are rewarded, learning becomes a game of compliance in an attempt to give the teacher what he or she wants so as to get an A. Today, one of my core beliefs was tested because our faculty discussed whether or not to continue having an awards ceremony. The principal raised the question because of complaints from teachers, students, and parents about the two-hour assembly that we have every year in front of the entire school. I was in a difficult position because I was afraid that if I said anything against the ceremony people would resent my comments because I am a new member of the faculty. But, I was afraid if I didn't share, the others would not consider the perspective that such awards can damage the learning of many children.

In essence, I needed to balance my core belief with my status on the faculty. I decided to watch and listen. I established a compromise in my mind. The compromise for me was that the awards ceremony be held at night and students who were getting awards would be invited to attend. That way the entire student population wouldn't have to sit by while a small percentage of students were honored.

April 10, Beliefs About Leadership

Writing about my beliefs is like being in quicksand made of words. The more I write, the deeper I sink. I agonized over each word and the meaning each conveyed. The act of putting my ideas into writing forced me to look at them with a different lens than if I were just spouting off to some of my colleagues in a local pub.

I discovered a couple of things about my beliefs as I drafted a statement for a job application. When I started, I didn't see how teaching, learning, and leadership were connected. I knew they were, but I didn't see how strong the connection was until now. I now believe that success in leadership and teaching are dependent upon one's understanding of learning. I don't believe a person can be a successful educational leader if he or she does not have a deep understanding of how people learn. This discovery caused me to pare my core beliefs about leadership down to one: School leaders need to be effective teachers.

I think I stay true to many of my beliefs as a classroom teacher. I have created a classroom free of rewards, punishments, and labels. Although there are outside forces always pushing against my beliefs, I am able to hold myself to the practices I value. I care about students, set personal goals, and assess the way I believe students should be assessed. As a leader of students and of teachers, I am able to incorporate strategies that make me an effective teacher into how I lead. I promote learning with adults the same way I do it with students every day.

Introduction to
"Works Well With Others:
The Nurturing of a
Teacher Leader"

*I*t is easy to forget how formative are the first years of teaching with regard to establishing connections and relationships with colleagues. That is why mentoring colleagues is a vital role of teacher leaders. Barbara Bolton urges young teachers to take seriously what happens in their classrooms, of course, but also to realize how important it is to learn from and with other adults. Linda Lambert and her colleagues (Part II) as well as Eleanor Drago-Severson (Part IV) demonstrate the importance of teacher learning as the foundation of good teaching. The isolation of the job can often lead people to shy away from observation and critique by other teachers. Teachers view their teaching as personal, so they feel vulnerable when any aspect of their practice is on display. Because teachers are so personally connected to their work, it is vital that beginning teachers find colleagues who share their views and with whom they can be safe and trustworthy critical friends.

—SVM

17

Works Well With Others: The Nurturing of a Teacher Leader

Excerpts From Your First, First Grade: Advice to NYC Teaching Fellows and Others Who Are About to Begin Teaching

Barbara McGillicuddy Bolton

Before the first day for the children, you will have at least one day of staff meetings. These may take place in your own school, or in another. They may involve only staff from your school or they may be districtwide, with teachers grouped according to grade or discipline. One presenter may be dressed like a TV anchorperson. Another may have on an orange tank top that leaves her midriff exposed, pea green capris, flip-flops, and nose and tongue rings. Just as you will need to suspend judgment on what others wear, so too on how they speak. Perhaps you pride yourself on a heartland accent and keen grasp of language and see those attributes as marks of the educated person. Perhaps you are not musical;

perhaps you have lousy handwriting; perhaps you're not a big reader, or the scientific method eludes you, or math fusses you up. Something. Something to remind you that the job of teaching has too many parts to it for any one person to be wonderful at all of them. So overlook the deficiencies you see around you. That gentleman at the next table may have good cause for putting his head in his hands and shutting his eyes during the presentation. Those two middle-aged women may have serious reason to talk together throughout the meeting.

It doesn't take long into the school year to realize that for all the other adults in the system, you are spending acres of time alone with the children in your class. Yes, your school has cluster teachers, reading specialists, a social worker, a guidance counselor, staff developers, secretaries, and a principal, but when Roger has a very bad day and won't get out from under the author's chair where he is setting up a howl, none of these folks may be available to help you. This is your job. This is what you are paid for. Later you can fill out a form referring Roger for counseling. Maybe you have already done this, but these things take time, and while Roger's papers crawl through the process, you are left with Roger. Even if the process is finished and Roger gets taken out for counseling one hour a week, all those other hours you are left with Roger.

This is when it would be helpful to have another adult in the room. That person could oversee the rest of the class while you deal with Roger, or better yet, that person could squat next to him and redirect his attention to the work at hand, freeing you to carry on with the rest of the class. Or even better, that person might have sensed his mood and forestalled an eruption by sitting beside him with an arm soothingly around his shoulders. Usually, however, no such other person is in the room. It's you and Roger and the rest of the class.

The other adults most available to you may be Demeter, the veteran teacher on your grade level, or Diana, your fellow novice. You and Diana, in fact, may have an agreement to swap certain students whenever life in the classroom becomes too much for any of them. On this day, for instance, you may ignore Roger—if you can—until he stops yelling and crawls out from the under his lair. Then you may give him a choice of working nicely in your room or taking his paper and pencil to Diana's ("Ms. Woodsprite" to Roger). He may welcome the chance to move temporarily to neutral territory, or he may prefer to stay with his class. At any rate, you hope that the power to make a choice will redirect his energy into a socially acceptable pursuit. And when Damian or Britney appear at your door with book or paper and pencil in hand, you wave them to a seat, fulfilling your part of the bargain with Diana.

Another part of the bargain you have with Diana and the other teachers is affirming one another publicly. When improvising a scene, actors employ a skill called "Yes, and . . . ." One actor starts with a provocative question such as, "Are you planning to wear those shoes to the wedding?" The other actor picks up on the information supplied and furthers the narrative: "Yes, and I want you to forget about that silly fight and come with me" would be a sporting answer. "No" would be a spoiler. Remember to look for supportive acting when you see teachers in your building playing a variation on this game in front of the children. When you and Diana walk through the gym and see Demeter's class practicing for a performance and Demeter says, "Oh, Ms. Woodsprite, don't we look ready for tomorrow?" Diana is expected to say, "Wow! I can hardly wait to see you in costume! This is terrific!" Then when you see Diana's class lined up nicely for lunch and you happen to know she's had trouble in the line-up department recently, you won't even have to wait for her opening sally to say, "Wow! This is a first grade? I thought you guys were second graders. You look so grown up!"

Aim to keep your remarks positive. If on another occasion Diana is so exasperated that she actually asks for negative feedback ("Isn't this line awful?") artfully sidestep by saying, "Well, the boy in the blue shirt certainly looks grown up, and the girl beside him is ready." This will provide time for Diana to gather her wits and for the children to emulate the boy in the blue shirt and the girl beside him. There may occur out-of-control situations that call for a veteran teacher or an administrator to quash, but unless it's your own class you will not be called on to play the heavy. So stay positive and develop the theme.

This kind of play-acting may strike you as manipulative and phony, and, of course, it is. The proper test, however, is whether it works. Most of the time it's you against the kids. Lining up with the rest of the faculty and staff gives you a fighting chance. Another way in which faculty support each other is in exchanging information. The one other adult in the school who knows Kaily as well as or better than you is her kindergarten teacher. Although you don't want to run the topic into the ground, you might on occasion give this teacher an update and seek her opinion. She may remember that Kaily was more apt to be contrary on a Monday if she'd spent the weekend with her father. She may advise you that building with blocks has a soothing effect on Kaily. Although you deplore gossip—and you hear plenty of it in the teachers' room—this kind of information is so helpful that it deserves a better name. Maybe you can draw a distinction between, on the one hand, idle or malicious gossip and, on the other hand, useful gossip.

On the subject of gossip, in some situations you are going to have to think carefully about these distinctions. A parent–teacher conference with Soosie's mother about Soosie can morph into her criticism of Soosie's brother's third-grade teacher, Mr. Mercury. You are on thin ice here. Listen—sympathize, even—but don't play the "Yes, and . . ." game. Suggest that Ms. Van Pelt talk directly to the teacher. Maybe using you as a sounding board will help Ms. VP clarify her complaints so that she can be specific when she speaks to Mr. Mercury. A good working relationship with Joe Mercury, moreover, may enhance your school day.

Extra adults are welcome, and there are several ways to find them. You may have a few parents who are willing to volunteer for special projects or during a reading or writing session. Your principal, Jim Janus, may offer you a parent volunteer whose child is not in your class. There is a certain advantage to having someone who is no one's mom and can therefore be spread around equally among the children. Although you don't want to act bossy, most adults would welcome a specific assignment.

Jim Janus may assign a special-interest teacher to your class, or he may put out a memo offering the same. Say yes. Whether it be chess, dance, or civics, it will mean a second adult. That person may be an educator in the arts or a volunteer from corporate America. She may have wonderfully conceived lesson plans or not. The point is that you will have help with your class. You will see them led by a different adult. If the other adult is weak, you can help with planning and play a strong supporting role. If she is strong, you will learn from her and get insights into managing your class. In all likelihood, you will have much to offer each other, not the least being adult companionship in the classroom.

You might experience this same kind of give-and-take with a student teacher. Unless your school is overrun with them, however, it is unlikely that you will be assigned one. They are reserved for veteran teachers like Demeter, who have more to offer them. You may find yourself a teeny bit jealous of Demeter's student teacher because she gets to ease her way into the school day and to be rescued by Demeter. You may find yourself a teeny bit jealous whenever you see two adults working together.

One way of mixing professionally with other members of the faculty is to serve on a committee. In fact, you may be assigned to one. Assigned or voluntary, these committees vary greatly. You remember student council in high school. In all likelihood the campaigns were the highlight, and the council, due to collusion of administration and faculty, was limited to a very narrow exercise of power—choosing the snacks for sale during lunch, for instance. Many committees you might find yourself on will suffer from this kind of diminished effect. Serve on one committee at a time, one semester at a time, until you find one that accomplishes a mission or makes you think or whose members you enjoy. If, as a semester nears its end, you find that your committee is still dithering over the bylaws or the mission statement, surrender your membership and try for one that has momentum.

Every time you enter the faculty room, of course, you will find a committee meeting of sorts. The agenda will consist of chit-chat, gripes, and war stories. If your faculty is like that of most elementary schools across the country it will be top heavy with middle-aged women, and that constituency's topics, such as menopause and the dating habits of their young adult children, may rule. You may find it possible, nevertheless, to discuss serious concerns of the classroom. You may find another teacher or two who want to trade ideas for lessons, and you may decide to visit each other's classes to see how a particular subject is handled. You don't have to limit yourself to first grade. It may interest you particularly to look at kindergarten or second-grade classes to see where your students have come from and where they are going. This kind of collaboration is free. And the other teacher may be as starved for professional adult companionship as you are.

Introduction to *"The Code of Silence"*

*B*etsy Webb's story, although not ostensibly about teacher leadership, strikes a chord with all who read it. Most teachers have a similar story to tell about how they encountered the culture of schools and discovered the "undiscussables" of a particular environment early in their careers. Our hearts go out to the struggling veteran and the new teacher who falls in line with "how we do things here" even as she cringes at what the isolation and silence mean to students and adults alike. No wonder Morgaen Donaldson (Part IV) found such ambivalence about leadership in her study of newly tenured teachers. She effectively captures the tension new teachers feel: Do they really want to leave their classrooms at all? It's much safer inside with the students. On the other hand, sometimes an incident like this one or one that similarly affects students can lead teachers to speak out, to act, to find a role for themselves as leaders. That is, if they don't recoil in horror and leave the profession entirely.

—SVM

18

The Code of Silence

Betsy Webb

As a young teacher, I quickly learned the importance of getting along with other teachers and staff members. There appeared to be an unspoken rule of protecting the profession and not mentioning the weaknesses of those teachers who really struggled in the classroom. This unspoken rule was the professional code of courtesy. At least that's all I can think to call it.

In one of my first teaching assignments, I taught next door to a 20-plus-year veteran male music teacher. He was teaching a music appreciation class, and I was teaching an advanced programming class. The teacher of music was put into a computer lab because there were no other rooms available for his class. The other computer department teachers often complained about this music teacher's lack of classroom discipline and how his incompetence was going to end up destroying "our" computer lab. I often wondered why the administration did not address the issue.

Each day as I taught my class, I would hear what appeared to be loud, out-of-control behavior from the room next door. Even the students in my class would comment on the noises and they would ask, "What is going on in there?" Some student in our class would make a sarcastic comment like, "What do you expect? It's Mr. B." I would carry on and work to get my class back on task. It was hard to keep my students respectful of the teacher behind the door because of their peers' descriptions of their experiences and the noise next door that seemed to confirm their beliefs.

I never really spoke to the teacher except to smile and say hello in the hallway on the way into my classroom. However, I noticed from this person's body language in the hallways that he was not happy. Whenever he made a comment at staff meetings, others seem to roll their eyes in a way that said, "Can you believe this guy?" From my assessment, this man was struggling in all aspects of his work at the school. Yet, no one appeared to talk about the matter or to do anything.

One day as I was teaching my class I heard a loud crash, like furniture overturning, from the next room. Then we heard screams, screeching, silence, and then sobbing. I didn't care anymore about the silent rule of professional courtesy. I went right through the adjoining classroom door and entered his classroom. It was an unbelievable situation. I found the teacher on the floor sobbing. The computer tables were turned over; the majority of the computers were strewn about on the floor. Some of the students threw paper and pencils at the teacher as he sat in the middle of the floor. Although some students were not actively participating, it still appeared to be a mob scene. No one stopped the behavior of the student bullies in the room.

I told the students to stop immediately and to take their seats. I then pushed the intercom button and called the Main Office. I informed the secretary that there was an emergency situation in this room and I would be keeping all students present until the administration came to the room. I helped the teacher up and brought him back to his desk. I told the students to sit silently and think about their actions until the administration arrived.

The teacher had an emotional breakdown precipitated by the events of that day and was hospitalized for a period of time. He never came back to teaching because he decided to take an early retirement. Life went on in the school. A substitute was hired, and then another teacher took over for the rest of the year. For a while I stopped thinking about the man.

One afternoon many months later, as I worked in my classroom after school, the male music teacher entered my room. He gave me a beautiful pin to thank me, he said, "for caring enough to act." He told me that I was the only person who reached out to help. I do not know if this is true. It certainly could be only his perception of the situation. I often think of him and the terrible silence that surrounded him in that time of need, and I wonder what might have happened if I had reached out earlier. I still have the pin that he gave me and use it as a reminder of the balance that must be found between the "professional" code and the tipping point at which the code no longer matters for the good of all involved, students and teachers alike.

Introduction to
"Confessions of a Teacher Leader"

*M*uch of the writing in this section could be called "confessions": People acknowledge flaws that keep them from being as effective as they want to be in the role of leader. The intrapersonal dimension of leadership development involves leaders reflecting on their behavior, examining their strengths and weaknesses, and working toward enhancing the former and mitigating the latter. All the while, though, they must continue to put themselves in a leadership arena, so their inner work is constantly affected by their outer work with colleagues. Just as one improves her teaching through reflection, leadership learning comes from reflecting in, on, and from practice.

Liz Murray's piece describes the self-understanding that leaders develop. She describes her teacher leadership learning cycle:

> As a teacher leader, understanding more about how adults make meaning and what different adults need has helped me to avoid disasters, or at least to be more strategic in my interactions with adults. In my classroom, I accepted very quickly the reality that classroom teachers are always learning and that each new understanding unleashes a hundred new questions. Only recently, have I begun to approach my work as a teacher leader learning about adults in the same way. (Murray, personal communication, November 2005)

In Jed Lippard's charter school (Part V), she finds the right context for leading and learning, even as she wonders about the sustainability of her intense brand of leadership.

—SVM

193

Confessions of a Teacher Leader

Liz Murray

W hen I began teaching 7 years ago, I was a living breathing cliché. My plan was to make a difference. I unhappily worked as a paralegal at a law firm and sought a position that I hoped would bring me closer to finding my life's work. I applied for teaching jobs and eventually landed one at a small Catholic school in Boston. I am in debt to that principal, who took a chance on me, a young uncertified and untrained teacher, who knew nothing of the lingo and vocabulary of curriculum and instruction.

My first taste of teacher leadership came in that little Catholic school, in which teachers were typically isolated and had few formal opportunities to collaborate. Fortunately, a handful of veteran teachers had taken me under their wings and often invited me into their conversations after school. One afternoon, our conversation turned to the school's struggles with discipline, which we believed were rooted in the absence of a school-wide vision of appropriate behavior. Our group wondered what might happen if we offered to write and present a Code of Conduct for our school. We became excited at what might change for teachers and students and decided to try. The chance that our work might lead to improvement was a more powerful force than the fear of rejection or disapproval, and we pressed on.

After earning my master's degree in a Teacher Education program, I joined the teaching staff of an urban charter school in the midst of a dramatic transition. The school had been run by a private management company whose trademark features were teacher-centered instruction, weekly testing in all subjects, and a "teacher-proof" prescribed curriculum. When I was hired at the start of the transition 4 years ago, I was eager to be part of the work of changing the direction and culture of the school. The principal who hired me was crystal clear about what life in a charter-school-in-change might be like, and I was more than game for the workload, the uncertainty, and the frantic pace. Fresh from a year in graduate school and filled with idealism and hope, I was thrilled to be a contributor to the process of change.

When the faculty gathered together in August for a week of professional work, I was ready and armed for battle. *Change* was in the air, and I was a willing soldier. I remember the first morning of orientation, when the faculty, new hires and returning teachers, gathered for introductions and opening presentations. A new administrator stood and presented the concept of backwards planning and introduced the work of Grant Wiggins to the faculty. In my head, I thought, "Yes, yes, of course. How could it be any other way? Brilliant. Now, we'll all be on the same page." The work of our first Humanities department meeting that afternoon taught me that change does not happen as quickly or as easily as I had imagined. I sat at the table with my new colleagues expecting to discuss *how* we would work to "backwards plan" the English and Social Studies curricula from twelfth grade down to my sixth-grade course. I was a believer and was ready for the work to begin.

The next couple of hours became an exercise in disillusionment and disappointment. Our conversation was not about backwards planning at all. The discussion was unfocused, and teachers started talking about books that they wanted to teach. I boldly and suddenly ventured, "What do we think students should *know*?" I thought Grant Wiggins would be rather proud of me, but I was met with empty stares. A returning English teacher looked at me dismissively, turned to the group, and passed out his course syllabus. He said, "Well, here's what I'm teaching this year." I was shocked. Hadn't he heard the presentation about Grant Wiggins's work? Thankfully, I was not alone at the table. I had a strong ally, a friend from my graduate school program—a gifted teacher, a fearless teacher leader in her own right—who at the time was ready to blaze the same path that I had my sights on. Without her, I would have thought that I was losing my mind, at that meeting and throughout our first years at the school. At that first meeting, I refused to give up, and shifted into what I thought was a clever maneuver to get the group refocused. Although my previous questions had been met with blank stares, I plowed forward with, "Okay then, what do we think students should be able to *do*?" Although I was pretty impressed with myself, my brilliant approach was met with more silence, and the stares that were once blank became filled with clear signs of impatience. Body language clearly indicated that I was starting to annoy some of my new colleagues. "Irrelevant." I thought. I was not there to make friends; my mission was bigger than anyone at the table and certainly bigger than myself. Change might be uncomfortable, and I was ready for that possibility. After all, I had read all about it in grad school. So that afternoon, I kept going. And going. And going. My friend and I even broke out chart papers and colored markers, thinking that if we could guide the group with visuals, it would all make sense, and the backwards planning could begin. We were teaching the teachers, the ultimate form of teacher leadership in our minds. And we would not give up.

When I replay that scene in my mind 4 years later, I watch us running around the table, taping up chart paper, talking and telling, talking and telling, explaining how things needed to work, and repeating the same things over and over again. I now refer to that mode as the *Bulldozer Effect*. I operated in that mode for much of my first two years at that charter school and walked away from many conversations as I did after that first meeting, red in the face, having stated my ideas as articulately and firmly as possible, but without having made even a dent. During those first years, I bulldozed my way through meetings and informal conversations, critiqued and analyzed my heart out, and in doing so, burned some important bridges. When I hammered my colleagues with critiques and new ideas, I failed to acknowledge the hard work of the teachers who had worked at the school before me and unwittingly dismissed the efforts that came before the new direction of the school. My friends and I truly believed that we could move the school forward simply by saying smart things and by repeating clever ideas. If we kept saying them or said them *louder*, they would happen, right? We believed that smart people should just be able to sit around a table together, say smart things, and make change happen. We were wrong.

I still notice myself operating in the Bulldozer Effect mode more often than I should, and sometimes I even choose it in order to make things happen. But I've also learned some tough lessons about listening to colleagues and building relationships since that first department meeting. Years later, I began to understand that burning bridges with new colleagues actually slowed the process of change down. When I stepped away from my bulldozing episodes and looked at what was happening, I realized that colleagues got quiet and my speeches were frequently met with silence. I've learned that I have the power to silence a discussion with my insights and remarks, but that my bulldozing rarely leads to change. Do I still bulldoze? Yes, often. It comes from my passion and determination. It's rooted in my impatience and anger toward an educational system that fails the kids whom I love and the desire to fight against that with everything I have. It's a mode that feels familiar and comfortable to me, but I've learned that it's one of the least effective tools for making change happen.

Over the years, I've become better at building relationships and learning the importance of listening. This has not come so naturally to me, so

I have learned to watch more experienced leaders as they listen to colleagues and work to build relationships. Years ago, this angered me. I would get frustrated as I watched colleagues become empowered to complain and to criticize changes in which I was intellectually and emotionally invested. I've come to understand why these skillful leaders invested time and energy in listening. I watched as colleagues with whom I clashed softened when they felt that they were being listened to and heard by leaders in my school. Without that sense of validation, they could not hear. They could not engage in the teamwork required to make real change happen until they were valued as part of the team. Watching my mentors in action has helped me to learn the difference between having your say and actually being heard. I've learned much about the power of listening as a critical ingredient in getting my ideas to be heard, and processed, and sometimes even implemented. I've learned to dial down the bulldozer in myself, and to invest energy in building relationships instead of jumping on opportunities to blast people with my opinions. I still bulldoze. I bulldoze my allies, I bulldoze new colleagues, I bulldoze my ever-patient principal, but I have learned to hold back, to wait for the best moment. I've also learned the power of listening.

When I started to understand that being *heard* is not the same as simply *saying* it, I began to watch people and wonder what they might need in order to hear what I'm saying. The understanding of this distinction has changed my work as a teacher leader. I have built a wonderful relationship with one of my toughest critics, one of the teachers at that first department meeting 4 years ago. He has actually become a close ally, but that relationship has grown out of a great deal of listening. I noticed that when I give him my ideas in writing, whether it's a rubric, an assignment, an idea regarding writing expectations, and I step away and give him time to process, he's much more open to having a genuine exchange. I can also see how much he has to offer me. Until I learned to stop blasting him with my ideas and tried to figure out what needs to be in place for him to hear me, our exchanges were artificial and we both walked away doing exactly what we had been doing all along anyway. No change. No real learning from one another. We still disagree frequently, but our conversations now are real exchanges in which we listen, hear, and trust that when we walk away we'll remain open to thinking about the other's ideas.

After 7 years in the profession, my love for teaching has not waned, nor has my commitment to my role as a teacher leader working to make change within my school. However, my sense of duty and obligation to honor my students and to build a school that is worthy of them does create real tension for my work as a teacher leader. I struggle with defining boundaries in this work. There are no limits to the number of projects or initiatives that might improve a school, and I struggle with saying no. Identifying a need or a problem is easy; developing a solution is much harder but profoundly exciting. For now, I am hooked on this cycle in my life as a teacher leader. But this makes for an exhausting existence. As a classroom teacher, I learned quickly that the work of a teacher knows no boundaries and that a teacher's to-do list only moves in one direction. Learning to create balance has always been a difficult lesson for me, and it is one that I have not yet mastered. Working as a teacher leader to make change outside of my classroom has compounded this problem. Looking outside of my classroom into the hallways, offices, and classrooms of my school takes my to-do list into the realm of the nearly impossible. Saying no, declining invitations for more work, opting out of projects and initiatives are things I've trained myself to do out of necessity. While my emotional investment in the work keeps me looking outward, creating solutions, and pushing forward, being a teacher leader becomes a full-time job-*plus*, and defining how large I am willing to let the *plus* grow is a challenge. I wonder for how long my 13-hour-a-day-approach to teacher leadership will be sustainable. It's a question that I am unable to answer yet, but it's a question that's on my mind more often as each year passes.

Several years ago, I scoffed at those who raised the question of sustainability. During my first year at my current school, a veteran teacher repeatedly asked if I could sustain working as much as I did. I took this very personally. Long hours and multiple projects and committees beyond a full-time teaching load have been trademarks of my work as a teacher leader. I was angry at him for suggesting that we should work less or that there might be some other less passionate, less dedicated, less consuming way to approach the work. I viewed him as complacent and unwilling to participate in the effort to transform and reform our school. I judged him and grew angrier each time I heard him pose the question.

A few years later, though, I'm the one asking the question. I listen to friends who started teaching with me echo similar thoughts. A mere 7 years into the profession, we sound tired—still committed, but definitely tired. I look around and watch friends get married and have children, and I wonder how long I can sustain this work-around-the-clock-to make-the-world-better approach of mine. When all of my hours fill up with "teacher leader-like" commitments and responsibilities, when colleagues seek my ear and my advice at 8 o'clock on a Tuesday night and my papers have yet to be graded, I hear a truthful and honest voice inside my head wondering if it really *is* sustainable.

What keeps me going? It always comes back to the kids and the world inside my classroom. Being with them, laughing with them, and learning with them inside the laboratory that is my classroom keep me going. This year, I have a new formal leadership position inducting our new hires, of which there are many, and mentoring novice teachers, of which there are also many. The work is stimulating, invigorating, and perpetually interesting. But it simply cannot compete with teaching and time with my students. The kids still surprise me and challenge me in a way that captures my heart and my mind completely. Even as I listen to myself describing my feelings about being in my classroom, I can hear that I am just as goofy and emotional about my students and my teaching as I was 7 years ago. They keep me going and pushing forward. That emotional connection to my kids keeps me looking outward and recharges my batteries daily. The little voice in my head that wonders about the sustainability of my work is silent when I am with the students watching them create, explore, succeed, and stumble.

In my new role as a mentor, I spend much of my time observing in the classrooms of novice teachers. I am able to watch my former sixth graders grow and learn through middle school into high school. Watching them inspires me to push onward and reminds me of how much work is left to be done. In my mentoring work, I see new ways to create change and to work toward improving our school for our students and for the teachers who serve them.

Introduction to
"Reaching Out to Parents"

I make a lot of friends among librarians by admitting to them that I went back to the classroom after a few years as a school librarian because I found the job too hard. I disliked the lack of control—over people and events—I had in the library. As a high school librarian, I didn't have to deal with parent volunteers, but I am familiar with teachers' discomfort with parents.

Deborah Vose captures the essence of informal teacher leadership described by Donaldson (Part II) as influencing the practice of others by modeling, demonstrating effective strategies, and helping others find their own way into improving teaching and learning in their classrooms. In her development as a person and a teacher, Deborah has come to see the importance of collaboration—with colleagues as well as parents—as opposed to the isolation and incestuous professionalism often found in schools. Deborah points out the community-wide benefits of taking a stand and encouraging other professionals to embrace her point of view about the importance of connecting with parents.

—SVM

20

Reaching Out to Parents

Deborah Vose

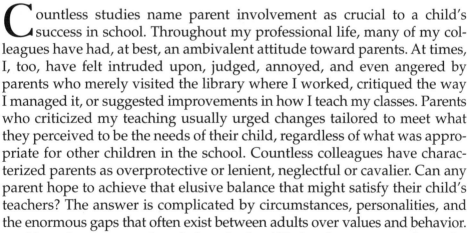

Countless studies name parent involvement as crucial to a child's success in school. Throughout my professional life, many of my colleagues have had, at best, an ambivalent attitude toward parents. At times, I, too, have felt intruded upon, judged, annoyed, and even angered by parents who merely visited the library where I worked, critiqued the way I managed it, or suggested improvements in how I teach my classes. Parents who criticized my teaching usually urged changes tailored to meet what they perceived to be the needs of their child, regardless of what was appropriate for other children in the school. Countless colleagues have characterized parents as overprotective or lenient, neglectful or cavalier. Can any parent hope to achieve that elusive balance that might satisfy their child's teachers? The answer is complicated by circumstances, personalities, and the enormous gaps that often exist between adults over values and behavior.

I have become convinced, though, that if I give the parent-teacher relationship the same scrutiny that I devote to the student-teacher relationship, everyone benefits. It has taken years, and both successes and failures in responding to parents' concerns, complaints, and compliments for me to reach a level of assurance where I truly welcome parent participation in my library/media program. Likewise, it has taken years of experience, my own parenthood, confidence in my beliefs, and trust in my competence to make me feel as if I can model for my colleagues effective approaches with parents. I have learned how to capitalize on parents' best intentions without letting them subvert my well-laid plans for student learning.

As a library/media specialist in a public elementary school, I see 400 students weekly, often for 6 years running, from the time they are kindergartners until they are fifth graders. The nature of my job means that my relationships with students and parents are almost always less intense than a classroom teacher's. I feel fortunate that I have a chance to rejoice in the growth and achievement of all students from ages 5 to 11. I crave authentic connections with every one of my students. If I notice behavioral changes, I have a network of people I respect from whom I can seek help. Sharing anecdotes with parents is one of my favorite ways to forge a connection with them. I want them to realize that I know their child, I take their reading interests seriously, and I cherish their individuality.

Many parents do not realize I prepare and teach classes in addition to my other duties. Even among my fellow professionals, I often feel that my job is misunderstood and undervalued. Some administrators express shock that a librarian wants to collaborate with colleagues. Occasionally a teacher asks, "What do you do during all your breaks?" It can be argued that we librarians have nothing to lose and much to gain by having parent volunteers become acquainted with what we do. We can't be valued any less, so we may gain some support. Many library chores are time-consuming routines that can be done by volunteers with little training and supervision.

On the other hand, having another adult observe you as you work with children in a classroom setting can be stressful. After more than 20 years, I am now rarely uncomfortable when others observe me carrying out my professional duties. I am surer of myself and feel I can effectively explain my strategies and decisions. In my first few years as a school librarian, I must have done some things competently, but I vividly remember frequent feelings of insecurity.

In early September a few years ago, my district eliminated all the media paraprofessional positions, so I knew I would have to depend on parent volunteers to help replace my assistant's 25 hours work per week. Conducting six to eight meaningful classes with time for book borrowing in 30 minutes on each of the three days in my schedule had been a challenge even with a paraprofessional helping me. Several of my fellow librarians spoke of enlisting volunteers in dire tones. They would rather soldier on alone than open the floodgates and have parents come in and "take over." "They don't want to shelve books, they want to read to the children, as if we just pick up a book at random and read it without any planning!" they warned.

I, too, was wary. More than a few volunteers had critiqued my "performance" in the past. One cautioned me that I was rewarding negative behavior by paying attention to disruptive students. "Just ignore those students," she commanded. Another volunteer told me that initially she thought my system of organizing books was ridiculous, but she came to appreciate it. Even when told that Melville Dewey had developed his decimal system in the 1800's, she persisted in assigning credit and blame for its idiosyncrasies to me!

I wondered if I was doing the right thing as I scrambled to solicit, train, and schedule parent volunteers. A discussion with my principal, who supported the idea of using volunteers, convinced me that I had to assert my authority and ensure that parents respected the integrity of my program and the spirit of the school's mission. Volunteers were urged to attend an orientation session and required to sign a confidentiality pledge.

As for the radical change in my work situation, my colleagues expressed their sympathy almost exclusively in terms of my having to deal with "all those parents" all day, every day. Initially, I used humor to deflect the negative comments. "I've never been so organized," I would say. "I feel as if I'm undergoing a tenure evaluation every class!" Then, when the comments kept up, it struck me that teachers feel unnecessarily threatened by parents. They're overlooking a pool of potent allies. Parents can be inappropriate, and having additional adults in a teaching space changes the dynamic; however, I have learned to appreciate the positive results even more fully this year. Most adults want the best education for all children. I admit this sounds idealistic, but it is a rare, and likely disturbed, person, who volunteers with ill intentions. However, I must admit that I still faced some difficult situations.

One such scene unfolded when four parents—all women—showed up to volunteer for a kindergarten class in October. Three of them had attended my orientation, and signed the sheet that spelled out the confidentiality requirements, so I felt pretty confident that they would quietly dive into their chores. They whispered instructions to the uninitiated volunteer, which was only mildly distracting to me and my young students. Midway through the class, as I was reading a book, the four of them assembled behind me in a phalanx-like line and began talking in normal conversational tones. I looked over my shoulder, trying to make eye contact to indicate, "Please stop distracting the kids."

One mother noticed my distress and moved away from the group. The others carried on. I kept on reading, aware that I was losing several students and in danger of losing more. I was seething. I resented this situation forced on me. "Why should I have to figure out a tactful way to stop this rude behavior?" vibrated through my brain. I was sweating profusely. I got through the book. I was still upset, even trembling, but managed to supervise the book checkout. I pondered what to say to the parents to prevent this from ever happening again.

I seized the chance to accompany the students to their room when the class ended. Because no other class was scheduled, I could focus on what I had to do—confront these adults who were not helping, but interfering, with the rapport their children and I had as we created our learning environment. I was calmer, but still shaky, as I returned to the library, but the message I had to deliver was so apparent to me that I spoke with conviction when I entered the room, "Thanks for your help today, but it's clear that only one, at most two, parent volunteers, are needed in this small space. Here's a calendar so you can work out a schedule."

The parent who understood my dilemma apologized, "I'm sorry we were so involved in our conversation that we forgot you were teaching a class." Two other parents added their apologies, and I felt a wave of relief sweep over me. I knew then that I had the power—the power to establish the rules for the conduct of not only students but other adults in my space. I told all the parents the new policy and used humor to emphasize my point, "I can't compete with you—I'm like day-old bread. The students find you much more riveting." I am still blindsided at times by an adult—not only parents, but also staff members—who does not respect the environment that my students and I have created. I am not constantly on guard, but I am vigilant. I work hard to create a congenial atmosphere conducive to exploring and learning, and I refuse to let anyone else subvert it.

Now, when my fellow teachers offer me sympathy because of "all those parents I must put up with," I take the conversation in a different direction. "Actually," I say, "I don't know what I'd do without them." I am honest and admit that there was some adjusting, but that I expect volunteers to honor the rules of my space, and if they don't, I diplomatically outline what has to change. So far, it has worked much better than expected. I make it clear from the outset that I am in charge. I tell skeptical teachers the spiel I've developed for volunteers who don't respect the boundaries: "This is my job and I love it. I spend hours selecting the books for the collection and plan my classes with care. I'm very grateful for your help, but I can't expect you to be involved in managing the library or disciplining students. It's not fair to you, to the students, or to me."

I also look for opportunities to tout the unanticipated benefits. Many parents have become strong advocates of the library program. Also, after the novelty wore off, two of my most difficult students behave better when their parents are present. In addition, I now realize that these parents do understand that their children are challenging, but they also see that their children's quirks are acknowledged and even appreciated. I am comfortable in setting a tone and requiring that everyone honor the guidelines I've established.

As a specialist, I feel I am more effective if I have a positive relationship with every classroom teacher. I jump at the chance to pass on parents' compliments to my colleagues for their exemplary efforts. Reflexively, I halt parents' inappropriate comments about staff members by calmly stating, "It would be unprofessional for me to discuss my fellow teachers, so I don't." If I can, I leave, if not, I change the topic. I am pleased to say that the negative comments are very rare.

This may sound simplistic, but I believe that I have helped change the attitudes of at least some of my colleagues about parent volunteers. Parents are not the enemy. They are impressed with the way teachers manage large groups of children much more often than not. I believe that when parents see, firsthand, what we are attempting and how hard we work, we make powerful allies. We need those allies to help our children become lifelong learners.

Introduction to
"A Roaring Silence"

*K*atzenmeyer and Moller say "awakening the sleeping giant" of one's teacher leadership involves figuring out "Who Am I?" (Part I). Wendy Lessard explains how her analysis of her readiness for leadership coupled with the assessment of others regarding her potential led her through excitement to anguish. Truly in touch with herself having explored her own family and school experiences, she saw a conflict brewing between the system she and her colleagues were putting in place in her school and the needs of what we often call "at-risk" students. As a leader, how could she deny the truth she knew about her own family background and how it had shaped her response to her students? Her burgeoning leadership understanding pushed her to give voice to this truth. She shows that part of leadership is not just voicing beliefs but being able to stay the course as she strategizes for ways to deepen and expand others' understanding of thorny issues.

—SVM

21

A Roaring Silence

Wendy Lessard

I have always loved literature and the transformative learning that can happen around it, and this is what I attempted to create in my classroom as a high school English teacher. Yet there has always been a part of me that has been interested in leading and managing. So after a decade as a classroom teacher, the opportunity arose for me to become a department head at our school. I was eager to take on the challenge in another area of academic life. The role of department head came a bit earlier than I had expected it to in my career, and I knew that there were many skills I needed to identify and acquire to be an effective leader, so I decided to embark on another run of college courses to fill those needs. I was fortunate (more fortunate than I could imagine or appreciate at the time) to find a program focusing not only on the typical cognitive work expected of graduate students in educational leadership but on interpersonal and intrapersonal dimensions as well. The program helped me dig into my core beliefs, rationalize my stances, and understand myself and relationships with others more fully.

My school is an open, professionally nurturing environment, and we pride ourselves on our ability to center on what we think is best for student learning, which creates many deeply rewarding conversations around educational issues and problem solving. I am lucky to have leaders who were comfortable enough in their own roles and within themselves to let me "cut my teeth" on meaty issues with them. I have always been able to share with them a professional challenge and to ask for advice. When the administration asked me to consider taking on a curriculum coordinator role, I was thrilled by the possibility of embarking on an even more formal and full-time leadership and administrative position.

I was excited as I thought about new projects and challenges, not to mention the impact on even more students. I knew my contact with students would be more removed, something I always considered the downside of leaving the classroom. But the opportunity to shape students' educational experiences, especially in a time of deep reform at our school, was energizing. I felt, validated, too, when I thought of the leaders I respected encouraging me to consider this move into a formal leadership position. The excitement and anticipation caused an adrenaline rush that had me brainstorming countless ideas on the commute from work or on the cardio machines at the gym and into the wakeful hours of the early morning.

It was during one of those dark hours as I lay awake that I turned my focus from the future, with all its possibilities, to the now. I wondered why I was spending so many early morning hours with this burning anticipation. I began to recognize conflicting emotions were clutching my solar plexus. My emotions had become a physical sensation, a knot in my upper chest; once I stopped feeling the adrenaline, I realized that the excitement and anticipation were outweighed by a growing anxiety. Over the next few days I listened to this anxiety and traced its origins.

What I realized is that my role as a collaborator on and spokesperson for a local assessment system that includes certifying for standards *and* a senior exhibition created a fundamental conflict for me as a person and as a teacher. Serious doubts emerged. I worried about equity.

Were we building an insurmountable system of hoops that many students would not be able to jump through? I am comfortable with requiring students to demonstrate identified skills in order to graduate. These skills should be (and are at my high school) embedded in classroom work, and our assessment of those skills is accompanied by teacher support and many possibilities for student voice and choice. Yet one facet of the new local assessment system was not part of the regular curriculum, and I realized it could be seen as a hoop. Senior exhibitions, with their emphasis on research, independent learning, and presentation outside of the curriculum, would add an extra layer overwhelming to those students we deem most at risk. I could see where students from a certain socioeconomic background, when faced with so many daunting—and perhaps irrelevant to them—requirements to graduate, would drop out sooner.

There was more than professional unease gripping my abdomen, however. The American school system until some recent reforms had failed a significant proportion of my immigrant family. The system failed them, not by placing a string of "F's" on report cards, but by its inability to meet their needs. By instructing my family members in the middle class values and norms of American society, schools failed to demonstrate that their family's values were valid and important to maintain. Schools were an unfriendly place for children of immigrants who spoke English with a foreign accent, if they spoke English at all. A curriculum that focused on obedience, compliance, and rigid expectations without opportunities for students to make their own meaning out of what was being learned became a dead-end street for many of my aunts and uncles, and even for my parents. For many of them, even the promise of assimilation and a shot at the American Dream was not enough to keep them in school, and they dropped out, even though they are some of the smartest people I know. Lack of formal schooling and all that it can offer, from a diploma to indoctrination into the language and structures of power available in American society, created some challenges for my relatives that a number could not overcome in spite of their native intelligence. Even when they tried to break out of the working poor status that they were destined for by dropping out, they did not know how.

Journaling in the early morning hours led me to articulate something I had never consciously acknowledged but knew was there because it had made me the teacher I am. I valued the ability of formal education to connect my students to the wisdom and stunning creations in literature of the past, but I knew that past would have no meaning unless I could connect it to my students, to their realities, and to who they wanted to be. I tried to create classes that were exploratory learning groups, with me as guide. As one student put it, "You (as our teacher) actually treated us as people. We weren't just children to you . . . being tolerated at best." I love and honor the power of the written and spoken word and try to model that in my classes, but I do not teach solely for the love of demonstrating my own learning. I coach my students to find their own style, voice, passion, goals, and meaning in their lives.

Knowing my relatives as I do, I could see that the system failed them in a myriad of ways. I wondered how they would function, and how I could function, in the accountability system we were in the process of building. I felt like a traitor: to my heritage, to my family, to who I was as an educator. At my school we were creating a structure without conversations about how a new piece that was not part of the established curriculum would be made valid to those who were barely hanging on already. Without articulating a rationale to each other, how could we ever establish validity with those who already challenge so much of what school tries to do? The deeply burrowed anxiety resulted from realizing how much we had ignored the needs of these students, the very people whose learning experiences we were attempting to transform.

It is one thing to know where we come from and why we have the particular stances that we do, but it is another to voice concerns, to risk a group's complacency, to be an agent of change. I have always felt supported in my school, and thus when I presented my final portfolio for my graduate program to a small group in our school, I felt nervous but confident that

I could speak my mind. I knew the only reason I had been able to arrive at my awareness for what resided in me was the work I had done in the program. I also knew that the intent of the program was preparation for moments like this; I had to voice my concerns to leaders who could effect change, the very people in my audience. Close peers and confidants, my mentors and formal administrative leaders, and my professors observed my presentation. I closed with the apprehension I felt about where our school was heading and my own discomfort with the layers we were adding. I shared that many members of my immigrant family dropped out of a system that failed them; I have seen firsthand how challenging American life is for people the educational system fails. I said I knew I would find a way to reconcile my misgivings with the school's current direction to find a way to make school work more effectively for *all* our students, but until then, I had deep reservations about being able to be an effective leader in shaping that change.

I felt gutsy sharing my thoughts. It was a different kind of adrenaline rush that lasted as I heard the commendations and observations of the audience. I trusted my words would open dialogue about my fears for our students; and I believed that I would have my fears allayed either by plans in place that I was not aware of or by building an even stronger system.

Yet as the weeks elapsed after the presentation and the commendations from our school's leaders petered out, I heard . . . silence. Silence around the deeply rooted and personal concerns I had voiced. Silence about what I had revealed about my family, my personal stance, and my fears. Silence about what the system could do to our most at-risk students. A silence that roared.

I was taken aback. This was not the culture I thought I knew; where was the professional dialogue, the focus on what was best for student learning? Had I broken some unwritten law about not bringing the ultra-personal into my professional life and aspirations? Had I so disappointed my mentors in some way that I had ruptured our working relationship? In reflecting on the lack of response, I have come to believe the most significant cause of the silence is I brought up an issue that no one is currently willing to address: matters of class and disadvantage. Yes, there are some technical conversations around raising aspirations and reading levels, but where are the conversations that address the values that create this friction? There are no conversations about our poorest students. Nor are there conversations about our nontraditional and creative students who are finding other ways to advance their own learning and contribute to our society. Nor is there conversation around the lifelong learners who emerge from those who drop out, the students for whom the educational system does not work. We need to be able to discuss the bias these standards hold for students from socioeconomically challenged families, about the choice we set up for these students: school values or family values. Educators are perhaps too busy creating assessments and evaluating student work to remember, for they are silent about these underlying issues. This silence on class issues and nontraditional forms of lifelong learning is one begging acknowledgement and discussion.

The silence on this topic has continued for me at my school. I have let it, until now, because I needed the time to process it. At first I felt constrained because I shared such a personal aspect of myself and of those I love the best. I feel protective of them, and I feel protective of my students. Because this is an issue that strikes at the core of who I am as a person, a teacher, and a school leader, I know that I need to delve into it. I need to have it make sense to me, and I need to do something about it, because schools are supposed to be a place in which we honor diversity and nurture individuals, and I believe that. My role will not be to point the finger of blame to create shame, which is an easy and unprofitable trap, I know. I do know that this concern for my students and my values will cause me to use my voice again, and I will think hard before I do to find a way to encourage all voices, rather than a conspicuous silence.

Introduction to
"Education's Glass Ceiling"

*W*illiam Ferriter laments the lack of staging of the teaching career that Dan Lortie *(1975) described several decades ago. Unless one leaves the classroom for quite a different role, teachers do the same job every year. Their expertise increases, as does their confidence, but they find they must seek challenges out of the classroom to garner status for themselves. They may find, as Hank Ogilby says (Part III), that they end up doing neither job—teaching or leading—very well. And, granted, male teachers may feel this tug more than women in spite of all that is open to women now. Flatter organizations may solve some problems—perhaps more so for principals than teachers—but they may not solve this one.*

On the other hand, it may be possible as I discovered in my study of teacher leaders who have transitioned to administration (Part IV) that it is possible to bring one's teacher leader mind-set to other roles. Growth in an education career does not necessarily mean that one needs to move into administrative leadership, but ideally we should see any move as an evolution that builds on one's capabilities and interests.

—SVM

Lortie, D. (1975). School teacher: A sociological study. *Chicago: University of Chicago Press.*

22

Education's Glass Ceiling

William Ferriter

Not long ago, I had a reunion with one of my favorite students. Michael was only 10 when I met him as a fifth grader in one of my first classes as a teacher. He was someone that I hit it off with instantly, and I grew to know him and his family quite well over the past 11 years. Michael is now on the edge of graduating from college himself, and we got together to catch up.

As our conversation drifted toward careers, Michael surprised me by asking, "When are you moving out of middle school? You could teach somewhere else easily. Maybe you could go to a high school or college?"

"I'm not," I said. "I really love my sixth graders."

"But is that what you want to be doing when you're 50?" he pressed, "Don't you think it would be weird to still be just a teacher when you're 50?"

And for the first time in my career, I struggled to answer. "Teaching is what I do," was my first reaction. "I love my students, and knowing that I'm making a difference in their lives drives me."

I've even taken steps to make staying in the classroom a better financial decision. Several years ago, I earned National Board Certification, which carries a significant pay raise in our state. I then added a master's degree, further increasing my pay. Combined, National Board Certification and a master's degree have made staying in the classroom almost affordable.

But is being "just a teacher" enough? Is it what I want to be doing when I'm 50?

Honestly, the answer is, "I'm just not sure anymore," and that saddens me.

It's not that I'm "burned out," tired by the daily demands of meeting the needs of middle schoolers. In fact, I still thrive on my interactions with my students. It's also not that I feel "disrespected" by society as a whole. Although the criticisms of public schooling can be trying, I know that I have been successful within my school and community.

What has me doubting my decision to finish my career in the classroom is that despite great successes, I've recognized that I am still "just a teacher" in the eyes of most people. My day-to-day responsibilities haven't changed in 12 years and are no different from the responsibilities of the first-year teachers in my building. Although I am currently working for an administrative team that believes in empowering teachers, I still find myself wanting more input in conversations related to education at all levels.

Teaching is truly a "flat profession." There are no real opportunities for teachers to advance and remain classroom teachers at the same time. To get the additional influence that I want, I'm going to have to leave my classroom for a career in school administration or educational policy—and lose my connection with my students. That is incredibly frustrating.

It is time to break education's "glass ceiling" and to stratify teaching. If we hope to retain our most accomplished teachers, we must work to create school-level leadership positions for teachers who want to stay in the classroom and advance as well. There are successful stratification models being tried across the country, and several have been proposed here in our state. All have the potential to inspire teachers looking for opportunities to grow professionally.

But these initial efforts are slow to develop and to be embraced by a society that largely still views teaching as something slightly less than professional work. Until these perceptions change, teachers will continue to be forced to make the difficult decision to remain "just a teacher" or leave the part of the profession that they love the most.

As for me, what will I be doing when I'm 50? I don't know. I haven't decided yet.

Introduction to
"Learning in the Risk Zone"

S tephanie Marshall's reflection is connected to Linda Bowe's "It Isn't Just a Dream" (Part V). Linda was Stephanie's leadership coach. She helped Stephanie "peel the onion" of her resignation and withdrawal from leadership responsibilities in her school and district. Linda acknowledges her skill in coaching teacher leaders comes from her own experience of stepping out from the group and making herself heard. To be an effective coach, she herself experienced the "holding environment" described by Eleanor Drago-Severson, Jennifer Roloff Welch, and Anne E. Jones (Part V). Those authors provide safety in the "convening" they do; Linda and Stephanie found it in the coaching relationship.

One could argue that teachers themselves create a risk-averse culture, which makes it even harder to summon courage and find oneself continually pushing against the status quo. Because the greatest learning comes from situations neither too comfortable nor too dangerous, teacher leaders must push themselves to work in areas that are risky in order to grow and change. They must also have supportive guides to feel safe enough to reflect honestly, plan for next moves, and receive constructive feedback.

—SVM

23

Learning in the Risk Zone

Stephanie Marshall

I have been a teacher in the same district for many years. Throughout my career I have been an active participant and leader on many different school and district initiatives. I am currently a teacher leader in English Language Arts. A few years ago, my superintendent suggested that I apply to a two-year leadership development program for teachers and administrators. I worked closely with a leadership coach who was a facilitator in the program. It was the beginning of a transformational relationship for both of us.

Our journey together started out in a "danger zone." I had come to a professional and personal impasse while attending the first summer's institute. While working to gear up for the intensive leadership experience ahead of me, I realized that I might not be able to continue. I felt I could not learn because I was too confused and disheartened. My years of leading teachers in my school had left me fatigued and disillusioned as to whether any of our efforts were getting us anywhere. I doubted that I had either the commitment or the energy to complete the program, and I wondered whether I could even continue my current teacher leadership roles come fall. Two weeks after the institute, it was time for me to meet with Linda, the facilitator and coach of the program, to discuss my situation.

I now realize how close I was to "burning out" of my profession. I was a committed, highly respected teacher with 20 years of experience. I had been on numerous committees, given many presentations, developed new programs, and put in hours of work. Because I was so focused on all the work that needed to be done, I felt overwhelmed. Other teachers at the school relied on me. I listened to their struggles and offered support and empathy; yet I felt I couldn't go to anyone about my feelings of despair and inadequacy as a teacher.

I had no way of putting my teaching life, my home life, and my own goals into balance. I felt that my participation in the program was going to be more work. I was too emotionally tired to do it. In the time between the summer institute and when I met with my coach, my doubts about the program had only increased. I thought about canceling the meeting. My husband encouraged me to meet with her in spite of my doubts.

When I met with Linda, I realized it was the first time I had really talked to anyone about my inner teaching life. I expressed my doubts about entering the program, and she listened. She offered support to explore the issues that were facing me; she encouraged me to stay and promised that the experience could indeed provide me with a safe and instructive place. I was relieved that I could work through my despair with her assistance. That conversation with Linda was a turning point for me. "Perhaps it would be okay to be in turmoil and still continue with the program," I thought. It felt risky, but at the same time, I knew that the way that I had been proceeding was dangerous to my health and psyche.

Linda encouraged me to write about my hectic life. I took up her suggestion, and as I did, it soon became apparent that I had to change the way I was thinking about my leadership role in school. I felt I needed to be on all the committees, and the word "no" was not in my vocabulary. To change this energy-draining situation and regain some balance in my work life and home life, I had to create some priorities for myself. Through subsequent conversations with my colleague critic team and Linda, I had a better sense of what I wanted as a teacher leader. By identifying some filtering questions, I could clearly assert my voice and my needs as well as maintain a leadership role at the school. These questions guide my work as a teacher leader and maximize my learning instead of shutting me down:

Does this activity, role, course, or committee
- fit in with my other commitments? (In regard to time and frequency of meetings)
- provide me with new learning or insight?
- excite me?
- fit in with my leadership development plan and my school's greater goals?
- demand too much of my time? If I add this _____, what will I let go?

These questions are now integrated into my life as a teacher leader and have helped me to contribute to my school in ways that revitalize me. They have helped me to balance my professional and personal goals. I started to understand the many forces that impinge on authentic change in schools.

Some of these forces are within my control, such as interpersonal relationships, my own beliefs, and my conceptual frameworks. I realized that I had been operating in a school system that was highly politicized and that I had taken many of its conflicts to heart. I gradually learned to depersonalize some of the conflicts; therefore, my intrapersonal energies are refocused on those things over which I do have control.

In the past, I had taken on many leadership responsibilities, but I always had a lot of self-doubt. I would think, "I am a sham"; "leadership is for someone else who has got it together and I don't; therefore I can't really be a leader." What was most difficult for me to overcome was thinking that somehow good leadership was special. I was obviously not a good leader because I didn't think that leaders had *any* doubts. With my coach's help, I learned to take "little risks" in my school. I identified the risk I wanted to take, made an action plan, got feedback, and then reflected on it. I built up successes bit by bit instead of taking on too much and being overwhelmed by it all. I transformed my interior landscape. My self-talk now is very different. We're all leaders. I am a leader of 19 children in a second-grade classroom, and so, by the very nature of being a teacher, I am a leader. I facilitate an environment that allows learners to further their understanding. This statement is the kernel of teacher leadership.

As a teacher leader, I have one foot in the classroom and one foot as a leader in the greater life of the school. I have the best of both worlds. Although I do not have an administrator's authority, I do have more freedom. I can forge my own path. My authority comes from how I act. My colleagues know what to expect from me—I guess you could call that integrity. My coach has integrity. I knew what kind of a person she was by what she said and did. Because she values me and my experience, it is easier for me to value the experiences of people I come in contact with every day. It is the unspoken part of professional relationships. When someone is true to herself and who she is, can express that and allow others to *be* who they are, then that, to me, is leadership.

It is difficult to grow on your own. Conflict and risk are where learning happens, but I need support, encouragement, and challenge to be able to learn from them. I'm not the leader I was 2 years ago, and I haven't developed into the leader I will be 3 years from now. I need to learn from people who are further along in their path. My self-talk now is "Where do I want to go on my path? Be open to the possibilities."

Introduction to
"Hard Lessons About Leadership"

*I*n this piece, Jennifer Ribeiro, an accomplished midcareer teacher, examines her beliefs about her leadership practice. She espouses the views of Lambert, Collay, Dietz, Kent, and Richert (Part II), so she sees herself as attempting to be a constructivist leader. She has to fight her tendency to accomplish tasks alone, however, especially tasks set by others in the school district. Her understanding of herself leads her to deeper appreciation of the skills she has, but she is frustrated by her lack of patience with the amount of time it takes to make meaning with adults so they truly understand and own their learning. One could argue that she is caught between models of leadership: She aspires to include everyone and nurture relationships as they develop ideas together, but she has a role in the district hierarchy that places expectations and constraints on what it takes to construct a true learning community. As Jennifer reflects on this situation, she promises to delve more fully into what actions she can take to ameliorate this inner tension.

—SVM

24

Hard Lessons About Leadership

Jennifer Ribeiro

I am always ready to learn, but I do not always like to be taught.

—Winston Churchill

I hate to admit how let down I was when I realized there was no magic book or complicated scientific formula that leads to highly skilled leadership ability. It is more than just what you know; it is what you can do with what you know. One thing that helped me learn some things about myself was the Myers-Briggs Type Indicator (MBTI). I never really understood my preferences or strengths and weaknesses. I cannot say that I enjoy having this new knowledge. I feel more responsible for my shortcomings since I'm aware of them. Knowing my preferences, though, means I need to make choices about my behavior. Learning some things about myself has helped me develop more confidence, which affects how I work with others both individually and in groups.

Understanding how I am a leader has been empowering. One of my challenges lies in dealing with uncomfortable situations with colleagues rather than avoiding a conflict or accommodating their needs and not my own. I want to keep things moving so badly that I do not collaborate very well. This year I worked on a three-person grade-level team with a woman who has caused me some anxiety over the past few years. A group of three does not work well in a third grade classroom, so why should I expect it to work well with three independent adults? The anxiety was not a result of working in a triad, however; when there is a person in the middle, I find it is easy to leave someone out. These behaviors make relationships more complicated than they need to be, as happened with our team. One improvement that occurred in the working relationship of our team was our commitment to discussing items that required decision making only when all of us were present. More important for me was my commitment to be positive or neutral unless I had specific comments that I was willing to share with everyone.

Another breakthrough in my relationship with my colleague came when I explored the cause of my anxiety. I have learned that I find group process to be an important component in how things get accomplished; my colleague likes quick, simple decisions. She was confident and forthright in her opinions, which is what I both envied and found disconcerting. Our different approaches were a major cause of my difficulties. Once I was able to identify the issue, I was able to prepare myself for encounters. I could be more flexible and understanding in our working relationship without feeling as if I should bend to her wishes all the time.

Buoyed by some success in my relationship with her, I explored my role on a districtwide curriculum design team. I am still working on it. During our meetings last year, I often found myself offering to help with projects and speaking out at meetings. Others on the team were less involved. I assumed I should do more because I liked this work better than others. I realized that some of my decisions may have helped get the work done, yet much of the team failed to keep up with my learning. On more than one occasion, I offered to assist in the organization and presentation of new information about our district's local assessment system for a districtwide meeting. I read and synthesized information with the committee leader, and people saw me as knowledgeable. These things were positive; however, by volunteering so readily each time, I was filling a role that others might have been encouraged to fill. I soon found myself in a position in which it was more difficult to collaborate and easier to just do things for the team. My excitement and impatience went a bit too far and led to less collaboration.

Although we had a mission statement and other documents that stated specific jobs for which we were responsible, I felt that some of us, me in particular, were taking on a lot more responsibility. I was uncomfortable with my role because I couldn't define it. I joked with my friends on the team that it was about wanting to have more control. Then I worried about having said that because it sounded negative and wasn't really that simple. I did not feel collaborative because of the extra work I was doing, yet I found it hard to get others to pitch in at times. So I was occasionally frustrated by our lack of accomplishment. It was that darn "can-do" attitude getting me in trouble and affecting my priorities.

Conversations about clarifying roles led the assistant superintendent to create a position to help her run the committee. She asked for applications from anyone on the committee who felt he or she could assist her with leading the work. I knew I had to apply since it would help me deal with the uncertainty about my role. I had become quite knowledgeable, yet I was doing too much of the work independently. I wrote up my proposal, yet I didn't feel I should take the job on my own. I lacked confidence, but more important, I wanted to be more collaborative. I approached a colleague on the committee who I felt could handle the position as well. He and I discussed our ideas about how we could assist the team and sent in a joint proposal. At the time I considered this a good idea: Because I would have support from someone whose style would balance mine, we could better lead the team. In choosing to work with a partner, I had drawn someone else into the work at a higher level.

In spite of the success I enjoyed collaborating with my coleader, I did not do very well encouraging greater collaboration with the team. For example, our committee was asked to finish creating assessments for the local system by the end of the year. This sounded like a simple task; however, it created quite a bit of distress for the district teachers and the teacher leaders on our committee. Instead of working with the leaders to help them facilitate decision making with their groups, we chose to make suggestions for the leaders ahead of time. I was doing the work for them in an effort to make it easier for the groups. The result was an assessment list that was completed without enough group ownership. Many of the teacher leaders from the committee were unable to fully explain how particular items became part of our assessment system. My co-chair and I were more concerned with accomplishing the task presented to us than we were with fully engaging the group in solving the problems.

I learned about the need to balance efficiency with collaboration, which I find to be a continuing challenge because it is unclear to me, even in retrospect, how much efficiency could be sacrificed to focus on the group's working together. Because I am one of the people responsible for accomplishing an agenda, I feel a different sense of obligation. Some members felt the leaders would make sure the work got completed so they were less involved. Once again, I ponder how things could have happened differently to keep everyone involved and focused on the vision while allowing "leaders" to streamline some of the work to be more efficient.

I now ask myself these questions: What should collaboration look like? How much collaboration is enough? How do you effectively encourage collaboration? I could look at these questions and feel like a failure, yet I have come a long way in understanding the concept of collaboration and feel that many teachers struggle to define it. Part of that struggle comes from a fear of having to collaborate. Working together toward a shared goal or project requires trust, effort, time, and motivation. People who work together are often at different stages of commitment to engaging in collaborative relationships. I know my strengths and weaknesses pretty well. I strive to be a collaborative leader, yet I struggle to feel highly effective with this model. I believe in many constructivist leadership principles, yet I am unsure if I really have the patience. I strive to be positive and exude a "can-do" attitude, but I learned that I have to accept some things about myself. I need to continue to accentuate the positive and use that perspective to encourage others to help us all move forward.

Introduction to "I, Leader"

*P*oetry in its economy of words packs a lot of emotion. The Teacher Formation work inspired by Parker Palmer and described by Sam Intrator (Part V) uses poetry to help participants get in touch with emotions they may have repressed or that have never surfaced.

Gary Chapin's poem came from his confrontation with his deeply held beliefs about teaching, learning, and, ultimately, leadership. Often teacher leaders recognize that confidence is what they lack. They have to come to grips with their core—their strengths and weaknesses as well as the fundamental principles that guide their work. Gary calls his assurance about himself and his beliefs "arrogance," a more powerful and pejorative word than confidence or courage. To summon what it takes to feel useful—to be useful—he must be forceful and overconfident in order to be influential in the arenas where he sees his participation making a difference.

—SVM

25

I, Leader

Gary Chapin

I am a leader.

I lead in a predictable way.

I lead in my family.

I lead in my classroom.

I lead in my school.

I am the chair of the District, K–12, social studies curriculum committee.

I lead in an unpredictable way, merely by acting when others are indecisive.

> Then, as if I were moving through brackish water, the others fall into my wake, appreciating the momentum.

I lead in an unpredictable way, when confronted by improbable, implausible, unpalatable, unlikable, unlikely, or intolerable options. There's that sick feeling when I know I have to say something and say it well.

Clarity is courage. Don't abandon rhetoric! Persuasion trumps all. Yes, in this unpredictable moment, I'm nervous.

Because I can lead, I have to. Opportunity is the obligation.

Do people like being led? Are followers even a part of the model anymore, or has the follower been homogenously grouped out of existence? Are we all above average? Is this what we want, or only what we can stomach?

When I lead, predictably or not, my leadership is spent on process and content. To coax every team member to contribute—why must they be coaxed?—to articulate the will of the group, to accentuate the team's will.

But there are things that I want, and things that I believe. I have a will.

Does the fact that I've articulated these beliefs, honed and sharpened them, and believed them—really believed them—make them righter?

Do people like to be led?

I used to dress my twin girls identically. Not because I thought it was very cute, but because I wanted one less decision in my day. Does fatigue create followers?

I used to allow friends to choose the restaurant we'd eat at just because I didn't care and if we're going to have a fight why not have a fight about something that matters. Does indifference create followers?

I have a model in my head of discipleship where you go to the master and say, "teach me." Do deference, respect, trust, and reverence create followers?

And then there's Principal Steve. He's earned my loyalty and respect. I believe he can take the part that I am, and, by leadership, fold it into something—it becomes more than the sum of itself. His leadership adds value to my teaching. As good as I am, existing within the context of the schools, transforms my teaching into a better thing.

T'ain't easy.

There are leaders like me.

We believe in the democratic process. We believe in the power of the collective.

No. Really. We do.

But—damn them—they make it hard.

The followers.

You know.

I'm elitist.

There's arrogance in me.

How could there not be?

How could you commit the act of attempting leadership without a store-house of arrogance behind you?

How could you scratch a word into a piece of paper unless you believed your words deserve to be read?

> How could you persuade unless you believed others would be better if only they thought more like you?

Arrogance!

I am elitist. There is a best. We can approach it. We should.

I can see it. I can see. I can help.

In the district, K–12, social studies curriculum committee

In my school

In my classroom

In my family

In ways both predictable and not

I can add value.

Questions for Reflection and Conversation

- Which entries resonate with your experience? Why? Have you had similar moments of awareness about your beliefs, your dispositions, your behavior, or your understanding of leadership?
- Running through these stories is tension—between people and within people, most often related to their dealings with others. In your work, where do you see these tensions?
- The National School Reform Faculty's Critical Event Protocol can be helpful for individuals as they analyze the importance of an incident, but sharing the information with a group provides a richness of reflection that is hard to achieve on one's own.

As you consider your leadership, think about an incident that stands out for you—one that you thought about on the way home or that has revisited you during the night. The incident can be about something that happened that was particularly rewarding, or puzzling, or devastating. The event could have been an epiphany, a crisis, or a moment of revealing insight. More likely, though, it was merely a small event that seemed unremarkable at the time, but somehow it made its way into your reflections. Write about the event in as much detail as possible. Simply tell the story of the incident. What happened? Where? When? Who was involved? Stop writing as soon as you find yourself raising questions about the incident or analyzing it in some way.

In conversation with others or in writing for yourself, what reflective or analytical questions does this piece suggest? What might this incident mean in the context of your work as a leader? Are there any implications for your practice or for your listeners' practice? What new insights occurred to you and to the other participants in the protocol?

PART IV

Keeping the Teacher in the Leader

Part IV provides more evidence of the vexations of teacher leaders even as they lean into the challenges and soldier on. They are usually able to celebrate the small successes of their learning about and in leadership. They also gain tremendous sustenance from their teaching while they live for the dream of feeling part of a collective, collaborative enterprise. They are part of something larger than themselves. Their strength comes from the classroom, yet unless they venture out from it, connecting and relating to the other adults in the organization, they are not fulfilling the power implicit in their teaching role. Granted, those teachers who stay in their classrooms exert some power, too. If we think of the push-pull or binary school leadership (Evans, 1996) of top-down and ground-up, the individualists or isolationists are part of that tension, too. It can be pretty messy, as such leadership involves relationships as well as ideas and ideals.

In Part I, Crowther, Kaagan, Ferguson, and Hann (2002) highlight the messiness by categorizing some of the many teacher leader roles, tasks, or stances in their Teachers as Leaders Framework. Almost all of the aspects of the framework involve taking themselves outside the classroom or putting their inner selves out for others to encounter in deep and powerful ways. For example, the framework describes teacher leaders as individuals who "facilitate communities of learning through organization-wide processes . . . confront barriers to the school's culture and structures, (and) . . . nurture a culture of success" (Table 4.1). Although school environment implies more than the school community itself (and teacher leaders have many roles in the larger school and educational community), much of the work of such leaders is with their colleagues and their principals (York-Barr & Duke, 2004).

The pieces in this section gently move us from the individual teacher leader and his or her story to the leadership arena where the stories occur. The authors, having studied teacher leaders, attempt to make sense of the meaning making and occasional struggle of teacher leaders as they interact with other adults in the school context. All of these writers have themselves experienced the tensions of teacher leadership which, in fact, give rise to their curiosity and the desire to explore the phenomenon of teacher leadership more fully. These pieces are more personal than those in the first two parts of this book because of the nature of what the authors are exploring and the way they have chosen to do so—making extensive use of the voices of teacher leaders much in the way Barth does in his monograph in Part I. We want and need both, and this collection seems a logical way to ease out of the intensity of the individual stories of Part III.

George Marnik's chapter is a reflection on his personal leadership development through teacher, principal, and now professor. Principals often talk about supporting teacher leadership, but many fewer actually do so fully or effectively (York-Barr & Duke, 2004). Marnik shows how delicate a balance it requires. The principal must come to grips with his or her own role in the leadership dynamic and, to a large extent, trust, nurture, and let go. Being able to cultivate interpersonal relationships comes from knowing oneself well and having strong beliefs in the capabilities of others. It sounds like good teaching, and it is. An effective principal is a leader and teacher of adults.

JoAnne Dowd in her study of 15 teacher leaders captures their frustration and, occasionally, sorrow that the job of moving people to change—even in the best interests of students—is so hard. The tensions they feel echo the ones Marnik describes. Dowd argues for new ways to think about teacher leaders in schools not to obliterate the tensions but to support and strengthen the leaders who understand so well what the tensions are.

Morgaen Donaldson studied teachers at the cusp of a major turning point in their careers, early on just after they received tenure. She admits that she herself left K–12 education—at least for the time being—to pursue further study. The attrition rate for this cadre of teachers is still high, so she investigates how the members of this group consider leadership in their teaching careers. She finds the teachers contemplating what being a teacher leader might mean—especially as they hone their craft and feel compelled to share their enthusiasm and expertise—but no one thinks about the role of administrator as a way to fulfill their hopes and dreams for schools.

Sarah Mackenzie's chapter, on the other hand, delves into the thinking and experience of teacher leaders as they transition to administrative roles. Her participants are at a different stage from those in Donaldson's study, but unlike those in Dowd's, they have decided to take on another leadership role after years as both teacher and leader. She finds these new administrators determined to hold on not just to their beliefs but also to the attitudes and understandings they developed as teacher leaders. Could they be creating the environment that Dowd advocates? Or will the context in which they work subvert their commitment?

Eleanor Drago-Severson studied principals, but she found that what she had to say about their efforts to promote teachers' growth were also applicable to the work of teacher leaders. Her analysis of the different ways of knowing and how they influence collegial inquiry provides a lens through which all leaders in schools can view individual teachers' learning. She offers powerful examples of strategies to promote teacher development that can become part of a leader's toolbox no matter what the context.

In the final chapter, Mary Ann Minard, a curriculum coordinator, reminds us how other people in a school system play a role in ensuring that teacher leaders find a niche that connects their work with others and makes a difference in their students' learning.

REFERENCES

Crowther, F., Kaagan, S. S., Ferguson, M., & Hann, L. (2002). *Developing teacher leaders: How teacher leadership enhances school success.* Thousand Oaks, CA: Corwin Press.

Evans, R. (1996). *The human side of school change: Reform, resistance, and the real-life problems of innovation.* San Francisco: Jossey-Bass.

York-Barr, J., & Duke, K. (2004, Fall). What do we know about teacher leadership? Findings from two decades of scholarship. *Review of Educational Research, 74* (3), 255–316.

26

Looking Within

A Principal's Thoughts About Teacher Leadership

George F. Marnik

I was not always a principal, nor am I now. However, I was for many years, and over those years I learned a lot about leadership in schools from my varied experiences and from those with whom I worked most closely, teachers. As a teacher, director of an alternative school, principal, facilitator of a leadership development program, and university professor, I was primarily a learner. As I sit here today I recall many of the times that influenced my thinking about leadership and how I acted on those emerging beliefs as a school leader.

It was 1970, and I remember my first summer of "real" work in an early childhood education program in North Philadelphia. Waves of heat wafted skyward from the hot pavement of the playground outside the run-down school building. Children played, as children do, despite the surroundings. What was intended to be a cooling mist of water meant to provide relief just trickled from the nozzle at the end of the garden hose. In a few minutes students would return to the stuffy, overheated building to resume their studies. My just-out-of-college idealism was already being tested by the hard lessons of poverty and the realities of urban life.

Fall came sooner than expected as I began my first high school teaching position. I now had two graduate courses in education to my credit in the university internship teaching program to which I had been accepted. To the sea of Black and Hispanic students in my class I was probably just another young White teacher passing through on the way to something better. What immediately struck me about the school was its size: two stories high with a basement, full of classrooms on all three levels, an auditorium with a balcony, a shop area, and a gym. It covered a full city block and was patrolled by armed police officers. With 4,000 students in a building built for at best half that number, students attended in double shifts. To me, as an adult, it was overwhelming. How could it be any different for these young adolescents? As the months marched by it became increasingly apparent that it wasn't. There were significant numbers of youngsters who felt as disconnected from this structure called school as I did. Many were making it through by doing what was expected of them, whereas many others were falling by the wayside. How could learning take place in such an environment?

THE POWER OF A GOOD IDEA

A small group of teachers began to meet and talk about our frustrations, the devastating impact on students that we saw each day, and what, if any, options existed. With a supportive assistant principal to guide us through the labyrinth of school politics when needed, we developed a proposal to work with a few dozen students in a smaller, more individualized setting in the hopes that we could make a difference in the lives of these needy youngsters. We found housing in a community center a few blocks away and two of us took the leap into the world of alternative schools. It was my first taste of the power of a good idea, starting small yet thinking big, and the influence a group of teachers can exert on others. In short, it was teacher leadership.

Within a couple of years I left this program and moved to another alternative school. The work of this staff with gang members from throughout the city was the most challenging and the most rewarding I've ever been engaged in. Under the guidance of a director who nurtured students and staff alike, we were encouraged, supported, and ultimately expected to be creative in our work, collaborate with other adults on staff, and expose students to new horizons. We worked as one with a depth of sincerity and common commitment seldom felt in public schools. We thrived in an atmosphere of collegiality and risk-taking, devoting our lives to a single mission on behalf of the teenagers with whom we worked. There were certainly many sad moments along the way as we lost students to the violence that permeated their lives. But there were also many joyous ones as they grew beyond our wildest expectations to meet challenges and blossom into adults making contributions of immense proportion to their communities.

SHARED COMMITMENT

What I learned about teaching and leading during this time of my life was that a tremendous sense of community evolves from shared work and commitment to a common cause. I also learned that teaching is not the exclusive purview of those who are certified. I learned much from those on staff who had been raised on the streets of the city and could teach and build relationships with youngsters in ways I could only begin to comprehend. I learned that you share the good times and the bad and that you come back the next day, because for many kids this was their home and we needed to be there. Finally, I learned that much of what had been accomplished would have been nearly impossible without the support, encouragement, and unfailing devotion to a dream of the enlightened director of the school. Her willingness to work side by side with staff and to share what it meant to take risks and to lead in order to benefit our students and their learning and growth set an example undiminished over the years. Time and again she demonstrated the art of relinquishing control over others while not abandoning the responsibilities of her position.

I wanted to be this kind of leader. When the opportunity came along I moved across the river to Camden to begin, with a trusted friend and colleague, a similar program in a city just beginning to recognize its unwanted youth. I couldn't have taken such a step, though, without the guidance and support of mentors. Not mentors in the classic sense of learning while sitting at their knee, but mentors who led from behind with a gentle hand on the shoulder guiding and encouraging me to learn by doing and by sailing into uncharted waters. The time that it takes to listen carefully, to talk through the challenges of school life with another, to make sense of what has occurred and learn from those experiences, and to commiserate when needed are at the core of a mentoring relationship. This was being there for him or her, in the purist sense of the phrase. Leadership in schools is being there for one another as we take steps ranging from innovation to systemic change. In moving across the river I hoped I could be there for others and nurture their capacity to lead as others had me.

I moved to Maine in 1979, exhausted from the intensity of working in cities with youth plagued by the inequities of our society. A teacher on our staff who had shown particular enthusiasm and promise as a school leader replaced me. She would carry on the work of building a collaborative approach to learning in our program. Prior to leaving I had hired a young man who had been a student a few years earlier in Philadelphia. The value of working with others in ways that encourage their own growth as leaders had come full circle.

MAKING A DIFFERENCE AS A SCHOOL LEADER

It took a few years after moving to Maine to reenter education. I did as a teacher at the local high school. But it wasn't long before I felt the pangs that had once touched me years ago and saw in the faces of these rural students much of the same frustration that I had seen years earlier in city youth. The color of the faces had changed, but many other issues remained the same. Leadership at the school had been a revolving door over the past several years, and I soon found myself stepping into my first formal role as a school leader when I became the part-time assistant principal. Within a year, I was the principal in a school where principals came and went every year or two. I stayed for eleven.

How? Why? The challenges were abundant in this small school, but I soon learned that I had a few assets that would serve me well. First, I had a wealth of varied experience in my past to call on, both as a teacher leader and as a director of a small alternative school. Second, I had learned through these experiences the critical importance of valuing positive working relationships based on trust with teachers and among teachers. Third, I had lived and worked in the community for 3 years and, even though "from away," had a non-educator sense of what community members viewed as important in their local schools. Combining these assets magnified their potential for making a difference as a school leader in this setting. I hoped to address issues left festering from years of avoidance and build bridges among staff, with students, and with parents, all within a community often torn apart by its adversarial (or was it love-hate?) relationship with its schools.

Over the Christmas break when I moved into the principal's office I realized in one day how different it felt for me to sit in this chair. With it came the formal authority and power that come with the position. I felt somewhat awed, somewhat uncertain, but in the end relatively confident in my abilities to step into the role. What kind of principal would I be? It was the 1980s, and I saw myself as the instructional leader that I should be, based on the professional reading I had done and the few courses I had taken to become certified as a principal. Steeped in the effective schools literature of the time, I clearly understood the importance of the principal in moving a school forward in its efforts to improve student learning.

However, I had never been a "power over" kind of person. Too many examples of the strength of relationships built "through" others permeated my professional life. Thus I entered this new stage with "me-as-leader" seeking to provide the strong leadership the school required while at the same time encouraging teachers to take more active roles in the life of the school outside of their classrooms. I was certainly willing and able to provide direction but immediately ran into the refrain that "time spent out of the classroom was time taken away from students, and of course that is why I became a teacher, to work with kids, not with adults." The challenge of involving others to look beyond their own classroom and think about the school as a larger entity and the importance of the interplay between the school and classroom manifested itself to me on a daily basis during those early days of my tenure.

Persistence over time counts. Just being there as principal month after month, year after year, allowed me to build a working relationship with many members of the staff. This was fertile ground to till after years of high turnover in the principalship. Taking advantage of the enthusiasm of a few teachers to test the waters beyond the classroom and broaden their responsibilities allowed these pioneers to stretch in terms of their own learning and provide models for others. Their development followed a typical pattern: holding individual conversations about hot-button issues leading to informal small group meetings about such issues or about challenging students; becoming members of task committees evolving into chairing such work; then taking on primary leadership responsibility for special projects and initiatives. There was nothing magical about the process, just small steps leading toward a larger goal. The value of persistence coupled with ways to recognize and reward staff for such effort turned the tide. Teacher-led suggestions and initiatives surfaced and benefited students in ways that justified the commitment beyond the classroom.

In the 1990s, my professional study enhanced my understanding of leadership. I had the opportunity to take a leave of absence from my principalship for a year and work with a cohort of teachers, principals, university professors, and other school leaders in a unique, federally funded leadership development program. As one of the two facilitators in the program, riding circuit from school to school, working with a variety of school leaders, my understanding grew tremendously. I was excited about exploring models of shared leadership in schools and examining the tremendous potential of personal growth. The program emphasized the importance of interpersonal relationships when leading and building collegial communities of leaders and learners. The dynamic power of relational influence was at the heart of the learning for many involved in the program.

Funding, though, was short-lived, and after the completion of one cycle of the program I returned to my school district. I was even more aware of some of the inherent pitfalls, contradictions, and, at times, overwhelming responsibility in the role of principal as the sole instructional leader working with others to encourage leadership toward common school goals. The conundrum that increasingly puzzled me, stated simply, was, Whose vision, goals, and school improvement initiatives were these? Whose should they be? Could the responsibility for developing them be shared to build ownership in them and to lessen the burden I was increasingly feeling?

Principals are expected to steer the ship of school. At the same time, they're expected to negotiate the hazards of the sea and not rock the boat too severely. As my thinking progressed, this image was challenged as

I saw "me-as-leader' diminish and "us-as-leaders" begin to emerge. However such an evolution of thinking and acting on such thoughts threatens the traditional structure of the principalship as we know it. How does one effectively relinquish control while still being "captain" of the ship and begin to share "power with" others?

DEMOCRATIC LEADERSHIP

In the mid-1990s, I moved to another high school, one that was progressive in its philosophy and well supported by its community. It was one of the few high schools in the state that I would even consider moving to since I so enjoyed the school and community that I had lived in for the past 17 years. Once there, though, I began to understand and experience leadership with others ever more deeply.

In the move to the new school I entered one that had three times the number of faculty members than the previous school. It meant a challenging adjustment and a significant learning curve for me. My direct, hands-on approach would not work in such a setting, and I quickly realized that I would have to rely on, and trust, others to a much greater extent than ever before. This reality certainly pushed me even more quickly than anticipated in the direction of letting go of even greater amounts of direct involvement and leadership than I had been contemplating a short time ago.

I have a hard time imagining a more conducive environment in which to do so. One of the school's cornerstones of success was a history of whole-school engagement. Faculty members were actively immersed in the decision-making process in the school already, so I was able to take this readiness one step further and move toward even more egalitarian forms of problem identification, discussion, and school improvement initiatives. Structures already existed within the school for active teacher leadership, and we took steps to genuinely involve students in leadership roles in a wide variety of ways. Where structures didn't exist to address a need, teachers readily came forward with their thoughts and willingly put vast amounts of time into making these new ideas a reality. "Us-as-leaders" became the norm. As a facilitative leader in such a setting, I needed to take a step back, trust others, stay out of the way of creative people, and do my best to foster the opportunities and provide the resources they needed to do their work on behalf of students. There was no student that the faculty felt they couldn't work with if they put their hearts and minds to it. Such a plethora of possibilities existed that I thought I was decades younger and back in Philadelphia again.

Why would I leave a school where such shared responsibility for leading, teaching, and learning was the norm? A combination of circumstances conspired to thrust me into a new and different role. The opportunity arose, first to work in a statewide leadership role on issues of high school reform and then shortly thereafter the chance to help resurrect and create anew the school-based leadership development program for both teachers and principals. The program focused on teachers and principals learning within the action of their schools as well as from one another. A central tenet of the program was that leadership was not role bound. Remembering the sense of excitement in exploring these waters, I left the principalship and entered a world in which I would be working with teachers and principals to help them find their own leadership paths.

In this new role, I felt I could influence learning about and experiencing leadership in new and different ways. In turn, the individuals with whom I worked could influence others in their own schools and districts. Over the decades my thinking about leadership and my ability to put those thoughts into action with others had evolved. There were stories and experiences to be shared with others so that they might benefit just as I had benefited from working with other school leaders who came before me. From the hot, stifling pavement of Philadelphia in summer to the cold, snowy roads of Maine in winter, there are lessons about leadership for all of us to share so that we might grow together and share the leadership of our schools on behalf of our students.

27

Taking on Teacher Leadership

A Foray Into Netherland

JoAnne C. Dowd

Good teacher leaders know how to negotiate, and sometimes they have to for the greater good and vision of the school. Good teacher leaders must demonstrate moral courage and take a stand when needed. Good teacher leaders know that they walk in the netherland between teacher and administrator. Good teacher leaders have an innate understanding that how we need to do school now is not in alignment with how principals traditionally work. We cannot allow the administration to shoulder the whole burden and responsibility for change.

—Rural high school English teacher

The purpose of this chapter is to help the reader understand the complexities of current structures in schools, structures that do not allow for the comfortable existence of teacher leadership. This chapter acknowledges the existence of informal leadership for change, leadership that happens in every school building, regardless of where the school is in terms of change. Even schools that are not actively engaged in reform have a handful of passionate and committed teacher leaders who want change to happen on behalf of students.

Individuals who emerge as teacher leaders are action-oriented. They are passionate, successful classroom teachers who understand that the needs of their students go beyond the four walls of the classroom. This understanding compels them to become involved in initiatives and to act as advocates on behalf of students. Although they do a commendable job of meeting the needs of their students in the classroom, they are not content to stay within those boundaries. Because they understand their students so well, they feel obligated to reach beyond their classroom walls. They recognize that the structures of schools do not always serve to benefit students. This awareness, coupled with a strong desire to help their students, urges them to act.

Who are these teachers? What impels them to take on these roles? What frustrations do they experience as they undertake leadership activities? What structures seem to get in the way of reform? Why, despite resistance, do they persist? In order to explore these questions I sought out teacher leaders from a variety of schools. The schools vary in size and in their public pursuit of change. The smallest school is in a rural, impoverished town, the largest a highly traditional urban high school. The teachers are men and women in various stages of their careers. I have tried to remain true to the ideas presented to me by these teachers, though at times I have summarized their words and combined their thoughts for clarity. I interviewed and scripted the responses of 15 teacher leaders using the same set of questions in each interview. I traced patterns that appeared in their comments and emerged with a clear picture of what type of teacher becomes a teacher leader, what drives them to take on leadership roles, and why they persist (or not). This chapter will flesh out the patterns and categories with voices of the teacher leaders asked to elucidate their commitment to ensure that their schools meet the needs of all young people.

Teacher leadership in the context of this chapter includes a range of experiences. There are teacher leaders who have simply started asking difficult questions out loud about the structures of their school that may not work for all students. Some have started discussion groups among colleagues, with or without official sanction, whereas some have been appointed department head by the principal. Included are teachers engaged in a graduate program on teacher leadership who are trying new techniques in their school and teachers who are on leadership teams in their buildings who facilitate professional development for their colleagues. In most cases teacher leaders are not paid above and beyond their teaching responsibilities.

A SENSE OF MISSION

*In the end I feel that what I am doing is right. If I am going to step out
on a limb, I have to have a moral belief that what I am doing is right.*

—Urban high school English teacher

The teacher leaders interviewed have in common a strong inner drive and
a compulsion to take action on the behalf of students. Their need to do
what they feel is right overpowers any sense of hesitancy about how they
will be perceived by their colleagues. Although they are aware that their
actions at times cause consternation among their peers and even at times
their administrators, their sense of urgency is powerful. One teacher said,
"I feel school simply does not work for all students. What motivates me is
the students and their achievement."

The teachers interviewed come from a place of moral fortitude rather
than one of ego or self-aggrandizement. They are willing to take risks. One
teacher requires her seniors to apply to a college, despite the fact that the
school traditionally has sent only 30% of its students on to higher education. Although criticized by colleagues, she believes she is doing the right
thing on behalf of her students.

Teacher leaders have an awareness of purpose larger than themselves
and their individual classrooms. They have an investment in changing the
educational system while simultaneously reaching students in their individual classrooms. One teacher saw a pitfall in not becoming involved. "A
leadership role keeps me from being isolated. I might sink into complacency
and isolation; staying involved makes me a better teacher and leader." They
see themselves as pathmakers, questioning the possibilities among many
avenues the school could follow. They are interested in making school a relevant experience for all students. Even as they try to inject a different point
of view, they know their views are not always appreciated.

A TEACHER FIRST

*We must find ways to share the burden as teacher leaders and still work
to teach successfully in our classrooms.*

—Rural high school social studies teacher

The driving force for this group of dedicated educators is service to
students. They involve themselves in the aspects of schooling that will
most benefit all students. Leadership activities are secondary to their work
as teachers. Lifelong learners, they take lessons from their work with
adults and use them to become better teachers. One social studies teacher

said, "Good teacher leaders will invest in making good students great. It is important to model what you want to see happen."

Many teacher leaders notice a strong positive correlation between their leadership work and their teaching. "In the process of sharing ideas with colleagues, I become more reflective and thus improve my own teaching." Taking on leadership roles has a positive effect on how these teachers work with their students. "I'm a much better teacher. I am running a more effective classroom. Students' needs are more clearly met because I am involving them in decision making . . . because I realize the traditional ways of 'doing school' don't necessarily make sense." One interviewee noted, "I need to remember to keep student learning at the center of all my thoughts when it comes to how schools are organized and how they function." At times taking on leadership roles reminds these teachers of the ultimate goal of education. "It is my job to keep students at the center of my influence and thinking." One teacher said, "Being involved in teacher leadership makes my classroom experience richer."

Teachers who become leaders often cite the problems of time and competing priorities. The work of school can be draining and frustrating. One teacher says, "Sometimes I just feel overwhelmed, sad, and frustrated, because I am not always the best person I can be with my students." Many of the teachers interviewed note that these additional commitments, such as committee work, community meetings, creation and facilitation of professional development, and work at the district level, are carved out of personal time, family time, and sleep.

Despite these drawbacks, most of those interviewed preferred their nebulous teacher leader roles over becoming administrators. "That aspect of the profession is unappealing to me. I most enjoy being with students; I would find the current day-to-day bureaucracy very discouraging." They express joy in their current positions and view administrative work as thankless, consuming, and overwhelming. They find their time with students uplifting.

COURAGE, RISK, AND SELF-AWARENESS

Act from the love in your heart, and together we can move in a direction that is good for our kids.

—Rural high school social studies teacher

This group of teachers describes how they become aware that a need exists and they self-select a teacher leadership position to help meet that perceived need. They are passionate educators who have the needs of their students at the forefront of their minds at all times. They also expressed personal qualities such as curiosity, a need to understand the *why* of the organization, a desire for action, and even "bossiness." Despite the lack of definition, status, and parameters, they make the choice to become and remain involved in the work of the school outside of their classrooms. They forge ahead in this educational netherland. Whereas many teachers are content to remain in the classroom without becoming involved in the school at large, as a group these teacher leaders feel compelled to do something more than spending their days and careers in the classroom, alone, with the door closed. One teacher leader who voluntarily took on rewriting the curriculum for her grade level said, "I am not one to sit back and watch things happen around me. I want to make things happen. I like to be involved and see things from all different points of view."

Willing to take on the difficult task of understanding the alternative points of view of their colleagues, the group honors the diversity of voices that exists in a school community. "I like challenging myself to suspend judgment and truly hear others' voices." One teacher leader who volunteered to take over facilitation of the school's barely functioning leadership team stated, "I am always asking myself, 'How can I lead and keep open, but also have my own voice within the conversation?' An important part of leadership is allowing others to grow and come to a new place."

Many interviewees recognize that keys to successful leadership are feeling empathy, listening to colleagues, and accepting views different from one's own. A teacher who began informal dialogue groups among her colleagues said, "It is important to start with people where they are. They need to be on the road with you."

RELATIONSHIPS AND THE HUMAN FACTOR

I have content knowledge and teaching experience, but I have never had training in how to deal with the relationship aspect of things. I have had to learn how to deal with groups and individual people.

—Suburban high school mathematics department head

These teacher leaders understand the importance of modeling positive behaviors for their colleagues and their students. They understand the power of "walking the talk" and often take risks in their classrooms by making their classrooms democratic, interactive places for students. They also model taking risks with their colleagues by their willingness to speak out; join and lead committees and work teams; and identify, research, plan, and implement professional development for colleagues. They are willing to state the need for, create, join, and even facilitate, school leadership teams. They exhibit behaviors such as a willingness to understand others, courage to take risks, and willingness to ask hard questions even though they might make others uncomfortable. These teachers have an awareness of good communication skills and an understanding of relationships and group dynamics. "Potential leaders have the courage to take risks, be supportive, and be aware of colleagues who look at things differently but may not always be good at expressing themselves." One teacher called it the human factor.

Other skills important to success in teacher leadership are organization, willingness to follow through, and commitment to a democratic process. Also mentioned are the ability to set goals, solve problems, and elicit the best from colleagues by recognizing their skills and knowledge. A leader knows how to access resources. Not to be underestimated, these new leaders need to be able to brush off verbal and nonverbal challenges from their colleagues. One interviewee stated that the skills for effective teacher leadership are the same as those for good leadership at any level. "The skills of a teacher are the same as those of a good principal or assistant: strong communication, vision, a deep understanding of systems and how they work, and always, always the desire to serve students, the community, and the faculty." One teacher pointed out the importance of modeling: "It is harder to be the one that has to model the changes you propose for the school. Whatever decisions I come to, I actually have to go back in my classroom and do it."

LEADERSHIP AT THE BUILDING LEVEL

The relationship that administration has with teacher leaders will affect the relationship that teachers have with their students.

—Suburban high school mathematics teacher

An important factor in the success of teacher leadership is strong modeling at the building level. The work of teacher leaders is nearly impossible without someone who is competent and visionary at the forefront. Teacher leaders that are most positive and enthusiastic about their undertakings have mentors who are equally enthusiastic and encouraging. Principals they work for ask difficult questions, have high expectations of themselves and their staff, are strong communicators and have a long-range vision for the school that includes meeting the needs of all students. These principals exhibit courage by saying difficult things out loud and articulating the direction of the school. Compensation appears to have very little to do with whether or not teacher leaders feel their efforts are worthwhile. In most cases all they need is support from their building leader and from their colleagues. "I can make suggestions, write a proposal, organize an initiative, and get a timely response from our principal. I actually think I am an influential member of the staff."

In situations where administrators were not as supportive, teacher leaders express frustration and despair. One interviewee outlined her experience in a school that held onto its very traditional top-down structure and atmosphere of complacence. As a person who was willing to ask hard questions out loud, she did not feel at all validated. "I am not supported or understood by my principal. She doesn't understand the role of teacher leadership."

Another teacher leader, who worked in a building that had a significant grassroots movement to more effectively meet the needs of its impoverished students by trying to increase the percentage of students who pursued postsecondary education said, "My administrator did not see a need to communicate differently or to think systemically. I could not handle the added responsibilities in addition to the negativity of some staff."

Many interviewees questioned the current structure and hierarchy in schools, saying that collaborative work involving more voices would be effective and efficient. The very structures themselves seem to be a hindrance to the emergence of multiple voices for change. "Unless we redesign the role of administration, we will find these positions to be more and more hazardous and short term. Collaborative work is what excites me."

This group had advice for both building-level and district-level leadership. They embraced the idea of creating more opportunities for teachers to take on leadership roles both formally and informally: for example, creating action teams, leadership teams, smaller learning communities, advisory boards, professional learning communities, and groups to design and implement professional development. They also had suggestions for how administrators communicate and do business. "Don't just assume teacher leadership will happen without structural support to allow it to develop." They strongly suggested that administrators ask for input, use it, and let people know how suggestions were implemented. "Designate others to complete tasks. If teachers, like students, are challenged with authentic leadership tasks and given the tools to complete them, they will learn better leadership skills."

TREADING INTO NETHERLAND

We have a culture that cannot reward or celebrate each other's good work. Our faculty does not understand how to work in this model. They are more used to a patriarchal/hierarchical approach. This view disallows the faculty from taking responsibility for decisions. They don't see leading as their job.

—Rural high school English teacher

There is something about the structure of the teaching profession, as well as perhaps the type of people that gravitate toward the profession, that doesn't allow for formal and informal leadership to be authentically pursued or acknowledged. Almost every interviewee described a scenario in which some colleagues were supportive and grateful for their leadership pursuits. Others were suspicious and even outright hostile toward them. It is an interesting phenomenon. Teachers don't want to be singled out or to single themselves out. Often colleagues question the motives or express jealousy of those pursuing leadership in their perceived elevated status. "The faculty perceives my work as some kind of access to power. They don't think outside the box. They don't want power or change. The faculty believes I have some other agenda."

The questioning attitude of, "Who made you the boss?" seems to pervade, especially in larger schools and in schools with weaker or more traditional leadership structures. "Sometimes I experience resentfulness from peers, resentfulness from my administrator, reflected in the words: 'How dare you question. You are being insubordinate.'"

The work of teacher leadership, informal and without title or label, takes place in an ill-defined space that is wide open for miscommunication and misinterpretation by colleagues. "I had to learn the hard way what is true versus what is false. I need to become more adept at thoughtfully responding in unfamiliar and challenging situations." Almost all interviewees describe a sense of being caught between two worlds, where motives are questioned and assumptions made about accepting leadership roles. The strength of leadership in the building and the amount of time a school has been engaged in the reform process play a role in skepticism and hostility of colleagues and administrators. The involvement of teachers in reform often reveals an undercurrent of "us" versus "them" that is not publicly expressed. "I am perceived by colleagues as no longer upholding the interest of teachers and of changing allegiance."

Most interviewees mention a split in the faculty, with one segment being appreciative and the other resentful. One teacher celebrates the ability to be more reflective with his colleagues, and another speaks about the painful loneliness that can result from attempting to lead change. "I lost friends and found out that teacher leadership means one is alone. It is scary and lonely to deal with adults in this building."

"What advice would you give to colleagues interested in taking on teacher leadership roles?" I asked. The responses included the following: "There's not enough time. You have to be willing to extend yourself." "The more staff members are involved in decision making, the greater is the acceptance of change." "It is added work and time, but it is nice to be part of something positive."

CONCLUSION

Courageous teacher leaders bridge the gap between schools as they are and schools as they might be. They remain committed to their students, whom they teach every day, but are able to engage simultaneously in a larger discussion about what needs to happen in schools to make them more effective for all students. Often school structures are too rigid to allow teachers to successfully navigate both roles. Many schools do not acknowledge or value the work done by these dual-role professionals. Too often, schools' decision-making structures remain entirely top-down with little room for alternative views or solutions. We must reexamine the current structure of schools to make room for more teachers at the decision-making table. Without this voice, we are missing a vital link to successful schools for all students.

28

To Lead or Not to Lead?

A Quandary for Newly Tenured Teachers

Morgaen L. Donaldson

THE PERFECT NEXT STEP

It was the day before the winter break, and I fell into step with my principal as we walked through the snow to the auditorium, the site of our school's annual Winter Fest concert. As a third-year high school teacher, I had just started to feel at ease in the classroom. I knew how to plan a curriculum backwards, starting with the course objectives; I could develop a strong lesson; I had talked to students about everything from their academics to their behavior to serious issues that were affecting their lives, like sexual harassment or their parents' divorce. Although I was far from an expert pedagogue, I was beginning to feel comfortable as a teacher.

"So what are you going to do next?" asked my principal, startling me. I had been planning my Christmas shopping, not considering my next career move. "Well," I thought a moment, "I'm not sure. I like teaching, and I love the kids. But there is a part of me that wants to be involved on a larger scale, in writing and research." "You have to be a principal," my principal declared, "It's the perfect next step for you."

So began my interest in teachers' careers. As a teacher, I faced a number of career choices. Should I follow my principal's advice and enroll in an administrative certification program? Should I become a department head? Should I try out this mysterious new thing called National Board

Certification? Could I remain in the classroom and "lead" by developing my expertise in instruction itself? Ultimately, drawn by the lure of books and the challenge of conducting original research, I left teaching after 5 years to pursue a doctorate.

As a researcher, I now study teachers, including those who have received tenure but are still in their early careers. Among other things, I have inquired into how these early-career teachers conceive of a career in teaching and how they make career choices. Predictably, perhaps, I have asked them some of the very questions with which I struggled as a teacher. This chapter focuses on several questions that recurred in the narratives of early-career teachers whom I interviewed in 2004: If they continue to work in schools, are they more interested in becoming a principal or a teacher leader? Why do they see one route as more realistic or rewarding than the other? Are they interested in both types of roles, or does neither appeal to them?

NEEDED: A NEW GENERATION OF SCHOOL LEADERS

As a researcher, I knew that such questions were not only personally interesting to me but also important more broadly, to policy and practice. Our schools need good leaders and research suggests that they may be in short supply. Based on numerous accounts, the educator workforce is aging. Principals and teachers are growing older, on average, and retirements from both the classroom and the front office have increased in recent years (e.g., Cusick, 2003; Gates, Ringel, Santibanez, Ross, & Chung, 2003; Whiting & National Education Association, 2003; Young, 2003). Researchers and school leaders have begun to ask who will take the place of these veterans, many of whom have spent decades educating the nation's children.

Schools and districts need capable leaders, both principals and teachers, to function well. Yet, as retirements slowly deplete the ranks of these leaders, there is some evidence that today's early-career teachers—those who might step into those roles—eschew administrative positions (Cusick, 2003; Stricherz, 2001) but are attracted to formal teacher leadership roles (Johnson & the Project on the Next Generation of Teachers, 2004).

Outside of these studies, however, the research community has produced little empirical evidence that considers in detail how current, early-career teachers weigh the option of entering administration and the option of pursuing teacher leadership. Specifically, we know little about how early-career teachers assess leadership roles in urban schools and districts, where, arguably, consistent and effective leadership is most needed. In urban schools the retention of principals (Gates et al., 2003; Rand Corporation, 2004; Stricherz, 2001) and teachers (Hanushek, Kain, & Rivkin, 2004; Lankford, Loeb, & Wyckoff, 2002; Loeb & Reininger, 2004) is particularly difficult, which makes the question of principal and teacher leader recruitment in urban settings especially pressing.

Currently, many important questions stand unanswered. Do early-career teachers see the option to become a principal and the option to become a teacher leader as mutually exclusive or as steps on a logical career progression? In an urban context, what sorts of leadership roles appeal more than others and why? How, in the view of these teachers, do leadership roles compare with classroom teaching? Do these teachers believe it is possible to lead without leaving the classroom to enter a formal leadership role?

Therefore, on a pragmatic level, research is needed to inform efforts to recruit high-quality administrative and teacher leaders to guide urban schools and districts in the coming decades. Research is also needed to inform efforts to reform principals' and teacher leaders' jobs in ways that are likely to support and sustain the people who take these jobs and make them their most productive. Thus, my personal interest is also of larger interest to teachers, principals, policymakers, and researchers.

The Teachers

Convinced that this topic was worth investigating, in 2004, I conducted a study based on interviews with 12 teachers who were newly tenured, which I defined as having taught between 4 and 6 years. I chose to focus on newly tenured teachers for two reasons. First, these teachers have invested several years in teaching and, statistics suggest, are more committed to staying in teaching than their less-experienced counterparts (Murnane, Singer, Willett, Kemple, & Olsen, 1991). Second, newly tenured teachers have passed the only formal milestone of the traditional teaching career: tenure. Having earned tenure, they may be wondering what to do next and may be logical candidates for teacher leadership and administrative positions in the future.

Because I was interested in how these teachers were experiencing their careers within their schools, I first selected five urban high schools within a large metropolitan area in the northeastern United States. These schools enrolled between 1,200 and 1,900 students, many of whom were students of color from low-income households. I then carefully selected a sample of teachers within these high schools (2–3 per school) who were relatively diverse in gender, race, age, and subject matter. I collected data through 60- to 90-minute interviews with each of the 12 teachers. I followed a semi-structured interview protocol that included questions about how these teachers wanted to develop their teaching careers and whether they had found support for the careers they envisioned in their schools. Because I was examining these teachers' conceptions of professional growth within a teaching career, I did not explicitly inquire into their definitions of teacher leadership. Instead, I asked them about whether and how they were building a long-term career in teaching, what they found appealing in terms of career development, and the extent to which they believed their school and district provided what they would need to construct a satisfying teaching career.

To Lead or Not to Lead, and How?

In analyzing the data, I found that most teachers in this sample were not interested in pursuing a position in administration but were attracted to particular teacher leadership roles. Overall, the teachers felt principals had less control over their own work than classroom teachers; did less meaningful work than teachers; and encountered more challenges to their integrity than classroom teachers did. In contrast, these teachers felt teacher leadership roles such as union representative or faculty senate president would allow them an opportunity to influence their schools while continuing to do meaningful work in teaching students. A few teachers were not interested in pursuing formal leadership roles of any sort and preferred instead to focus within their classrooms, developing relationships with their students and honing their craft.

Dislike for the Principalship

The teachers I interviewed generally were not interested in becoming principals. They came to this decision based on observing and working with principals in their own schools. Admittedly, several of these teachers said they did not know what principals did on a day-to-day basis. Yet, despite their lack of information, these teachers had generally decided not to pursue a position in the front office. Frank, a White, sixth-year science teacher said directly, "I don't want to be an administrator." Similarly, Mac, a White 50-year-old former Air Force major, summed it up, saying that he had "no desire whatsoever" to become a principal.

Lacking Control

One reason that these teachers rejected the principalship as a career option was that they felt that principals, compared to teachers, had less control over their work. Julius, a fourth-year African American math teacher, had applied for his district's principal-preparation program. He was rejected, but he said he would not apply elsewhere. At the time of his interview, Julius was not interested in becoming a principal. He said this was due to principals' lack of control, which he described this way:

> The principal doesn't run that building. The principal is just a sergeant executing the plans of the superintendent. The superintendent only cares about numbers, results. "Is your school performing

well on the state tests? Yes or no." If you say "no," then you have a hundred legitimate reasons, "90% of my school is special ed." He [the superintendent] doesn't take that into consideration. It's just "Did you pass the state test? Yes or no."

Julius concluded that he would not pursue administration because, as a principal in his large, urban district, he felt he would not "directly have input on the environment that I'm in."

Another teacher I interviewed, Agatha, also thought the principal had little power. This fourth-year White special education teacher said, "I think our principal is micromanaged from the superintendent. And his hands are tied. I think there's a lot of things he'd rather see, but she's [the superintendent] in the building." She believed the principal was "being watched" by the superintendent, who occupied an office in the high school building. For this reason, she said the job of principal did not appeal to her.

Overall, many teachers felt that principals had, in one teacher's words, "their hands tied behind their back." Based on this perception, these teachers did not consider the principalship to be a viable career option. In general, they recognized that their schools needed positive change but felt that principals had little power to make such alterations. Instead, these teachers felt that principals took their orders from superintendents and had little freedom to implement their own solutions to the problems their schools encountered.

Lacking Meaning

These teachers perceived the work of the principal as lacking meaning as well as being devoid of real power. Some teachers felt that being a principal meant devoting countless hours to completing mundane paperwork. Mac explained his choice not to pursue administration: "Because of my experience in procurement, which was administrative minutiae, I realized not only what I want but what I don't want, and I just hate paperwork, you know?" Similarly, Frank said he would not pursue administration because he felt administrators' work was "tedious . . . I don't like forms. I don't like papers."

Some teachers extended this logic, reasoning that, as a principal, they would be consumed by tedious and even absurd tasks that took them away from the more meaningful work of educating young people. Lacey, a White fourth-year social studies teacher, captured this view:

The state department of education is a mess. And they keep changing, you know, the lawmakers come in and change all the rules, and you [as a principal] have to do this and jump through that. And I just think having to deal with all the constituencies is not something that I would enjoy. And plus, you're so removed from the kids. And I definitely enjoy that interaction. It gives me a lot of energy.

Similarly, when asked whether she wanted to become a principal, Jasmine, an African American fifth-year math teacher, said:

> No, no. No way, principal. You know, walk around with a walkie [talkie]. No. Not even a dean in a high school. Because they're too far away from the kids . . . when you're teaching, you get to know that 60 or 100 kids that are yours, and you get to really bond with them. That's why if I became an administrator or any more leadership role, I'd have to be teaching, or else I wouldn't do it because I wouldn't get the interpersonal relations with the kids that I would just really miss. As much as they get on my nerves, I love them anyway.

In choosing whether to spend time responding to ever-changing state directives and prowling the school halls with a walkie-talkie or teaching students, Lacey and Jasmine emphatically chose the latter.

Lacking Integrity

A third reason these teachers gave for avoiding the principalship was their view that principals served so many constituencies that their values were inevitably compromised. Many teachers said they would not consider pursuing administration because of the "politics" that engulfed the front office. Others recounted times in which their own principals seemed to cave in the face of pressure from various interest groups.

Lacey had thought about pursuing administration and felt that she could be a good principal. However, she commented, "I don't think I'd want to be an administrator. It's much too political a job . . . the fact that the school committee, everybody's got their agenda, which, you know, everybody cases each other for which kids they're looking out for." Thus, she avoided taking this career path because of her aversion to "politics."

Julius also characterized administration as political in a negative sense. He questioned the selection of principals, ultimately concluding that people who were connected politically received appointments, rather than those best suited to the job. He explained his view of how the superintendent tried to fire one principal whom Julius respected:

> The district sends stuff down to him. He looks at them and says, "Okay, these are the rules, how are they going to apply to my school?" And then he applies it. But at the same time he backs his teachers 100%, he backs his students 100%. The superintendent? Trying to get rid of him. So I see a trend . . . of bad principals in buildings. They're more business people instead of managers. . . . So I'm done with it.

Amy, a White fourth-year English teacher, felt that becoming a principal required a person to compromise her values for, as she described, "political" ends. Based on this assessment, she said she could not become a principal because, she explained, "I have high standards, I think I'd ruffle a lot of feathers." She frowned on her principal's decision not to discipline certain students, particularly star athletes, and felt that he had capitulated to parental pressure. She recalled incidents in which "kids [came to] dances who are three sheets to the wind, and nothing's done about it. There's no consequence." In contrast, she said, "I'm a very 'Hey, let's make a rule, consequence, action.'" For this reason, Amy preferred not to become an administrator since she felt doing so would subject her to pressure from parents and other community members to bend rules. Instead of becoming a principal and battling to act in accordance with her values, Amy preferred to maintain integrity within her own classroom.

Some teachers I interviewed had little respect for the principals with whom they had worked. Julius declared,

> I've come across in my three schools one administrator that I can respect 100%, one out of three principals . . . and the reason I could respect her 100% is because she put her kids first and for her it was all about the kids. I've seen her take the hit from the union about removing a teacher that didn't want to teach. She had those qualities because in order for her kids to be okay, her teachers had to be okay.

By contrast, the other principals and assistant principals with whom he had worked had not made decisions based on students' best interests, and he respected them less as a result. Deb, a White fifth-year, science teacher, was even more biting in her critique of principals' integrity. She declared that she would "never" pursue a principal's position. In her view, principals "are usually slimy. They usually have stabbed someone in the back." Deb, like many of the other teachers I interviewed, preferred to continue teaching and become involved in some form of teacher leadership.

An Enticing Opportunity

A few teachers I interviewed were interested in pursuing the principalship. These teachers felt that their schools needed change and that they could lead such change from the principal's office. Importantly, each of the teachers who viewed an administrative career path favorably identified a strong principal role model—someone who showed them that principals could make a difference, do important work, and maintain their integrity. Interestingly, both of these teachers were African American, and, in both cases, these teachers' principal role models were of the same race and gender. The opportunity to connect with a principal of the same race and gender may be what made these teachers more interested in pursuing administration than the other teachers I interviewed, some of whom worked in the same schools, with the same administrators, as these teachers.

Generally, however, the teachers I interviewed felt that the front office had less to offer them than the classroom. Becoming a principal, they felt, would make them less autonomous, their work less meaningful, and might require them to compromise their values. They preferred to continue teaching, at least for the short term.

The Appeal of Particular Teacher Leadership Roles

Although most teachers I interviewed did not find becoming a principal appealing, many said they were interested in pursuing certain teacher leadership roles. In fact, several of those teachers who wanted to make teaching a long-term career saw teacher leadership roles as critical to sustaining them.[1] However, these teachers wanted to remain in the classroom at least part-time while taking on a special role. These teachers tended to avoid teacher leadership roles that they judged to lack meaning, control, or integrity—the very characteristics that caused them to shun principals' roles. As discussed elsewhere (Donaldson, 2005), instructionally focused roles such as literacy coach also appealed less to the whole sample than roles such as union representative, which were less directly focused on instruction.

In general, these teachers found teacher leadership roles that enabled them to influence school processes appealing. Mac, for instance, served on one committee to reorganize his comprehensive high school into smaller units and another that analyzed standardized-test data. He explained, "I always like to have some control or influence over [things]; at least I want to know what's going to happen before it happens." At the same time, he emphasized his interest in the classroom:

> We used to have a saying in the Air Force. There were some guys who were pilots who never wanted to go to the Pentagon, but they knew in order to get promoted, they had to go to the Pentagon. And they say, "Look. I'm a good stick. I'm a good pilot. Why can't I just get promoted, being good at what I do?" And that's kind of the way I feel about the classroom. You know? I'm a good teacher. And I can be a great teacher. And that's what I want to do.

Many of these teachers had already taken on leadership roles, in addition to their classroom teaching, to influence the work of their schools.

"Having a Say" in School Practices and Policies

Several teachers pursued teacher leadership roles to change how their schools functioned. For some, this meant becoming involved with their local teachers union. For others, it meant working on committees responsible for reforming the structure or policies of the school.

Agatha was one teacher who had become a union representative early in her teaching career. She decided to get involved because, as an expectant mother, she felt the district's family leave policy was inadequate. She explained,

> I was so disgusted with our policies regarding maternity leave, you know, family leave. [The way the policy] was worded, you know, I think when the majority of women didn't go back to work after they had a child, and it bothered me. And no one could give me clear-cut answers on how much leave I had, what time I could use. And I was frustrated because there's a lot of young teachers here now, all having children. So we just wanted something in the contract more concrete. We just wanted people to recognize that there should be leave for fathers, too. My husband's in the system. He's a teacher. They said, "Okay, you have three personal days." When we had our first child, I didn't think three personal days was enough. And that was my major issue. And now that I'm there, you know, I enjoy knowing what's going on. I enjoy having a say in it.

Agatha became involved in the teachers union to change school policies that directly affected her.

Like Agatha, Paul, a White fourth-year math teacher, was not interested in pursuing a principalship but had volunteered to be a union representative. He did so specifically because he was interested in reforming teachers' pay to compensate them for their performance in the classroom.

Deb also was interested in getting involved with her local teachers union. She said, "Part of the reason I left being a chemist [her first career] was because I was interested in being a union activist. And I believe that the unions really can change and shape social policy." However, Deb, like Agatha and Paul, wanted her union to change. She singled out the traditional secrecy of the union as one of many things that "aren't going to really fly any longer with the younger people." By becoming involved with her union, Deb felt she could make a difference within the union and in the wider world.

Other teachers found other opportunities to influence reforms under way in their schools. Lacey volunteered to represent her colleagues on her school's council. She did this "to understand how everything works: the administration, the relationships with the community, the parents and the administration, the school committee, and the state department of education." In addition to serving as a union representative, Agatha had been involved in efforts to make her school's discipline policies clearer and more consistent by reforming the student handbook. She took on these roles because, as she said, "I like being involved in things that potentially could change the school . . . things that are going to strengthen our school." Mac echoed her comment: "I like to get outside of my classroom and find out what else is going on in the school."

Pursuing New Challenges

The second reason the teachers I interviewed were interested in teacher leadership was to pursue new challenges as they progressed in a teaching career. Some of these teachers were in their 30s and willing to devote up to 30 more years to a teaching career. Other teachers, who had entered teaching after spending considerable time in another line of work, were facing a shorter period in the classroom. Both first-career and midcareer entrants to teaching agreed that teachers would need new roles to sustain a lengthy career in the classroom.

Terrence was an African American midcareer entrant to teaching who pursued teacher leadership roles because they provided intellectual challenges. In his school, Terrence had already served as faculty senate chairperson and participated on a committee that designed the new block schedule. He explained that he took on these roles because he

> enjoy[ed] that adult interaction and the problem solving, I guess sort of my research background coming out there, and I thought that I'd made a positive contribution on trying to troubleshoot, you know, what are we dealing with, where are we headed, what type of clientele do we serve, and where do we think we want to take these folks?

Terrence enjoyed the opportunity to apply the skills he had developed in his previous job as a biomedical researcher. This taste of leadership left him hungry for more opportunities. Asked to become a leader in the science department, Terrence said, "I welcome that."

Whereas many of these teachers enjoyed holding leadership roles currently, some teachers saw them as a way to stay engaged in teaching long term. Lacey said leadership opportunities would play a critical role in keeping her in teaching. She bemoaned the flatness of the traditional teaching career and worried that she would get bored after 5 or 10 more years in teaching. She saw teacher leadership opportunities as a way to satisfy her need for "change" and variation. Lacey said she would be interested in a role that would take her "on-the-ground experience, you know, in the trenches," and allow her to apply it "to help schools change the bigger picture." She and several other teachers were interested in becoming districtwide curriculum coordinators or instructional coaches.

Mac was a midcareer entrant who felt that leadership roles were especially critical to people who came to teaching relatively soon after college. He said that had he come into teaching as a first career, he would have needed leadership opportunities to stay engaged. He explained, for the person coming in straight out of college for teaching, I think that they, they should have some sort of other [roles]. They're going to need something . . . 35, 40 years doing the same thing, you're going to get stale. It's just human nature . . . I think teachers need other avenues.

Thus, leadership roles seemed to offer these teachers new challenges while allowing them to continue to do what they love: teach.

Roles With Little Allure

Particular roles held little allure for the teachers I interviewed. Many of these teachers rarely mentioned instructionally focused roles like literacy coach or professional development provider as positions that attracted them. They voiced stronger aversion to roles that they felt exhibited the worst qualities that they identified in the principal's job.

In particular, the teachers in this sample who had made a long-term commitment to teaching were not interested in taking on instructionally focused roles at this stage in their careers. Many of these teachers did not talk much about this type of role, but Deb confided, "I look at what they do, and I'm just not impressed." She felt that these roles "suck resources" and divert good teachers' focus away from their own classrooms, where they more directly benefit students.

These teachers also rejected roles that they thought lacked meaning, control, or integrity. For instance, when asked if becoming department head appealed to her, Lacey said, "the way the job is set up now, I wouldn't want to do it. He doesn't get to teach. He doesn't get a lot of interaction with students." Instead of having meaningful interactions with students, Lacey observed, "he just tries to shield us from a lot of that so we can teach and try to help us be good teachers. It's political again. And I don't know that I want to do that." Julius also avoided some leadership roles because he felt they, like administrative roles, were highly political. He explained,

I try to stay away from the politics of school as much as possible, and when you take a leadership role in school you have to deal with politics. Would I like to be on the school senate? Yes. Would I like to be on the school parent council? Yes. All those other things yes, but that means involving yourself in politics of the school. I don't need that. That takes away from my teaching.

Thus, it seemed that these teachers avoided teacher leadership roles that, in design and in practice, seemed to exhibit some of the same negative characteristics they associated with principals' roles. Although they embraced roles that allowed them voice in school policy and practice and presented new challenges over time, they seemed to avoid roles that entangled them in power struggles, buried them in paperwork, or limited their contact with students.

One teacher exemplified this perspective and, in fact, preferred to focus exclusively on his classroom and pursue no formal leadership positions. Although Frank had led professional development in the past, he said he had done this "just to pitch in." As he considered a future in teaching, Frank was not interested in taking on formal leadership roles and preferred instead to work with students and develop a deeper knowledge of science.

TO LEAD

U.S. schools are poised on the brink of a transition: Large numbers of teachers and principals retire annually, and, increasingly, communities look to early-career teachers for leadership and vision. My interviews with a small sample of newly tenured teachers in urban high schools suggest that many of these teachers are ready to offer such leadership and vision, but as teacher leaders rather than principals. In a way, the fact that many of these teachers are engaged by teaching and teacher leadership is good news. We want our students to have teachers who love to teach, after all, and are good at it.

Yet our schools also need caring, committed, and skilled principals. These interviews suggest that the job of the principal might require some targeted public relations efforts, at the least, and deliberate restructuring, at the most. If teachers' negative perceptions about the principalship do not match reality, school leaders need to do a better job of educating teachers about what principals actually do. However, if teachers' negative perceptions about principals' work are accurate, the principal's job may need to be revised to allow these school leaders more contact with students and more freedom to make fair and reasoned decisions without undue regard to political pressures. To persuade teachers to become principals, schools may have to work to make the principal's job more autonomous, more meaningful, and more sheltered from politics.

Many of these teachers also voiced a desire for particular teacher leadership opportunities, especially as they progressed in their careers. But will these roles truly offer the influence, challenge, and variation that may be necessary to retain the teachers in this group who are willing to consider a long-term career in teaching? Lacey and Julius's lack of interest in particular positions suggests that not all teacher leadership roles are equal in their potential to make teachers' careers satisfying. Roles that offer true opportunities to influence school policy and practice seem to appeal more to teachers who want to make teaching their long-term profession. This sort of role may also have greater influence over these teachers' retention.

In response to the need for leadership roles that allow teachers to have a voice and new challenges, teacher leaders may play a key part in creating change not only in their schools but also in their profession itself. These teachers can push their schools to recognize individuals' talents and place people in positions that enable them to share their expertise with others. Teacher leaders are also well positioned to examine how current roles play out in their schools, whether these roles appeal to teachers, and whether they serve their intended purpose. They can then recommend adjustments accordingly. More broadly, these teachers can lead their teacher and administrator colleagues in looking carefully and critically at how the teaching career is enacted in their schools and what new opportunities might be offered to teachers that help them be their most productive throughout their careers.

For decades, the teaching career has offered a teacher basically the same experience on her first day in teaching as on her last. By custom, it has also failed to recognize teachers for individual talents. Although this is a very small study, it adds to the growing body of evidence that the teaching career as traditionally structured offers a few opportunities to newly tenured teachers, but not a range of legitimate, substantive roles to which they might aspire. From this study, it appears that some early-career teachers want to be teacher leaders because they think such leaders make a difference. It is up to current teacher leaders to take this desire as a starting point and to chip away at the structure of the teaching career to create a range of legitimate opportunities where teachers can contribute. In this way, they might make teacher leadership a rewarding option for the next generation of union representatives as well as curriculum coordinators, literacy coaches, and department heads.

Note

1. Some teachers in this sample had made a short-term commitment to teaching and were preparing to exit the profession when I interviewed them. Compared to their counterparts with longer-term commitment to teaching, these teachers pursued a broader range of teacher leadership roles, including instructionally focused roles. In this chapter, analysis for the most part focuses on what I have called "potential long-termers," people in the sample who were considering teaching for the remainder of their adult working lives. A broader analysis of teachers' initial commitment to the profession, their professional growth needs, the extent to which their schools supported these needs, and implications for their retention in teaching can be found in Donaldson (2005).

REFERENCES

Cusick, P. (2003). *A study of Michigan's school principal shortage.* East Lansing, MI: Education Policy Center at Michigan State University.

Donaldson, M. L. (2005, April). *On barren ground: How urban high schools fail to support and retain newly tenured teachers.* Paper presented at the 2005 Annual Meeting of the American Educational Research Association, Montréal, Québec, Canada.

Gates, S. M., Ringel, J. S., Santibanez, L., Ross, K., & Chung, C. (2003). *Who is leading our schools? An overview of school principals and their careers.* Santa Monica, CA: Rand Corporation.

Hanushek, E. A., Kain, J. F., & Rivkin, S. G. (2004). Why public schools lose teachers. *Journal of Human Resources, 39*(2), 326–354.

Johnson, S. M., & The Project on the Next Generation of Teachers. (2004). *Finders and keepers: Helping new teachers survive and thrive in our schools.* San Francisco: Jossey-Bass.

Lankford, H., Loeb, S., & Wyckoff, J. (2002). Teacher sorting and the plight of urban schools: A descriptive analysis. *Educational Evaluation and Policy Analysis, 24*(1), 37–62.

Loeb, S., & Reininger, M. (2004). *Public policy and teacher labor markets: What we know and why it matters* (policy report). East Lansing: The Education Policy Center at Michigan State University.

Murnane, R. J., Singer, J. D., Willett, J. B., Kemple, J. J., & Olsen, R. J. (1991). *Who will teach? Policies that matter.* Cambridge: Harvard University Press.

Rand Corporation. (2004). *The careers of public school principals: Policy implications from an analysis of state-level data.* Santa Monica, CA: Author.

Stricherz, M. (2001). Despite retirements, "baby busters" scarce in principal's positions. *Education Week, 21,* 6–8.

Whiting, B. E., & National Education Association. (2003). *National Education Association: Status of the American public school teacher 2000–2001.* Washington, DC: National Education Association.

Young, B. (2003). Public *school student, staff, and graduate counts by state, school year 2001–02* (NCES 2003–358). Washington DC: National Center of Educational Statistics.

29

The Continuum of Leadership Development

Teacher Leaders Move to Administration

Sarah V. Mackenzie

Many teacher leaders work closely with principals, so their colleagues often consider them mini-administrators because they take on supervisory roles for curriculum and occasionally instruction. Although most teacher leaders are not administrative wannabes, some decide to assume such a role in schools. They want to be influential in a school by becoming an administrator even though it means accepting responsibilities that are not seen as "teacherly." Although there are certainly teacher leaders whose career plans assume a move to administration, many other teacher leaders struggle with the decision to take on such a role because they truly enjoy, and feel they need, the close contact with and oversight of the learning of a small group of students.

When teacher leaders make the move to administration, they vow to maintain connections with students, but they often find they must concentrate on what adults are doing and learning in order to fulfill the goals and purpose of the school. Effective administrators must always keep the learning of students their priority (Barth, 1990b, 2001; Cotton, 2000; Darling-Hammond,

2001) although they realize their goals must be assumed by many others involved in the actual implementation. Furthermore, they must take responsibility for the tasks that give administration its name.

When teachers move to administration, they experience a period of transition just as anyone does who undertakes a job that requires different responsibilities. The transition can be compared with the move from student teacher to beginning teacher, although administrators have greater visibility. They have more maturity and experience in the field, but the identity change may be even greater than becoming a teacher primarily because of the traditional hierarchal structure of schools. Teachers moving to administration participate in the "legitimate peripheral practice" of newcomers as they strive to learn in context the culture of the school as well as the expectations of the new role (Lave & Wenger, 1991).

Often people moving from teacher to administrator are cautioned about maintaining friendships with former colleagues because they are seen as crossing a barrier to another place in the hierarchy whose values and goals may be different from the rank and file of teachers and even of teacher leaders. They leave behind the isolation of teaching for the loneliness of the administrator (Langer & Schacter, 2003). In the new role, therefore, administrators have to decipher for themselves how and where they can apply some influence, which they envisioned as teacher leaders, as well as dress themselves in the new role even if they are not sure what it entails for them.

Effective teachers whose leadership is based on firm beliefs about practice that they share with colleagues and are assured make a difference in student learning may be particularly hopeful about their new role as administrator. They see themselves as able to influence more people to achieve results more quickly. Nevertheless, they still must struggle with their newcomer status—often in a school different from the one in which they had success as a teacher leader. Are they able to have the kind of influence they envisioned in the new role? To what extent are they able to act on the core beliefs about teaching, learning, and leadership they developed and exercised as teacher leaders? How much of the mind-set of a teacher are they able to bring to administration? These questions are plumbed by probing the intrapersonal dimension of transitioning leaders. Exploring the reflections of some teacher leaders immersed in transitioning to administrative roles can provide insights to guide teacher leaders in their growth as leaders and offer some assurance to those contemplating a change in role.

A STUDY OF NEW ADMINISTRATORS

I conducted interviews with five teacher leaders who had recently become administrators. All of the teacher leaders had at least 10 years of experience as classroom teachers and were at different stages in their development as leaders, but each one felt ready to take on a different role. A teacher leader who had held several formal and informal leadership roles in her school (including being interim principal for 3 months), Harriet became the principal of an elementary school in another district. Lisa held a quasi-administrative teacher leader role in her middle school and became an assistant principal in an elementary school in the same district. Ruth moved from teacher to coordinator of a districtwide English Language Learners program. Two men moved from being teachers who had filled various formal and informal teacher leader roles in schools to administrative positions: Larry as an assistant principal and Tim as a principal in elementary schools in other districts. All of the participants have or are completing master's degrees. Two have Certificates of Advanced Study, and one is working on a doctorate.

I met with them in their schools during the late Fall of 2003, the first year in their new positions, and I taped the hour-long interviews and afterwards transcribed them. I had access to journals they wrote during the first half of that year. I have followed up with e-mails to check in on how they are seeing their leadership develop and their perspectives change—or not. All but one of the study participants are in the same positions now; one moved to a central office job in his former district; a few have started to think about changing jobs—moving to another principalship or taking on a principalship.

I coached these individuals for a few years either in their teacher leader roles or in their transition to administration as part of a leadership development program they participated in. This role gave me access through their writing, conversations, and observations in their schools to the progress of their thinking about their deeply held beliefs about teaching, learning, and leadership, as well as to their analyses of their growth in cognitive, interpersonal, and intrapersonal dimensions. Although they may not represent the norm of teacher leaders moving to administration, they can articulate some of the personal difficulties of the shift. Their ability to tease out how their thinking, believing, and acting evolved can provide some insight to teacher leaders who may contemplate a similar move or who may be learning to work effectively with new administrators.

INTRODUCING THE TRANSITIONING TEACHER LEADERS

After high school, Harriet took a job as a kindergarten teacher's assistant. While in that position, she completed her bachelor's degree in 9 years. After a year of student teaching, she taught in middle school and had some of the same students she had had in kindergarten. She left that position to look for one in the primary grades, which she found after a year or so. She was a multiage K–1 teacher for 9 years and was active in her school's curriculum alignment and assessment work. She worked hard to obtain her principal's credentials and sought assistant principal jobs before she completed the degree. Her first administrative job was as the principal of a large elementary school in a sizable district. She says of her transition to the new role,

> I did a lot of reading of books, which has always been my way of exploring. I also think applying for jobs the year prior got me mentally ready to transition. My transition from my previous school to here was not as emotionally trying as I expected it to be. Because mentally I was ready to be here. I think talking to other principals was really helpful. . . . I did a lot of reflecting, written reflection. I think I had to. A lot about this position that made it easier opposed to accepting a job in house was I didn't know the players. So I had to concentrate on what information I would need to know and made lists. (Harriet, interview, November 2003)

Her organization and systematic approach are what made Harriet successful as a teacher leader. I have to insert here that a mere 3 years before, Harriet had not talked about herself in leadership terms. She saw herself as a teacher who worked with others to accomplish the team and school-wide tasks that needed to be completed.

Lisa began her career as a special education teacher, and she taught in three different middle schools for 12 years. She became a team leader and consulting teacher for the special education program at her last school. She had no specific teaching duties per se, but she worked closely with the teachers and students in her department and with the teams of teachers with whom her teachers collaborated. She had strong beliefs about inclusion of special education students and used data to back up her claims. After Lisa spent 4 years in the consulting teacher position, her superintendent tapped her to be an assistant principal in one of the district's elementary schools. Lisa knew the principal well, so her qualms about moving to another level were somewhat assuaged.

Because she was staying in the same system and felt her beliefs were in sync with her principal's, she thought the transition to a new position would be an easy one and her teacher leader skills could easily be put to use. She realized, though, that she needed to focus on familiarizing herself with the social, behavioral, and academic needs of much younger children.

> When they come in, they know nothing. . . . I just forgot how little they are. You sort of take it for granted at the middle level that they have always known how to write and read and you just have to teach them to do it better. How much more respect I have for elementary teachers. . . . There is just so much you have to send them

to the next level with. That's besides trying to encourage them to be independent and solve problems and not tattle. All this emotional behavior and social stuff. (Lisa, interview, November 2003)

Ruth had a varied career before she became an English Language Learners (ELL) coordinator. She started as a special education teacher and worked in a few private elementary schools for children with specific disabilities and behavioral impairments. When she started a family, she tutored children, then taught English classes in an adult education program ultimately specializing in teaching adults whose first language was not English. She soon moved to elementary ELL. As the number of ELL students and thus the number of teachers required in her city increased, Ruth was the logical person for the position of K–12 coordinator.

Ruth explained that she knew the need for a coordinator was coming, so she wanted to be prepared by enrolling in a graduate program in educational leadership.

> Knowing that eventually they will need somebody to do this job, I wanted to have the education to be able to move into this position. I didn't want to work for somebody else who was going to come in with a very different philosophy after investing so much into developing this program. . . . The other piece was to try to understand more of the goings-on in the bigger picture. (Ruth, interview, November 2003)

Ruth did not have to transition to a new school because her base was still at the school where she had taught. In addition to maintaining close contact with teachers and students in the elementary school, she had to travel to other schools, though, and hire and oversee staff and programs in the middle and high schools as the elementary students moved on. She said,

> I have worked at the middle school for several years popping in and out. But now, I have had to learn more about the inner workings to help the teachers be effective in their jobs. For example, trying to help teachers right now understand when they have siblings in the system and they have parent conferences, they need to coordinate the times, especially when they need a translator. . . . To me it seems like a real simple thing, and to them it is foreign. It's more encountering the culture and helping to influence it. I have to figure out what they don't know. (Ruth, interview, November 2003)

Like Harriet, Larry took an indirect route to teacher leadership. After college, Larry was the assistant manager of a mall. He had wanted to get into real estate development, and this seemed like a good way to do that. He discovered this kind of work was not for him, at least at the age of 22, so he went to work as a paralegal because he wanted to see if law school was a good investment for him. It wasn't, he decided. He saw an ad for a kindergarten position in a private school and took the job even though it meant a large pay cut. After a year he went to graduate school in education because he had fallen in love with teaching. His teaching experience ranged from primary through middle school.

Larry had significant experience in curriculum development. His last teacher leader endeavor, though, was as cofacilitator (with a principal) of a districtwide committee creating a teacher evaluation system. He says of his new position as assistant principal in a large elementary school,

> I felt I was ready for it. . . . What I really wanted to do was to try and maintain the perspective of a teacher, while at the same time, honoring the fact I was in a new role. I wanted to stay true to what it is like to be teacher and what kinds of things teachers need from administrators. And as I have been here more I see how all the experiences I have had, from the mall to the law firm to teaching, have really put me in a position so that I was ready for this job, because things like budget don't intimidate me and things like problems in school because that's part of my job. (Larry, interview, November 2003)

After 26 years of teaching, Tim took a half-year sabbatical. Because his district did not have an administrative position for him after he had been back for a year, he left his job. He found the perfect opportunity for a teacher leader unsure of what leadership direction he wanted to follow: He became a part-time curriculum coordinator, part-time principal (while the principal pursued university coursework). He described his previous experience this way:

> I spent a lot of years at the vocational school, and I started in their expeditionary programs with Outward Bound. It was a heterogeneously grouped program aimed at ninth and tenth graders. Developing and teaching this program lead me to rethink my position on assessment, curriculum, and instruction. I did some work with the district on assessment, and I was director of a project which helped teachers to revise assessment. (Tim, interview, December 2003)

Tim had spent some time consulting on assessment of the curriculum in his new district during his sabbatical, so he was somewhat familiar with people and structures. He was hired for the position in late August. He moved from high school to elementary school and from being a teacher leader to sharing a principal's position and being a curriculum coordinator. "I was ready for this. So it wasn't like, 'Do I really want to do this?'

No, I didn't hesitate. I didn't have to say, 'Can I do this?' I actually didn't have any doubts." (Tim, interview, December 2003)

BELIEFS AND BEHAVIORS AS TEACHER LEADERS

Teacher leaders stand on a solid platform of beliefs about teaching and learning. Philosophies of teaching are often drafted in their preprofessional experience and then modified, perhaps, but certainly elaborated on through their teaching experience, though not often in writing. When these teacher leaders wrote their platforms, they fleshed out the nuances in the fundamental statements related to their specific teaching situations, school level, or particular population of learners. As experienced teachers, they agreed on the ability of all children to learn, which to them means that schools need to provide a great variety of learning experiences and assessments to ensure and demonstrate student learning. They also agreed that learning standards are important in guiding the teaching and learning process if used generally and assessed wisely. Students must be treated with trust and respect in a community that values everyone's potential for learning and promotes a lifelong commitment to learning. These teacher leaders' beliefs about school leadership were more difficult to articulate because they did not see themselves as leaders separate from teachers or a group of teachers. They honed their beliefs to express the "I in we" as well as their ideal of leadership apart from what a leader does.

They each expressed a commitment to collaboration and a desire to promote collaborative leadership. Each school situation, though, presented a varied cultural context for teacher leaders. In their different arenas, these leaders identified specific skills they wanted to develop or improve because they observed other leaders being more effective in certain circumstances or because they saw one dimension of their personality had been developed at the expense of another. They were not focused on preparing for a new job at all; they simply knew they needed to be better at the one they had. Although they continued to learn from the many challenges their classrooms posed, they concentrated on learning and developing leadership skills in order to bring the ideal of collaborative leadership to fruition among the adults in the school.

When she wrote her platform as a teacher leader, Harriet based her ideas on reading as much as observations of others and experience. She was influenced by Meier's (1995) writing about school culture, Katzenmeyer and Moller (2001) on the role of teacher leaders in promoting collaboration, Sergiovanni (1996) with regard to authenticity, and Barth (1990a) on the subject of vision. Her beliefs were fully fleshed out, but this sampling of action principles and rationales for a culture of collaboration provides a snapshot of her thinking about leadership as she worked as a teacher leader:

> To transfer the understanding of the power of many to "our" work would be my goal in creating collaborative relationships. Collaboration in connection with vision provides a powerful focus on all work. And one person cannot do it alone.
>
> To allow and encourage *teacher* thinking to expand into a more diverse term as it relates to improving student learning opportunities involves the passionate exchange of possibilities to create an energized environment not only for the teacher but also the student. (Harriet, Platform, March 2001)

She traced the implications of her leadership beliefs from the collegial relationships among teachers to their work with students in the classroom. She always wrote about the "we" of leadership; however, she acknowledged how much the culture has to do with creating the possibility for that ideal to be realized.

At the same time that Harriet could be contemplative and serious, she was struggling with her behavior in groups. She describes it in this e-mail message to me.

> I don't want to change who I am necessarily. I want to be who I am. However, what I have been sensing for a while is a need to consider how I act in relationship to the environment I am in and make some conscious choices on how to respond, react, or behave. My natural instinct, which is definitely defensive, is to be humorous, quick witted—(at times, almost sarcastic) with an eye on being in an active, verbally expressive/processing mode. What it creates is a buffer for my real responses that usually arrive later, under my breath, or among a group conversation and thus, lost to the general ear. . . . Because with a quick joke I usually get a response. And with plain ramblings to myself that eventually get confirmed through hearing other people say what I would have said, I protect myself. In an effort to be a part of a group, I have a strong need to connect to the bigger project but I have used mechanisms which may not fit all the time. . . . This is attached to confidence, which most people feel I have but I don't think it is real confidence in the professional sense. I think the confidence people feel I have is connected to the risk taker and the extrovert. (Harriet, e-mail, August 2001)

She even referred to herself as having "three faces." Her struggle, then, was to be sure her behavior matched the seriousness of her views so that she could be a more effective leader. She understood, having been in her school for many years, that others knew her, saw her with children, and appreciated her style. She realized she needed to come across differently in a new situation with professionals with whom she was not familiar. At the same time, though, she knew her humor was a strength and useful in some situations.

Lisa needed to confront a similar issue. Like the other teacher leaders, she expressed beliefs in collaborative leadership and supportive climate. But, she felt her ability to influence other teachers was through her "weaselly ways," humoring, cajoling, and flattering people rather than using straight talk. To her, these were not legitimate leadership behaviors because they depended so much on long-term relationships with peers. Her colleagues were able to help her see how important relationships—with a group or individuals—are to promoting a collaborative culture. Nevertheless, to expand her repertoire and grow, she knew she needed to move out of her comfort zone. Although her goal of directness had to do with her behavior with others, she knew there was an intrapersonal dimension also, so she created these complementary goals:

> Interpersonal Objective: I will be more assertive and use direct confrontation because there are times when direct confrontation is necessary in a leadership position in order to make change occur in the best interest of students.
>
> Intrapersonal Objective: To explore and understand why it is difficult for me to be assertive and use direct confrontation. By exploring why direct confrontation is difficult for me, I can begin to overcome the difficulty and be more effective in instituting change in my position as a school leader in special education. (Lisa, Leadership Development Plan, January, 2001)

In spite of her attention to this new behavior, she was concerned about how she would lead in a different context and different role.

Ruth, likewise, struggled with how to be more confident and assertive in working with her supervisors. She was at ease in situations in which she acted as an advocate for her students or taught others about what it means to work with communities whose native language is not English, but when it came to her and leadership, she did not feel able to speak compellingly. She deferred to others because she believed administrators have a better grasp of the big picture than she.

> I have become aware that I tend to defer to position and need to be more assertive in expressing my views and opinions with administrative leaders in our school community and school system. I have found that by stating what I know or offering information without regard to, "is it my place to say this?" I have been more successful at communicating within the school community. It is when I am

challenged that I have to work at not backing down from what I want or believe. (Ruth, Reflection, December 2002)

Like many teacher leaders, Ruth has strong beliefs about what is right for her students, but she assumes she does not have a role in the ultimate decision-making process in spite of these strong beliefs.

Larry's teacher leader struggle was on the same continuum as the others, but he describes the rub for him differently. He realized he shut down in meetings if a discussion got off track and lost direction. He says, "I am energized by people who agree with me, but left stagnant by people who disagree with me. I think in some ways it is a defense mechanism because I am fearful that some will consider me too passionate. I get lost in all the jabber. I have trouble when people are more assertive than I am. I need to maintain an involvement in the conversation without zoning out during a discussion that I view as useless" (Larry, Reflection, December 2002).

In the midst of focusing on this inter-/intrapersonal problem, he came across another stickier point in his cofacilitation of a systemwide committee. If he can stay in the discussion with colleagues, he wields a lot of influence; as with Ruth, though, the power and authority of administrators shuts him down. He analyzed his withdrawal among teachers and his intimidation by hierarchy as feeling that he can find "no middle ground. I feel that if I am not 'in charge' at the front of the room then I am either withdrawn or yelling. I *know* that a lot of this is my own perception and not true, but this is how it feels" (Larry, Reflection, December 2002).

He focused on changing his behavior—both internally and externally, and he found some success. "When I met with the other cofacilitator, I realized that I was in for a long year. I sat down beside his desk, and he took out the agenda for the first meeting. I listened respectfully and left at the conclusion of the meeting with my tail between my legs. It was obvious that the administrator saw me more as a 'rookie' in training and not as an equal." Larry's critical friends recommended he resign from the committee because he felt the committee was not accomplishing much and teachers were mere tokens. Larry chose to stay. Aware of his tendencies, he developed assertiveness. He discovered he was more able to express himself to administrators whom he knew and trusted, but he continued to find his feelings about the power and authority of administrators daunting.

Tim describes his passage to teacher leadership as "meeting a leader who taught me that one should never sit and watch the world go by." As he improved teaching and learning in his classroom, he shared his success with others and occasionally met surprising resistance. He said,

I nearly retreated back to my closed classroom, but the leader of the school encouraged me to take a leadership role that would model good teaching and learning, and more importantly, to continue to take risks. In my years spent in school improvement I gained insight that would later prove extremely useful. . . . On the one hand, I felt proud to be asked to take on such roles, but on the other hand, my work was rarely appreciated. I discovered that, in my system, those that claimed they were collaborative didn't always practice collaboration. (Tim, Reflection, May 2002)

Tim's work in a large district provided many opportunities to develop skills and understanding. His ascent up the hierarchy, though, was stalled. He knew he wanted to affect the teaching and learning of more children; furthermore, he had confidence in his skills with a wide variety of groups of adults. It made sense for him to take another risk, leave his job, and wait to see what would happen. That is how he became an interim principal and curriculum and assessment coordinator for a small district nearby.

These teacher leaders had varying opportunities to develop their leadership skill, but they all had a sense of what it would mean for them to move to an administrative role. Because they looked at their careers and themselves as constantly changing, they saw the various roles they played as teacher leaders as part of a leadership continuum irrespective of their formal position. None of them, with the exception of Tim, was determined to move to a new position immediately. As a result, they found the right "fit" for them at the time, even if that fit would challenge them in ways the classroom had not for many years.

STEEP LEARNING CURVES

The teacher leaders transformed into administrators as soon as they walked in the door of their schools with the new title. They had varying amounts of time to prepare: Harriet and Ruth, about 4 months; Larry and Lisa, 1 month; Tim, 1 day. Harriet and Larry had detailed entry plans, which they said helped them structure their first encounters with individuals and groups. For all of them, the first few weeks involved gathering information about the people, the culture, and the expectations of the position. None of them mentioned any difficulty in leaving teaching behind or in leaving their previous school behind. This group, and probably most teacher leaders who make the transition to new roles, see their careers as evolutionary.

The most important part of their entry into the new position involved people. Larry describes his modus operandi in getting to know his colleagues.

I remember a CEO of a company gave a speech where he said, "Your first year on a job, keep your mouth shut and listen." That made sense, and it is something that I have really always done.

> I was kind of worried about that because here I was thinking there are going to be situations were I have to talk more, where I have to show what I think more, when I have to share, and I can't always just be a listener, which is what I would do. It would help me identify people that I thought were safe, not safe, and so on. I think the entry plan helped, and then on top of it, I was able to do a lot of listening. . . . Understanding the culture is how I think you survive in an organization. (Larry, interview, November 2003)

Lisa described how she "played dumb" and asked a lot of questions, even if it created in her, as Larry also implies, some tension because she did not want to appear incompetent as a new administrator. In fact, she experienced greater incompetence when she had to deal with first grade students who did not take her seriously as an authority figure. The culture, she found, was vastly different from middle school, and she needed to temper her sense of humor in dealing with teachers and students. Like Lisa, Tim said he asked naïve questions to encourage people to open up to him and reveal how they did things at the school.

In addition to analyzing the culture and discovering what their staff members wanted from them as leaders, the teacher leaders-turned-administrators had to learn new information. Harriet devoured books and periodicals about reform, literacy, assessment, for herself but also so that she could provide resources she thought teachers could use or, in some cases, needed to use. She said she wanted to be a model for both teachers and students of someone who is always learning, so she distributed books and articles from her professional library.

Lisa had the steepest learning curve because she had to immerse herself in many different curricula and, to a certain extent, different teaching methods. Although Tim moved to a different level, he was confident in his understanding of curriculum and assessment at the elementary level because of his K–12 work as a teacher leader and his complementary role as curriculum and assessment director. Ruth felt her cognitive learning gaps were in the areas of personnel (hiring, especially) and budgeting.

The new administrators faced many challenges, but they did not have to do with the job itself or their ability to do it. As is so often the case, the challenges were interpersonal. Lisa alludes to a situation in which she realized not only that the culture of her new school was very different from the middle schools where she had worked but also that she had a different role now:

> I've taught at three different middle schools, and they've all kind of basically had the same culture—maybe not the same climate, but the same culture. And it's a totally different culture from elementary school. I was just at a grade-level meeting, and one of the new teachers made a joke. A veteran teacher overreacted, handling it

very inappropriately and way too harshly. It was so uncomfortable and awkward. Maybe there were episodes like that at the middle school, but I didn't really pay attention to them because I didn't have to. And now I realize I need to address this because her reaction was really unprofessional. Before I would complain about it maybe to my husband, but I never had to deal with it. (Lisa, interview, December 2003)

Most of the participants' insights, though, were more general. Lisa talked about how much she appreciates elementary school teachers now because she sees how much they have to do and how hard it is to work so intensely with young children. Harriet, who had been a K–1 multiage teacher, is amazed at how exhausted she is compared with how she felt dealing with young children:

I was busy as a classroom teacher plus the extra stuff I was doing like classroom work, but this is busy because I'm people-oriented all the time. Adult people–oriented all the time. I've had a harder time de-processing that type of energy loss from constant adult interaction. The other part is, I hope that every time I show up it is not a complaint, that it is more on instruction, caring, and kids. But at this point I've gone from a maybe 75% complaints to maybe 50% complaints. I'm getting down, but I'm not where I want to be. (Harriet, interview, November 2003)

Whereas Harriet said she was tired, Larry found his job as an administrator easier than when he was a teacher:

When I consider how much time I put into being a quality teacher and on top of it how much time I spent thinking about school culture and school reform, school change, all these things, I was exhausted as a teacher. Now I don't focus on being the best classroom teacher I can be. I focus on being the best support of classroom teachers that I can be. Teachers just have stuff constantly coming at them, but they have no control over the flow. It's like the shutoff valve on your sink doesn't work and the water just keeps coming. As an administrator, I feel more in control to shut it off and turn it on when I want. That's not across the board, but with these mandates that are coming down, I feel like I have time and I am in a position to question them. And I didn't feel like I had that time before. (Larry, interview, November 2003)

Tim echoes this idea, in commenting about his work both as a principal and with principals in planning for staff development:

I get to do the good stuff. I get to work with the people rather than trying to figure out what you are going to spend and cut. But I want to say this, I have a different respect for principals. But I also have little tolerance for their excuses because I can say that I have been in their position, and I know that some of the excuses they use aren't real, about how hard it is and about time. I always found time to do the things I needed to do. I know that budget is a big part. But it can't be that much. You don't have to sit in there all day and do it. It is your own personal choice. (Tim, interview, December 2003)

Ruth felt she was fortunate to be in a job that she had shaped and defined. Ruth's insights had to do with the expansion of a role she felt she always had as an ELL teacher. She felt obligated to connect with members of the community who were not native speakers as well as help teachers be more mindful of that population and their differing needs. What she has had to contend with, though, is how much she is responsible for the messages sent out to all the stakeholders of the community and how much she is looked to as the expert on a topic both within and outside the school system.

The way these individuals started their new jobs and their reactions to them show their differences based on temperament and personality. When it comes to how they felt grounded in their beliefs and how they were or were not able to enact them, however, they show many similarities.

ENACTING THEIR BELIEFS AS NEW ADMINISTRATORS

The new administrators did not express any conflict within themselves about their beliefs in their new role. In fact, they described a heightened sense of their beliefs about teaching and learning, which, on the whole, seemed to surprise them. Larry told me that having to express his beliefs in writing prepared him best for his administrator role (personal communication, February 2005). Although they had articulated their beliefs about leadership as teacher leaders, they imagined enacting them would be easier as administrators. They discovered power in the role, of course, but also many of the same constraints and even more tensions than they had previously experienced.

Influencing Others

Lisa expressed most strongly the sense of responsibility she felt for ensuring effective teaching in her school. She said,

The biggest change and biggest understanding for me has been never before did I feel the pressure to make good teaching happen. I feel like there is so much more at stake if there are not good teachers. Before, I knew who was terrible and felt the school could just get rid of them. Now I feel it's directly connected to me and I have a responsibility, and it's such a pressure for me. (Lisa, interview, December 2003)

In his new role, Larry sees how much pressure is on teachers to do a good job. He is sympathetic because he appreciates how easy it is to make recommendations of best practice to teachers who may not have access to resources or who have to spend a great amount of time gathering and planning for using them. Tim, too, says in his new role he is more conscious of the "day-to-day struggles of teachers." His role, he says, is to support them as much as he can because he feels they want to do a good job even if they complain or initially resist changes in expectations for results.

Harriet's entry plan called for her to gather information about teachers and their practice as well as about individual students. Her interview revealed what she had found about the gap between her beliefs about best practices in teaching and what she observed in her school. She saw teacher-directed learning coupled with lack of student ownership. Her thorough exploration, she hopes, will give legitimacy to her recommendations for teams and individuals; nevertheless, she is mindful that the test scores of the pupils in the school have been steadily good.

Insights and observations, then, lead to leadership challenges that bring to light the tensions between beliefs and enactment. These new administrators dreamed of having greater influence on teaching and learning, but much of the influence was still through one-to-one relationships. Many of them felt they could be influential with individual students as they dealt with discipline issues, and they could, thus, influence teachers by helping them deal with particular students.

Although they mentioned the drag of administrative duties, they all described their strong commitment to attending team meetings and planning faculty meetings that enhance instruction. They were aware of their new role in those meetings even as they worked hard at being collegial. Tim emphasizes "we" in his conversations in meetings; Harriet attends not only team meetings but also outside workshops with teachers from her school so she can stay on top of curriculum. Because Ruth remained in the same school and the same program, she feels greater confidence in making suggestions to other teachers:

I think as an ESL teacher I always felt like the classroom teacher had the last word. And I now feel if there is something that needs to happen, then the classroom teacher is a part of the decision making, the planning, but I am more direct. I think in the past maybe

I would have said, "Gee, you might have to . . ." or "Do you think you could?" Now I say, "You need to." (Ruth, interview, 2003)

All interviewees voiced the feeling that their collegial connection with teachers has changed. They are providing, as Lisa and Tim say, the "outside perspective" teachers need; however, they miss the insider status that allowed for greater congeniality with their peers:

I ask a lot of questions. It has been to my advantage to do that, I think; it's less threatening. . . . I was thinking that my special education background would help me, but honestly I have not used it very much. (Lisa, interview, December 2003)

They do not know, however, how those comments are viewed. Larry says,

I don't feel I can be as connected to people as I could as a teacher on the same level. I feel like I have to be professionally responsible, and it's not the same. When I am in the parking lot I don't have people coming over to me asking what I thought of the meeting because I did the meeting. (Larry, interview, November 2003)

Lisa felt the pressure to do something about what she considered ineffective practices even as she felt less authoritative in her suggestions. That may explain her sense that she has less influence in her new role than she did as a teacher leader. "I don't know if it is just inevitable when you cross that line. . . . I feel like I was much more of a leader in my last position. . . . I feel like I am more of a manager dealing with the student issues and a problem solver."

The other interviewees, though, say they feel they are more able to influence others in their new positions. Tim says he does it by pushing principals, and supporting them as he does so, to be more purposeful about the changes they want to see in curriculum and instruction. The ability to influence others is solidly connected to how they envision the ethos of the school.

Shaping Culture

Obviously the big change for these new administrators is the time they have to spend developing the climate for the leadership they want in the school. Their challenges are similar to the ones they had as teacher leaders: how to encourage collegial relationships, how to develop capacity for collaboration and collaborative leadership in individuals and groups, how to balance the need to accomplish tasks with ownership of the process and the product. They experience varying levels of ability to influence these individuals and groups as well as different perspectives on the kind of authority they have in their new role. Larry says,

> When I first looked at administration, I thought it was enough to be an effective teacher. If you were an effective teacher, I thought you could be an effective school leader. Because there are lots of things that go with being an effective teacher that I think would cross over. I think there are other things now, like I think you need to be able build the culture. . . . You can have a greater impact than when you are the teacher, you can be a contributor to the culture, but you can't set the tone. Everyone can influence it, and I think everyone can promote it, but I think it's easier in this role because you have more time to focus on school culture and community; you don't have that in the classroom. . . . It's like a whole separate job. If you don't have a healthy culture, then it can negatively impact everybody. (Larry, interview, November 2003)

Larry's view of the importance of administrators influencing the culture dovetails with his feeling that his role as assistant principal is easier than that of a teacher leader. Teacher leaders have all of the responsibilities of the classroom in addition to school and system tasks, all of which contribute to the organization. Because they are so busy doing things, they have to rely on others who work on the larger pieces of the school community, including the culture.

Larry sees how his rapport with individual teachers and participation in meetings help to maintain a collaborative culture. Harriet, too, is working on relationships. She struggles to find the right pressure points to move people forward in examining their practice because her school has the aura of collaboration but not the reality. Larry and his principal, a woman who has much experience as a principal but who is also new to the building, used the first faculty meeting to ask teachers how they would know the two administrators were successful in their leadership. The faculty enumerated behaviors they wanted to see.

Harriet in her one-on-one conversations with staff members found visibility was what they wanted:

> I guess my first couple of months I wanted to emphasize myself as a certain type of person. Which I think I had to do by being very physically available in rooms frequently, learning kids' names, that type of thing. But what I think I need to change is to be more purposeful in our direction. But what I have been is more setting the stage of who I am and how I operate. Now I'm feeling the need to change my pose to be a little bit more forceful, more clear, more focused. . . . It's not that I haven't done that inadvertently, but I haven't done it purposefully. (Harriet, interview, November 2003)

Just as Harriet analyzes her situation and develops a strategy for next steps, Tim, in his role as systemwide curriculum coordinator, engages in a similar process:

> I realized that I needed to pass the responsibilities along to the principals because it is their building, but I need to support them, when they have questions from their staff or they need some guidance. So I don't do a lot with their buildings, because I can see it happening that if I did, I would be disturbing the power of the principals. So I did the planning with the principals, but they did the staff development. I think that they (the principals) needed somebody to hold their hands sometimes, to argue with them sometimes, to bring the bad news to them sometimes, and to fight for them sometimes. (Tim, interview, December 2003)

Building Capacity

Leaders have to move back and forth from big-picture strategies to the everyday tasks of moving toward goals both concrete and intangible. To save themselves time and to help build capacity in others, both Harriet and Ruth found they had to disengage from certain conversations in team meetings because they did not want to micromanage. Harriet and Lisa described the pileup of seemingly insignificant managerial tasks. Lisa described the familiar tension of facilitation versus direction exacerbated for her in this new role:

> Sometimes I want to go back to being that teacher leader because I had so much more of a positive impact and didn't have all the pressure. . . . It is making me work harder. I definitely used my interpersonal skills to get things that I wanted and to get things done that I wanted to get done. I don't have that advantage here. I can't do that, and I have to work a lot harder. It is almost like I am fighting against my role because I am still trying to think about how I can do this without coming off as the administrator and without coming off as the supervisor and the boss and that I am giving a directive. It's like I am always trying to figure out a way not to weasel, which I have been doing for years. (Lisa, interview, December 2003)

All the interviewees mentioned finding or developing teacher leaders. Their comments were not about manipulating or overpowering others, but finding comrades and colleagues who share their vision and can help move the school forward. They acknowledged their new authority, but shied away from, as Lisa does, wanting to exercise it. She says she and her veteran principal have a solid working relationship, but Lisa has to be encouraged to delve into some of the thornier situations that may require directives.

Compromising

The new administrators discovered quickly the compromises they have to make in enacting their beliefs about leadership. Both Larry and Tim say their nonnegotiables have to do with standards and how they may be implemented. Both described their patience, for the moment, with how their school systems are progressing. Ruth and Lisa both mentioned some of the ways they had to bend a bit to be on the same page as other administrators in the school or system. Harriet found herself adjusting as she worked to understand the system's philosophy of accountability, but she stood firm by resisting central office requests to attend meetings when she needed to be at her school for team meetings. Ruth discovered, as many teacher leaders do, the right-versus-right dilemmas of what is good for the individual versus what is good for the whole. Her discovery also had to do with leadership strategies based on different priorities.

> [My telling my Ed techs they had to help out in newly inaugurated study sessions] was in conflict with what the principal had told staff members. I was just going from the leadership point of view of "This is what is best for the kids" and was not asking too much extra of staff members. She was looking at it as facing a new program, and it's sort of getting people to buy into it. We have so many kids that need so much help, and I'm just trying to do anything we can do to help the kids. (Ruth, interview, December 2003)

In always looking at what is best for students, administrators face the same challenge teachers do in their classrooms: How to manage the tension between group and individual needs. Teacher leaders' greatest insights often come from discovering the "big picture," the system and all its parts that are constantly changing but, they hope, moving in the same direction. Administrators have more "needs" to balance, as they keep the school community and the stakeholders focused on the learning of students. Harriet says,

> I am changing my posture with parents only because I am trying to be consistent and fair. I'm trying to base my decisions not so much on the individual to individual, which is what I would do as a teacher. If I make this one decision for this one parent I have to multiply that by all my parents and say this is viable. Could I make this same accommodation for this child and this parent for every child and parent? (Harriet, interview, November 2003)

The teacher in the classroom is central to student learning, so teacher needs, teacher voices, and teacher learning have to be close to the surface of administrators' consciousness. On the other hand, they know part of their function is to help individuals understand their part in the whole system and to mediate the competing needs of individuals and groups of teachers. Rather than draw some lines around their old and new roles, these new administrators have attempted to keep the teacher in them viable as they grow into leaders with a different title.

KEEPING THE TEACHER IN THEIR LEADERSHIP

One of the major reasons teacher leaders say they do not want to become an administrator is that they will lose touch with children (Donaldson, this volume; Mackenzie, Cook, & Morrell, 2004). These new administrators mentioned various ways they developed to stay connected to children: studying files, learning names of children, choosing a few students to make close connections with and following their progress, teaching units or lessons, sponsoring or coaching extracurricular activities, to name a few. Getting to know students as learners is easier than it used to be for administrators because there are numerous opportunities in such things as Critical Friends Groups or team meetings for examining student work, assessing progress of groups, and discussing learning needs.

Not only must administrators stay connected to students and their learning, administrators must stay connected to teachers and their learning. In addition to reading voraciously and passing on articles and books, Harriet kept abreast of new developments in literacy and assessment by attending ongoing staff development. Larry's return of disciplined students to classrooms entailed conversations with teachers about strategies they both generated for helping students learn more effectively in their classrooms. All participants mentioned ways they hope that they model a desire to learn and to teach what they know effectively.

Having vast experience as a teacher is certainly important because it provides many avenues into conversations with faculty. They can leverage their knowledge in a variety of ways. On the other hand, they recognize that their experience may make them cynical about certain responses of teachers, so they have to guard against being too heavy handed in alluding to their teaching experience.

As these teachers moved into administration, they were highly committed to making a "seamless" transition in that they did not want their teacher mind-set to be vastly altered, modified, or reshaped. Ruth's move was within her venue of ELL, so she could more easily, perhaps, keep her teacher voice. All the interviewees claimed that thinking like a teacher and understanding teachers' needs was a driver for them in the new role. Tim said he wanted to make public not just teaching practice but also principal practice so everyone understands, appreciates, and can critique not just what others do, but why they do it. Lisa brought up some concerns about not wanting to fall into an us-against-them situation, but they all expressed largely what Harriet says here:

> I'm making my routine more "teachery" than more "principalery." The funny thing is I have no experience of seeing what that is supposed to look like. I know what I don't want it to look like. But I think that I've been able to keep my behavior more teacherish, as I wanted it to be. I've been able to stay in contact with teachers and with what they are doing. Our conversations are very meaningful. They're not just small talk. I can talk about certain kids with certain issues and have something to offer. When I am in a Pupil Evaluation Team as a principal I am only there in name. I am there physically as a teacher thinking about a child who is struggling in a classroom. And what I suggest usually is from the teacher position. I have a new title and more authority. I have to say that the title has allowed me to be the teacher's voice. . . . Personally my behavior and how I operate hasn't changed that much. I don't feel like a different person. I don't feel like when I engage with others I am putting on some type of different performance. I am trying to be very real, very authentic. So in that case I feel like even though I've changed in my operating style because of certain situations I don't feel I've changed my person and who I am. (Harriet, interview, November 2003)

In her second year, Harriet felt she often "was a colleague, not a person who had all the answers, and we solved the issues together." In some instances, though, her teacher stance had to change because on certain issues she had to take a stand that differed from what the teachers wanted to do. She says,

> I have the same ideals I had as a teacher. My beliefs about education have remained the same. What I have come to realize is my staff doesn't have the same ideals and at times, they have opposing ideals. I am struggling to create the climate where it is OK to have different ideals, but we need to have the same mission with the same purpose and done in a manner that is good for kids and their learning. (Harriet, Reflection, June 2005)

She acknowledges that these circumstances are no different from ones she encountered as a teacher leader; however, she has more authority to make decisions based on her own beliefs, which, of course, produces other kinds of challenges in terms of interpersonal relationships in the school.

Teacher leaders who have articulated their fundamental beliefs about both teaching and learning and leadership have a strong basis on which to operate in many arenas. Tim points out,

Leadership in schools takes many forms. I am not sure that one necessarily needs to be a principal before becoming a good curriculum coordinator, nor do I believe that a curriculum coordinator would necessarily make a good principal. At the core of these leadership positions, and in fact any leadership position, are skills one gains through a variety of experiences. It is what we take away from these experiences that paves the road to better leadership. It is having the skill to keep the car on the track even though you have never gone that fast around a curve before. (Tim, Reflection, May 2002)

Larry acknowledges, though, the issue for positional leaders in schools. "When you have a title, everyone assumes that you have the answer to every question." He describes how he attempts to change people's views and help them find the leader in themselves.

The challenge is in prodding people into transforming their traditional views of a school as an organization. People need to see the "leader" not as someone who has all of the right answers but as someone who is adept at facilitating individuals or groups of people at coming to the right answers and to believe in their own abilities as professionals to do what is right for themselves as professionals and for the students they teach. (Larry, Reflection, December 2003)

A CONTINUUM OF LEADERSHIP DEVELOPMENT

These new administrators did not seem to experience an identity crisis. They moved, as all leaders do, along a continuum of development that changes with locations and roles, surely, but also with knowledge, skills, and understandings of self. They have to establish and maintain relationships with children and adults. They have to observe and analyze situations and help solve problems. They must stay in touch with their deeply held beliefs as they influence others and allow themselves to be influenced in return. Their desire was to have a greater influence on the learning of more students by working more closely and constantly with teachers. Although their challenges seem more intense than those of teacher leaders because they have greater responsibility and higher visibility, the work of school leaders—no matter what the role—remains largely the same.

The lesson for teacher leaders is to remain open themselves and reach out to establish collegial connections with administrators. Learn with them. Be a critical friend just as you expect they would be to you. Help each other break down the isolation of teaching and the isolation of leadership. Tim describes his vision of his work.

While traditionally school leadership has been portrayed as a lonely, unrecognized position, I believe that leaders who seek out and learn from others become effective and happier. It is a matter of discovering that school issues are the issues of the whole and not the one. Once the burden of taking care of problems alone is lifted, school leadership becomes the collaborative institution it was designed to be. (Tim, Reflection, May 2002)

All school leaders—no matter what role they play—are doing the same work from slightly different perspectives. Teachers are doing the core work of the school in their classrooms, but they cannot accomplish the learning work of the school alone. They are dependent on the good work of the other teachers who are moving steadily toward the same goals. The hierarchical nature of the organization means that the administrator is outside the core work but, nevertheless, is coordinating curriculum, nurturing teachers, helping students participate effectively, supporting parents, and maintaining a focus on the learning needs of the school. Of course, these are all aspects of the teachers' work, too. The authentic educational leader, then, merely extends his or her scope in the shift from teacher to administrator (Starrat, 2004). Building and maintaining relationships that respect each person's commitment to student learning is the essence of school leadership.

REFERENCES

Barth, R. (1990a, March). A personal vision of a good school. *Phi Delta Kappan, 71*, 512–516.

Barth, R. (1990b). *Improving schools from within: Teachers, parents, and principals can make the difference.* San Francisco: Jossey-Bass.

Barth, R. (2001). *Learning by heart.* San Francisco: Jossey-Bass.

Cotton, K. (2000). *The schooling practices that matter most.* Portland, OR: Northwest Regional Educational Lab.

Darling-Hammond, L. (2001). *The right to learn: A blueprint for creating schools that work.* San Francisco: Jossey-Bass.

Katzenmeyer, M., & Moller, G. (2001). *Awakening the sleeping giant: Helping teachers develop as leaders* (2nd ed.). Thousand Oaks, CA: Corwin Press.

Langer, S., & Boris-Schacter, S. (2003, September-October). The embattled principal. *National Association of Elementary School Principals, 83*(1), 14–18.

Lave, J., & Wenger, E. (1991). *Situated learning: Legitimate peripheral participation.* Cambridge, UK: Cambridge University Press.

Mackenzie, S. V., Cook, S., & Morrell, B. (2004). *A view from the inside: Continuing the conversation about teaching in Maine schools.* Augusta, ME: Maine Educational Leadership Consortium.

Meier, D. (1995). *The power of their ideas: Lessons from America from a small school in Harlem.* Boston: Beacon Press.

Sergiovanni, T. J. (1996). *Moral leadership: Getting to the heart of school improvement.* San Francisco: Jossey-Bass.

Starrat, R. J. (2004). *Ethical leadership.* San Francisco: Jossey-Bass.

30

Working Together Through Learning-Oriented Leadership

Promising Practices for Supporting Teacher Leadership and Growth

Eleanor E. Drago-Severson

S chools need to be places where the adults as well as the children can grow. To this end, teachers need ongoing contexts for reflection to develop practices to support their growth. I am a professor and researcher in a university where teachers and other school leaders come to study leadership for adult learning. In addition to working with these graduate students, I also dedicate myself to helping practicing teachers, principals, and other school leaders who dedicate themselves to educating youth in our schools. Having served as a middle and high school teacher, I know how magnificent schools can be when they are fertile, invigorating, and inspiring places for the ongoing development of children, youth, and adults alike. Children thrive. Adults grow. Both experience high levels of satisfaction and learning. I also know how challenging it can be to create such school contexts.

Recently, I had the privilege of working with a group of experienced teacher leaders during a two-day professional development institute in which they assessed their past goals and drafted future intentions for their work. At the start of the workshop, these professionals reflected on their hopes for the workshop. John, who had been teaching for 22 years, seemed to capture the others' experiences. He wanted to create a space where he felt "intellectually fed" and "nurtured" by the workshop. "I love teaching," he continued. "I love my work. And I also feel that it is so rare that I have a chance to reflect on my own needs for growth and learning because I am so invested in caring for my students. I need this time and wish for more of it." John's sentiments and needs are emblematic of what other teachers have shared during similar workshops I have delivered.

ADULT GROWTH IN A TOUGH SCHOOL CLIMATE: MEETING DIVERSE INDIVIDUAL NEEDS

Listening to and learning from teachers like John inspires me, and I am honored to help them to enhance their leadership by creating contexts to support their work and growth. Many tough issues combine to challenge teacher leadership and development. Improving student achievement, implementing democratic initiatives to improve school conditions, strengthening assessment, attending to the needs of an increasingly diverse population, and enriching professional development for teachers and principals are at the forefront of our educational agenda. Teacher leaders, principals, and other leaders struggle with the challenge of shaping school cultures that support adult learning and improve practice in a context of more extensive assessments and increased accountability (Ackerman & Maslin-Ostrowski, 2002; Elmore, 2004; Fullan, 2005). At the same time, we are searching for ways to build schools as learning centers that can effectively nurture adult and youth development. Today teachers, not just principals, are called upon to assist in building these collaborative learning organizations.

Educational challenges such as those named above place new, complex demands on teachers who dedicate themselves to educating children and youth. We know that there is a direct link between supporting adult learning and enhanced student achievement (Guskey, 1999; Moller & Pankake, 2006). This means that we must change how we work and learn together. As teachers committed to supporting student learning and achievement, organizational change and adult learning, first we must understand that authentic change starts with us. Recent research shows that teacher leaders (a) navigate the complex structures of schools, (b) cultivate relationships with each other, (c) help each other manage change, and (d) challenge conditions in schools by illuminating children's needs and voices (Silva,

Gimbert & Nolan, 2000). How can we build high-performing, high-equity, and democratic schools? To enhance teacher leadership and build high-performing, high-equity schools, we need more effective practices for supporting adult learning *within* schools. One way to accomplish this is to assist teachers in effectively shaping school cultures to be collaborative learning communities supportive of teacher learning and leadership (Boles & Troen, 2005; Drago-Severson, 2004b; Fullan, 2005; Little, 2001; Spillane, 2005). Leading and learning together will help us meet this challenge.

The best professional development practices ignite and sustain teachers' excitement for learning and growing (Drago-Severson, 2004b). Yet how can we create opportunities for growth and lifelong learning that meet the needs of adults with different preferences and developmental orientations? Teachers' needs do not come in the same shapes and sizes. In addition, although teachers must take on various roles to support themselves and other adults with differing needs, developmental orientations, and preferences, many are not given the support to fulfill the demands of these roles. Learning together is essential to teachers' ability to manage the complex changes of school environments and to meet the needs of children. We must create contexts—new school cultures—where we learn together and are supported in our own growth and development. Teacher leadership can make the difference in this task.

Teacher leaders will benefit from learning about adults' differing developmental needs and preferences. Admittedly, there may be other reasons for differences among teachers' preferences for engagement in particular types of practices (e.g., age, educational background, career phase). However, this kind of developmental mindfulness will enable teachers to better support themselves and each other as they strive to improve practice, work collegially on issues of practice, and create contexts in which adults and children can grow (Drago-Severson, 2004b). My hope is that the practices I present below (i.e., teaming, providing teachers with leadership roles, engaging in collegial inquiry, and mentoring) will enable teachers to support their own and each other's growth in more effective ways—so that they do not have to leave schools in order to grow. Learning together and employing the practices that follow are one fruitful path to enhancing teacher leadership and creating schools where teachers, our most precious resource, thrive.

THE CONTEXT AND THE STUDY: LEADERSHIP WORK IN SUPPORT OF TEACHER LEARNING

When a teacher leader or principal committed to children's learning employs practices that support teacher learning, adults flourish. However, we need more knowledge about effective programs that support adult learning by focusing on the ways that adults make sense of their experience (Drago-Severson, 2004a, 2004b; Kegan, 1994, 2000). My research responds by identifying effective practices that can be employed to support teacher learning and leadership. Specifically my research examined the practices that 25 successful principals serving in U.S. public, Catholic, and independent schools (elementary, middle, high school, and K–12 with varying levels of financial resources) employed to effectively support adult learning within their schools (see Drago-Severson, 2004b). This work addressed the questions: What do principals do to support adult learning? How do they shape leadership practices that support transformational learning (i.e., learning that increases adults' cognitive and affective capacities to better manage the complexity of work and life)? What developmental principles underlie practices that support transformational learning?

I suggest that teacher leaders can also employ these practices to support their own and each other's growth and learning. In this chapter I discuss:

1. Constructive-developmental theory and how it informs adult growth and development;

2. A new model of learning-oriented leadership; and

3. Four pillar practices-for-growth that can be tailored to any teacher leader's particular setting and work to support the growth of adults working in schools.

THEORIES INFORMING THIS RESEARCH

Researchers and practitioners have long recognized that attention to the role of the principal is *one* key to school improvement because leadership supportive of adult development makes schools better places of learning for children (Barth, 1980, 1990, 2001; Howe, 1993; Sergiovanni, 1995). More recently, the need for teacher leadership has occupied national attention because we know that teachers are essential to making schools contexts for growth (Hargreaves & Fink, 2004; Lambert, 2003; Spillane, 2005). Three kinds of literature informed this research: (a) literature on leadership for teachers' development, (b) professional development literature, and (c) adult developmental theory. Taken together, these writings provide a foundation for generating a new model of learning-oriented school leadership. I briefly summarize these here (for an in-depth discussion, please see Drago-Severson, 2004b).

The literature suggests three ways school leaders can support teacher learning: (a) creating a developmentally oriented school culture (Evans, 1996; Sarason, 1995), (b) building interpersonal relationships among teachers (Barth, 1990; Bolman & Deal, 1995), and (c) emphasizing teacher learning (Elmore, 2002; Johnson, 1990, 1996; Johnson et al., 2001, 2004).

However, this research is almost entirely theoretical, and the question of how specific leadership practices support teacher growth within a school has not been investigated (Donaldson, 2001, 2006; Levine, 1989; Lieberman & Miller, 2001). Furthermore, there is a lack of consensus as to what constitutes teacher development and how to support it; current models operate on divergent assumptions (Cochran-Smith & Lytle, 2001; Darling-Hammond, 2003). Conspicuously missing from many professional development models is attention to teachers' different ways of knowing, or the meaning-making system through which all experience is filtered and understood (Drago-Severson, 1994, 2004b).

Drawing on adult developmental theory, I define growth increases in cognitive and affective capacities that enable adults to manage better the demands of teaching, learning, and life (Drago-Severson, 2004b). An increase in these capacities enables us to take broader perspectives on others and ourselves. I employed constructive-developmental theory to highlight developmental underpinnings of the practices of the principals in my study and to understand how adults develop in learning-oriented programs. As noted earlier, adults with different preferences, needs, and developmental orientations need different forms of support and challenge to grow through participation in learning opportunities.

Constructive-Developmental Theory and Our Ways of Knowing

Robert Kegan's (1982, 1994, 2000) constructive-developmental theory centers on two fundamental premises: (a) As human beings, we actively make sense of our experiences, and (b) the ways we make meaning of our experiences can change over time. Research suggests that in any school, it is likely that adults will be making sense of their experiences in developmentally different ways (Drago-Severson, 2004a, 2004b; Kegan, 1994; Kegan et al., 2001). Therefore, teacher leaders need to attend to this type of developmental diversity, in addition to other important forms of diversity. To do this, it is necessary to incorporate learning-oriented leadership practices that will support and challenge adults with different ways of knowing.

Also referred to as a "developmental level" or a "meaning-making system" (Kegan, 1982) or an "order of consciousness" (Kegan, 1994), one's way of knowing dictates how learning experiences—and all experiences—will be understood, managed, and used. In other words, a person's way of knowing organizes how he or she understands his or her experience of the self, others, teaching, working collaboratively, and all life situations. Each way of knowing has its own logic, which is different from and builds upon the previous logic by incorporating the former into its new system. Moving from one way of knowing to the next is a progression of increasing complexity in an individual's cognitive and affective capacities. Put simply, a person's way of knowing shapes how he or she understands his or her role and responsibilities as a teacher, leader, and learner, and how he or she thinks about what makes a good teacher, what makes a good leader, what constitutes effective teaching practice, and the types of supports he or she needs from colleagues in order to engage effectively in various forms of adult collaboration.

There are three qualitatively different ways of knowing that are most common in adulthood: the *instrumental,* the *socializing,* and the *self-authoring* way of knowing. Here, I describe some of the key characteristics of these ways of knowing; however, it is important to note that there are also four discernible transition stages between each of them (for a fuller description, please see Drago-Severson, 2004a, 2004b). Growing from one way of knowing to another is a progression of increasing complexity in an individual's developmental capacities. Growth of this type is dependent on available and needed supports and challenges. Each way of knowing has developmental strengths and limitations.

The Instrumental Way of Knowing

A person who has an instrumental way of knowing has a "what do you have that can help me/what do I have that can help you" perspective and orientation to teaching, learning, and life. A strength of this way of knowing is that a person understands that visible events, processes, and situations have a reality separate from his own point of view, although he understands the world in very concrete terms (Drago-Severson, 2004b, 2006a, 2006b). Although instrumental knowers have the developmental capacity to take perspective on and control their impulses, they do not have this same perspective on their needs, desires, and interests. In general, another person's interests are important only if they interfere with one's own. A limitation to this way of knowing is that a person cannot yet take on another's perspective fully. Instrumental knowers do not have the capacity to think abstractly, nor can they make generalizations from one context to another.

The Socializing Way of Knowing

A person who makes meaning mostly with a socializing way of knowing has an enhanced capacity for reflection. Unlike adults who are instrumental knowers, socializing knowers have the developmental capacity to think abstractly and to reflect on their own and others' actions. With this way of knowing, a person is able to subordinate her own needs and desires to the needs and desires of others. However, she is not yet able to have a perspective on her relationships. Others' approval and acceptance are of utmost importance to socializing knowers. A valued authority's expectations, for example, become one's *own* expectations. In other words, other people, and often societal expectations, are understood and experienced not simply as resources to be used by the self (as they are for instrumental knowers), but rather as the origin of internal confirmation or authority (Drago-Severson, 2004b, 2006a). Socializing knowers orient to their internal states. They feel responsible for other people's feelings and hold others responsible for their own feelings.

The Self-Authoring Way of Knowing

Adults with a self-authoring way of knowing have the developmental capacity to generate their own internal value system, and they take responsibility for and ownership of their own internal authority (Drago-Severson, 2004b, 2006). They can identify (and are identified *with*) abstract values, principles, and longer-term purposes and are able to prioritize and integrate competing values. Self-authoring knowers can assess other people's expectations and demands and compare them to their own internal standards and judgment. A person who makes meaning with a self-authoring way of knowing internally generates his own system of beliefs or personal philosophy. He has the capacity to reflect on and regulate his interpersonal relationships, but is limited by an inability to take perspective on his own autonomy, or self-system, which manages relationships, because it is embedded in his own assertions, theories, and standards.

Why Do Our Ways of Knowing Matter When Supporting Adult Growth and Teacher Leadership?

A developmental stance helps us understand the developmental basis of practices that support adult learning as well as how teachers and other adults will experience participation in the four pillar practices-for-growth. It also shows how a "holding environment" (Kegan, 1982)—or the context in and out of which a person grows—can be created within these practices to facilitate adults' transformational learning, or growth that signifies a change in their capacities to handle the complexities of their work and lives (Drago-Severson, 2004b).

A good holding environment, which can be a relationship, a series of relationships, an organization, or a group, serves three important functions. First, it needs to "hold well" by recognizing and confirming who a person is. This means meeting a person where he or she is, without an urgent need to push for change. This first purpose includes providing developmentally appropriate supports to accommodate the way a person is presently making meaning and organizing his or her experience. Second, and only when a person is ready, a holding environment needs to "let go" and provide challenge, enabling the person to grow beyond his or her current way of organizing reality to a new, more complex way of knowing. Finally, a robust holding environment needs to remain in place and provide continuity and stability to the person as he or she reemerges so that relationships can be re-known and re-created in a way that supports who the person has grown to become (Drago-Severson, 2004a, 2004b, 2006a, 2006b; Drago-Severson et al., 2001a; Kegan, 1982, 1994). Notably, the most effective holding environments provide individuals with developmentally appropriate forms of high support *and* high challenge in order to support growth. Any one of the pillar practices-for-growth can serve as a "holding environment" for adults who make meaning with different ways of knowing (Drago-Severson, 2004b, 2006).

For example, some professional development initiatives, such as engaging in teacher collaboration, invite adults to share decision making in order to make informed decisions about practice. However, adults will experience this kind of invitation differently because they have different capacities for self-reflection and perspective taking (Drago-Severson, 2004b, 2006). For teachers who are instrumental knowers, establishing rules for conversation while engaging in shared decision making will be experienced as supportive. Encouraging these adults to move beyond what they see as the "right answers" and toward open-ended dialogue wherein multiple perspectives are discussed and considered will broaden their perspectives and support growth in thinking. Teachers who are *socializing* knowers, for instance, look to valued colleagues or authorities for direction in their decision making. They will need to be supportively challenged, over time, to gradually look to themselves *first* for direction in decision making. In contrast, adults who are *self-authoring* knowers look internally—to their own set of values—when making decisions. Teachers, and all adults, for that matter, with this way of knowing are able to hold and coordinate multiple perspectives when making decisions or voicing their views. Conflict is experienced as a natural part of dialogue for adults with this way of knowing. In contrast, adults who are socializing knowers experience conflict with the opinions of valued colleagues as a threat to the self and their relationships. This means that the way in which adults will be able to engage in collaborative work or in shared decision making will vary according to *how* they make sense of the process. It also means that with appropriate supports and challenges adults can grow to participate in these processes even more effectively (for a full discussion, please see Drago-Severson 2004b).

HOW TEACHER LEADERSHIP CAN SUPPORT ADULT LEARNING: KEY LESSONS

Here I focus on the four pillar practices-for-growth identified by my research to assist teacher leaders in supporting their own and others' transformational learning (Drago-Severson, 2004b).

Successful principals in my research employed four broad practices aimed at transformational learning: (a) teaming, (b) providing other adults with leadership roles, (c) collegial inquiry, and (d) mentoring (Drago-Severson, 2004b). All four of these practices centered on adult collaboration. In their application, these initiatives ranged from newly implemented to mastery, and created opportunities for using reflective practice as a tool for professional and personal development. Often, practitioners have difficulty doing more than responding from assumption and instinct because the time and tools for reflection are limited. Reflective practice supports adults in developing the capacities to better manage the complexities of their work. Through systematic reflection with colleagues, teachers *and* principals become better able to view their thinking through the lenses of others, which can lead to alternative frameworks and the reframing of assumptions. Any one of these pillar practices can serve as a holding environment (Kegan, 1982) for growth. As a teacher leader, you can benefit from employing these four practices in your school.

First Pillar: Teaming

Teaming promotes sharing perspectives, providing opportunities for individuals to understand their own and other people's thinking and assumptions. As a teacher leader, working with colleagues in teams can help you to support your own and your colleagues' learning and growth. Almost all of the leaders in my study used teaming to promote personal and organizational learning through various forms of adult collaboration, including curriculum, literacy, technology teams, teaching, and diversity teams. Many organized their schools for teamwork. They described how teaming opens communication, decreases isolation, enables the sharing of leadership, and enhances the implementation of changes (Drago-Severson, 2004b).

Working in teams can create a safe place for teachers to experiment with their own thinking and challenge each other's perspectives as a means to growth. For example, each team member can be encouraged to have a voice in ongoing dialogues about practice and student work and to envision alternative ways of acting. Individuals working in teams can also provide support to each other, thus potentially creating a "holding environment" (Kegan, 1982) in which people take risks by sharing their own and opening up to other people's perspectives. Learning to appreciate others' perspectives can enhance the potential for teachers to better manage situations with multiple viewpoints. Importantly, though, voicing opinions and beliefs could be perceived as risky for individuals at different developmental levels. Instrumental knowers might find it difficult and need support as they grow to be able to consider and understand multiple perspectives. Teachers who are socializing knowers could find it uncomfortable initially, especially when conflict emerges. These adults would need to be encouraged, over time, to understand that conflict can be a means to developing better and more effective initiatives or solutions. In contrast, learning from conflict and diverse perspectives would be experienced as stimulating and supportive to self-authoring knowers. Encouraging and gently challenging these adults to consider perspectives that diametrically oppose their own would support their growth—and their growing edge. The team structure can thus provide a safe context within which to experiment with one's thinking, improve teaching practices, and grow.

Second Pillar: Providing Leadership Roles

Encouraging adults to assume leadership roles supports growth and learning through sharing power and decision-making authority. In many of the schools in my study, teachers, staff, and administrators were invited to embrace leadership roles. Successful principals reported that leadership roles provided teachers (and themselves) with opportunities for transformational learning. In their view, people grow and develop from being responsible for an idea's development or implementation (Drago-Severson, 2004b). For example, many of these school leaders stressed their efforts to support teachers' ideas for implementation. Some principals asked teachers who proposed ideas to develop a written proposal and share it with the school community. Even developing the proposal can encourage the development of certain skills or capacities in community members.

Working with others in a leadership role helps adults to uncover their assumptions and to test out new ways of acting. Principals understand this practice as inviting teachers to share authority and ideas as teachers, curriculum developers, or school administrators as they work toward building community and promoting change. Their stories highlight the rewards and challenges faced by both principals and teachers (please see Drago-Severson, 2004b). Leadership roles can help teacher leaders to negotiate the sometimes-competing demands of supporting oneself and each other while attending to practice and larger school needs. Engaging in leadership roles and supporting other teacher leaders in these roles create opportunities to tailor forms of support and challenge to individual needs. These roles offer opportunities for transformational learning.

Like teaming, though, leadership roles can be perceived differently by teachers with distinct ways of knowing. Whereas those who are challenged by assuming their own authority—instrumental and socializing knowers— might initially require considerable support as they take on leadership roles, self-authoring knowers might appreciate the opportunity to put their plans into action. Still, leadership roles can serve as effective and rich holding environments for adults with diverse ways of knowing, especially if supports and challenges are offered to the person assuming the role so that he or she can grow from it.

Third Pillar: Collegial Inquiry

Collegial inquiry is a shared dialogue directed toward helping oneself and others become more aware of their own guiding assumptions and their influence on the teaching and learning process. Principals in the study used this to engage themselves and other adults in conflict resolution, decision making, and learning about key developmental issues (e.g., diversity). Examples include:

- Reflecting privately in writing in response to probing questions followed by public discussion;
- Collaborating in the process of goal setting and evaluation with others;
- Sharing thinking in response to questions related to a school's mission and practices; and
- Reflecting collectively when engaging with conflict toward resolution.

Creating situations for adults to regularly think and talk about practice in the context of supportive relationships encourages self-analysis and can improve the individual's and the school's practice. An example helps to bring this practice and its potential for supporting adult growth to life.

Receiving Feedback and Goal Setting: A Developmental View

What kinds of feedback best support your own and other teacher's learning? Since teachers—and all adults—bring various developmental needs and orientations with them to the goal setting and evaluation process, we need to understand adults' reactions to feedback through a developmental lens in order to best help support and challenge that individual's learning and help them grow (Drago-Severson, 2004b, 2006).

Adults will experience—and understand feedback—in developmentally different ways. As explained earlier, how teachers make meaning of their experiences varies at different developmental levels. For example, as Table 30.1 illuminates, adults with an *instrumental way* of knowing will likely experience a colleague's feedback on their teaching practices as if they are doing things the right or wrong way. Teachers with a *socializing way* of knowing see valued colleagues as individuals who have information that they should know to meet their own or the group's goals and expectations. Colleagues' expectations for their work and practice become their own expectations. Teachers with a *self-authoring way* of knowing, in contrast, generate their own expectations for their work. They have grown to have the developmental capacity to weigh their colleagues' perspectives and suggestions and then look to their own internal authority to decide how to improve their teaching practice. These individuals see themselves and colleagues as knowledge generators, such that domains of knowledge

Table 30.1 How Adults With Different Ways of Knowing Experience the Pillar Practice of Collegial Inquiry

Way of knowing	Supports	Challenges (Growing edge)
Instrumental knowers	Establishing step-by-step guidelines or rules for how to engage in discussion. Sharing the concrete details of their practice and whether it is "right" or "wrong." Engaging in conversation with others is supportive when it provides concrete advice, skills, and information about practice. Colleagues are experienced as resources with information and skills. Addressing concrete needs for improving practice (e.g., learning better skills or more effective rules to follow).	Thinking more abstractly by discussing and reflecting on one's own practice and other people's practices to understand and evaluate themselves through another person's point of view.
Socializing knowers	Meeting the expectations of valued others and evaluating themselves based upon what the other important people think of their ideas. Acceptance from colleagues and principals will help these teachers feel recognized and safe in taking risks and sharing their own perspectives. Sharing their own perspectives in pairs or smaller groups before sharing their perspectives with larger groups. Differences of opinion will be experienced as being okay as long as colleagues remain connected and the interpersonal relationships are not jeopardized.	Developing their own beliefs and values independent of what valued others think they should be thinking or doing; becoming less dependent on the approval of others.
Self-authoring knowers	Learning from the process of growing their own capabilities and competencies. Evaluating and critiquing their own practices, decisions, vision, and internally generated standards within the larger context of the school. Emphasizing becoming more competent and extending their own options in order to achieve their self-determined goals. Inviting these teachers to create some structures for how to proceed with the process of collegial inquiry, (i.e., allowing them to demonstrate their competencies). Conflict as a natural part of dialogue that can help the group arrive at better solutions, more effective practice, and/or ideas for implementation.	To be less invested in their own identities, standards, perspectives, and more open to standards, values, and perspectives that are directly opposed to their own; to experience themselves as being process driven.

From *Helping Teachers Learn: Principal Leadership for Adult Growth and Development*, by E. Drago-Severson, 2004, Thousand Oaks, CA: Corwin Press. www.corwinpress.com. Reproduction authorized only for the local school site that has purchased this book.

are context dependent and come from an internal source. Each of these ways of making sense of goal setting, collaboration, and receiving feedback influences how a teacher will perceive and understand feedback. Thus it is vital for teacher leaders to consider the various ways their colleagues make sense of these and other learning experiences in order to consider how to best support each other's learning and growth.

Collegial inquiry is a practice that holds the potential to provide a supportive, safe learning environment in which teachers can develop greater awareness of their beliefs and assumptions and reflect with others in ways that may allow them to envision alternative ways of thinking or behaving. In summary, a teacher, like all adults, will experience collaborative work, goal setting, and feedback in an individual and unique way that is related to how she makes sense of her experience. When providing feedback to teachers it is important to consider how to offer feedback that supports the individual teacher based on assessment of her needs and also challenges to her thinking in order to support growth.

Fourth Pillar: Mentoring

Mentoring is a relational practice that traditionally offers a more private way of supporting development and growth. It can help teachers build school cultures that facilitate their own and each other's growth. Across school types and resource levels, the principals in my study talked about how the purposes of mentoring programs varied from "mission spreading" to exchanging information to providing emotional support to new *and* experienced teachers and staff (Drago-Severson, 2004b). Principals selected mentors according to different criteria, including understanding of the mission, teaching experience, disciplinary focus, and nonacademic characteristics, and these programs worked differently in each school. In all cases, principals valued this practice and shared how they think it supports their own and other adults' learning.

Teacher leaders can create robust and highly effective mentoring programs. One important element to consider when conceptualizing mentoring programs is the goodness of fit between the mentor and mentee and adults' developmentally different needs for different types of support and challenge when engaging in this practice (Drago-Severson, 2004b, 2006). Although a pair of teachers need not necessarily be matched for developmental orientation, mentors should probably not be operating with a dominant instrumental way of knowing, in order to best facilitate the learning of the mentee.

Our ways of knowing will influence what we need from mentoring relationships and the kinds of expectations we have for our mentors. For example, instrumental knowers will feel supported by mentors who help them meet their concrete needs and who patiently explain the step-by-step procedures for achieving the "right solutions" and concrete goals. Over time, a mentor will want to encourage an adult with this way of knowing to move beyond what he sees as the "right answers" and toward engaging in open-ended discussion, which will broaden his perspective and stretch his thinking. A socializing knower will feel supported by a mentor's explicit acknowledgment of his beliefs and points of view. Feeling known and accepted by mentors will be of great importance to adults with this way of knowing. To support growth, a mentor would want to encourage his mentee to consider and voice his own perspective before learning about other people's perspectives. Also important would be to demonstrate, by modeling, that conflict of opinion is okay, does not threaten the relationship, and can support growth. Self-authoring knowers will feel supported in mentoring relationships that enable them to learn about diverse perspectives, critique and analyze their own and their mentor's practice, and provide opportunities to demonstrate their competencies. To support growth, over time mentors can encourage self-authoring mentees to let go of their investment in and identification with their own understanding or strategies without feeling internally conflicted (Drago-Severson).

IMPLICATIONS FOR LEARNING-ORIENTED TEACHER LEADERS

This work introduces a new way of enhancing teacher leadership and supporting adult development and learning, which I call *learning-oriented school leadership*. By drawing on current research and adult developmental theory, it offers specific practices supportive of adults' transformational learning (Drago-Severson, 2004b). Importantly, each practice can be modified to meet the needs and conditions of your school. This research provides insight and concrete practices for creating opportunities to supporting your own and your colleagues' learning and development. As developmental practices, teaming, leadership roles, collegial inquiry, and mentoring can be adapted to meet the needs and conditions of your particular school and staff. By presenting a variety of practices, I hope to help teacher leaders find multiple options that suit their preferences and their own school contexts.

Learning-oriented school leadership needs to attend to developing adults' capacities to manage the complexities of their teaching work. Learning-oriented school leadership needs to be about more than practice and improvement: It needs to attend to developing ongoing capacities for handling complexities within adults. The four *pillar* practices that compose this model can assist teacher leaders as they work to build collegial relationships, strengthen collaboration, and enhance their own and other people's practice. Understanding and nurturing this, in my view, is directly tied to improving teaching and teacher leadership in support of children's growth and improved achievement.

There are four important implications that I would like to highlight from this model.

1. Teacher leaders can benefit from a developmental perspective when supporting colleagues with different ways of knowing because they will experience practices in different ways.

2. A developmental vocabulary helps us to *understand* adults' experiences and better support adults with different needs.

3. Teachers, like all adults, need *different* supports and challenges to grow. These supports and challenges can be embedded in the four pillar practices.

4. Consideration of the developmental match between the expectations of a school culture and adults' capacity to meet such expectations will help shape collaborative school cultures that support adult growth and lifelong learning (Drago-Severson, 2004b).

The four pillar practices take into account how a person makes meaning of the experience in order to grow from participation (Drago-Severson, 2004b, 2006). The best way of supporting adult learning and teacher leadership resembles the ways we support the growth and development of children and youth. By this I mean that when we consider how to best support development, we think carefully about developmentally appropriate supports and challenges. This helps us to see how differences in behaviors and thinking are often related to differences in how a person *constructs* his experience, and it provides us with a language for discussing development. It helps us to understand that we need to look beneath behaviors to understand a person's meaning making.

This work offers a range of practices that are supportive of individuals at different stages of their careers and with different developmental orientations. It also points to the need for and promise of reflective practice for teacher leaders (Drago-Severson, 2004b). At the end of the professional development workshop I introduced at the start of this chapter, we discussed how these experienced teachers might use some of the pillar practices to strengthen their leadership and teaching practice. In addition to voicing a common need for more time to collaborate, they unanimously agreed on what one participant, Katie, proposed: "All along, we've known that our primary concern and agenda has been to support children's growth, learning, and development. It occurs to me, now, how rarely I've thought about the need to support adult learning. This is really important and needs to be part of our shared agenda in our school."

I hope that learning about these pillar practices and the developmental principles underlying them is helpful to you and your leadership work in support of transformational learning. Learning-oriented leadership can successfully support adults with different needs, preferences, and developmental orientations. Vital to student success and to teachers themselves is professional development that can renew in adults an excitement for learning, growing, and teaching. Learning-oriented leadership and the four pillar practices can help us achieve these goals and meet the challenges of 21st-century schooling.

REFERENCES

Ackerman, R. H., & Maslin-Ostrowski, P. (2002). *The wounded leader: How real leadership emerges in times of crisis.* San Francisco: Jossey-Bass.

Barth, R. S. (1980). *Run school run.* Cambridge: Harvard University Press.

Barth, R. S. (1990). *Improving schools from within: Teachers, parents, and principals can make the difference.* San Francisco: Jossey-Bass.

Barth, R. S. (2001). *Learning by heart.* San Francisco: Jossey-Bass.

Boles, K., & Troen, V. (2005, January/February). Let's professionalize teaching. *Principal Magazine* (National Association of Elementary School Principals), *84*(3), 34–37.

Bolman, L. G., & Deal, T. (1995). *Leading with soul: An uncommon journey of spirit.* San Francisco: Jossey Bass.

Cochran-Smith, M., & Lytle, S. (2001). Beyond certainty: Taking an inquiry stance on practice. In A. Lieberman & L. Miller (Eds.), *Teachers caught in the action: Professional development that matters* (pp. 45–58). New York: Teachers College Press.

Darling-Hammond, L. (2003). Enhancing teaching. In W. Owens & L. S. Kaplan (Eds.), *Best practices, best thinking, and emerging issues in leadership* (pp. 75–87). Thousand Oaks, CA: Corwin Press.

Donaldson, G. A. (2001). *Cultivating leadership in schools: Connecting people, purpose, and practice.* New York: Teachers College Press.

Donaldson, G. A. (2006). *Cultivating leadership in schools: Connecting people, purpose, and practice* (2nd Edition). New York: Teachers College Press.

Drago-Severson, E. (1994). *What does "staff development" develop? How the staff development literature conceives adult growth.* Cambridge, MA: Harvard Graduate School of Education.

Drago-Severson, E. (2004a). *Becoming adult learners: Principles and practices for effective development.* New York: Teachers College Press.

Drago-Severson, E. (2004b). *Helping teachers learn: Principal leadership for adult growth and development.* Thousand Oaks: Corwin Press.

Drago-Severson, E. (2006a). How can you better support teachers' growth? *The Learning Principal, 1*(6), 1, 6–7.

Drago-Severson, E. (2006b, Summer). Learning-oriented leadership. *Independent School Journal,* pp. 58–61 & 64.

Drago-Severson, E. (in press). *Leading adult learning: Promising practices for supporting adult growth and development.* Thousand Oaks, CA: Corwin Press.

Elmore, R. (2002, January/February). The limits of change. *Harvard Education Letter,* 1–4.

Elmore, R. F. (2004). *Educating educators: A promising partnership between HGSE and public school leaders.* Retrieved from http://www.gse.harvard.edu/news/features/elmore 07012004.html on August 23, 2006.

Evans, R. (1996). *The human side of change: Reform, resistance, and the real-life problems of innovation.* San Francisco: Jossey-Bass.

Fullan, M. (2005). *Leadership and sustainability: System thinkers in action.* Thousand Oaks, CA and Ontario: Corwin Press and The Ontario Principals' Center.

Guskey, T. R. (1999). *Evaluating professional development.* Thousand Oaks, CA: Corwin Press.

Hargreaves, A., & Fink, D. (2004). The seven principles of sustainable leadership. *Educational Leadership, 61*(7), 8–15.

Howe, H. (1993). *Thinking about our kids: An agenda for American education.* New York: Free Press.

Johnson, S. M. (1990). *Teachers at work: Achieving success in our schools.* New York: Basic Books.

Johnson, S. M. (1996). *Leading to change: The challenge of the new superintendency.* San Francisco: Jossey-Bass.

Johnson, S. M., Birkeland, S., Kardos, S. M., Kauffman, D., Liu, E., & Peske, H. G. (2004). *Finders and keepers: Helping new teachers survive and thrive in our schools.* San Francisco: Jossey-Bass.

Johnson, S. M., Birkeland, S., Kardos, S. M., Kauffman, D., Liu, E., & Peske, H. G. (2001, July/August). Retaining the next generation of teachers: The importance of school-based support. *Harvard Education Letter, 17*(4), 8 & 6.

Kegan, R. (1982). *The evolving self: Problems and process in human development.* Cambridge, MA: Harvard University Press.

Kegan, R. (1994). *In over our heads: The mental demands of modern life.* Cambridge, MA: Harvard University Press.

Kegan, R. (2000). What "form" transforms? A constructive-developmental approach to transformative learning. In J. Mezirow and Associates (Eds.), *Learning as transformation* (pp. 35–70). San Francisco: Jossey-Bass.

Kegan, R., Broderick, M., Drago-Severson, E., Helsing, D., Popp, N., & Portnow, K. (2001). *Toward a "new pluralism" in the ABE/ESOL classroom: Teaching to multiple "cultures of mind"* (NCSALL Monograph No. 19). Boston: World Education.

Lambert, L. (2003). *Leadership capacity for lasting school improvement.* Alexandria, VA: Association for Supervision and Curriculum Development.

Levine, S. L. (1989). *Promoting adult development in schools: The promise of professional development.* Boston: Allyn & Bacon.

Lieberman, A., & Miller, L. (Eds.). (2001). *Teachers caught in the action: Professional development that matters.* New York: Teachers College Press.

Little, J. W. (2001). Professional development in pursuit of school reform. In A. Lieberman & L. Miller (Eds.), *Teachers caught in the action: Professional development that matters* (pp. 23–44). New York: Teachers College Press.

Moller, G., & Pankake, A. (2006). *Lead with me: A principal's guide to teacher leadership.* Larchmont, NY: Eye on Education.

Sarason, S. B. (1995). *Revisiting the culture of schools and the problem of change.* New York: Teachers College Press.

Sergiovanni, T. J. (1995). *The principalship: A reflective practice perspective.* Needham Heights, MA: Allyn & Bacon.

Silva, D. Y., Gimbert, B., & Nolan, J. (2000). Sliding the doors: Locking and unlocking possibilities for teacher leadership. *Teachers College Record, 102*(4), 779–804.

Spillane, J. (2005). Primary school leadership practice: How the subject matters. *School Leadership & Management,* 383–397.

31

Encouraging Districtwide Teacher Leadership

Mary Ann Minard

The room is crowded as the last school committee meeting of the year gets under way. Three reporters sit with pencils poised; the television technician makes his final adjustments for the live broadcast; and two groups of teachers prepare to make their public presentations of the newly created K–12 Visual and Performing Arts and Career Preparation curricula. Despite the fact that the morning will bring the final day of school, the teachers are energized, their conversations and actions relaxed and punctuated with laughter. I am proud to work with such a group of dedicated professionals, and I am grateful, as the district's curriculum coordinator, for their knowledge, their commitment, and their expertise. In 4 years our school system has created K–12 vertical teams in eight subject areas, resulting in collegiality among members of each of the teams as teachers developed cohesive curricula. The tasks have been daunting, the timeline compressed, the struggles evident; yet the teachers' proud faces serve to remind me that our work is important and valued. How did the teachers move from being isolated strangers in separate buildings to becoming friends and coleaders in these curricular efforts? As I study the faces before me, I wonder what administrative actions empowered them to assume leadership roles, and how did we encourage the development of the multiple voices of teacher leadership?

Communicating expectations and setting the stage for change were important first steps in increasing teacher leadership in our district. Designing and promoting a vision of excellence on the basis of system-wide continuity was a priority for us in a system that had long prided itself on its building-level autonomy. The superintendent and I developed a strategic plan based on the New American Schools model. We created a 5-year map for K–12 curriculum and assessment development and designed a system for K–12 curriculum teams as well as a districtwide K–12 Teacher Leadership Team designed to serve in an advisory capacity to the central office administrators. This team designs the district's professional development, which incorporates school change efforts.

All curricular areas have K–12 teams in place. School principals expect teachers to participate in at least one districtwide team. Teachers set their own norms and schedules for team meetings and work collaboratively on K–12 initiatives. The team members share their building-level successes and struggles while supporting each other's efforts. In math, for example, the move to a standards-based program at the middle school level was initially met with parental resistance. The K–12 Math Team organized a parent information meeting at which high school team members were instrumental in garnering parental support for the middle school program because they spoke clearly about the success of the students at the high school level who had been involved in the math pilot program. Likewise, when the fifth-grade teachers expressed their concern about the new program, the K–12 Math Team requested a meeting with the group. At one point during the meeting, a fifth-grade teacher commented, "Fifth-grade teachers need to solve this matter because this is a fifth-grade problem." Immediately, an eighth-grade teacher responded, "No, this is a middle school problem." The words were hardly spoken before a high school teacher declared firmly, "No, this is a K–12 problem." Activities such as cross-school visits, meetings, and observations have created a true district-wide team.

Professional development is an important element in developing the voices of our teacher leaders. Teachers and administrators share a common language and knowledge based on the principles of *The Skillful Teacher*. Learning more about the challenges of teaching at the various levels has increased respect among educators, helped faculty members to expand their circle of colleagues, and encouraged conversation about instruction that extends beyond the school walls.

Offering in-district courses taught by our own faculty members recognizes the value of the voices of experienced educators as instructors. We hold a Summer Institute during the week immediately following the final days of the school year. Our teachers and others offer a menu of courses that are opportunities for in-depth conversations about teaching and learning. Wellness options, including massage and Reiki, and celebratory luncheons punctuate the Summer Institute and create an environment conducive to collegiality. In this relaxed atmosphere, teachers share ideas, learn from each other, and have the time to reflect on their instruction and their roles as teacher leaders.

We value collaborative inquiry, which has long been recognized as critical to sustained change and the development of shared leadership. Administrators and teacher leaders have participated in Critical Friends Group training and use the protocols regularly in administrative team meetings and in small school-based voluntary groups (see chapter 36 for more about Critical Friends Groups). Teachers identify the foci for the Critical Friends Groups. The system supports them through release time or funding for meetings after school. Although these groups are organized at the building level, the K–12 application of the principles and protocols of the Critical Friends Groups helps to validate the complexity of the work that is taking place in each building and encourages the voices of teacher leaders to ask difficult questions of themselves and their peers. Because principals understand Critical Friends Group processes, they can employ protocols in faculty meetings and problem-solving sessions at the building levels.

The voices of teachers, so confident in classrooms, sound less self-assured when they engage in discussions with peers. We have strengthened the voices of teacher leaders by establishing the expectation of professional interaction through K–12 teams; by designing opportunities for teachers to collaborate on meaningful, important work; and by providing professional development to support teacher leadership and learning. We hear teacher leaders' voices as they engage in inquiry, debate, decision making, and espousal of district initiatives.

Questions for Reflection and Conversation

- Have you worked with principals who have kept the teacher leader alive in their practice of leadership? What qualities did they have? Did they make you think it easier or harder to be this kind of leader?
- Describe your vision of a 'teacherly' school—that is, one that focuses on teaching and learning and the needs of that essential activity of the school. What would it look like and feel like? How could your school take a few steps closer to this ideal?
- Consider using a consultancy protocol. This one is designed for use with others. Essentially, you present to a small group the context of your work, some major issues or problems with which you are struggling, and a question for the consultancy group to consider. The goal is not for them to give you advice, but rather it is to help you understand the issues more fully as they push and probe your thinking about the problem or dilemma.

As is typical in protocols of this type, after the members of the group ask you clarifying and probing questions, you remain silent as you listen to them discuss your problem and their insights about it. They do not discuss their own situations at all. They focus on you as they provide feedback, analyze your situation, and offer conjectures about aspects of the problem they hope will enlarge your understanding. You then respond to them, if you wish, about what was useful or how you are thinking about the situation having heard their comments.

PART V

Nurturing Teacher Leaders

This section of the book might, at first glance, be considered a technical one. It tries to get at answers to the question of how to make teacher leadership a viable reality. We provide chapters here that describe how schools or other organizations nurture teacher leaders—that is, how they support and sustain teacher leadership. Coupled with the nourishment and encouragement of individuals is the cultivation of teacher leadership, creating cultures and structures that make it safe for people to feel they are leaders or have a role in leadership. The pieces we have compiled focus on the former, which is appropriate in a book devoted to the inner world of individuals. When educational reformers speak about building capacity, to us, they refer to the notion that developing individuals—their teaching and their leadership practice—has exponential effects on the ability of the school to meet its goal of improving learning for all students. The important point, though, is not to picture the principal, the curriculum coordinator, or any other administrator as *the* leader bringing other little leaders along. The development process is dynamic so everyone coaches, bolsters, champions, pushes, sustains other school leaders as they learn and grow together.

We begin with Linda Bowe's reflection on her coaching of teacher leaders that builds on her experience being similarly coached. Granted, her coach was not a colleague or principal from her school, but the process of coaching is the same, and it moves a bit away from mentoring. Coaching means "support[ing] the colleague in developing his or her expertise in planning, reflecting, problem solving, and decision making. . . . By focusing on the perceptions, thinking, and decision-making processes of the other person, the skillful coach develops the colleague's resources for self-directed learning" (Garmston & Wellman, 1999, p. 28). This concept is very much in keeping with constructive leadership; moreover, skillful leadership means helping others discover inner resources so they, reciprocally, can refine, enhance, and build on them in enacting their leadership.

Sam Intrator highlights the idea of nourishing the spirits of teachers and teacher leaders in his chapter describing the Teacher Formation work inspired by Parker Palmer. Ellie Drago-Severson, Jennifer Roloff Welch, and Anne E. Jones suggest another way to think about stimulating the teacher leader's heart. They describe a course in teacher leadership that delves into both the intellectual and the emotional needs of teacher leaders. Barnett Berry and John Norton describe a third way of helping individual teacher leaders connect with others outside their own venues and find ways to sustain themselves.

The next two pieces present group-oriented, and therefore, more school-based, ways of both supporting and encouraging teacher leaders and, thus, promoting teacher leadership. Deborah Bambino offers a look into the benefits of Critical Friends Groups, which portray the kind of support for and facilitation of adult learning that focuses the energies of educational leaders on improving learning and the conditions for learning in their schools. Jed Frank Lippard tells the story of his professional life to demonstrate both the kind of leader-learner he is and to suggest that charter school educators, in their willingness to explore different ways of leading, provide food for thought about where and how teacher leadership can be nourished and implemented effectively.

Finally, Martha McFarland Williams, a retired teacher, concludes this section with a poignant reminiscence of her career. She found her teacher leadership role in her last years as an informal mentor to novice teachers. Such a teacher leader role is the building block of the collegiality and collaboration we hope for all teachers. Schools are a community of teachers, learners, and leaders, and therein lies the potential for their meaningful improvement.

REFERENCE

Garmston, R., & Wellman, B. (1999). *The adaptive school: A source book for developing collaborative groups.* Norwood, MA: Christopher-Gordon.

32

It Isn't Just a Dream

Linda Bowe

During the past 7 years, I have worked with aspiring teacher leaders and principals in various educational leadership preparation programs. Some were more traditional, university-based programs, and others were field-based experiences, but all were designed to improve schools by increasing the leadership capacity of their personnel. Coaching emerging teacher leaders in the field has been particularly satisfying for me because this approach takes into account the highly contextualized nature of school leadership. Over the years, I have pinpointed a common thread that for me captures the essence of this role. Much like the characters in the *Wizard of Oz* (Baum, 1900) who embark on a journey down the "yellow brick road" seeking a magical person who will grant them the attributes they believe they lack, my primary role is to help teachers more clearly appreciate and actualize the leadership dispositions and qualities they already possess.

My job as coach is to support, guide, and inspire emerging teacher leaders to learn new skills and competencies as they take on the task of improving student learning in their school communities. Often the most formidable challenges they face, however, are intrapersonal; they often lack the self-confidence and assurance that they need in order to make a difference in the larger context of their school. As a result, their growth processes are highly individualized and require care and attention over time.

Like the Tin Man looking for a heart, the Scarecrow looking for a brain, the Lion looking for his nerve, or Dorothy looking for home, I know that developing the heart, head, and hands of leadership is a risky and complex endeavor; these characters' experiences highlight the importance of having someone who can guide them to look deeply inside themselves to discover the attributes they already possess. As I see it, my primary role is to assist the teacher leader to realize his or her strengths and accomplish leadership goals in an atmosphere of supported risk, thus enlarging the home of self.

My own experiences as a teacher leader trying to "find home" taught me much about the power of this kind of transformational journey. Though the journey is fiercely personal, paradoxically, it is not a completely private journey. Rather, the process relies heavily on the relationships developed between the teacher leader and coach over time, a relationship built on trust, integrity, and the endeavor of seeking knowledge together.

Teachers have traditionally held much autonomy within their class-room but have had little professional interaction with their colleagues. This isolation often inhibits their ability to grow as leaders within the greater school community. A coach can help them to bridge into this new world of professional discourse and collaboration. I vividly remember my own for-ays as a resource room teacher venturing into the larger workings of my school. I was just beginning to emerge from the cocoon of the resource room where I had taught for 5 years. I set out to study the effects that the inclu-sion model had on students with special needs in the regular classroom, an initiative I had spearheaded in the previous 2 years. As I laid out my plans for approaching the teachers in my school, I found a parallel between the isolation that my resource students experienced from their peers and my own isolation from the other teachers. Because we had so little experience in talking about our work together, I feared that my inquiries would open me up to their criticism of my advocacy for this change. Although I wanted the feedback, I was frightened by the prospect of receiving it.

My coach listened to my concerns and suggested that I lay out a regu-lar schedule in which to meet these teachers. More important, he offered encouragement to continue the process, despite the intrapersonal chal-lenges of doing so. As a result of our collaborative efforts, my colleagues and I improved our communication and executed some effective ways to teach special education students in the regular education classroom, strategies that we built upon during the years to come. What I discovered was that I did possess the commitment, knowledge, and skill to engage in this collaborative work, but I needed someone who recognized that I had these qualities to encourage me. This experience, and others that followed, taught me the value of having a trusted guardian who could guide and support me, someone who could help me to illuminate the strengths I already had in order to overcome my weaknesses. This is the essence of what I can now offer to the teacher leaders with whom I work.

Even in a school where they are delineated as such, teachers often feel insecure about taking on leadership roles; they think they need to "be" a leader in order to act as one. Not unlike the Tin Man, the Scarecrow, the

Lion, and the lost girl searching for a wizard to grant them traits which they think they lack, many teacher leaders initially look for someone outside themselves to grant them authority as leaders. However, what I and many others have discovered is that their true power as leaders comes from a complex bonding of moral conviction, intention, and action, a process that is intensely personal and dynamic. Many times I have had the experience of working with a teacher leader who has reached out to colleagues who were fearful of change, challenged organizational barriers, or confronted individuals not willing to alter their teaching practices to reach more students. In so doing they have had to reach deeply within themselves to connect with their beliefs so they then acted in principled and disciplined ways. It is often during a quiet moment together, as they share their victories and apprehensions with me, that I have seen a palpable change come over them as they strive to make sense of their experiences. A puzzled look changes to an excited one. "I AM a leader!" they declare, with a conviction that is strong and sincere. They have clarity about what they are contributing to their schools and to themselves. I find that once they have crossed this threshold, these teacher leaders exhibit a confidence that no one could have imparted to them. It is as if they have arrived home.

My primary offerings to these teacher leaders are encouragement, probing questions, and deep listening. My presence and these skills provide the setting for them to explore their inner thoughts and feelings with me. To be of assistance to them, however, I myself must continually build on my own leadership strengths and work to moderate weaknesses. I strive to be vulnerable and open to change myself, for I can only ask them to do what I am willing to do myself. It is through the dynamic relationship between coach and leader that transformational change can occur. Like Dorothy, everything we ever wanted was right in our own backyard, but we have to struggle together to actualize that. We get to go home together, knowing that we have worked our insides out to get there.

REFERENCE

Baum, L.F. (1900). *The wonderful wizard of Oz*. Chicago: George M. Hill Co.

33

The Heart of Teaching

Making the Connection Between Teaching, Leadership, and Inner Life

Sam M. Intrator

THE SOURCE OF GOOD TEACHING AND LEADERSHIP

A few years ago, I interviewed a veteran teacher from South Carolina about her work. She struck me as the embodiment of the very best teachers I've known. She spoke reverentially of the mystery and complexity of learning and how she struggled to understand the "rivers" of her "students' minds." She talked about herself as a quilter—as somebody who knits connections among her students, her colleagues, their families, and the community. At the end of the interview, she added, "One more thing. Maybe the most important thing—

> Like the old saying, "If Momma ain't happy, ain't nobody happy."
> If you get a teacher in the classroom who's not happy, then look
> out, little children.

This bit of wisdom, offered in the homespun vernacular of the American South, has become a touchstone for how I think about efforts to mobilize for educational reform: We can't teach children well if our teachers aren't well. We can't be supportive and engaged colleagues if we are worn down.

It's worth lingering on the cold implications of this teacher's observation. If our teachers are unwell—weary, unhappy, or demoralized—then our children will suffer. If our teachers feel resentful and disconnected from their work in schools, then these teachers withdraw from their colleagues or—even worse—devote their energy to complaining or undermining efforts to make school better. Conversely, available, energized, and soulful teachers provide opportunities for our children and colleagues to thrive because—as teachers—our moral energy matters, our idealism matters, our capacity to be fully present for students and colleagues matters. In other words—who we are matters.

Let me frame this encounter a little more broadly: If schools, youth groups, and other educational enterprises are to be places that promote academic, social, and personal development for students, everything hinges on the presence of intelligent, passionate, caring adults working as teachers and mentors toward the common good.

Parents intuitively understand the critical importance of having a qualified, connected, and humane teacher in the classroom. Now social science researchers have explored the link between the quality and experience of a teacher and educational outcomes, and the evidence is compelling. The American Council of Education synthesizes these findings in a report, *To Touch the Future*:

> The success of the student depends most of all on the quality of the teacher. We know from empirical data what our intuition has always told us: Teachers make a difference. We now know that teachers make *the* difference. (American Council of Education, 1999)

The quality of the teacher is the most important in-school factor for improving student achievement: Who the teacher is matters more than what curriculum is taught or what methods are used (Nye, Konstantopoulos, & Hedges, 2004). In other words, a competent, caring, and qualified teacher leaves an enduring trace of his or her legacy. Conversely, less-qualified, unprepared, or worn-out teachers leave a different kind of legacy in the life of a child.

Likewise, we know that schools that function the best for students, parents, and teachers are open and relational settings characterized by collegiality, trust, and a willingness to share expertise (Bryk & Schneider, 2002; Little, 1990; Rosenholtz, 1989). Habits of individualism and privatism have long held sway in schools. These norms intensify the pressure teachers feel and derail opportunities for the sharing of wisdom and support that can be so sustaining of growth. When teachers abandon their privateness and resist well-established norms of adversarial relationships between their fellow teachers and administrators and embrace a way of being in school that encourages collegiality, shared decision making, and the co-creation of more effective instructional practices, teachers can be at the vanguard of enduring change.

FROM RESEARCH TO PRACTICE

The upshot of this important research turns us toward asking: What can we do to ensure that our teachers work with an orientation toward leadership and practice that engages colleagues in experimentation and then examination of more powerful instructional practices in the service of more engaged student learning (Wasley, 1991)? Likewise, what can we do to heed the insight of the teacher from South Carolina who understood that a teacher's emotional and spiritual wellness is a critical element of good practice? And how do we operationalize programs that recognize that a critical dimension of quality teaching involves the condition of a teacher's inner and emotional life?

As a researcher who studies the forms of professional development available to teachers, I have come to believe that there are at least four ways that we organize opportunities for teachers to learn and grow in their own practice and in service of their colleagues. I will briefly consider the first three, but focus on "the way of heart" or "the way of the inner life."

The way of the subject: Familiar to all of us who work on improving teachers' practice is professional development focused on expanding a teacher's understanding of content and subject matter. Exploration of key concepts and principles at the core of a subject is necessary if teachers are to advance student learning. Done well, such exploration means teachers learn not only about key ideas within the subject area but also about strategies for bringing these ideas to students in developmentally appropriate ways.

The way of the method: A second critical approach is to support the growth and refinement of our methods. Our focus on expanding teachers' practices and refining their techniques seeks to augment their instructional capacity. Professional development organized in this way introduces teachers to systems of instruction such as cooperative learning, reciprocal teaching, and similar approaches.

The way of understanding students: A third approach to working with teachers asks who our students are and how we develop more complex and appreciative ways of understanding how they think and live. Our focus is to introduce teachers to cutting-edge findings in learning theory and child development.

Obviously, there is no single way forward. Teachers need a combination of professional development experiences to continue to grow and develop. The first three approaches can be understood to focus on questions integral to the teaching and learning process: What do I teach? How do I teach? Whom do I teach? I would like to now consider what I call a fourth way to be of use to teachers.

This way forward is inspired by the South Carolina teacher's observation: We can't teach children well if our teachers aren't well. It is reflected in comments of Denis Sparks, Executive Director of the National Staff Development Council, who contends that "teachers' vitality and engagement in their work improves school performance" (Sparks, 2004). It is grounded in Parker J. Palmer's best-selling book *The Courage to Teach*, in which he argues that if we're serious about improving schools then we must address the heart and soul of a teacher. As Palmer reminds us,

> In our rush to reform education, we have forgotten a simple truth: reform will never be achieved by renewing appropriations, restructuring schools, rewriting curricula, and revising texts if we continue to demand and dishearten the resource called the teacher on whom so much depends. Teachers must be better compensated, freed from bureaucratic harassment, given a role in academic governance and provided with the best possible methods and materials. But none of that will transform education if we fail to cherish—and challenge—the human heart that is the source of good teaching. (Palmer, 1998, p. 3)

The way of the heart: The way of the heart means that even as we work with teachers on deepening their content knowledge, expanding their methods, understanding their students, and probing their sense of purpose, we strive to "cherish—and challenge—the human heart that is the source of good teaching."

A TEACHER'S HEART

The heart of the teacher bespeaks mystery and ineffability; it hints of romanticism and connotes hard-to-codify qualities and elusive constructs such as emotion, intuition, and passions. As a researcher, I know it is my duty to try to pin down a definition of what I mean when I say "a teacher's heart," but I move to this task with utter humility knowing that no word or concept in the gallery of language and human thought has garnered as much attention as the idea of "heart." For example, the *Oxford English Dictionary* offers 56 distinctions of heart in its noun form, beginning with heart as a biological organism. While the denotation of heart interests me, the connotation is what intrigues me. Heart is implicated as the center of vital functions: the seat of life and mind, of feeling, understanding, and thought. The heart is the setting for one's innermost being and one's soul. It is the core of our human self and according to those who study the self's role, the coordinating center for our action in the world. Thus it is not merely an ethereal concept but a pragmatic force: It goads us to action, to make choices, and to take responsibility. It is the guide for our executive functions (Baumeister, 1998).

For a teacher, the role of the self plays out not only in those decisions and actions of everyday practice but also in regard to larger questions of calling and mission. The Dutch researcher Fred Korthagen describes this place of heart as the setting for the "core qualities" of a teacher: qualities such as creativity, courage, kindness, and spirituality (Korthagen, 2004). Importantly, Andy Hargreaves reminds us that this core place, or what he calls the "emotional geography" of teaching, also includes the shadow emotions of shame, jealousy, frustration, boredom, and other dark sentiments (Hargreaves, 2001).

In short, my contention is that inspired, memorable teaching irretrievably depends on the condition of a teacher's heart. Our capacity to engage students, connect them to the subjects we teach, intervene in their lives, discern their needs, attend to their development, and cultivate constructive relationships with colleagues and parents depends on the condition of that "core place" of the teacher.

This brings me back to "the way of the heart." Most teachers enter the profession with a vision of themselves as potent agents of change in the lives and learning of their students. Across the long stretch of a career or a school year, teachers face a steady stream of external challenges and institutional limitations that erode their idealism, energy, and purpose. There is much that teachers can do to support themselves and many initiatives that can be developed by educational leaders committed to deepening the adult community at their school site in an effort to renew the vitality of their teachers. One formal professional development program explicitly devoted to cherishing and challenging the heart of the teacher is The Courage to Teach program.

THE COURAGE TO TEACH

The Courage to Teach is a program of retreats designed to support educators on the journey to reclaim and deepen their professional identity and vocational integrity. It focuses on bringing teachers and educational leaders together into supportive communities to explore their teachers' hearts and examine how their inner lives play out in their work as teachers. Each group consists of 20 to 30 educators who gather for three-day retreats over a one- or two-year period. In large-group, small-group, and solitary settings, "the heart of a teacher" is explored, making use of personal stories, reflections on classroom practice, and insights from poets, storytellers, and various wisdom traditions. The intent of the retreat activities is to support teachers on a journey to reclaim their passion for teaching and find the balance so critical for sustaining their work.

The program operates under the premise that teachers choose the vocation for reasons of the heart, because they care deeply about their students and about their subject. But the demands of teaching cause too many educators to lose heart. The personal and communal process of the retreats seeks to create quiet and disciplined spaces, often called circles of trust, where teachers can hear their own inner voices and begin to claim what it will take for them to do their work with integrity and wholeness. Let me give a short taste of what these programs look like in practice:

> Twenty-five teachers and administrators sit in a circle, giving their full attention as an elementary teacher speaks passionately, and poignantly, about her love for her students and her commitment to reach each and every one of them. She goes on to tearfully describe the personal toll this is taking on her own life—creeping guilt at not having enough time or emotional energy to give to her own family, bone-deep exhaustion, nonstop worrying about the safety of some of her students, the weariness of facing an always burgeoning mountain of papers and projects to grade, a sense of increasing isolation from friends and colleagues because there is simply no more to give. The listeners sit quietly, respectfully, as she finishes, each reflecting on their own version of her story. (Jackson & Jackson, 2003, p. 283)

As this vignette illustrates, the planners of these professional development retreats deeply understand that "the way of the heart" matters. The retreats do not focus on pedagogical methods, content knowledge, or child development, but on the exploration of personal and professional beliefs. Here is one participant describing the experience:

> A poem about fear led to an amazing conversation about the fear in our own lives. Very capable and accomplished professionals shared openly and honestly. People with multiple graduate degrees and years of experience and awards in their professions shared their fear of being inadequate. Their fear of failure. Their fear of letting people down. Sharing that vulnerability, in a way I still don't completely understand, helped strengthen all of us. But somehow knowing we were all indeed quite human and quite apprehensive about being able to meet the challenge of educational leadership actually made us bold to keep on trying. (Jackson & Jackson, 2005, pp. 190–191)

Ultimately, "the way of the heart" attempts to go public with an alternative way "to be of use" for teachers. It contends that our greatest challenge is to sustain, motivate, and deepen a teacher's understanding of true self. It is an approach that believes that what teachers need is not simply a refill of energy and vigor, but careful exploration of the question: How should I allocate my energy in ways that are consistent with the deepest values I have about myself as a teacher and a person? It is an approach grounded in the simple homespun words of that South Carolinian teacher: "If you get a teacher in the classroom who's not happy, then look out, little children."

REFERENCES

American Council of Education. (1999). *To touch the future: Transforming the way teachers are taught.* Washington, DC: Author.

Baumeister, R. F. (1998). The self. In D. T. Gilbert, S. T. Fiske, & G. Lindzey (Eds.), *Handbook of social psychology* (pp. 680–740). New York: McGraw Hill.

Bryk, A., & Schneider, B. (2002). *Trust in schools: A core resource for improvement.* New York: Russell Sage Foundation.

Hargreaves, A. (2001). Emotional geographies of teaching. *Teachers College Record, 103* (6), 1056–1080.

Jackson, M., & Jackson, R. (2003). Courage to teach: A retreat program of personal and professional renewal for educators. In S. M. Intrator (Ed.), *Stories of the courage to teach: Honoring the teacher's heart* (pp. 282–308). San Francisco: Jossey-Bass.

Jackson, M., & Jackson, R. (2005). The threads we follow. In S. M. Intrator (Ed.), *Living the questions: Essays inspired by the work of Parker J. Palmer* (pp. 179–193). San Francisco: Jossey-Bass.

Korthagen, F. (2004). In search of the essence of a good teacher: Towards a more holistic approach in teacher education. *Teaching and Teacher Education, 20,* 77–97.

Little, J. W. (1990). The persistence of privacy: Autonomy and initiative in teachers' professional relations. *Teachers College Record, 91*(4), 509–536.

Nye, B., Konstantopoulos, S., & Hedges, L. (2004). How large are teacher effects? *Educational Evaluation and Policy Analysis, 26*(3), 336–345.

Palmer, P. (1998). *Courage to teach: Exploring the inner landscape of a teacher's life.* San Francisco: Jossey-Bass.

Rosenholtz, S. (1989). *Teachers' workplace: The social organization of schools.* New York: Teachers College Press.

Sparks, D. (2004). Look for ways to ignite the energy within: An interview with Jane E. Dutton. *Journal of Staff Development, 25*(3), 38–42.

Wasley, P. A. (1991). *Teachers who lead: The rhetoric of reform and the realities of practice.* New York: Teachers College Press.

34

Learning and Growing From Convening

A Context for Reflecting on Teacher Practice

Eleanor E. Drago-Severson,
Jennifer Roloff Welch, and Anne E. Jones

INTRODUCTION

The convening process itself was amazing. Convenings were safe environments built around practical problems and peer sharing. Having the opportunity to participate in convenings was such a gift, and I learned so much from it.

—Teacher, Spring 2005

Supporting children and adolescents' learning, development, and emotional well-being has been the primary focus of educators' attention for centuries. In recent years, however, as a nation, we have realized that there is an urgent need to find more effective ways to support teacher learning and teacher leadership. This is not only important because research has proven that supporting teacher learning is directly and positively linked to supporting children's achievement (Guskey, 1999; Sindelar,

Yendal-Silva, Dow, & Gonzales, 2002). It is also crucial, given the demands of teaching and leading in the 21st century. Whereas many practices have focused on how to support teacher learning *outside* of schools, we believe that more effective practices are needed to support teacher learning and the development of their reflective capacities *within* schools. This will support teachers, strengthen leadership, and build more effective learning communities. Recently, there has been a great deal of discussion about the need for teacher leadership—in order to strengthen schools so they can be contexts where both the children and adults can grow. Yet this literature reveals high variation as to how schools can enhance teacher learning and bolster leadership and little clarity around what constitutes best practices.

The nature of teaching and leadership in the 21st century places complex demands on teachers and schools (Drago-Severson, 2006a, 2006b, in press; McLaughlin & Talbert, 2001; Wagner et al., 2006). In addition, today's educational context requires teachers and other school leaders to assume even greater leadership responsibilities within and beyond their classrooms. This often means that not only are teachers asked to assume even greater leadership responsibility, but they must also develop the skills and competencies needed to negotiate complex relationships with other adults (fellow teachers, administrators, parents, and community members; Donaldson et al., 2005). Yet many adults are not adequately prepared for assuming these kinds of leadership responsibilities and do not yet have the developmental capacities needed to meet such challenges (Drago-Severson, 2004b; Kegan & Lahey, 2001). Further, the long-standing problem of teacher isolation (Kardos, 2004; Lortie, 1975) leaves teachers to address these demands on their own. However, such complex demands cannot be addressed in isolation.

We need more effective ways to support teachers as *individuals,* as teacher leaders in relationship with other adults, and in their organizations. One promising path is to create collaborative contexts *within* schools where teachers have regular, ongoing, structured opportunities to reflect on their practice. This can support teacher growth, teacher learning, and the development of enhanced instructional practices (Guskey, 1999). Such practices have been shown to decrease feelings of isolation, increase a deeper sense of community, and increase leadership capacities (Drago-Severson, 2004b; Guskey, 1999, Sindelar et al., 2002). Teachers need time to reflect on their practice in order to improve it. We argue that, in order for such reflection to be most effective, teachers must do this in the company of colleagues. But what kinds of practices and structures can create a rich soil for teacher reflection and the enhancement of collegial relationships among teachers? How might such practices benefit teachers, their instruction, their students' learning, and achievement and our schools? How might these practices support and challenge teachers as they work to improve instructional practice? In this chapter we present one practice, convening (Drago-Severson, in press), that can serve these needs and discuss how it addresses these questions.

CONVENING: A PROMISING PRACTICE FOR SUPPORTING TEACHER LEARNING AND LEADERSHIP

What can we do to better support teacher learning and the development of their leadership—in service to their own and their students' learning? Our university course, entitled *Leadership for Transformational Learning* (hereafter LTL) dedicated to serving as a context that supports the development of teacher leaders, purposefully introduced teachers to theories of adult learning and development and created spaces in which they were given opportunities to reflect on their practice and to receive support for their development, learning, and leadership growth. One of these spaces was called *convening* (Drago-Severson, in press; Kegan, 1991). The practice of convening used in this course was adapted from a similar practice used by Robert Kegan to help teachers reflect on difficult teaching moments. The first author expresses gratitude to Robert Kegan for his teachings.

As the opening quote from a graduate student who participated in the practice of convening indicates, engaging in convening can support teacher learning and enhanced leadership. Her words echo sentiments that other graduate students who enrolled in the course expressed over five years of teaching LTL. Having regular opportunities to discuss real-life experiences (cases) and benefit from other people's perspectives on issues and struggles of practice supported teacher learning and the development of greater leadership capacities. By this we mean that teachers who participated in the course reported greater reflective capacities and the courage to share their perspectives and judgments about practice to a greater extent with colleagues and administrators to benefit their schools and improved performance. In other words, we found that a focus on teacher learning through reflective practice in convening builds individual leadership development and, in turn, strengthens organizational capacity.

We, the authors of this chapter, are Ellie Drago-Severson, a university professor, who designed the course and the practice of convening (Drago-Severson, 2004b; 2006a; in press), and Jennifer Roloff Welch, and Anne E. Jones, two Teaching Fellows, who taught the course along with Ellie during the spring of 2005. Like the students in our graduate course *Leadership for Transformational Learning*, we benefited from reflecting on our practice, as we worked as a team to support teacher learning and leadership development within the context of a one-semester course. Our collective reflective practice mirrors the power of reflection to improve our teaching practices. Ellie, a university professor and an adult developmentalist, designed LTL and has taught it for five years. She created convening practice for LTL (Drago-Severson, in press). Ellie teaches and conducts research on supporting adult learning and leadership for professional development in K–12 and in adult education programs. Jennifer is a teaching fellow and a doctoral student studying adult literacy, learning, and development. She was an LTL teaching fellow for three years. Anne is a teaching fellow who is a doctoral student studying instructional capacity and teacher collaboration. She was an LTL teaching fellow for one year. Each week of the semester we engaged in shared reflection and dialogue after class, as we considered how to improve convening as a practice that might better serve our students in terms of supporting their learning and leadership development. This shared reflective practice strengthened our individual and collective work and enhanced our teaching practice.

Adult learning and adult development theories are powerful tools for supporting teacher learning, leadership, and growth. Yet they have been underutilized in K–12 schools. Using these theories (Kegan, 1982, 1994, 2000; Mezirow, 1991; Mezirow & Associates, 2000; Osterman & Kottkamp, 2004) to inform practice can strengthen teacher learning and leadership *in schools*. Teaching teacher leaders in a university context has allowed us to learn that many teachers feel that they need to leave schools in order to grow. We believe that schools need to be places where adults as well as children can grow. We have found that engaging in convening is a practice that supports teacher learning and helps them to develop their leadership capacities.

In this chapter, our purposes are to (a) describe the practice of convening in order to provide an understanding of how we used it to support teacher learning and leadership in the context of a university course; (b) illuminate the benefits and challenges of creating ongoing, structured contexts in which teachers can engage with their own cases in convening in order to learn from their experiences and improve practice; and (c) highlight effective practices (e.g., writing and learning from alternative perspectives) embedded in the practice of convening that support powerful individual development, more effective teaching, and enhanced capacities for teacher leadership within groups and within schools as learning organizations. In so doing, we hope that teacher leaders can use this practice in their schools as a support to their own and other teachers' learning and leadership. Ultimately, we hope that more and more teachers experience schools *as* places in which they can grow and learn as they work to support children's increased achievement.

Toward this end, we present (a) a brief overview of the course design to situate the practice of convening in the larger context of LTL; (b) central principles from the literature, theory, and research that informed the course design and the practice of convening; and (c) an in-depth look at the structure of convening, the process of engagement in it, and why it serves as a rich learning context for enhancing practice, attending to teacher learning, and developing increased leadership. Our aim is to show how the practice of engaging in convening creates a structure supportive of teacher learning and leadership development. Although the practice of convening requires time and energy, we believe that the rewards—enhancing teacher learning and growth—make it worthy of the investment. We will highlight the power of convening as a mechanism that supports teacher learning and the development of leadership capacities and how it can be employed in schools.

THEORETICAL CONTEXT

Leadership for Transformational Learning (LTL): Course Design, Structure, and Goals

Who Enrolled in LTL?

LTL was aimed at expanding notions of leadership to include leadership in support of teacher learning and development. Many of the graduate students enrolled in LTL were interested in leadership in support of adult growth in a variety of settings (K–12 schools, ministry, university contexts, and consulting and for-profit settings). The majority of participants were teachers who told us that they entered the course this year because they wanted to assume greater leadership in their schools and classrooms. In addition to teachers, former and future department chairs, aspiring and seated principals, superintendents, clergy, consultants, and other leaders enrolled.

Course Aims and Goals

LTL focused on presenting the theory and research of transformational learning (i.e., learning that helps us develop improved capacities to better manage the "complexities of teaching work and life" Drago-Severson, 2004b). We considered questions such as: How can teachers and other leaders create contexts that better support adults' transformational learning? What developmental principles inform practices that better support adults' transformational learning (Drago-Severson, course syllabus, 2003, 2004, 2005a, 2003, 2004, 2005a, 2005b)?

The Structure of LTL

Through lectures, readings, group discussions, case analyses, convening, and interactive exercises, we examined (a) conceptions of leadership in support of adult learning and development; (b) theories of adult learning (central concepts) and constructive-developmental theory (Brookfield, 1987, 1995; Daloz, 1983, 1986, 1999; Kegan, 1982, 1994, 2000); (c) essential elements for creating positive learning environments for adults; (d) practices that can support adults' transformational learning (e.g., teaming, assuming leadership roles, reflective practice, and mentoring) (Drago-Severson, 2004b) and the developmental principles informing them; and (e) the importance of caring for one's own professional development and learning while caring for the learning of others (Drago-Severson, Course Syllabus, 2005a, 2005b). Participants expressed an interest in supporting adult development and learning in various contexts (e.g., schools, non-profits, organizations) (Drago-Severson, Course Syllabus, 2003, 2004, 2003, 2004, 2005a, 2005b; Drago-Severson, in press).

LTL focused on supporting adults' learning as they engaged with, reflected on, and refined their ideas about practice and leadership in support of their own and their colleagues' learning. As a teaching team, we worked to complement and build on learners' knowledge, experience, and skills by providing them with theoretical frameworks and practices informed by adult learning and development theories to support them in their learning and leadership work. We—authors of this chapter—worked as a team (hereafter the teaching team) throughout the semester. Our aim was to facilitate student learning.

Adult Learning and Adult Developmental Theories

In this section we briefly describe two theories that informed course structure and specifically the design of the practice of convening (Drago-Severson, in press).

Malcolm Knowles's Theory of Androgogy

Malcolm Knowles (1970, 1975, 1980, 1984) was one of the first scholars to articulate a theory of adult learning. Central tenets of his framework inform LTL and our teaching in support of adult learning. His seminal work identifies four characteristics that must be considered when supporting adult learning. These are as follows:

1. Adults must understand *why* they need to learn something.

2. Adults need to learn *experientially*.

3. Adults approach learning as *problem solving*.

4. Adults learn best when the topic is of immediate *value*.

Throughout LTL, and especially during the convening process, we aligned pedagogy with the four characteristics Knowles identified. For example, we were explicit about why we were presenting theory and literature. In other words, we discussed why theories were presented and how we thought they could inform instructional practice and efforts to support adult learning and development within schools. In addition, we named for learners how course structures (e.g., convening) connected to theories of adult learning and centered on experiential learning.

For example, during convening, learners engaged in discussion about real-life cases that had "immediate value" for the convener. We asked that group members provide their own perspectives on the problem, struggle, or unresolved dilemma that was presented in the convener's case. Group members also had the opportunity to apply their learning from various theories (discussed in the course), their own experiences, and the literature to the case that was under discussion. Writing a convening case was an opportunity for students to select topics of immediate value to them. In other words, it mattered to them and their teaching and leadership practices. These are some of the ways in which principles aligned with Knowles's theory were threaded into the practice of convening. The overarching goals were to meet the adults where they were and to support them in their learning and leadership by offering alternative perspectives on the case under discussion.

Robert Kegan's Constructive-Developmental Theory

Robert Kegan's (1982, 1994, 2000) constructive-developmental theory presents a hopeful lens for considering how to best support teacher growth and the development of enhanced leadership capacities. According to his theory, growth involves a renegotiation between what constitutes the self and what constitutes others. In this chapter, growth is defined as an increase in a person's cognitive capacities, enabling him or her to manage better the complexities of teaching and leadership (Drago-Severson 2004a, 2004b, 2006a, in press). Kegan's theory centers on two key premises: (a) people actively *construct* their experiences, and (b) the *ways* in which people make meaning of their experiences can change or *develop*, provided that appropriate supports and challenges are offered to support development. We suggest that the practice of convening serves as a "holding environment" (Kegan, 1982) that provides both supports and challenges, which are needed for growth and learning (Drago-Severson, 2006a, 2006b, in press).

Kegan's (1982, 1994, 2000) theory informed the design of LTL and guided the structure of a particularly promising practice for supporting and challenging adult growth in LTL: convening. The practice of convening is a way for teachers and teacher leaders to learn from their own and each other's experiences in schools within a supportive context.

What Is a "Holding Environment"? The Importance of Context

To support learning and growth, we must consider the context. Put simply, the context of the school, relationships within it, and the practice of convening can serve as a "holding environment" (Kegan, 1982) for growth, learning and leadership development. D. W. Winnicott (1965) originally used the term *holding environment* in reference to special relationships and different types of supports and challenges needed to support an infant through early life. Robert Kegan (1982) extended Winnicott's notion of a holding environment to include adults. Kegan refers to a holding environment as the "form of the world in which the person is, at this moment in his or her evolution embedded" (pp. 115–116). In other words, just as infants and children learn and grow through relationships within their environments, so too do adults continue to learn and grow throughout their lives (Drago-Severson, 2004a, 2004b, 2006b, in press; Kegan, 1982, 1994, 2000).

What Does a Holding Environment Do?

According to Kegan (1982), "a holding environment must hold— where holding refers not to keeping or confining but to supporting . . . the exercises of who the person is. To hold without constraining may be the first requirement of care" (p. 162). Kegan suggests that a holding environment is a "supporting system" which may be a "single individual (like a mother) or a complex organization (like a school)."

A good holding environment serves three functions. Like the teaching and learning process, it needs to "hold well," meeting a person by recognizing and confirming who that person is, without need for urgent change. This means that it must provide appropriate supports to accommodate the way the person is currently making meaning. Second, when an adult is ready, it needs to "let go," by challenging adults and permitting them to grow beyond their existing perceptions to a new way of knowing. Last, a strong holding environment needs to stay in place, providing continuity, stability, and availability to the person in the process of growth so that relationships can be re-known and reconstructed in a new way, a way that supports who the person has grown to become (Drago-Severson, 2004a, 2004b, 2006a, 2006b, in press; Drago-Severson et al., 2001a; Kegan, 1982, 1994).

The role of the holding environment remains the same whether the individual being supported is an adolescent or an adult. However, to support growth, a holding environment must be a place where individuals experience various kinds of supports and challenges. According to Drago-Severson (2004b),

> *Support* can be defined in terms of recognizing and acknowledging and affirming who the person is and how the person is making sense (thinking and feeling) of his or her experiences. *Challenge* can take the form of supportively posing questions to a person in order to gently push the edges of a person's thinking and/or feeling so as to expose the individual to new ways of thinking. These needed combinations of challenge and support bring into being what Kegan (1982) calls the "holding environment." (p. 33)

Providing needed combinations of support and challenge in holding environments can (a) help teachers grow to better manage the complexities of learning, teaching, and leadership; and (b) be spacious enough to provide developmentally appropriate support and challenge to teachers who make sense of their experiences in *developmentally different* ways (Drago-Severson, 2004b). But how can schools and professional practices support teacher learning and growth? Our work has taught us that the practice of convening can serve this purpose (Drago-Severson, 2006b, in press).

LEARNING AND GROWING FROM CONVENING

What Is Convening?

The practice of convening is a structured opportunity to come together with colleagues and reflect on one group member's written case during each session (Drago-Severson, in press). Each group member has the opportunity to write a case based on an experience from practice. The *convener*, or case writer, then distributes the case to the other group members. The goal of convening is to listen to and hear from the group members about the case writer's experience. This kind of hearing out and listening is designed to help the case writer move one step further in his or her thinking about and relationship to the presented case. For example, as a result of the convening, the case writer may be able to see the experience from others' perspectives or realize that his actions in the case do not match his stated beliefs about practice. This shift in thinking represents an increase in capacity to deal with the complexity of the dilemma presented in the case because the convener is able to see his or her experience in a more robust way. Below we outline this practice of convening that we believe supports adult learning and growth in schools.

It is important to note that before the first case is discussed in convening, the members discuss and agree upon group norms in order to establish a context that is safe for sharing experiences (Drago-Severson, in press). Some examples of group norms developed by LTL students in the past include the following: rules about confidentiality; consensus to share only two to three comments during a convening session, especially if others in the group have not yet spoken; ideas about how to share positive feedback before offering critical insights; and reminders to keep a sense of humor while sharing and receiving feedback. Once these norms are agreed upon, a group member creates a one-page document summarizing the norms and provides hard copies for all members.

The process of convening is composed of two main components: a self-selected case and group discussion about the case. In the sections that follow, we describe both.

Writing the Case

The case is a descriptive account of an individual's experience involving support for adult learning. In the case, the convener can be the person providing support for adult learning or receiving the support. The case includes a brief written description of the relevant context surrounding the experience, a description of the experience, the convener's thoughts and feelings about the experience, and questions about the experience on which the convener would like his colleagues to focus (Drago-Severson, 2006b, in press). In order that the convener have some distance from the case and be able to better listen to colleagues, members are encouraged to select experiences that occurred in the past. Cases are submitted to the group one week before the discussion so that members can read the case, prepare comments for the discussion, and provide written feedback to the convener.

Discussing the Case

The discussion of the case can be up to 45 minutes long. At the start of the convening, a few minutes are set aside for clarifying questions and a brief introduction by the convener about his case (Drago-Severson, in press). The majority of time is spent discussing the case. During this discussion, the convener is asked to only listen. The rest of the group discusses the case among themselves, referring to the convener by name. Group members focus their comments on the convener's questions, which are included at the end of the case. The intention of the convening session is for group members to provide alternative interpretations of the data presented in the case, identify assumptions that the convener may hold, and point out potential discrepancies between the convener's espoused beliefs and the actual actions taken in the case. The convening closes with a few minutes of final reflections from the convener.

LTL and Convening as Holding Environments

Just as the larger context of this course provided a holding environment, so too did the convening. The class itself (LTL) provided a holding environment with supports and challenges, including learning about adult learning and adult development through lectures, doing both structured and free writing, sharing ideas in pairs and small groups, discussing the relevance of theoretical lenses to teaching practice in schools, receiving feedback on writing from the teaching team and peers, and participating in convening (Drago-Severson, in press). *Convening* was one particularly powerful practice within the structure of the class that functioned as a holding environment for the students' learning and growth.

Support

The convening provided powerful supports and challenges in various forms to individuals and the group as a whole. Support within convening came in many forms. First, individual students wrote their personal cases and were invited to share their cases with the teaching team (the authors of this chapter) prior to distributing it to the rest of the group. In this way, students were supported through the writing process. Whether they needed help formulating their experiences in writing or articulating their feelings and thoughts about a particular experience, the teaching team was available to read their drafts and provide feedback to support the students in their learning.

Second, when conveners shared their cases with the rest of their convening group, they knew that their words and work would be held in confidence, that the group members would not discuss their cases beyond the walls of the convening room. In this way, students could make themselves vulnerable through writing within a safe and trustworthy environment. Third, when group members shared their perspectives on each convener's case, their goal was not to show how they would have "done things differently" or better, but to offer their unique perspectives on the case (Drago-Severson, in press). In these ways, the context of convening provides support in the form of "recognizing and acknowledging and affirming who the person is and how the person is making sense (thinking and feeling) of his or her experiences" (Drago-Severson, 2004b, p. 33).

Challenge

Shaping a context for learning and growth requires not only support but also challenge. Members of the convening group provide challenge in various forms, including through verbal and written feedback. For example, during a convening, members might point out where they saw inconsistencies in the logic and behavior of different actors in the case, thus helping the convener to see the events or experience from different perspectives. This kind of learning from alternative perspectives oftentimes helps individuals to see and understand their experiences in new ways (Drago-Severson, 2004a, 2004b, 2006a, 2006b, in press; Kegan, 2000; Mezirow, 2000).

Because it is often difficult for an individual to examine the underlying beliefs behind his or her actions without another's help, an alternative way to provide challenge within this context is to help the convener uncover the assumptions behind her actions. In this way, the role of the members of the group would be to provide a context in which the convener could take a step back from the events of the case and examine the beliefs and assumptions that may have been implicitly or explicitly driving her behavior. By posing questions in written and verbal form to the convener, members of the group are able to "gently push the edges of a person's thinking and/or feeling so as to expose the individual to new ways of thinking" (Drago-Severson, 2004b, p. 33).

By providing various forms of supports and challenges, the convening functions as a holding environment for learning and growth for adults who wish to share their experiences with others and gain new perspectives on their experiences in practice (Drago-Severson, 2004b, 2006a, 2006b, in press). This kind of reflection enables adults to step forward with new ways of thinking about their work as teachers and teacher leaders in schools.

Benefits of Convening

Because of its focus on creating a nurturing context for growth, the practice of engaging in convening has many benefits. These benefits apply to the individual practitioner, the convening group, and the organization as a whole.

Individual Benefits

For the individual, benefits of convening include empowerment, reducing isolation, translating theory to practice, and moving to a new relationship with his or her thinking (Drago-Severson, 2004b, 2006a, 2006b, in press). First, empowerment is a result of providing individuals the opportunity to have an active say in what they do and in how they shape their experience. In convening, this opportunity is provided by asking people to examine their own questions about practice and leadership. Although they will be taking the lead in writing their case, it is also important that the teaching team is walking right next to them, ready to provide support in the form of feedback, encouragement, or questions on their case in advance of distributing the case to group members if needed.

Second, the practice of convening reduces teacher isolation by creating a collaborative structure that brings many perspectives to bear on one member's experience. It also provides the members with a sense of belonging to a community (Westheimer, 1998) and a sense of support from his colleagues. The effect of being in a cohort, a group that works together over a period of time, can provide powerful supports and challenges for the group members (Drago-Severson, 2004a). Research has shown that this kind of structure is a support to adult learning, emotional well-being, and perspective broadening (Drago-Severson, 2004a, 2006a, 2006b, in press). Third, convening acts as a model for how to translate theories of adult development (Drago-Severson, 2004a, 2004b, in press; Kegan, 1982, 1994, 2000; Mezirow, 2000) and reflection (Osterman & Kottkamp, 2004) into practice. It is built on the idea that for adults to grow and develop, they need to be in a context that promotes growth, a context that provides supports and challenges. Furthermore, convening offers a clear, structured reflective model by making the components and processes explicit through handouts, direct instruction, and the opportunity to experience it (Drago-Severson, in press).

A final benefit of convening to the individual is that it moves the person into a new relationship with his or her thinking. For example, as a result of the convening, the convener may be able to see the experience with a fresh perspective and perhaps notice for the first time how his or her assumptions or beliefs differ from actions in the case. This complex shift in thinking happens as the result of the convening process. Three components of convening are designed to facilitate this learning: Opportunities for self-reflection, opportunities to consider new ways of thinking and acting, and the sense that one is learning and growing while being "well held" in a safe holding environment.

In the convening process, the primary opportunity for self-reflection is the writing of the case. Writing is a unique act that provides one with the time and sustained attention needed to identify individual thoughts, feelings, beliefs, and assumptions about one's experience. It also helps the writer to gain some emotional distance from the actual experience. Through the process of writing a case, the convener has the opportunity to think through the events of a particular experience and, with some distance and the support from other group members, may gain new perspective on a troublesome or problematic experience or dilemma of practice (Drago-Severson, in press). Hashweh (2004), a researcher, engaged in a project in which he asked teachers to write cases about their experiences of teaching about democracy in Ramallah. He suggests that cases could be useful for educators "to promote, to describe, and to explain teacher and educational change" (p. 229). He adds that "While some researchers have themselves written narratives about teachers in the form of cases, case studies, or biographies, others have supported teachers writing their own stories, in an effort to give more emphasis to the teacher's voice" (p. 230). We agree with Hashweh that there is power in the act of writing itself. And we believe that case writing can be a transformative tool that helps the teacher-writer to see his or her experience from a distance, perhaps for the first time more objectively, and eventually to view it from multiple perspectives. Writing and then sharing a case can be the impetus for individuals coming to a new understanding of former experiences or sorting through options for action in the future.

The written case also serves as a way to communicate one's experience to others who can then help the writer make a shift in his or her relationship to the case by offering new ways of thinking about it. These opportunities include the convener's receiving verbal and written feedback from the group and giving verbal and written feedback to fellow conveners about their cases. While the convener's case is being discussed, he has the unique opportunity to play the role of listener. Although some find it difficult to resist the urge to respond to comments and questions offered by group members during group discussion, it is important to practice listening as it provides a wonderful space to consider how trusted colleagues view and discuss the events in one's case (Drago-Severson, in press).

The convener may hear others offer alternate interpretations of the experience, thoughtful new questions, different views about assumptions driving behaviors, or discrepancies between beliefs and actions. The observations and thoughts offered by the group are valuable because typically, one person would not be able to see the experience as robustly as the group. Group members who offer their views on another person's case also benefit because they are, in a sense, practicing the development of new ways of thinking and acting in relationship to a case.

It is important to point out that a shift in relationship to one's thinking is nurtured by the context of convening, which is purposefully designed to support growth (Drago-Severson, in press). At the start of the convening process, the group collectively creates and agrees upon norms of engagement (Drago-Severson, 2004b). This is done to establish an environment that is safe for the risk-taking that is involved in transformational learning. Furthermore, the culture of this LTL course, the context in which convening exists, is also based on respecting others, balancing advocacy and inquiry, taking collective responsibility for individual and community learning, and valuing diversity (for an in-depth discussion, please see Drago-Severson, in press). Trust is also a critical element of convening, as it requires a great deal of trust to share one's deepest thoughts and feelings about a troubling or problematic experience from one's practice. The act of disclosing such experiences is in and of itself a trust-building act, which serves each group member who benefits from the convening process.

Benefits to the Convening Group

Benefits of convening extend beyond the individual to the group. Group members learn not only from their own cases but also from other people's cases. They can develop deeper insight and use learning from other's cases to inform their own practice. Furthermore, members of the group feel less isolated as they realize that the dilemmas presented in cases are similar to their own. Members also feel less isolated because they are offered a structured time and space in which to engage with their colleagues. This increased collegiality helps develop relationships within the context of the group that can support the development of the community. This community, in turn, provides a structure in which learning, emotional well-being, and perspective broadening are supported by the cohort (Drago-Severson, 2004b).

Benefits to the Organization

The practice of convening can also benefit the entire organization by building organizational capacity for learning, growth, and leadership. "Organizational capacity entails building organizational structures and systems that support and value personal learning and that facilitate and encourage collective learning" (Sackney, Mitchell, & Walker, 2005, p. 3). The collaborative nature of convening reinforces the importance of learning from colleagues and provides a supportive and challenging context in which this learning can take place (Drago-Severson, course syllabus, 2003, 2004, 2005a, 2005b, 2006a, 2006b, in press). Additional benefits to the organization include strengthening teacher leadership, building stronger school communities, increasing personal and professional satisfaction, and developing enhanced practices.

Challenges to Implementing the Practice of Convening

As with all meaningful growth opportunities, there are challenges associated with implementing the practice of convening in schools. However, we believe that the rewards of the practice of convening far outweigh such challenges.

Individual Challenges

First, the individuals who participate in convening face certain challenges, including investing time to write up a personal case based on an experience from their practice, which still sticks in their minds. After the case is written, the individual or case writer takes an important risk, or leap of faith, by sharing his or her written case, based on a personal experience, with the rest of the group. Putting one's experiences on paper can be scary, especially since usually the person has kept the experience private, and the context of convening may be the first time he or she is sharing his or her experience with others. Sharing these kinds of experiences with other people takes courage—and can be a rich and rewarding learning experience. Oftentimes, the cases individuals write revolve around experiences that were thought provoking, troublesome or problematic in some way. For these reasons, the writing and sharing process may feel like a risk or pose a challenge to the case writers. The intention of the convening group, though, is to help the members learn and grow from their experiences through this process.

Challenges to the Group

The group itself can face challenges within the convening process. Two such challenges may include examples such as adhering to norms set by the group and providing thoughtful and attentive feedback to the case writer.

To address the first possible challenge, it is important that individual group members adhere to the group norms set at the beginning of the process. Such norms help the group to maintain focus and order and to maintain a respectful, safe learning context (Drago-Severson, 2004b, 2006b, in press). Group norms pertaining to the nature of feedback can be helpful for keeping the convening momentum going while staying on a focused topic. For example, the group may have decided that each person would speak only two to three times within a convening session, which allows other group members to have the chance to share their perspectives. This kind of shared norm enables group members to speak freely and eliminates the possibility of one or two people dominating the conversation.

The second example of a challenge pertains to providing verbal and written feedback to the case writer. When discussing the case during convening, it is important that all group members point to specific examples when referring to the case. So, a person who wishes to share his or her thoughts on a case would refer directly to the page number in the case in order to point out for the rest of the group what evidence in the case supports her statements. With regard to written feedback, it is very important that the members of the convening groups invest time in reading the case carefully and in writing comments and questions to the convener to help further her thinking. At the end of the convening session, conveners receive their cases back, with the written comments, which can be invaluable to helping the convener retrace what might have been said during the convening or to further process their fellow members' comments and questions regarding their case.

Challenges to the School or Organization

Finally, of course, we understand that in schools the biggest challenge is time. The convening practice itself lasts approximately 45 minutes for each session; therefore, it could be worked into a school day or after school. Groups may choose to meet once a week, once every two weeks, or monthly, for example. It is our belief that learning and growth, which can take place during convening, justifies the time needed to invest in reflective practice, teacher learning, and leadership.

APPLICATIONS AND IMPLICATIONS

We know that engaging in convening is hard yet rewarding work. We also know that time is a precious commodity in schools. Yet we believe that this practice is important and that allocating time to engage in the convening process will yield tremendous benefits for teachers as individuals, for groups of teachers, and for schools as organizations. We have witnessed this in our classroom. We have observed the benefits of this in schools. When teachers have ongoing contexts to reflect on their practice in the company of colleagues, they (a) feel less isolated and more a part of a supportive community, (b) demonstrate a greater understanding of themselves, and (c) improve teaching practice and enhance leadership development (see Drago-Severson, 2006b, in press). Teachers will develop tools to learn and grow in order to better support and learn from other adults in schools and to foster better practices that ultimately support student achievement. Furthermore, the context of an ongoing holding environment (Kegan, 1982) created by convening will enable teachers and teacher leaders to build strong, positive relationships within the school and improve their collaborative skills. The group provides the support necessary to sustain teachers in their practice and the challenges necessary for teachers and teacher leaders to feel that they can learn and grow within schools without having to leave. In effect, schools become more successful as learning organizations. Reflective practice will become part of the fabric of the school, and schools can become healthy, vibrant learning centers where both the adults and children are growing (Drago-Severson, 2004a; Drago-Severson, in press).

REFERENCES

Brookfield, S. (1987). *Developing critical thinkers.* San Francisco: Jossey-Bass.

Brookfield, S. (1995). *Becoming a reflective teacher critically.* San Francisco: Jossey-Bass.

Daloz, L. A. (1983). Mentors: Teachers who make a difference. *Change, 15*(6), 24–27.

Daloz, L. (1986). *Effective teaching and mentoring.* San Francisco: Jossey-Bass.

Daloz, L. (1999). *Mentor.* San Francisco: Jossey-Bass.

Donaldson, M. L., Kirkpatrick, C. L., Marinell, W. H., Steele, J. L., Szczesiul, S. A., & Johnson, S. M. (2005, April). *"Hot shots" and "principals pets": How colleagues influence second-stage teachers' experience of differentiated roles.* Paper presented at the annual meeting of the American Educational Research Association, Montreal, Canada.

Drago-Severson, E. (2004a). *Becoming adult learners: Principles and practices for effective development.* New York: Teachers College Press.

Drago-Severson, E. (2004b). *Helping teachers learn: Principal leadership for adult growth and development.* Thousand Oaks, CA: Corwin Press.

Drago-Severson, E. (2003, 2004, 2005a). *Leadership for transformational learning* (Course syllabus). Cambridge, MA: Harvard Graduate School of Education.

Drago-Severson, E. (2005b). *Creating learning communities* (Course syllabus). New York: Columbia University, Teachers College.

Drago-Severson, E. (2006a). How can you better support teachers' growth? *The Learning Principal, 1*(6), 1, 6–7.

Drago-Severson, E. (2006b, Summer). Learning-oriented leadership: Transforming a school through a program of adult learning. *Independent School Journal,* pp. 58–61 & 64.

Drago-Severson, E. (in press). *Leading adult learning: Promising practices for supporting adult growth and development.* Thousand Oaks, CA: Corwin Press.

Drago-Severson, E., Helsing, D., Kegan, R., Popp, N., Broderick, M., & Portnow, K. (2001a). The power of a cohort and of collaborative groups. *Focus on Basics, 5*(B), 15–22.

Guskey, T.R. (1999, April). *New perspectives on evaluating professional development.* Paper presented at the annual meeting of the American Educational Research Association, Montreal, Canada.

Hashweh, M. (2004). Case writing as border-crossing: Describing, explaining and promoting teacher change. *Teachers and teaching: Theory and practice, 10*(3), 229–246.

Kardos, S. M. (2004). *Supporting and sustaining new teachers in schools: The importance of professional culture and mentoring.* Unpublished dissertation, Harvard University, Cambridge, Massachusetts.

Kegan, R. (1982). *The evolving self: Problems and process in human development.* Cambridge, MA: Harvard University Press.

Kegan, R. (1991). *Reflecting on our teaching practice: A seminar* (Course syllabus). Cambridge: Harvard Graduate School of Education.

Kegan, R. (1994). *In over our heads: The mental demands of modern life*. Cambridge, MA: Harvard University Press.

Kegan, R. (2000). What "form" transforms? A constructive-developmental approach to transformative learning. In J. Mezirow & Associates (Eds.), *Learning as transformation* (pp. 35–70). San Francisco: Jossey-Bass.

Kegan, R., & Lahey, L. L. (2001). *How the way we talk can change the way we work: Seven languages for transformation*. San Francisco: Jossey-Bass/Wiley.

Knowles, M. S. (1970). *The modern practice of adult education: Andragogy versus pedagogy*. New York: Association Press.

Knowles, M. S. (1975). *Self-directed learning: A guide for learners and teachers*. New York: Association Press.

Knowles, M. S. (1980). *The modern practice of adult education: From pedagogy to andragogy*. New York: Association Press.

Knowles, M. (1984). *The adult learner: A neglected species* (3rd ed.). Houston, TX: Gulf.

Lortie, D. C. (1975). *Schoolteacher: A sociological study*. Chicago: University of Chicago Press.

McLaughlin, M. W., & Talbert, J. E. (2001). *Professional communities and the work of high school teaching*. Chicago: University of Chicago Press.

Mezirow, J. (1991). *Transformative dimensions of adult learning*. San Francisco: Jossey-Bass.

Mezirow, J., & Associates. (2000). *Learning as transformation: Critical perspectives on a theory in progress* (pp. 3–33). San Francisco: Jossey-Bass.

Mezirow, J. (2000). Learning to think like an adult: Core concepts of transformation theory. In J. Mezirow & Associates (Eds.), *Learning as transformation: Critical perspectives on a theory in progress* (pp. 3–33). San Francisco: Jossey-Bass.

Osterman, K. F., & Kottkamp, R. B. (2004). *Reflective practice for educators: Professional development to improve student learning*. Thousand Oaks, CA: Corwin Press.

Sackney, L., Mitchell, C., & Walker, K. (2005, April). *Building capacity for learning communities: A case study of fifteen successful schools*. Paper presented at the annual meeting of the American Educational Research Association, Montreal, Canada.

Sindelar, P. T., Yendal-Silva, D., Dow, J., & Gonzales, L. D. (2002, April). *School culture: Can it be a predictor of student achievement?* Paper presented at the annual meeting of the American Educational Researcher Association, New Orleans, LA.

Wagner, T., Kegan, R., Lahey, L., Lemons, R. W., Garnier, J., Helsing, D., Howell, A., & Rasmussen, H. T. (2006). *Change leadership: A practical guide to transforming our schools*. San Francisco: Jossey-Bass/Wiley.

Westheimer, J. (1998). *Among school teachers*. New York: Teachers College Press.

Winnicott, D. (1965). *The maturation processes and the facilitating environment*. New York: International Universities Press.

35

America's Teaching Profession and the Teacher Leaders Network

Barnett Berry and John Norton

It is increasingly implausible that we could improve the performance of schools . . . without promoting leadership in teaching by teachers.

—Judith Warren Little (1988)

Teacher leadership is often discussed, sometimes touted, but rarely fully realized. Accomplished teachers who seek to become leaders are often brought up short by a system that still has difficulty accepting teachers as professionals deserving of the empowerment that comes with meaningful leadership roles.

America's teachers have a stormy and convoluted history—often framed by the struggle to determine who teaches what and how, and under what conditions. More than 200 years ago, America's teachers were hired to transmit values and, to some extent, the basic skills of the day. When women began to dominate the teaching workforce some 150 years ago, the occupation's status began to decline. Not much has changed since then. It's true that teachers have seen their salaries and working conditions improve. And we have experienced periods of time when national opinion-makers have called for a more highly educated, better prepared, and professionally paid teacher workforce. Recall the Sputnik panic in the late 1950s and, more recently, the "flat world" concerns growing out of global economic competition.

But relative to people in other professions, teachers still have to wrestle for status and respect, and while they often are expected to be smart and entrepreneurial, they also are expected to be compliant and conforming. At the dawn of the 21st century, good teaching and good schools are concepts defined *not* by successful teachers but by school boards, administrators, textbook companies, for-profit curriculum developers, and the testing industry.

For many years, teachers have served as department chairs, grade level leaders, and mentors—usually serving at the pleasure or direction of principals. Today, most teacher leadership roles are still best classified as *task du jour*. As such, teachers are expected to represent administrative purview, not to challenge "thinking as usual" or to transform schools. Scholars often write about how teachers are expected to adhere to leadership as traditionally defined in hierarchical organizations. Teachers, they say, are not expected to "take charge" (Lord & Miller, 2000). Ironically, despite legitimate criticism that too many local teacher unions have ignored issues of teaching quality and professionalism in favor of "bread and butter" issues, transformational teacher leaders have most often emerged from within teacher unions and associations, where genuine leadership development opportunities exist independent of administrative dictums. From time to time, the union model produces dynamic teacher leaders like Denver's Brad Jupp, who has spearheaded revolutionary changes in teacher professionalism tied to compensation (McGray, 2005).

The union model is a necessary but insufficient tool to make transformational leadership a widely accepted and respected role for American teachers. A big part of the problem is that the public, and the elected policymakers who serve them, have too few opportunities to hear from accomplished teachers who have a unique perspective on the core issues of school reform. Somehow, we have to convince decision makers that they will further their own school improvement goals by setting a place at the policy table for expert teachers who work every day in our nation's public schools.

Five years ago, the Institute for Educational Leadership issued a report, *Redefining the Teacher as Leader* (Task Force on Teacher Leadership, 2001), which called for teachers to be heard as well as understood and for their valuable insights to be taken seriously by policymakers. The report called for a new breed of teacher leader and for the elevation of teacher voice in the laws, rules, and regulations governing their profession and the students they teach. The distinguished members of the Institute for Educational Leadership's teacher leadership task force wrote:

> The infinite potential the nation's teachers possess for sharing their hard-earned knowledge and wisdom with players in education's decision-making circles—or even for becoming part of these circles—remains largely unexploited. There are a growing number of glittering exceptions, but they do not add up to much in American public education's universe of 46-plus million students, 15,000-odd school districts, and 100,000-plus schools . . . Except through the teacher organizations, most of the profession's members normally have little or no effective representation in the key organizational, political, and pedagogical decisions that affect their jobs, their profession, and, by extension, their personal lives. (pp. 1–2)

The task force concluded:

> It is not too late for education's policymakers to exploit a potentially splendid resource for leadership and reform that is now being squandered: the experience, ideas, and capacity to lead of the nation's schoolteachers. (p. 2)

Inspired by the Institute for Educational Leadership's call to action, in 2003 the Center for Teaching Quality began an unprecedented effort to identify and organize a diverse group of accomplished teachers interested in exploring issues of teacher leadership and teacher "voice." The result of this effort is the Teacher Leaders Network, a vibrant Internet-based professional community with a focus on enhancing and celebrating teacher leadership, spreading teaching expertise, and elevating the voices of highly accomplished teachers in matters related to their profession and the students they teach.

Using a simple Web site, e-mail listserv technology, and off-the-shelf e-communication platforms, the Teacher Leaders Network (www.teacher-leaders.org) connects and supports educators who agree that the nation's teachers are a "splendid resource for leadership and reform." At a time when top-down pressures threaten to overwhelm schools, the Teacher Leaders Network seeks to expand the roles of teacher leaders in achieving genuine school reform. By joining together, we believe, teachers can provide leadership to advance standards-based teaching and learning, close performance gaps among diverse students, raise public awareness of the teacher's critical role in student achievement, and help shape public education policy.

Our diverse group of more than 300 teacher leaders (more than 75% are National Board Certified) engage in ongoing daily conversations about teaching and learning, participate in periodic focused discussions of critical issues with national experts, organize book studies and action research projects, and serve as virtual mentors of novice teachers and teacher education students. In blogs and published conversations on our Web site, in media interviews and articles written for national publications, and through live presentations before influential national audiences, the highly skilled teacher leaders in our Network are demonstrating and publicizing to policymakers, practitioners, and the public what accomplished teachers know and can do.

At present, our network membership includes National Board Certified Teachers, Milken awardees, Presidential award winners, national and state teachers of the year, and other teachers identified as individuals with outstanding leadership potential. Our ultimate goal is to make it possible for interested teacher leaders in any school or district in the United States to learn from one another and expand their collective knowledge of teaching, learning, and leadership for change.

In our first 3 years, the Teacher Leader Network's progress has validated our belief in the potential of an Internet-based teacher network to overcome traditional barriers to teacher leadership development. Even more of that potential was realized in early 2006 when the Teacher Leader Network announced the creation of TeacherSolutions—a breakthrough initiative funded by the Joyce Foundation, with supplemental funding from the Gund and Stuart Foundations.

The TeacherSolutions model brings together a diverse cross-section of accomplished American teachers who work in teams to carefully examine critical issues facing public education and offer solutions based on their deep understanding of teaching and learning and how good schools really function. The TeacherSolutions team then translates their work into provocative and informative products and presents those products through the media and before influential national audiences. In our first TeacherSolutions project, 18 outstanding teachers from across the United States focused their attention on *professional compensation*, researching past efforts to create alternative pay models and recommending new and different designs based on their understanding of the professional work of teachers. It's a strategy we believe will become a powerful vehicle for demonstrating the unique policy insights that accomplished teacher leaders can offer.

The Institute for Educational Leadership report called for teachers to "get in the game." The Teacher Leader Network is on the field and ready to take the ball and score both for the teaching profession and for all the students who need to be served by knowledgeable and skilled teachers. As our Teacher Leader Network colleague Nancy Flanagan writes in this volume (Chapter 7): "If we want to make that transition, however, re-creating our beloved vocation into a nationally accepted profession, with all the respect and benefits accorded to professions in America, we must do it ourselves. Certainly, no one will do it for us."

When more teachers lead we are certain that America's students will be served by a teaching profession they so richly deserve.

REFERENCES

Little, J. W. (1988). Assessing the prospects for teacher leadership. In A. Lieberman (Ed.), *Building a professional culture in schools.* New York: Teachers College Press.

Lord, B., & Miller, B. (2000). *Teacher leadership: An appealing and inescapable force in school reform?* Boston: Education Development Center.

McGray. D. (2005, January 16). Working with the enemy. *New York Times Education Supplement.* Retrieved August 24, 2006 from http://select.nytimes.com/gst/abstract.html?res=FB0710FD345D0C758DDDA80894DD404482

Task Force on Teacher Leadership. (2001). *Leadership for student learning: Redefining the teacher as leader—School leadership for the 21st century initiative. A report of the Task Force on Teacher Leadership.* Washington, DC: Institute for Educational Leadership.

36

Teacher Leaders Redefining the Status Quo Through Critical Friends Groups

Deborah Bambino

Challenges make you discover things about yourself that you never really knew. They're what make the instrument stretch—what make you go beyond the norm.

—Cicely Tyson (1991)

Teachers know all about challenges and teacher leaders know about stretching, stretching alone and stretching together. When I stretch alone, I can sometimes hit a few high notes, but when I stretch with my colleagues in my Critical Friends Group, my/our thinking and practice begin to truly sing.

Traditional schools in our failing system are set up as a series of hierarchies in which the principal rules over the school and the teachers, and the teachers try to rule their classrooms and students. This unsuccessful system of "leadership" by mandate results in frustration and uneasy compliance or resistance all around. Principals feel isolated and beaten down by those issuing directives from above, and teachers feel victimized by an approach that treats them like robots who must teach from a standardized script and follow a standardized timetable, leaving them no time to build relationships with their students or experience the joys of shared learning that brought them into this profession in the first place.

Critical Friends Groups represent a shift from the leadership by mandate approach. In Critical Friends Groups teachers and administrators are challenged to find and use their minds and voices in search of equitable, high-quality learning experiences for all students. Critical Friends Groups offer teachers the skills, or tools, needed to resist and disrupt the status quo of the achievement gap and student disaffection. Critical Friends Groups signal a break with the culture of complaint and complicity that has left the masses of teachers flying solo, working in isolation, stretching to reach an occasional high note with this or that student, trying to forget the masses of students who are falling behind.

Critical Friends Groups stretch us as we seek shared leadership in our schools. Complaining is exhausting, but it is also comfortable. It is in fact easier to complain and blame than to reflect upon and disrupt the harsh realities of inequities in our own classrooms and schools. Serious reflection is hard work. What begins with looking at student work and wondering why a lesson or assessment did not work leads to introspection about our own beliefs and biases before it can ultimately lead to improved practices with kids.

We understand that real leadership starts when we accept that we don't know the answers and cannot find them alone. Although we believe we always work and lead better in concert with others, we recognize that in our urban schools in particular, our reflective, collaborative work is bound up with questions of race and class. Discussions about the role of bias in our own classrooms are uncomfortable. Critical Friends Groups provide the space and support where these tough conversations can occur, and where reflective, collaborative leadership can grow. Teachers and administrators who agree to "be disturbed," work together, over time, at uncovering previously held assumptions about each other, about their students and about their families, in order to co-construct new ways of creating equitable conditions for learning.

Given the current demographics of the teaching population, as a White woman I often find myself working with other adults who look mostly like me, in front of classrooms and schools where students of color predominate. Rather than adopt a "color-blind" or "color-mute" attitude that denies the existence of this fundamental difference, working in a Critical

Friends Groups creates a context for the careful examination of what it means to appreciate our differences and grow from them. I'm not talking about a celebration of heroes and holidays here; rather, I mean an exploration of cultural norms, styles, and strengths that can inform our teaching and support greater student engagement and success in our classrooms.

I'm reminded here of two recent examples in my work as a facilitator of seminars for new Critical Friends Group coaches. In the first session, we read an excerpt by Margaret Wheatley called "Willing to Be Disturbed" (2002). A 55-year-old African American female teacher, who said she is usually quiet in large groups, began to share her experiences and frustrations as a teacher of color who has often remained silent when faced with the good-old-boys network in our district. This conversation marked a turning point in this colleague's participation in the seminar, and a disruption for those of us, mostly White, mostly female, who saw Lynne as a reserved, quiet peer.

This example moved me to think about how the ways I am, with my quick way of speaking up and sharing, my assertive opinions, and my enthusiasm might contribute to the silencing of those who are "other" than I, both my colleagues and my students.

Critical Friends Group structures and processes create the context where the default hegemony of White leaders like me can be deconstructed and where we can begin to point to the ways new room can be made for the contributions of those other leaders that I and those most like me have been silencing, albeit unconsciously.

Another example of the ways our work creates a space for new leadership took place at a high school Critical Friends Group meeting that I was facilitating. Every teacher in the Critical Friends Group had brought some sample questions they had asked in their classrooms the week before to the table. As a group we charted the questions and examined them, looking for clues to student understanding, or misunderstanding. We examined our use of language and began to unravel our collective hunch that we were confusing our kids not only about the concepts we were addressing, but often in the very ways we were posing our questions. We began to share stories about student disengagement as a response to our framing of the questions as opposed to the facile excuse that "these" kids just don't care.

Finally, we examined our questions to assess our own expectations. Were we challenging our mostly poor, mostly minority students to think critically, or were we simply asking for recall from our own lectures? We found a mix of expectations and resolved to continue with our inquiry about questioning, vocabulary, and student engagement for the rest of the year.

In this Critical Friends Group, at a large urban vocational high school, this racially diverse group of teachers, some new, some veterans, some shop teachers and some academic instructors, are stepping up as teacher leaders. The school has a new principal, and the teachers are not sure how their input will be received, but their collaboration has bolstered their strength and is giving them voice, voice that they are now prepared to share with their students.

It is experiences like these that give me hope and strengthen my conviction that together we can educate all of our students in ways that challenge and stretch us all so that the "instrument" mentioned by Cicely Tyson can stretch and become an orchestra, composing a symphony of world music for all who care to listen.

REFERENCES

Tyson, C. (1991). *The quotable woman.* Philadelphia, PA: Running Press.

Wheatley, M. (2002). *Turning to one another: Simple conversations to restore hope to the future.* San Francisco, CA: Berrett-Koehler.

37

The Paradox of Teacher Leadership

Jed Frank Lippard

Throughout my first 6 years of teaching, I was perennially plagued by this elusive feeling that I needed something more, something bigger, something grander to achieve my true potential as a school person. I loved teaching, and unlike other young teachers—the infamous majority who don't make it beyond the third year—I was neither disillusioned, depleted, nor demoralized in my classroom practice. To the contrary, I was energized and impassioned, thriving on the brilliance of my students and constantly stimulated by the challenge of finding new ways to excite their curiosities. Still, I was not entirely satisfied.

As a founding teacher of the Francis W. Parker Charter Essential School in Devens, Massachusetts, one of the first 12 charter schools authorized by the Massachusetts Department of Education, my induction into the teaching profession was anything but typical. I had just completed the Undergraduate Teacher Education Program at Brown University, and whereas I had never really set my sights on being a middle school teacher, the opportunity to be one of 12 teachers on Parker's founding faculty was more compelling than teaching high school right away. Determined to put theory into practice and to be a part of a school community built around Ted Sizer's principles of "student as worker, teacher as coach," "less is more," and "learning to use one's mind well," I left my friends in

Providence and joined my new colleagues in June of 1995 for 2 months of planning our new school.

That first summer set the foundation for my 6 years at the Parker School. As charter school newbies, we were at once the masons, the brick-layers, and the travelers of this radical new path in public education. Determined to think and be "outside the box," we even had the delirious notion that we could run our school without a principal. Sure, we had some experienced teachers who defaulted to their prior years in schools to guide our decision making, but in truth, we were 12 individuals sharing 12 mostly equal pieces of the pie. At times, this arrangement was energizing, as we spent many animated hours hashing out important issues such as how to assess students without grades, how to honor student voice, and how to integrate the curriculum in authentic ways. On the other hand, we spent an equal number of excruciating hours debating minutiae such as the snowball policy, where (if at all) to place the microwave ovens, and whether or not to have vending machines in the student lounge. From the outset of my career as a teacher, I was intimately involved in leadership.

As the Parker School moved from idea to reality and the thrill of attending faculty meetings at the beginning and end of every day wore thin, we realized that for our work to be sustainable, we needed someone in charge. Too many late night meetings were taking their toll on our indi-vidual and collective well-being, relationships (in and out of school) were suffering, and in the end, our students were paying the price for our stress and exhaustion. For all of these reasons, we decided that for year 2, we would hire a principal teacher, someone who would be precisely that, half principal and half teacher.

Because this notion, the principal teacher, was still mostly outside the box, we were quick to pledge our support behind it. At the same time, it signaled a considerable shift in the way we did business at the Parker School. Feeling liberated from our administrative duties, the rest of us quickly defaulted to allowing the principal teacher to handle the minutiae that previously bogged us down. Within months, his job became impossi-ble, as the volume of stuff that landed on his principal's plate precluded him from being at all effective in his role as teacher. He struggled, and so did we, and for year 3, we finally got over ourselves and decided that the only viable solution to our leadership woes—even if it resided inside the box—was to hire a full-time principal. So we did.

For the next 2 years, I was able to zoom in on my teaching as I had never before had the liberty to do. No longer burdened by having, or wanting, to be a part of every decision, I worked tirelessly to expand my pedagogical repertoire, challenged myself and my students (who were now in high school!) to take demanding intellectual risks, and thrived on the thoughtful discourse of my classroom. By most accounts, life was good.

But still something was missing. The more established and confident I became as a teacher, the more I longed for something else. Although I had no desire to go back to the days of 11 p.m. meetings and making every decision by consensus, there was some force telling me that I had more to offer, that my sphere of influence ought to be bigger than my classroom, that I was limiting myself by being *just a teacher*. This restlessness propelled me to apply to graduate school, and after a teary and difficult goodbye, I left the Parker School in 2001 and went to graduate school to learn how to become a principal.

After a year of coursework and an internship at a large, high-achieving suburban high school outside of Boston, I returned to the charter school world as the Upper School (Grades 6–12) Director of Prospect Hill Academy in Cambridge, Massachusetts. Prospect Hill Academy had just undergone a major transformation, as only months before, the Board of Trustees had voted to sever ties with a private management company that had run school for more than 5 years. The parting was anything but harmonious, and I—along with a new Head of School and the people we hired—were charged with both cleaning up the residue and moving the school forward. No easy task.

If there was one phrase that permeated my consciousness like none other during my year in graduate school, it was that of *principal as instructional leader*. No matter the class we were in—supervision and evaluation, law, special education, or even budgeting—my classmates and I were constantly bombarded with this new paradigm for school principals. We were told to spend our time in the realm of leadership rather than management, to resist the tyranny of the urgent, and to establish our credibility as teachers first. Noble advice indeed, but easier said than done.

In my first weeks as principal, it became astonishingly clear that the administrative demands of running the school were irrepressible. Those rumors about principals not even being able to get from the car to the door without fielding hordes of "quick questions" (if I had a nickel for every time someone approached me with a "quick question . . .") weren't rumors at all; they became part of my daily existence. On most days, my "To Do" list got longer as the day progressed, and come evening, I had more e-mail messages to write, phone calls to make, and paperwork to process than I could have imagined even that same morning. As much as I longed to be the instructional leader, I was mired in the administrative purgatory that my well-meaning professors had so piously warned against.

To complicate matters more, since I came to Prospect Hill Academy as the *principal*—and an awfully young one at that—my colleagues had scarce opportunity to get to know me as a teacher. It was as if my track record at Parker meant nothing, for that was then, and this was now. Despite my ongoing and best efforts to deconstruct the us–them culture that toxically permeates so many schools, it was quite clear that in my role as an administrator, I simply was too far removed from the real action of my school.

After 2 years of indentured servitude to my nascent principalship, I made the calculated decision in year 3 to teach one section of eleventh-grade

English. Tired of being relegated to my office and feeling genuinely disconnected from my true passion, I knew that the only real way for me to emerge as the instructional leader of my school was to get back to doing what I did best. Sure, I had gained some cachet in the previous 2 years through my conversations with colleagues about *their* teaching, but I always sensed that there was an undercurrent of, "If only *you* knew what it was like to be in the classroom" or worse, "Who are *you* to be telling *me* how to teach?" So back into the classroom I went, determined not to perpetuate the same delusions of grandeur that emanated from my grad school professors.

It took no time for me to be humbled in my "new" role as teacher. I struggled with students who turned in mediocre work when they were capable of so much more. I grew tired of reminding high school juniors that they should not be engaging in side conversations when I, or one of their classmates, was talking. I resented giving up a whole day each weekend reading student essays and writing copious comments (often as long as the essays themselves), only to receive revisions with a few minor spelling corrections. I couldn't stand it when the Xerox machine broke down right before my class and my lesson plan depended on having those copies.

At the same time, I grew angry at Willy Loman's impenetrable lack of self-awareness. I was moved by Huck Finn's intuitive sense of right and wrong even in the face of society's misguided attempts to "sivilize" him. I became fascinated by what Zora Neale Hurston's Janie Mae Crawford might say to Nathaniel Hawthorne's Hester Prynne. And for one hour every day, I was impervious to the relentless and thankless demands of my other job. My time in the classroom was akin to my days as a young boy playing tag and running around in a big field, every so often touching base to regain my breath. Here, in so many ways that had been absent since I began my principalship, I was safe.

Perhaps more important than my own pleasure or satisfaction, last year I gained a real seat at the teachers' table. I attended English department meetings not as the boss but rather as a colleague. I shared and modeled my vulnerabilities, and in turn, teachers began to let down their guard with me. I too was at school until 11 p.m. the night before grades were due, and I was able to laugh and commiserate with my similarly last-minute colleagues about the absurdity of the whole situation. In conversations about learning and teaching, I found myself speaking in the first person plural rather the second person singular that had pervaded my discourse the previous two years. In sum, I was no longer one of "them"; I was a teacher who also happened to be the principal—or dare I say it, the *instructional leader.*

But if only it were so simple. I am back for my fourth year as principal, and just as strategically as I decided to teach a year ago, I decided *not* to teach this year. It's not that I didn't want to teach again or that I didn't enjoy teaching last year (in fact, it was more often than not the best hour of my day); it's that for me to do my job as *principal* well, I knew I had to recalibrate my priorities once again. In choosing to make sacred my time in the classroom and with my students, I was also choosing not to avail myself to my other constituents—parents, teachers, and fellow administrators—as readily as I had done before. Whereas some people understood and applauded my decision, others resented me for it. And truthfully, despite my best efforts to juggle all of my endless responsibilities, I did drop some (administrative) balls.

Paradoxically, it boils down to this. When I was teaching full time, I felt I had to *leave* the classroom to exercise my full potential as a school leader, yet as a principal, I felt compelled to *reenter* the classroom in order to exercise my full potential as a school leader. Am I really that hard to please? Or is it that the real mystery behind that elusive *something* lies somewhere in between, perhaps even in the form of the *teacher leader?*

Maybe we weren't that crazy at Parker after all.

38

The Times They Are A-changing

Martha McFarland Williams

For 32 years, I was a classroom teacher. The first years of my career were very different from the last. Schools got bigger, teachers' responsibilities grew, and communities changed. Size creates distance, and it was hard to maintain a sense of purpose. Increases in teacher responsibilities meant less student-teacher contact, and classrooms became less manageable. As a new teacher, I felt that I held a prestigious position and that the community held very positive views of the schools. I was so thrilled to be a staff member. I even saved detention lists that had my name on them. Now, it's not that simple, and many do not see teaching as a desirable profession, so I had mixed feelings as my daughter made her choice to teach special needs students. It's hard, she says, but she loves it. She is proud to be the third generation of her family to teach and looks forward to many years of service.

I wore many hats but was never a lead teacher, department head, or administrator. Rather, I found myself in leadership roles due to a number of other circumstances. I had many emotional ties to the school; my late father had taught there for 26 years; I had grown up in the town and attended its schools, so I was the go-to person for anyone seeking trivia from the past. It was a mixed blessing; like other veterans, I sometimes felt I had somehow overstayed my welcome. Many of the traditions we held dear are vanishing. Faculty members no longer feel compelled to buy fundraiser tickets, show up at basketball games, or advise cocurricular activities. I had directed plays, advised the cheerleaders, and enjoyed the sense of being a part of the students' lives.

Becoming yearbook advisor seemed a natural outgrowth of my interest in writing and personal history. It also offered considerable empowerment. On picture days, the schedule was all mine! If someone suffered an unflattering moment with the school photographer, I was the one to make substitutions. No one, even an administrator, wants to look like a "geek" for all posterity. I told the student editors we were personal historians and bound to a sacred trust. So, with some misgivings, I provided my true senior photo for the memories section—integrity at all costs! There were other benefits. We produced a tangible product each year. I made many pleasant connections with local businesses and never lost my belief in our mission.

It was both flattering and confusing to be selected as a member of a restructuring committee charged with the task of top to bottom reorganization of the school. The committee included parents, administrators, and students as well as teachers. This group met once a week during school hours, some evenings, and through the summer. Since I knew I was perceived as a traditionalist rather than an innovator, it didn't surprise me that my selection was based on the idea that I was to represent the skeptics in both the school and community. Committee members often disagreed on such issues as length of classes, off-site programs, and core education. We sent out surveys to parents and community leaders that revealed little support for change. When we met with these groups, their questions were always about "basics." They were concerned that the students' test scores were low, too many lacked essential skills, and schools were not communicating well. Parents, in particular, worried that newer methods were not working as well as the old for their children. I shared some of their concerns, so it was difficult to entertain some of the radical proposals some committee members suggested. For the most part, it was the nonteaching staff that encouraged sweeping change, so divisions developed and communication suffered. It was frustrating because although we shared the goal of better education, we were miles apart on how to go about it. In the end, we accomplished little. It felt wrong to have wasted so much time and so many resources, and sadly, the experience made me feel less like a leader.

In a more personal and satisfying way, I took on the role of teacher leader when I became an informal mentor to a group of young women with whom I shared a lunch period. I was motivated by my own memories of an older woman who had befriended me when I began my career. She was very candid in telling me about her own feelings of insecurity, something I would never have suspected. I felt obliged as a professional and maternal as a mother to these young women—come to think of it, I took the young man new to our department under my wing as well. In a way, I was hesitant because I didn't want to seem arrogant—that may be part of the reluctance veterans feel, and those age and experience differences seem more pronounced now. The new teachers were concerned about the supervision and evaluation process. They didn't need one more person to intimidate them.

These young teachers were enthusiastic, bright, and full of promise, but they needed support and direction. They felt there was so much to do and so little time. There were a few false starts. The new teachers were apprehensive about sharing problems, and I was not, after all, a designated leader. Both sides experienced plenty of insecurity. We talked generally, then more specifically, and learned from each other. I was able to share my experiences openly and honestly and feel gratified that they trusted me to share theirs. I was deeply sorry that none of the four stayed beyond that year. They would have contributed so much.

At the risk of sounding self-congratulatory, I'd say that teachers must be the most flexible people on the planet. We've always been asked to change with the times, fix whatever was wrong, keep a positive attitude in the face of tight budgets, and withstand a steady stream of constructive criticism. We all have had priceless moments—the popular athlete who befriended a disabled underclassman, the way we celebrated Guy Fawkes Day with an end-of-term pizza party, and the quiet satisfaction of seeing students—and, in my case, colleagues, grow. These rewards are still available, I hope, to our newer colleagues, but I worry they are being threatened by the distance teachers feel from other teachers and from their supervisors.

Throughout my teaching career, I have been affected by the emotional highs and lows of being involved in so many life changes that paralleled my own. I remember the conflicts that characterized my own adolescence and could easily empathize with my students' struggles. I see the experiences of my daughter, who has begun to work with young people, and many of those experiences feel familiar. With colleagues, some of whom became more like family than friends, I have shared the most important moments life offers. It's hard to think of any work that offers more opportunity to give and receive on such a human level.

I think of the many good days I enjoyed as a classroom teacher and sincerely hope that the future holds that possibility for my daughter and her classmates as they begin their careers. I also hope there are mentors and teacher leaders willing to help them find their stride in the classroom. When you think about it, there is hardly a more important task than theirs.

Questions for Reflection and Conversation

- What sustains you as a leader? How have you helped sustain others in their leadership roles?
- As you look back over your career so far, who have been your mentors or coaches? What did you learn from them—about teaching and leadership as well as the process of coaching or mentoring?
- A coaching protocol can be useful as you work with another person or small group of people to sort through what issues you or they want to tackle. The trick, ultimately, of using protocols—and this one in particular—is to internalize the approach so a conversation proceeds seamlessly. On the other hand, having a written procedure helps all participants understand and own responsibility for ensuring effective facilitation.

The coaching protocol follows the developmentally appropriate order for questioning in coaching or consulting situations. The progression follows the "ideal" progression a good coach uses by gathering more facts so he or she can understand the situation better, using active listening and interpretive listening, probing to help the presenter's understanding, and finally offering some advice and getting a response from the presenter at the end of the exchange. So the progression is

- Factual questions
- "What I hear you say . . ."
- "This is what I think you are saying . . . am I getting it right?"
- "What probing questions I now have . . ."
- "What ideas this brings to mind . . ."
- "What do you think?"

Following this basic outline ensures that many aspects of the situation are brought to the surface and that consultants resist the urge to give advice at the outset.

Conclusion

39

(How) Can a New Vision of Teacher Leadership Be Fulfilled?

Sarah V. Mackenzie

I want to conclude this book with some answers to another question about teacher leadership: "Can a new vision of school leadership be realized?" Wanting to end on a hopeful note, I cautiously ask, "How can it be realized?" Throughout my years in education, I have seen and experienced the growth of teacher leaders. Like the teacher leaders described by Wasley (1991), teacher leaders in the past felt a fair amount of stress in relationships with colleagues. Teacher leaders were not taken seriously in their own schools even if they were considered knowledgeable elsewhere. As a result, many teacher leaders denied their power and responsibility as leaders of their colleagues, let alone their schools.

But in the last decade, I have seen a change in teacher leadership. I assume it represents a change in the climate of schools and their colleagues' recognition that teachers have a vested interest in ensuring that their work is meaningful and important. I see colleagues more trusting of each other and teacher leaders more willing and able to acknowledge that they are leaders and have leadership skills and knowledge to share to help improve a school. Teacher leaders increasingly envision true *teacherly* leadership of their schools. Rather than individual teachers' participating in leadership activities in the school or other arena, the new vision of teacher leadership expands to all teachers fully involved in leading a school. Teachers want and need to make decisions that are meaningful to them because such decisions are relevant to their students' learning. Teacher leaders have come to know how important it is for all teachers to see their professional work as connected to that of their colleagues so the entire school benefits.

The latest reform efforts have emphasized common goals or guidelines, and, therefore, common curriculum and assessments. Although teachers may have some difficulty with the narrowness of the curriculum and the amount of assessing such changes entail, they generally embrace the concept of standards and the implications for improving learning for all students in the school. However, a collective responsibility for improvement represents a huge change for how teachers have viewed their work. Teachers are accustomed to focusing on the students in their own classrooms. When they emerge from the classroom to engage in planning or decision making with colleagues, they often consider their role to be an advocate for their own students' learning needs. Such advocacy is all well and good; however, it is often in tension with or may impinge on the learning of other students. Having a "big picture" of the needs of all students in the school, sharing goals that ensure the learning of those students, and seeing their work as encompassing the improvement of instruction for all students in a school are necessary beliefs enacted in the behavior of all teachers, not just administrators and teacher leaders.

There are places where teacher leadership in the sense of all teachers deeply engaged in leading an entire school has been firmly rooted or at least planted and nurtured (Gonzales, 2004; Meier, 1995). To a large extent, too, the latest reform efforts have pushed teachers and schools to embrace collaborative leadership or arrange structures that will promote it. Although organizations and expectations have much to do with shaping school culture, fundamental changes in beliefs about the job of teachers will have to occur before school culture can change. The vision of teacher leadership as every professional involved in priority setting and decision making describes changes in teacher behavior; however, these changes derive from intrapersonal adjustments that are necessary for collaborative leadership to take hold in schools.

Although the question of which must come first—the behavior or the belief—remains, as educators we know how important beliefs are in guiding action (Fullan, 1996; Starratt, 2004). The vision of all teachers as leaders involves the interaction of one's beliefs about one's ability as well as conceptions of the role of teacher (Bandura, 1997) and experience that involves having the opportunity to both engage in and learn from the practice of leadership of the school.

OPPORTUNITIES FOR TEACHERS IN LEADERSHIP

The newest educational reforms have meant that teachers have had to relinquish some of their favorite curricular and instructional activities. We have all heard about the struggle of the second-grade teacher who had been happily doing Egypt and the pyramids for years and sees the topic moved to fifth grade because it makes more sense in the developmental and conceptual scheme of learning organized by the teachers in the school. In addition, the kinds of assessments states administer or systems develop may well mean the seventh-grade science fair has to be modified or abandoned because the investigations were too diverse; there is no time in the present curriculum; or they represented parents' willingness to help their children instead of allowing students to learn themselves. The implication here is not just that teachers will have to submit to the will of the group of colleagues, whether it is the department, program, or entire teaching staff, but, more meaningfully, that they must consider and make decisions on content and pedagogy as a group. Such decision making will involve their understanding the goals of the school while seriously examining the logic of the curriculum and the developmental needs of all the students (Fullan, 1996; Newmann, Rutter, & Smith, 1989).

To align curriculum and develop assessments, teachers have to coordinate their work with their colleagues. They need to improve their skills of collaboration, which may well have been dormant or never, in fact, acquired. Teachers have to give up the isolation so characteristic of the work environment. The movement toward teaming has made inroads although some teachers still prefer to teach alone or, more often, find the structure of the school schedule such that they have little opportunity to collaborate with others except after school.

Gradually, though, teachers and administrators are coming to believe that structures and expectations for collaboration add up to time well spent (Donaldson, 2006; Short & Greer, 1997). One teacher leader experienced in and committed to collaboration recently moved into an administrative position. She had a directive from the school board to improve the culture of the school, but she encountered a faculty with a rigid view of the principal's role. She needed to get in touch with the flexibility she had as a teacher and teacher leader to relate to the teachers and alter their perspective of her role as well as theirs. She described her challenge this way:

> Within my building I have found some of my staff want me to basically make all the decisions, and others prefer being collaborative. At meetings when I insist upon input from the staff and that a decision be made together, I am sure some staff think I am not doing my job, where the others are happy to work together. It will take time for the staff to come together and work together as they should. I know I am

on the right track. A couple of staff members told me at the end of the year that this had been the best year in the building in a long time and that it was due to my leadership. I was pleased to hear it, but I realize it was because of their openness to seeing beyond what I wanted for the school and being willing to try new things. (Janice Twomey, personal communication, July 2005)

To ensure collaborative leadership, educational leaders have to be able to be flexible or "balanced" so they can create structures and situations for effective participation based on their assessment of what the school community needs in order to continue to move toward an ideal (Waters, Marzano, & McNulty, 2003).

BEHAVIOR OF TEACHERS

Collaborative task work and decision making require a skill set that teachers have been allowed to ignore or acquire only if interested in moving into administration or improving their teacher leadership. Furthermore, such activities often challenge teachers' deeply embedded identities. It is hard to imagine that teachers are considered competitive because the stakes are low and the rewards and resources thin. Proponents of merit-pay proposals have discovered how difficult it is to sell the idea as much to teachers as to politicians. Teachers, of course, want to be well paid, but for them the extrinsic rewards of the profession are not solely monetary. The extrinsic rewards they crave are respect and even love from their students and the other stakeholders of the school, especially parents. They cherish the unique place they hold in people's hearts. Is it any wonder, then, that they are unwilling to share new ideas, to give up effective curriculum and methods, to spend valuable time away from their classroom in discussions that will force them to do that?

The Prime of Miss Jean Brodie accurately represents both the martyr and the "teacher as hero" images of the profession, which derive from and are fostered by the isolation of the job. Some teachers will have to give up the isolation and territoriality they rail against, yet cherish, and all teachers will have to develop and practice skills of collaboration. Being able to participate effectively in collaborative decision making will push them even more. The skill and practice of managing conflict comes first from believing that conflict is a useful and necessary aspect of decision making (Hargreaves, 1995). Many teachers are actually quite adept at "straight talk"; however, plumbing the depths of others' deeply held beliefs and ideas about curriculum, examining them to see their alignment with one's own, and then being able to engage in discussion and dialogue to come to consensus about direction and next steps require beliefs and skills that will change teachers' conceptions of their job. The good news is that as teachers gain confidence in their interpersonal skills, have more experience struggling with the thorny issues schools face, and see their beliefs melded with the goals of the school, they will be leaders and see themselves as such (Barth, 1999).

BELIEFS OF TEACHERS

Since No Child Left Behind assesses school effectiveness on the basis of the adequate yearly progress of the students in the school, teachers have a stake in the outcomes of the whole school. Clear goals and clear objectives as well as common assessments provide the framework while the accountability measures drive the point home. We assume that teachers getting together and aligning curriculum will help them accept their responsibility for learning throughout the school. Shared goals are crucial (Fullan, 2004), but beliefs about how well the individual can participate in the planning and the delivery and the extent to which they believe their colleagues can are equally important (Bandura, 1997; Mackenzie & Donaldson, 2005; Tschannen-Moran & Barr, 2004).

Self-efficacy is not just the belief that a certain effort will produce an outcome, but it is "the conviction that one can successfully execute the behavior to produce the outcome" (Bandura, 1997, p. 193). Belief in a school's collective efficacy, on the other hand, comes from both an assessment of the ability of teachers in the school and a belief that all faculty members are important to the fulfillment of the school's goals. Teacher efficacy, like self-efficacy, is important, but collective efficacy is increasingly so (Tschannen-Moran & Barr, 2004; Tschannen-Moran, Hoy, & Hoy, 1998). As professionals in schools become more and more interdependent, the improvement of learning there will hinge on the strength and power of members' beliefs about their collective ability to organize and sustain significant change (Bandura, 1986).

The third wave of teacher leadership follows periods in which teacher leaders took on quasi-administrative roles or packaged and coordinated curriculum and instruction while teaching in the classroom (Silva, Gimbert, & Nolan, 2000). Whereas the other "waves" of teacher leadership entailed teachers working with colleagues outside the classroom and often on tasks unrelated to teaching practice or at least not closely connected to it, the new era of teacher leadership derives from teachers' central responsibility, teaching and learning in their classrooms. The opportunities and experiences of teachers (inside and now outside the classroom) have given them a strong foundation from which to enhance their capacity for leadership of the entire school.

Many teachers already know they are leaders because they can articulate their understanding of their practice and have opened themselves to learning how to improve it. Furthermore, they trust that teachers—as individuals and as a whole faculty—know best what their school's students need to meet the expectations the goals of the school imply. They are working on many levels. Their primary focus is, as always, their own students' learning while they also participate in and take responsibility for the learning of students in the entire school. They are "legitimate" leaders because of their knowledge of and clear focus on student learning. Their "big picture" encompasses trust in themselves and their colleagues to care deeply about how their practices affect student learning. They believe their willingness and ability both to share effectively with others their learning from practice and to learn from others about successful practices will strengthen learning in the whole school. They also believe their role as teachers involves constant dialogue about student learning so they can participate in collaborative decision making not just with colleagues but also with other stakeholders of the school.

If this change in attitude and behavior is happening with teachers as they transition to a new era of school leadership in which all teachers are leaders with increased responsibility and the disposition to accept it, what else must change? What do principals have to do—and believe—to fulfill the promise of this new order?

PRINCIPALS AND TEACHER LEADERSHIP OF THE SCHOOL

Scholars talk about distributed leadership (Spillane, 2005), binary leadership (Evans, 1998), and collaborative leadership as practitioners gradually embrace the structures that will enable their fulfillment. The vision of *teacherly* leadership, of true collaborative leadership of schools, involves changing beliefs about functions and roles of all the professionals in a school.

Some of the behaviors administrators need to demonstrate are obvious, but, like those of teachers, they are firmly rooted in beliefs about roles, capabilities, and responsibilities. If schools are to change to make the job of principal more doable, principals will have to struggle with some deeply held beliefs not just about their role but also about the role of teachers. The basis of resistance to true collaborative leadership with teachers from some principals and superintendents derives from their conception of the administrator role as protector of teachers. The essence of their job, they believe, is to keep teachers from having to wrestle with structural and political issues they feel it is their job alone to tackle. It is not necessarily about power; it seems to be more about keeping teachers focused on the important work of schools or, perhaps, each teacher's small part of it. Their behavior indicates they do not believe teachers need to understand how the pieces fit together as long as they fulfill their individual functions of ensuring student learning in their classrooms. These beliefs conflict with the ideal of developing a critical mass of systems thinkers in order to be able to effect fundamental improvements in student learning (Fullan, 2004).

PRINCIPALS' ACTIONS AND BELIEFS

Just as teachers have to experience new ways of doing things and have confidence in their beliefs about leadership as well as teaching and learning, so must principals and other administrators. Although principals recognize that teacher leaders are not eager for a new job, especially a totally administrative one, they need to appreciate the skills teachers have so they can help teacher leaders develop even more and take on other roles. Teacher leaders are, of course, good teachers who understand their craft and can communicate about their work with care and conviction with colleagues and other members of the school community. They have skills and knowledge about leadership, especially collaborative leadership. Principals need to recognize and congratulate teacher leaders' unique contributions and support the learning of these leaders as they manage the leadership of the school together. The roles of teacher leaders and principals complement each other while their relationships model for others the way all adults in the school should interact (Donaldson, 2006).

In spite of the different roles of teachers and administrators, everyone must be appreciated and expected to fulfill tasks in the best way he or she can, so that leadership is part of the responsibility of all members of the school community (Barth, 1988). Principals must believe that teachers are vital partners in decisions about curriculum, teaching practice, and school organization. Teachers can provide important information and insight for problem solving. Administrators may feel they do not have time to engage more people in discussions or they assume teachers do not want to be bothered, but when issues are shared, everyone feels increased responsibility for understanding and implementing solutions. Once developed, collaborative mechanisms for decision making and problem solving must be honored.

Ambivalence about teacher leadership of schools is understandable. Principals may know they need to support the leadership learning of their teachers and take the time required to practice collaborative decision making, but they also want good, solid teaching and learning for students all of the time. Teacher leaders are skilled in the classroom, so they are more able to take on other tasks. Because they are so committed to their teaching, the sheer volume of tasks and roles in a school and school system can overwhelm them. It can come across as whining if they sputter about all they must prepare for the classroom plus work on curriculum committees and extracurricular obligations. More often than not, they are silent martyrs.

To deal with the ambivalence of administrators and the silent or expressed feelings of beleaguered teacher leaders, there must be a meeting of the minds and hearts about their respective roles. Beliefs about inclusive, participative *teacherly* leadership of the school should lead to fundamental organizational and behavioral change. Partnerships evolve as both sides balance the work. Often principals are in the middle of demands on teacher leaders systemwide. They have to mediate those demands so that no one teacher leader is overburdened; at the same time, principals have to ensure that teacher leaders have the opportunities they want and deserve to fulfill many roles in the school, system, or larger professional community. Rather than protecting teachers from dealing with the demands in their priority-based decision-making process, principals and teachers can spread out expectations and requests for help among more teachers or pair evolving leaders with more experienced ones to complete a task. All partners must see building the capacity of the teacher corps as essential work.

Principals can no longer view their role as focusing on what is in the best interest of all members of the school community and mediating the narrower views of individual teachers and parents. Helping teachers see and appreciate the larger issues is a teaching job in its own right. Sharing an administrator's forest-for-the-trees perspective enlarges the leadership capacity of the school. In addition, although teachers already have strong ideas about good practice, they need opportunities "to talk the walk" (D. Ullman, personal communication, December 2003). Hearing themselves speak about their knowledge and beliefs about good practice builds confidence and capacity. They learn best when they *teach*, which is synonymous with *lead*. A new administrator describes his vision of teacherly administrative leadership in the following way:

> I have learned that it is important for teachers and students to see a school leader as an effective teacher. They need to be able to assess where teachers and students are with their learning and be able to instruct when appropriate. When school leaders aren't effective teachers and are unable to accurately assess the learning in their schools, they can actually shut the learning of students and teachers down because they cover the "leadership curriculum," by passing down mandates without thinking about how they "fit" with the philosophy of the learning community. I believe that now, more than ever, it is important for a leader to be an effective teacher, someone who accurately assesses their schools and filters mandates down to their staff. (Terry Young, personal communication, December 2004)

This new administrator helped the teachers focus on what was important and maintain a balance of stability and movement toward reform.

EVOLUTION OF *TEACHERLY* SCHOOL LEADERSHIP

Both teachers and administrators will need support to have confidence in themselves and the vision of *teacherly* leadership of a school. The concept of "The Four Hats of Shared Leadership" (Garmston & Wellman, 1999) can help school leaders see dimensions of leadership at which they are already proficient and to move into other realms that offer opportunities for challenge and risk-taking. Everyone involved in collaborative leadership needs some help with group dynamics. Administrators and teacher leaders can support each other as they attend to the process-product balance: It involves knowing how to help a group immerse itself in and trust group processes as well as knowing when and how to exert the push to produce.

Teachers have had different roles in task or governance groups from administrators. Individuals, no matter what role they have played, have their own areas of strength and needs for improvement as both teachers and leaders. In the new vision of school leadership, all participants will continue to struggle with authority and power issues. That is why the job description of both administrators and teachers must change. To make the work of schools doable and effective, everyone will have to work toward finding a comfort level with shared work, shared leadership, and shared responsibility for learning in their schools.

Raising the assumptions and tensions and addressing them as a school of leaders will help to clarify the purpose and promote guidelines for interactions, both interpersonal and procedural. As leadership evolves through the work, transparency of group decision-making processes will enable all teachers and administrators to feel as if they are equal members who have a stake in participating and implementing plans fully.

Collaborative leadership depends on what we do, not who we are and what role we have. It exists in the relationships among teachers and administrators to develop, implement, and be responsible for a shared vision of learning for all members of the school community. Because it is an interactive and ongoing process, school leadership will evolve as actions fulfill participants' beliefs while their beliefs are molded and deepened by the experience of leadership.

REFERENCES

Bandura, A. (1986). *Social foundations of thought and action: A social cognitive theory.* Englewood Cliffs, NJ: Prentice Hall.

Bandura, A. (1997). *Self-efficacy: The exercise of control.* New York: W.H. Freeman.

Barth, R. S. (1988). School: A community of leaders. In A. Lieberman (Ed.), *Building a professional culture in schools* (pp. 129–147). New York: Teachers College Press.

Barth, R. S. (1999). *The teacher leader.* Providence: The Rhode Island Foundation.

Donaldson, G. A., Jr. (2006). *Cultivating leadership in schools: Connecting people, purpose, and practice.* New York: Teachers College Press.

Evans, R. (1998). *The human side of school change.* San Francisco: Jossey-Bass.

Fullan, M. G. (1996, February). Turning systemic thinking on its head. *Phi Delta Kappan, 77,* 420–423.

Fullan, M. G. (2004). *Leadership and sustainability: System thinkers in action.* Thousand Oaks, CA: Corwin Press.

Garmston, R. J., & Wellman, B. M. (1999). *The adaptive school: A sourcebook for developing collaborative groups.* Norwood, MA: Christopher-Gordon.

Gonzales, L. D. (2004). *Sustaining teacher leadership: Beyond the boundaries of enabling school culture.* Lanham, MD: University Press of America.

Hargreaves, A. (1995). Development and desire: A postmodern perspective. In T. R. Guskey & M. Huberman (Eds.), *Professional development in education: New paradigms and practices* (pp. 9–34). New York: Teachers College Press.

Mackenzie, S. V., & Donaldson, G. D. (2005, April). *Collective efficacy, teacher efficacy, and collaborative climate in Maine high schools: Ingredients for change.* Paper presented at the annual meeting of the American Educational Research Association, Montreal, PQ.

Meier, D. (1995). *The power of their ideas: Lessons from America from a small school in Harlem.* Boston: Beacon Press.

Newmann, F., Rutter, R., & Smith, M. (1989). Organizational factors that affect school sense of efficacy, community, and expectations. *Sociology of Education, 62,* 221–238.

Short, P. M., & Greer, J. T. (1997). *Leadership in empowered schools: Themes from innovative efforts.* Englewood Cliffs, NJ: Prentice Hall.

Silva, D. Y., Gimbert, B., & Nolan, J. (2000). Sliding the doors: Locking and unlocking possibilities for teacher leadership. *Teachers College Record, 102*(4), 779–804.

Spillane , J. (2005). *Distributed leadership.* San Francisco: Jossey-Bass.

Starratt, R. (2004). *Ethical leadership.* San Francisco: Jossey-Bass.

Tschannen-Moran, M., Hoy, A.W., & Hoy, W. K. (1998). Teacher efficacy: Its meaning and measure. *Review of Educational Research, 68,* 202–248.

Tschannen-Moran, M., & Barr, M. (2004). Fostering student achievement: The relationship between collective teacher efficacy and student achievement. *Leadership and Policy in Schools, 3,* 187—207.

Wasley, P. (1991). *Teachers who lead: The rhetoric of reform and the realities of practice.* New York: Teachers College Press.

Waters, J. T., Marzano, R. J., & McNulty, B. A. (2003). *Balanced leadership: What 30 years of research tells us about the effect of leadership on student achievement.* Aurora, CO: Mid-continent Research for Education and Learning.

40

Leading From the Back

Richard H. Ackerman

I learned a great deal about teacher leadership by bushwhacking for 20 days through the Pisgah National Forest. I was part of a zealous group of out-of-shape administrators enrolled in a North Carolina Outward Bound Program. Each of us had somehow located 11 unaccounted personal summer days to spend crawling together through the jungles of North Carolina.

At the start of our journey, I frequently found myself in the front of the line, the "point" person, holding the map and compass, making the orienteering decisions and setting the pace. I was comfortable in the front and the others seemed happy with me there. I felt constrained by the frequent yell of the "sweep" (the person in the back) particularly when I was directed to stop and wait for everyone to catch up. Midway through the course, one of the instructors said to me, "Ackerman, if you want to know what real leadership is, try walking in the back for a while." I did.

The fellow directly in front of me was substantially out of shape. For endless stretches of time, I watched as he struggled, agonized, and oftentimes fell over every rock and protruding limb. Gradually, I found myself breathing with him, rooting for him, my nose pressed against the back of his sweat-soaked shirt. ("You can do it, you can do it.") He knew I was there. I admired his courage, and I began to understand our journey through his monumental pain and tenacity. I gradually became less concerned about when and how we would arrive at our destination. Others could figure out how to use the maps and compass. I was learning about leading from the back.

Successful leadership ultimately develops in the service of others. The notion of leading from the back is often undervalued, misunderstood, and seemingly paradoxical. Yet behind this paradox lies one of the mysteries of genuine achievement.

Index

About the Editors

Richard H. Ackerman, a former school teacher and school head, is currently Associate Professor of Educational Leadership at the University of Maine College of Education and Human Development. Ackerman is the coauthor of *The Wounded Leader: How Real Leadership Emerges in Times of Crisis.* He is the coauthor of *Making Sense as a School Leader: Persisting Questions, Creative Opportunities* with Gordon Donaldson and Rebecca van der Bogert. He was cofounder of the International Network of Principals' Centers, a 20-year collaboration of professional associations, universities, and education agencies working actively to strengthen leadership at the school level through professional development for leaders. Richard Ackerman leads retreats in Maine as well as nationally for the Center for Courage and Renewal, a program that invites teachers and leaders to explore the inner landscape of their lives as educators.

Sarah V. Mackenzie is Assistant Professor of Educational Leadership in the College of Education and Human Development at the University of Maine. She was a high school teacher and librarian for 18 years. She was a teacher leader for all of those years, but when she left the classroom she started to understand her own and others' teacher leadership. She worked for several years in undergraduate teacher preparation programs before she completed her doctorate and started teaching in graduate leadership development programs. She has coauthored several articles on leadership development with her colleagues in the Maine School Leadership Network and the University of Maine. Her recent article, coauthored with Richard Ackerman, "Uncovering Teacher Leadership," appeared in the May 2006 *Educational Leadership.*

About the Contributors

Deborah Bambino was a teacher in Philadelphia and is now a National School Reform Faculty Facilitator. She is the author of *Teaching Out Loud: A Middle Grades Diary* and has written many articles about her experiences as a teacher leader and Critical Friends Group coach.

Roland S. Barth, a renowned author of many books about leadership, is a former teacher, principal, and founder of the Harvard Principals' Center. His most recent books are *Lessons Learned: Shaping Relationships and Culture in the Workplace* and *Learning by Heart.*

Barnett Berry is the founder and president of the Center for Teaching Quality, Inc., based in Chapel Hill, North Carolina. He is author of numerous journal articles, book chapters, and commissioned reports on school reform, accountability, and the teaching profession, and serves on boards and in an advisory capacity to numerous organizations committed to teaching quality, equity, and social justice in America's schools.

Linda Bowe works as an educational consultant, helping administrators and teachers develop as leaders to create wholesome and effective learning environments for themselves and their students. She is completing work on her dissertation, which explores the ways in which teacher leaders use their relational influence with their colleagues to shape the teaching and learning practices in their schools. She enjoys the many benefits of living on Penobscot Bay on the coast of Maine, where she and her husband, Michael, have raised four children.

Gary Chapin teaches and leads, simultaneously and concurrently, at Hall-Dale High School in Farmingdale, Maine.

Michelle Collay is Associate Professor in the Department of Educational Leadership at California State University, East Bay, in Hayward, California. A former music teacher, she is a teacher-scholar who seeks to align teaching and scholarship in higher education and K–12 schools. Her research focus is teacher professional socialization with attention to how gender, class, and race shape teachers' lives. She coaches principals and teacher leaders engaged in professional learning communities, constructivist teaching and leading, and other school reform efforts.

Frank Crowther is an internationally respected scholar and researcher in educational management and leadership. He is Professor and Director of the Leadership Research Institute at the University of Southern Queensland, Australia. In 1997, he was awarded the Gold Medal of the Australian Council for Educational Administration in recognition of his services to educational leadership.

Mary E. Dietz is an international consultant specializing in assisting educators in building capacity to establish and facilitate learning communities. She is also cofounder of LearnCity, an educational technology firm offering a Web-based solution for designing, implementing, and assessing standards-based instruction, K–12. Her work is focused on coaching educational systems through the design and implementation of school reform efforts. Much of her work with educators has been in the areas of continuous improvement, professional development, coaching, and alternative performance assessments for educators. She established the Portfolio Network for the National Staff Development Council (NSDC), dedicated to promoting the portfolio process for professional learning. She has coached teachers, administrators, school boards, and communities in establishing the relationships necessary for systemic change. Most recently she served as designer and facilitator of an online Knowledge Management System for managing standards-based instruction in California.

JoAnne C. Dowd is a former teacher and administrator. She is affiliated with the National School Reform Faculty and the Coalition of Essential Schools. She is presently a Senior Partnership Associate at the Southern Maine Partnership.

Gordon A. Donaldson, Jr., is Professor of Educational Leadership in the College of Education and Human Development at the University of Maine. He has written extensively about leadership development, and his most recent book is *Cultivating Leadership in Schools: Connecting People, Purpose and Practice,* 2nd Edition.

Morgaen L. Donaldson A former high school teacher and teacher leader, Morgaen was a founding faculty member of the Boston Arts Academy. She is currently an advanced doctoral student at the Harvard Graduate School of Education and a researcher at the Project on the Next Generation of Teachers. Coauthor of *Finders and Keepers: Helping New Teachers Survive and*

Thrive in Our Schools (2004) and *Reflections of First-Year Teachers on School Culture: Questions, Hopes, and Challenges* (1999), Morgaen continues to research, write, and teach about how schools can become vibrant learning communities for children and adults.

Eleanor E. Drago-Severson is an Associate Professor of Educational Leadership at Columbia University's Teachers College. Her research interests include school leadership for adult learning, principal and faculty development, supporting adult development and learning in K–12 schools, Adult Basic Education/English for Speakers of Other Languages and university contexts, and qualitative research. Drago-Severson has authored two recent books, *Attending to Adult Learning* and *Helping Teachers Learn*, which was awarded the 2004 National Staff Development Council's Book of the Year Award.

Margaret Ferguson is District Manager of Education Services at Education Queensland. Her work focuses on capacity building, curriculum leadership, and pedagogical enhancement in schools. She has worked extensively in teacher leader development.

William Ferriter teaches sixth grade Language Arts and Social Studies at Salem Middle School in the Wake County (North Carolina) Public School System. Bill has taught for 13 years and earned his National Board Certification in 1997. He is a Senior Fellow of the Teacher Leaders Network. He recently cowrote an article with John Norton, "Creating a Culture of Excellence" for *Threshold* (Spring, 2004).

Nancy Flanagan retired after 30 years of teaching music in the Hartland, Michigan schools. She is National Board Certified and is presently pursuing a doctorate in Education Policy at Michigan State University.

Michael Fullan is the former Dean of the Ontario Institute for Studies in Education of the University of Toronto. He is recognized as an international authority on education reform. He is engaged in training in, consulting for, and evaluating change projects around the world. His ideas for managing change are used in many countries, and his books have been published in several languages. His books, which are widely acclaimed, include the *What's Worth Fighting For* trilogy (with Andy Hargreaves), the *Change Forces* trilogy, *The New Meaning of Educational Change*, and *Leading in a Culture of Change*, which was awarded the 2002 Book of the Year Award by the National Staff Development Council. His latest books in 2006 are *Breakthrough, Learning Places*, and *Turnaround Leadership*. In April 2004, he was appointed Special Adviser on Education to the Premier, and Minister of Education in Ontario.

Leonne Hann is Senior Research Associate in the Leadership Research Institute at the University of Southern Queensland. She has participated in national research projects in school innovation. Her recently completed postgraduate study deals with teacher leadership and successful school reform.

Sam M. Intrator is an associate professor of Education and Child Study at Smith College. A former high school teacher and administrator, he has published four books, including *Tuned in and Fired Up: How Teaching can Inspire Real Learning in the Classroom* and *Teaching With Fire: Poetry That Sustains the Courage to Teach.* Intrator currently codirects a youth leadership program called Project Coach, which trains inner city teens to run sports leagues and mentor elementary-aged youth.

Anne E. Jones is an advanced doctoral student in Administration, Planning, and Social Policy at the Harvard Graduate School of Education. Her research includes communities of practice, instructional capacity, second-stage teachers, retention, and data as a tool for instructional improvement.

Stephen S. Kaagan is Professor of Education at Michigan State University. His teaching interests are leadership, organizational analysis, and administrative practice. He has been honored with several awards, including membership in the Royal Society for the Encouragement of Arts, Manufactures and Commerce, London; and honorary doctorates from Williams College in Massachusetts and Green Mountain College in Vermont. He most recently authored *Leadership Games: Experiential Learning for Organizational Development* (1999, Sage).

Marilyn Katzenmeyer is currently President of Professional Development Center, Inc., in Tampa, Florida. She also serves the At Risk Institute and Institute for Instructional Research and Practice at the University of South Florida College of Education in Tampa, Florida. She was formerly Executive Director of the West Central Educational Leadership Network. The Network provided leadership training and school improvement assistance to educators throughout 13 school districts in Southwest Florida. Marilyn worked in Ohio and Florida as a secondary school teacher and as a human resource development professional. As director of the Broward County Human Resource Development Department (Fort Lauderdale, Florida), Marilyn created staff development programs for a large urban school district.

Karen Kent, EdD, is Director of the San Francisco Bay Region IV Professional Development Consortium. In her 16 years of experience in teacher-centered staff development, she has provided programs and participated in research focused on linking teacher involvement in whole school reform with professional development.

Linda Lambert is Professor Emeritus at California State University, East Bay, and founder of Lambert Leadership Development. Dr. Lambert has served in multiple leadership roles, including principal and director of numerous reform initiative and academies. Her pioneering work in leadership has led to invitations by the State Department, foreign ministries, and the Rockefeller Foundation to consult in Egypt, Asia, Australia, Canada, and Mexico. In addition to numerous articles and chapters, Dr. Lambert is the lead author of the 1995 and 2002 best-selling texts *The Constructivist Leader* (1st and 2nd editions) and *Who Will Save Our Schools?* (1997) and author of *Building Leadership Capacity in Schools* (1998); *Developing Leadership Capacity for School Improvement*, an adaptation of the 1998 text published in London (2003); and *Leadership Capacity for Lasting School Improvement* (2003). Awards include International Book of the Year (*The Constructivist Leader*), Outstanding California Educator, and Professor of the Year. Her major consulting and research areas involve constructivist leadership, leadership capacity, women in leadership, and organizational development.

Wendy Lessard is currently teaching high school English and is codepartment head in a Maine high school.

Ann Lieberman is Emeritus Professor at Teachers College, Columbia University, and a senior scholar at the Carnegie Foundation for the Advancement of Teaching. In addition to *Teacher Leadership*, she and Lynne Miller, both prolific writers, have cowritten five books, including *Teachers Transforming Their World and Their Work*.

Jed Frank Lippard is the Upper School Director of Prospect Hill Academy Charter School in Cambridge, Massachusetts. Having completed his doctoral coursework at Harvard, Jed has current research interests that include differentiated leadership for adult growth and development, the interaction between individual and institutional behaviors, and professional development for school leaders.

George F. Marnik is Clinical Instructor of Educational Leadership in the College of Education and Human Development at the University of Maine. He has authored or coauthored many articles about leadership. He coauthored with Gordon Donaldson *Becoming Better Leaders: The Challenge of Improving Student Learning.*

Stephanie Marshall lives and works in Camden, Maine.

Barbara McGillicuddy Bolton recently retired from elementary school teaching in New York City. She has rediscovered her interest in writing and has published several articles, most recently in *Puckerbrush Review.*

Lynne Miller is professor of educational leadership and coexecutive director of the Southern Maine Partnership of the University of Maine. Another book she cowrote with Ann Lieberman is *Teachers Caught in the Action: What Matters Most in Professional Development.*

Mary Ann Minard is the K–12 Curriculum Coordinator in York, Maine. She has taught in the public schools in Maine, Vermont, California, and for Department of Defense Dependent's Schools in Germany. She has a PhD in Educational Leadership and Policy Studies from the University of New Hampshire.

Gayle Moller is Associate Professor in the Department of Educational Leadership and Foundations in the College of Education and Allied Professions at Western Carolina University in Cullowhee, North Carolina. She was formerly Executive Director of the South Florida Center for Educational Leaders. The Center served large, urban school districts in South Florida. The Center provided staff development for school leaders who are working to improve schools. Gayle worked in the Broward County Public Schools (Ft. Lauderdale, Florida) for 19 years as a teacher, school administrator, and staff development administrator. For 6 years, Gayle developed and carried out an extensive leadership development program within the school system. She wrote "You Have to Want to Do This Job" in the *Journal of Staff Development* (Summer 1999). Recently, she coauthored a book with Anita Pankake—*Lead With Me: A Principal's Guide to Teacher Leadership.*

Samuel Moring lives and teaches in Bangor, Maine, with his wife and their growing family.

Liz Murray is a Social Studies/English teacher at the Upper School at Prospect Hill Academy Charter School in Cambridge, Massachusetts. She is also coordinator of Prospect Hill's Teacher Induction and Mentoring Programs K–12.

John Norton is the editor and moderator of the Teacher Leaders Network. John serves as editor of *Working Toward Excellence,* the journal of the Alabama Best Practices Center. John is also communications advisor for the Center for Teaching Quality, sponsor of the Teacher Leaders Network.

Hank Ogilby teaches ninth grade Social Studies in a Maine high school.

Laura Reasoner Jones manages a technology project for schools near her home in Virginia. In her spare time she makes oral history movies for her family.

Jennifer Ribeiro is an elementary teacher and curriculum coordinator for a school system in coastal Maine.

Anna Ershler Richert, PhD, is a professor of Education at Mills College, where she codirects the Teachers for Tomorrows Schools Credential Program. Currently she is a teacher education scholar with the Carnegie Foundation for the Advancement of Teaching and Learning and secretary of Division K of the American Education Research Association. Recent publications reflect her interest in narrative methodology for teacher education and teacher research. They include two book chapters: "Narratives That Teach: Learning About Teaching From the Stories Teachers Tell," in *Narrative Knowing in Teaching: Exemplars of Reflective Teaching, Research and Teacher Education* Nona Lyons and Vicki LaBoskey (Eds.), Teachers College Press (2002); and "Narratives as Experience Texts: Writing Themselves Back In," in *Teachers Caught in the Action: The Work of Professional Development*, Ann Lieberman and Lyme Miller (Eds.), Teachers College Press (2001).

Kathy Stockford teaches English in a high school in Maine.

Deborah Vose has worked in public and private school libraries in New York City, Brussels, Moscow, and several Boston suburbs for more than 20 years.

Betsy Webb is Assistant Superintendent of the Bangor, Maine Schools and a doctoral student in educational leadership at University of Maine. Her research is focused on the unwritten codes that guide behavior and their impact on schools.

Jennifer Roloff Welch is currently a doctoral student in Learning and Instruction at Harvard's Graduate School of Education. Her research interests include adult learning, literacy, and development with a focus on women's experiences in education.

Todd West is the Social Studies Learning Area Leader at Mount Desert Island High School in Bar Harbor, Maine.

Barbara H. White teaches English in a high school in Maine.

Elizabeth Wiley taught high school for many years before pursing her doctorate in American Studies at George Washington University. She lives in Falmouth, Maine.

Martha McFarland Williams, a retired teacher, enjoys personal history, English as a second language tutoring, and supporting human and animal rights.

Terry Young is an elementary school principal in Saco, Maine. He is a doctoral student in educational leadership. His interests include teacher leadership and standards-based learning.

CORWIN PRESS

The Corwin Press logo—a raven striding across an open book—represents the union of courage and learning. Corwin Press is committed to improving education for all learners by publishing books and other professional development resources for those serving the field of PreK–12 education. By providing practical, hands-on materials, Corwin Press continues to carry out the promise of its motto: **"Helping Educators Do Their Work Better."**